An Introduction To ADMINISTRATIVE JUSTICE In The United States

An Introduction To ADMINISTRATIVE JUSTICE In The United States

Peter L. Strauss

Carolina Academic Press

INTERNATIONAL STANDARD BOOK NUMBER 0-89089-353-5
LIBRARY OF CONGRESS CATALOG NUMBER 88-72170
MANUFACTURED IN THE UNITED STATES OF AMERICA

CAROLINA ACADEMIC PRESS
P.O. BOX 51879
DURHAM, NORTH CAROLINA 27717
(919) 489-7486

CONTENTS

TABLE OF CASES

PREFACE

This monograph was originally written for inclusion in a series entitled *Administrative Justice in the Western Democracies.* The series will include studies of administrative law and procedure in Sweden, West Germany, the United Kingdom, Belgium, France, Spain and Italy as well as the United States, each written by a leading university scholar in his respective country, and will be published shortly by Giuffre Press of Milan, Italy.

Subsequently, Carolina Academic Press persuaded me that this volume should also find an American audience. Although the original manuscript was written for the international reader, they felt that with revisions it would be useful for those who might not be versed in the subtleties of our administrative justice system or who might want a jumping-off place into the voluminous literature on the subject. To that end, we have adapted the original manuscript for this American audience. The original manuscript was completed in the spring of 1987. In the course of revision, I have tried to accommodate the important developments of the following year, but it is in the nature of such enterprises that the additions are supplementary.

Among the many who deserve thanks for their help, direct and indirect, a few are especially prominent: Walter Gellhorn, for getting me started; my colleagues Bruce Ackerman and George Bermann; Clark Byse, Todd Rakoff and, especially, Roy Schotland for his enthusiasm and many helpful suggestions. The series project, of which Professor Aldo Piras of the University of Rome is director, and the Abraham N. Buchman Fund for Administrative Law provided welcome financial support, and Dean Barbara Black of Columbia did everything a dean can to encourage and ease my way. Dan Ackman provided thoughtful, proficient help in research and contributed much that is in the footnotes. Marina Riedl cheerfully and efficiently typed, retyped, and typed yet once again, producing the index and other appurtenances as well. And without Joanna, Benjamin and Bethany, none of this would have seemed possible or worthwhile.

P.L.S.

August 1988   Hastings-on-Hudson, N.Y.

An Introduction To
ADMINISTRATIVE JUSTICE
In The United States

≡ 1
INTRODUCTION

A preliminary meeting among the editors of the series entitled *Administrative Justice in the Western Democracies* revealed what ought not be surprising, that each of us approaches the question of "administrative justice" in terms that reflect the distinctive features of our own legal systems. It seems useful at the start, then, to summarize some distinctive features of the American political and legal systems that will have to be kept in mind when reading this account of administrative justice in the United States.

- American government is *not* a parliamentary democracy. For this reason, the problem of controlling governmental action appears in a different context for Americans than for citizens of parliamentary governments.

- Under American ideas about "separation of powers," the legislature, the chief executive and the courts are kept sharply distinct. Each is given some role in controlling the acts of the others.

- Heads of the bodies that constitute the ordinary operating bureaucracy of government have no formal political connection to the legislature; they ordinarily do have such connections to the chief executive.

- Legal control over the acts of governmental bodies is ultimately effected by the separate, generalist judiciary rather than by court-like organs within the bureaucracy.

The pages that follow, then, may be concerned to a surprising degree with matters occurring in the "ministries" of American government rather than in its courts. Even when they are concerned with the role of the courts, these pages are likely to raise issues that may generate wonder concerning both the character of those institutions and some of the work they are asked to do. What follows is written in the hope of helping the reader unfamiliar with the details of the American legal system understand the more important characteristics and issues of our system of administrative justice. Its concern with the institutions and operation of the American bureaucracy is, itself, typical of the approach an American

3

lawyer might take. Indeed, American administrative lawyers often criticize teachers of administrative law for over-emphasizing the courts. The operative concerns of administrative justice in the United States are most often experienced at the agency level.

Bibliographic Note   The reader interested in pursuing issues of American administrative law in greater depth may find a variety of helpful sources. B. Mezines, J. Stein and J. Gruff, Administrative Law (Matthew Bender 1986), a five-volume looseleaf technical treatise, is the most extensive set of materials prepared specifically for practicing attorneys; three works prepared by professors of law trace the same ground in somewhat lesser detail, and with more attention to theoretical and critical issues: K.C. Davis, Administrative Law Treatise (2d Ed.)[1]; C. Koch, Administrative Law and Practice[2] (West 1985); and R. Pierce, S. Shapiro and P. Verkuil, Administrative Law and Process (Foundation Press 1985).[3] Somewhat less direct, but having the advantage of exposing the reader to a variety of primary materials in the field, are teaching materials such as Gellhorn, Byse, Strauss, Rakoff and Schotland, Administrative Law: Cases and Comments (8th ed. Foundation Press 1986) and Stewart and Breyer, Administrative Law and Regulatory Policy (2d ed. Little Brown 1984). Some of the more important works examining aspects of administrative law and its development are set out in the footnote.[4]

Another kind of reading is less technical, that which may introduce the reader to the variety of scholarly perspectives that can be brought to bear on understanding administrative justice in the modern American

---

1. The Treatise is published by Professor Davis himself, in five volumes with periodic updates. Professor Davis, one of the genuinely great older figures in administrative law scholarship, holds strong opinions on many issues, opinions which have long been influential in the field.

2. Professor Koch's two-volume treatise appears much stronger as an account of conventional legal relationships of control than of the political ones that, for rulemaking, are so important an element of the process.

3. This one-volume work is chiefly a text written for students, but at a useful level of detail and thought.

4. *Historical materials*: J. Landis, The Administrative Process (Yale University 1938); The Attorney General's Manual on the Administrative Procedure Act (1947); Report of the Attorney General's Committee on Administrative Procedure, S. Doc. 8, 77th Cong., 1st Sess. (1941). *Judicial review*: L. Jaffe, Judicial Review of Administrative Action (Little Brown 1965). *Rulemaking*: ACUS, A Guide to Federal Agency Rulemaking (1983); J. O'Reilly, Administrative Rulemaking (Sheppard's 1983). *Adjudication*: J. Mashaw, Bureaucratic Justice: Managing Social Security Disability Claims (Yale University 1983); J. Mashaw, Due Process in the Administrative State (Yale University 1985). *Freedom of Information*: J. O'Reilly, Federal Information Disclosure (Sheppard's 1977). *State Administrative Law*: F. Cooper, State Administrative Law (1965); A.E. Bonfield, State Law in Teaching of Administrative Law: A Critical Analysis of the Status Quo, 61 Tex. L. Rev. 95 (1982).

state. One interested in viewing the problems of administrative justice from the perspectives of judicial control would surely start with Professor Louis Jaffe's classic, although now somewhat dated treatment, Judicial Control of Administrative Action;[5] more recent studies have focused on the particular problems of judicial participation in the resolution of large social issues.[6] Alternatively, one could seek an historical perspective in the works of Professors McGraw,[7] Rabin,[8] Skowroneck,[9] or Stewart.[10] A third perspective, viewing the problems of administrative law as those of choosing suitable procedures or institutions for the carrying out of legislative policy, is exemplified by the work of Professors Breyer,[11] Kaufman,[12] and Mashaw.[13] Finally, increasing attention is being paid in the legal academy to the relationship of administration to the world of politics.[14]

---

5. See note 4, above.

6. R.S. Melnick, Regulation and the Courts: The Case of the Clean Air Act (Brookings 1983); D. Horowitz, The Courts and Social Policy (Brookings 1976).

7. Prophets of Regulation (Belknap Press, 1984).

8. Federal Regulation in Historical Perspective, 38 Stan. L. Rev. 1189 (1986).

9. Building a New American State: The Expansion of National Administrative Capacities (Cambridge University 1982).

10. The Reformation of American Administrative Law, 88 Harv. L. Rev. 1667 (1975).

11. Regulation and its Reform (Harvard University 1982).

12. The Administrative Behavior of Federal Bureau Chiefs (Brookings 1981); The Forest Ranger (Resources for the Future 1960).

13. Social Security Hearings and Appeals: A Study of the Social Security Administration Hearing System (Lexington Books 1978); Bureaucratic Justice (Yale University 1983); Due Process in the Administrative State (Yale University 1985).

14. B. Ackerman, Reconstructing American Law (Harvard University 1984); P. Strauss, The Place of Agencies in Government: Separation of Powers and the Fourth Branch, 84 Colum. L. Rev. 573; C. Sunstein, Interest Groups and American Public Law, 38 Stan. L. Rev. 29 (1985).

$\equiv 2$
CONSTITUTIONAL BACKGROUND

Any introductory assessment of American administrative law, and particularly one written with the reader not well-versed in our legal system in mind, appropriately begins with the legal system's fundamental legal document, the Constitution. The Constitution is a written document whose terms are, by its own provision, supreme in relation to any other law or undertaking (specifically including treaties to which the United States may be a party). The United States Supreme Court, early interpreted this provision for supremacy to mean that in case of conflict between the Constitution and other sources of domestic law, the Constitution must prevail.[1] An agency cannot act, nor can the legislature empower it to act, in a way that is contrary to the provisions of the Constitution. For this reason, constitutional arguments have a special priority in American jurisprudence, for administrative law no less than in other settings. A successful claim that an agency has acted (or been empowered) contrary to the provisions of the Constitution will defeat the action in an emphatic way. Note, too, the unusual authority this gives the Supreme Court: its constitutional judgments cannot be changed by ordinary legislation. Unless the Court itself can be persuaded that it has erred, they are subject to revision only by the formal (and cumbersome) processes of enacting a written amendment to the Constitution itself.

A second general characteristic of the constitutional system is that it is federal. It contemplates the individual states (for example, Massachusetts or California) as independent political entities having a defined relationship to the national government rather than as subordinate parts of the national government. Although the federal structure of American government has little practical importance for the powers of the national government,[2] it has special significance for understanding the limitations

---

1. Marbury v. Madison, 5 U.S. (1 Cranch) 137 (1803).
2. While the Constitution ostensibly defines those powers in a limited way, interpretation has been expansive over the years, and few doubt that Congress could now legislate on virtually any subject it chose to regard as having national importance; moreover, the supremacy principle makes any valid juridical act at the national level—whether Constitution, treaty, statute, executive or judicial decision, or subordinate legislation—prevail over any conflicting assertion of state law.

of this essay. Each of the fifty states has its own constitution and statutes creating its own distinctive governmental structures and administrative and judicial procedures. Many issues of interest to administrative lawyers are handled at the state and local[3] level. For example, most issues of land use control, professional licensing, and public utility rate regulation are controlled by the states. To outline contemporary issues in administrative law at the national level is a large enough task. Although this essay will discuss some issues of national law governing state administration (chiefly national constitutional requirements for fair procedure) and point out some contrasts between the national and state levels, it generally will *not* address the problems of state administrative law.

At perhaps the most general level, one may say that the Constitution sought to resolve two problems facing the nation when it was drafted in 1787: to increase the power and effectiveness of the national government, a government which under the previous arrangements was demonstrably ineffective; and at the same time to avoid creating so much power in a single place as to threaten a return of the tyranny that the states and their citizens had recently defeated. Many features of the national Constitution may be understood at least in part as means by which these potentially conflicting ends might both be secured—for example, the careful separation of legislative, executive and judicial power at the federal level, shortly to be discussed; the preservation of a federal form of government, with largely independent legal authority at the state level and a national government of defined, limited authority and independent political units; and the near-immediate adoption of a Bill of Rights. The writtenness of the Constitution, and the obstacles to its formal amendment,[4] further discourage altering the balance of power.

The fact that formal changes are so difficult[5] has posed obvious problems for the adaptability of constitutional government during the two centuries since the Constitution was adopted. A challenge of particular

---

3. Localities are subordinate units of state government, whose structure and authority is, in the first instance, a matter of state law.

4. Briefly, amendments require approval by a two-thirds majority in both houses of the American Congress *plus* approval by three fourths of the states; it is also possible for two thirds of the states to require Congress to call a convention for the purpose of proposing amendments, but thus far this procedure (which may open the whole of the Constitution to revision) has never been invoked. See W. Dellinger, The Legitimacy of Constitutional Change: Rethinking the Amendment Process, 97 Harv. L. Rev. 386 (1983).

5. In the two centuries since its ratification and the adoption of the Bill of Rights—ten amendments thought required for its ready acceptance—the Constitution has been amended only 16 times. The bulk of these amendments have been concerned with individual liberty or relatively minor issues of structural detail.

relevance for this essay was posed by the emergence of the modern administrative state in response to the social changes brought about by industrial and post-industrial economies. No one pretends that those who drafted the Constitution imagined either those changes or the enormous and variegated government apparatus that has been built in response to them.[6] Judges have responded to this challenge, on the whole, by interpreting the Constitution in ways that confirm the structural changes that have been made, and by reinterpreting citizens' rights in light of the changed arrangements. This history of recognition of expanded national powers and new structural arrangements, and adaptation of individual protections to the new circumstances of the modern age, might be regarded as having served as an informal or de facto amendment process for the Constitution.[7]

A good example of this "amendment" process lies in the development of the constitutional instruction that no person be deprived of life, liberty or property without due process of law.[8] As originally understood, this instruction chiefly concerned the ordinary processes of courts. It also embodied the sense of the earliest document of the English "constitution," the Magna Carta, committing the whole of government to the principle of legality. There was no reason to think it applied to procedures followed within the government bureaucracy—a bureaucracy that at the time hardly existed, and had few if any relationships with private persons that could be thought to require procedural norms. Not until the turn of the century, in a series of cases concerned with revenue collection, did an administrative jurisprudence of due process begin to emerge.[9]

While arguments about the necessary application and content of "due process" in the administrative context became increasingly common in both legislatures and courts during the first part of the twentieth century,[10] the most significant developments occurred after the Second World War,

----

6. That there would be change requiring adjustment *was* imagined, and that explains much of the document's openness of structure.

7. For a recent, general treatment, see B. Ackerman, The Storrs Lectures: Discovering the Constitution, 93 Yale L.J. 1013 (1984).

8. Unique among constitutional provisions, this one appears twice—as a command to the federal government in the Fifth Amendment, and to the states in the Fourteenth.

9. E.g., Londoner v. Denver, 210 U.S. 373 (1908).

10. Thus, debate over the Federal Administrative Procedure Act, enacted in 1946, was preceded by a decade's debate on the necessary content of administrative adjudication; and several important cases during this period established constitutional procedural norms for agencies deciding matters after hearing. Ohio Bell Telephone Co. v. Public Utilities Commission of Ohio, 301 U.S. 292 (1937); Morgan v. United States (Morgan I), 298 U.S. 468 (1936); Morgan v. United States (Morgan II), 304 U.S. 1 (1938).

beginning with the anti-communist campaigns of the 1950s and gathering true momentum during the 1970s. The courts then came to the conclusion—perhaps unsurprising to the reader but dramatic when first stated—that relationships with government (licenses, welfare entitlements, state employment, enrollment in public schools) must be recognized to have the dignity of "property" of which the citizen could not be deprived without "due process of law."[11] The courts, in the final instance, define what those procedures are. While they generally respect legislative choices (perhaps because legislative choices of appropriate procedure commonly reflect community notions about fair and necessary procedure), they do not always do so.

When courts find the legislative specification of procedure inadequate to provide "due process" the legislature must respect that judgment. Because it is based on the meaning of constitutional text, the legislature has no recognized authority to enact a statute inconsistent with it. Whatever one might believe about the justice of the results produced, the point for current purposes is that no one could pretend that the drafters of the Due Process clause envisioned courts telling school officials what procedures they must follow before suspending a student for ten days;[12] or telling welfare officials what sort of hearing they must give a recipient before suspending current payments, in advance of a formal, statutory hearing on the existence of grounds for terminating eligibility;[13] or telling the legislature, in effect, what procedural protections must be provided to government employees, once the legislature has decided to have a civil service program.[14]

This practice of judicial "amendment" of the Constitution, born of practical necessity and generally accepted though it may be, presents evident difficulties to legal theorists. American legal literature is filled with sophisticated efforts at criticism and/or rationalization. The very fact

---

11. Goldberg v. Kelly, 397 U.S. 254 (1970), discussed at some length within (text at pp. 38-40, below) was the initial decision; it drew upon a seminal article by Charles Reich, The New Property, 73 Yale L.J. 733 (1964), arguing that in modern society, much wealth consists of intangible entitlements such as those based on advantageous opportunities conferred by government. When a statute confers government benefits in an individual, those individuals should be recognized as having a property right in such benefits.

12. Goss v. Lopez, 419 U.S. 565 (1975).

13. Goldberg v. Kelly, note 11, above.

14. Cleveland Board of Education v. Loudermill, 470 U.S. 532 (1985). The legislature is free to adopt a civil service system—that is, a regime giving governmental employees statutory entitlement to their jobs during good and efficient behavior—or not; but once it chooses to create this sort of relationship between the government and its employees, the courts will have the final word concerning the adequacy of the procedures chosen.

that a judicial decision can have such a fundamental character, being reversible only by extraordinary means, gives rise to what has been described as the "countermajoritarian difficulty"—that the result of final judicial nullification of a statute frustrates what appears to be the popular will, as represented by the elected legislature's action.[15] More conservative constitutional theorists, often described as "interpretivists," take two lessons from this difficulty: first, that the courts are only justified in exercising their authority to declare legislation unconstitutional when they can link that judgment directly to the text of the constitution; second, that that authority should be invoked only rarely, and with utmost hesitation.

On the other hand, the particular (and historic) importance of the Court in protecting individual liberties and unpopular groups against the intolerance of legislatures and momentary public passions has led another group of scholars, loosely described as "noninterpretivists," to argue that the written text of the Constitution ought not be regarded as a necessary limit for judicial action. In their view, the use of analogy and reasoning from what judges perceive to be the emerging moral premises of contemporary society provide a sufficient basis for judicial action protecting individuals against state power.[16] Some recent opinions extending individual liberty claims[17] seem defensible only on some such grounds, and are roundly criticized by "interpretivists" for their failure to be grounded in text. The interpretivists, in turn, must struggle with making even a generally worded political text—as the Constitution is—relevant to today's vastly changed and uncontemplated circumstances.[18]

For administrative lawyers contemplating the possible application of the Constitution to an issue of interest, the important point to recognize

---

15. A. Bickel, The Least Dangerous Branch (Bobbs Merrill 1962); J. Ely, Democracy and Distrust, A Theory of Judicial Review (Harvard University 1980); L. Lusky, By What Right? (Michie 1975).

16. M. Perry, The Constitution, the Courts and Human Rights (1982); P. Brest, The Misconceived Quest for the Original Understanding, 60 B.U.L.Rev. 204 (1980).

17. In Roe v. Wade, 410 U.S. 113 (1973), the most prominent such case, the Court held that, because a woman's right to decide whether or not to end a pregnancy is fundamental, only a compelling interest can justify state regulators impinging in any way upon that right. No constitutional text directly addresses abortion (or like issues), and abortion had been regulated in varying ways for most of the nation's history.

18. See B. Ackerman, note 7, above. The problem was recently restated by Justice White of the Supreme Court, in an opinion for the Court refusing to extend reasoning like that in Roe v. Wade, note 17, above, to forbid state criminalization of homosexual acts between consenting adults: "The Court is most vulnerable and comes nearest to illegitimacy when it deals with judge-made Constitutional Law having little or no cognizable roots in the language or design of the Constitution." Bowers v. Hardwick, 106 S. Ct. 2841, 2846 (1986).

is that, while one begins with the text, the jurisprudence must also be consulted—and lively and current disputes persist respecting the limits and techniques appropriate to that jurisprudence. Whether the text constitutes a limit for the Court, and how textual meaning is to be derived (by reference to history? to governmental structure? to contemporary possibilities of meaning? to analogies between past and present problems?), remain surprisingly lively issues.[19] One might say that the writtenness of the Constitution, at least for judges, has been placed in significant doubt.

The separation of powers

A glance at the organization and provisions of the Constitution will confirm that the idea of separation of powers is central. Article I treats the legislative power and puts it in Congress, a two-house legislature of defined authority. Article II places a largely undefined executive power in a unitary executive, an elected President. Article III locates the judicial power in the Supreme Court, the state courts, and any lower federal courts Congress may choose to create. Article IV then touches in a variety of ways the other great separation of power already mentioned—that between the national government and the states.

As important as the idea of separation, and again serving the function of limited government, is the notion of checks and balances. Legislative power is divided between two houses in substantial part because that power was the most feared, and it was thought their jealousies would cause them to check one another. The President is able (within limits) to veto legislation; legislative bodies must approve appointments and can control executive behavior through denial of funds or impeachment; and so forth. By creating rivalries and jealousies, empowering each branch to place obstacles in the way of the others' full exercise of their powers, the draftsmen believed they lessened still further the chance that government would pass beyond the people's control.

While the Constitution defines and locates the three characteristic powers of government, it is striking to note that it does not define the government itself. That is to say, it does not define the bureaucracy, the specialist institutions that carry out the specific tasks of public affairs. The first three articles confer the "legislative," the "executive," and the

---

19. A good introductory source exposing these issues is a student text, P. Brest and S. Levinson, Processes of Constitutional Decisionmaking (2d ed. Little Brown 1983).

"judicial" powers upon *generalist* institutions lacking detailed responsibility for particular affairs, that might be imagined to sit at the head of the larger body of government itself. Although one can read between the lines a certain anticipation about the arrangements that would be made, the fact is that very little at all is said about the elements that would make up that larger body. The drafters agreed on a single head of the executive branch, reaching the judgment that unified political responsibility was essential. They did not agree, however, on a form of government beneath him. They left that to congressional definition.

Rejecting a plan that would have specified the cabinet departments in constitutional text, the drafters of the Constitution instead gave Congress authority to define the elements of government by enacting any law "necessary and proper" to carry out its general responsibilities for legislation. Thus, the Constitution is almost devoid of detailed specification of the relationship these elements are to have with the President or Court.[20] The principal constraints on Congress' judgment about what sorts of institutions are proper to create for the varied work of government may be those suggested by the separation of powers idea itself. Each of these generalist institutions—Congress, President, and Court—enjoys an uneasy relationship with the other two and a relationship with the operating bureaucracy that is given character by its own unique function. Very crudely, the Congress passes the statutes that establish the individual elements of the bureaucracy and empower them to act; the President oversees and guides their performance of function under those laws, as a policy or political matter; and the courts assure their adherence to legality.

From the outset (and as almost certainly anticipated) Congress has created a government that is distinct from the President and his personal office. It has vested responsibility for day-to-day administration of the nation's laws in these governmental units rather than in him. Article II provides that the President is to appoint the heads of any Department Congress may create and that he may call on them for written opinions

---

20. Aside from its general provision that a single, elected President is to wield the executive power, the Constitution says only (as to domestic matters) that the President or persons he selects will have responsibility for staffing government departments at the upper levels, and that he can call upon the heads of these bodies for advice. No part of the article conferring "the judicial power" on the Supreme Court discusses, specifically, its authority over the acts of government agencies or over the validity of congressional legislation, although the Court has asserted from the beginning that the article confers on it the power to enforce legality on the remainder of government, including specifically the power to find congressional acts inconsistent with the Constitution. H. Monaghan, *Marbury v. Madison* and the Administrative State, 83 Colum. L. Rev. 1 (1983) is a useful discussion of the latter aspect.

day, the Commissioners of a given agency may perform all the distinctive functions of government—adopting rules (subordinate legislation) on some matters within their charge, authorizing investigation of others, hearing argument in and deciding contested proceedings within the agency. These proceedings may even have begun with their ratification of staff recommendations for their initiation months earlier, and may often require interpretation of the agency's own rules.

It is hard to say as a theoretical matter why these arrangements satisfy the structural requirements of "separation of powers," although it is clear beyond doubt that in the eyes of the courts they do. In recent years, the Supreme Court has used "separation of powers" analysis in a surprising number of cases to strike down congressional legislation establishing governmental arrangements, on the general ground that one of the branches has encroached on functions reserved to another.[28] It has uniformly insisted, however, that the independent regulatory commissions are not challenged by this analysis.[29] Although the Court has been none too clear about its reasons, one may suggest at least two. First, these are now well-established instruments of government, which could not be thrown over without enormous inconvenience. More important, the Court could properly believe that they do not much threaten the relative authority of Congress, President and Court. Ordinarily these agencies have responsibilities for which, in any event, a certain distance from "political" control would generally be thought useful. Congress has tended to reflect this attitude in its own conduct toward them. Beyond this, the arrangements made do not create an imbalance among the three principals of the national government. The President retains (as do the courts) substantial relationships with them, even if not the full range of relationship he usually enjoys with executive departments.

As already suggested in discussing the combined functions of the Department of Agriculture—a cabinet department fully "attached" to

---

Commission and Federal Energy Regulatory Commission regulate rates and entry in their respective fields, but so does the Department of Agriculture for some purposes—an executive department headed by a cabinet Secretary; both the (independent) National Labor Relations Board and the (executive) Department of Labor regulate aspects of labor relations; the Federal Trade Commission and the Department of Justice, aspects of antitrust policy; the Nuclear Regulatory Commission and the Environmental Protection Agency, licensing of environmentally hazardous activities.

28. Buckley v. Valeo, 424 U.S. 1 (1976); Northern Pipeline Construction Co. v. Marathon Pipe Line Co., 458 U.S. 50 (1982); Immigration & Naturalization Service v. Chadha, 462 U.S. 919 (1983); Bowsher v. Synar, 106 S. Ct. 3181 (1986).

29. Bowsher v. Synar, 106 S. Ct. 3181 (1986); Commodity Futures Trading Commission v. Schor, 106 S. Ct. 3245 (1986); P. Strauss, Formal and Functional Approaches to Separation of Powers Questions—A Foolish Inconsistency? 72 Cornell L. Rev. 488 (1987).

the presidency—it is also possible to say, as a functional matter, that the combination in an "agency" of the three characteristic functions of government is not as threatening to the citizenry as that combination in the President, the Congress or the courts themselves. The element that neutralizes these apparent violations of "separation of power" principles is the presence of external controls. The agencies act subject to the legislation enacted by Congress, to review of the lawfulness of their behavior by the courts, and to the appointment and (uncertainly defined) political authorities of the President. Thus they do not present the spectre of government out of control that would be raised if the President or Congress were to attempt all these activities. By these means, it has thus far been concluded, the general fairness of agency actions can be sufficiently assured.[30]

Separation of powers issues do remain lively in circumstances where it might be concluded that the formal authority of one of the three designated principal actors (Congress, President, Court) has been threatened, insufficiently respected, or arguably displaced. Thus, Congress can give regulatory Commissioners fixed terms of office that put them somewhat beyond the President's disciplinary reach.[31] When Congress attempted to create a regulatory commission to which it rather than the President would make certain appointments,[32] however, or to give authority to an officer over whom it rather than the President enjoyed the prerogative of dismissal "for cause,"[33] the Supreme Court found these arrangements unconstitutional. Congress has long empowered agencies—both independent and executive—to decide matters that would otherwise be assigned to the courts, subject only to limited judicial review,[34] but when recently it embracively assigned judicial roles *and* judicial powers to bankruptcy officials (albeit subject to similar forms of review) the Court found this also excessive.[35] Congress and the President each employ a variety of political weapons in attempting to oversee agency

---

30. For a general treatment, see C. Sunstein, Constitutionalism After the New Deal, 101 Harv. L. Rev. 421 (1987). On the issue of individual fairness in having the same body that has adopted a rule and sought its enforcement decide its application in a particular case, see Withrow v. Larkin, 421 U.S. 35 (1975).

31. Humphrey's Executor v. United States, 295 U.S. 602 (1935); Morrison v. Olson, note 23 above, extended Humphrey's Executor (while reinterpreting its reasoning) to uphold a special prosecutor appointed and controlled by both the judiciary and the executive branch.

32. Buckley v. Valeo, 424 U.S. 1 (1976).

33. Bowsher v. Synar, 106 S. Ct. 3181 (1986).

34. Crowell v. Benson, 285 U.S. 22 (1932); Commodity Futures Trading Commission v. Schor, 106 S. Ct. 3245 (1986).

35. Northern Pipeline Construction Co. v. Marathon Pipe Line Co., 458 U.S. 50 (1982).

decisionmaking—especially the making of rules (subordinate legislation)—and this with apparent judicial approval.[36] Yet when Congress provided legislatively for a formal oversight device, the legislative veto, that would require agencies to lay their actions before Congress for possible disapproval but in which the President would not participate, this too was found offensive to separation of powers requirements.[37]

These decisions, all reached within the past decade, suggest a continued vitality for separation of powers ideas, although a brief theoretical exegesis is not readily to be made.[38] One may say, perhaps, that the central issue is the continued vitality of the three principal institutions of government as effectively competing nodes of differentiated power, each in relationship with the enormously variegated mass of government; "separation of powers" is invoked when the analyst (generally a court) is persuaded that an event or institution threatens that vitality—that is to say, threatens the exclusion of one of those institutions from its central role. Of course such judgments would be difficult in any circumstances, and the uncertainty surrounding the President's authority and role in government only complicates analysis where his role is concerned.

In the states, it may be briefly said, the same theories and a similar potpourri of institutions may be found. Again, it is not thought unusual or improper for state agencies to exercise, in a subordinate way, all of the distinctive functions of government. In many if not all states, however, the idea of a unitary executive is not established. In addition to their chief executive official, the Governor, competing or specialized executive figures may be elected and thus have an entirely independent political authority: the Attorney General, responsible for law enforcement in the strong sense; a chief financial officer, responsible for the regularity of official expenditures; even the membership of a public utility commission or local school board. Note that with federalism comes diversity: some state structures provide for very "strong" governors, others for very weak ones.

Legislation, sovereign and subordinate

The Constitution places all legislative authority in Congress, and addresses the legislative function at some length. It creates two Houses of

---

36. Sierra Club v. Costle, 657 F.2d 298 (D.C. Cir. 1981).
37. Immigration & Naturalization Service v. Chadha, 462 U.S. 919 (1983).
38. P. Strauss, The Place of Agencies in Government: Separation of Powers and the Fourth Branch, 84 Colum. L. Rev. 573 (1984); R. Fallon, Of Legislative Courts, Administrative Agencies, and Article III, 101 Harv. L. Rev. 916 (1988).

Congress (Senate and House of Representatives) and provides for their constituencies, their election cycles, the manner in which legislation is to be enacted (including its presentment to the President for possible veto) and the subjects on which legislation is proper.[39] Specific provision is made for a limited number of other functions—impeachment of executive or judicial officials for "high crimes or misdemeanors," responsibility to appropriate funds for governmental expenditures, senatorial participation in the approval of certain presidential appointments and treaties. Yet the dominant concern is with the legislative process, evidently viewed as both paramount and unique.

The contemporary functioning of the legislative process is rather different, however, from the picture this might suggest. Congress itself, or perhaps more properly its members, spends the great bulk of time on matters other than the enactment of legislation. To respond to the demands of a system that separates the legislature from the executive, and even requires them to compete with one another, Congress early found it necessary to create a system of legislative committees. These bodies exercise significant investigative functions. In addition to substantial investigations associated with the annual appropriations process, congressional committees conduct detailed oversight hearings of executive branch functioning and general investigations of perceived social ills or scandals. Such investigations have prompted enormous growth in congressional staff attached to the committees.[40] This growth, in turn, has fueled investigations: committee staffs, once assembled, have a continuing need for satisfying work and visibility in the political atmosphere of Washington.

An even more important part of the work of individual members of Congress is their casework, their assistance to particular constituents who become embroiled with one or another part of the federal establishment.

---

39. Section 8 of Article I of the Constitution enumerates Congress' power to legislate and holds that Congress may "make all laws which shall be necessary and proper for carrying into execution the foregoing powers." Section 9 then states specific limits on these powers. Two, in particular, emphasize the general and prospective character of legislation, as compared to adjudication. Congress may not pass bills of attainder, laws which in effect convict specific persons of crime for acts already committed. Similarly, it may not enact ex post facto laws, by which acts are made criminal after their occurrence.

40. The Congressional Quarterly's Guide to Congress reported that in 1982 3,278 congressional staff members were assigned to Congress' 298 standing, special and select committees and subcommittees. The overall congressional bureaucracy is much larger—each Senator has about 35 personal staff members; each Representative, about 17; and several thousand more are employed by legislative offices such as the General Accounting Office. Twenty-five years earlier, in 1947, total congressional committee staff numbered 399.

In the eyes of many contemporary political scientists, such casework is the basis on which a member's reelection is most likely to be won or lost.[41] As an activity, it too requires and is demanded by enlarged staffing (now, in the personal office of the member).

Current assessments make it seem more time-consuming than sinister, and rather like the function of ombudsmen in other systems. The member's staff may do little more than point the right direction, or assure that a matter is reviewed by agency officials. Here, the purpose is not to criticize that function (or others), but to point out that Congress has many distractions from legislation.

From an early point, Congress has used statutes to empower other parts of government to adopt rules governing matters within their competence—rules which, if valid, have the force of statutory law. The practice has been challenged for as many years as a delegation of the legislative authority that is solely Congress' under the Constitution, and those challenges have almost invariably failed.[42] At this writing, the annual compendium of rules published by the federal government occupies about 10 times as much shelf space in the law library as does the compendium of federal statutes. Various explanations have been essayed why so substantial a "legislative" process is acceptable in the face of the Constitution's clear assignment of legislative authority to Congress, and what if any limits there may be on Congress' capacity to create that process. None of the efforts to reduce to a formula precise limits on Congress' delegation has proved enforcible or commanded significant respect among commentators.[43]

Some observations may be appropriate, however, particularly in the context of the foregoing discussion of separation of powers. First, the two principal occasions in constitutional history when the Supreme Court found that an excessive delegation had been made[44] involved statutes that

41. M. Fiorina, Congressional Control on the Bureaucracy: A Mismatch of Incentives and Capabilities, in L. Lodd and B. Oppenheimer, Congress Reconsidered 332 (1981); R.D. Arnold, Congress and the Bureaucracy: A Theory of Influence (1979); A. Maass, Congress and the Common Good (1983).

42. The first challenge was to early rules adopted by the federal judiciary to govern judicial procedures, pursuant to the Judiciary Act of 1789. Wayman v. Southard, 23 U.S. (10 Wheat.) 1, 15-16 (1825).

43. See W. Gellhorn, C. Byse, P. Strauss, T. Rakoff and R. Schotland, Administrative Law: Cases and Comments 50-90 (8th ed. 1986) [Frequently cited hereafter as "Administrative Law: Cases and Comments"]; T. Lowi, The End of Liberalism: Ideology, Policy and the Crisis of Public Authority 129-46, 297-99 (1969) and J. Freeman, Crisis and Legitimacy, The Administrative Process and American Government 78-94 (1978) are full and influential commentaries.

44. Panama Refining Co. v. Ryan, 293 U.S. 388 (1935); Schechter Poultry Corp. v. United States, 295 U.S. 495 (1935). The Court, around this time, also invalidated

appeared to frustrate both legislative and judicial supervision of the resulting rules, and placed the authority to act in the office of the President himself. In the one case, it proved out, no one could tell what rule had been adopted; in the other, the President was given (in effect) a blank check to reorganize the entire national economy, with unusual power given private groups and no procedural safeguards provided. Particularly in the political context of the times,[45] a conclusion that presidential authority had been enlarged to the danger point was possible.

That conclusion differentiates those two cases from the ordinary instructions, say, to the Federal Communications Commission to allocate broadcast licenses in accordance with the "public interest," authorizing it to adopt rules that will express the standards by which those allocations will be made. The instructions to the FCC are, indeed, vague at best. Nonetheless, they designate a circumscribed field of action; the actor is not the President; the actions are taken publicly and according to prescribed law and procedures; and Congress, the Court and the President are each in a position to exercise their respective controls over the results.[46]

Second, there is the sheer necessity of the case. In fact the legislative process is not well suited to generating the multiplicity of highly detailed and often technical standards that modern times require, and courts and others well recognize this. Recent invocations of the delegation doctrine by individual Justices of the Supreme Court—and there have been a few—do not complain about the simple fact of rulemaking activity, but about political problems seen in the particular congressional action challenged: the power to set an annual fee for licensees, exercised in a way that seemed to favor one constituency over another, suggested a taxing power wielded on political principles;[47] the legislative history of a statute empowering the adoption of regulations to govern workplace safety revealed that the statute had been artfully worded to avoid decision of a sensitive political issue—whether and how to value the human lives the

---

one statute for excessive delegation to parties outside government. Carter v. Carter Coal Co., 298 U.S. 238 (1936).

45. Given European developments of the time, Congress' creation of a strong corporate-executive mechanism for governing the economy, in response to the severe economic depression and financial emergency, may have seemed especially alarming.

46. Similarly, separation of powers concerns underlay an invocation of "delegation" arguments in recent litigation concerning the legislative veto. Consumer Energy Council of America v. FERC, 673 F.2d 425 (D.C. Cir. 1982). If Congress could retain an unchecked political authority to approve or disapprove agency rulemaking, the court feared, the law-constrained character of rulemaking authority would be undermined.

47. National Cable Television Ass'n, Inc. v. FCC, 415 U.S. 336 (1974).

regulatory standards might protect, against the costs employers would face in complying with those standards.[48]

A recent case where such special factors were absent is more typical. A statute empowered the Environmental Protection Agency to adopt regulations governing the emission of air-borne pollutants. The EPA adopted a regulation that, *inter alia*, permitted a large factory site to treat all of its emissions as if they emanated from a single source (a "bubble") rather than having to control its emissions smoke-stack by smoke-stack, as some argued must be done. The statute empowering the agency to regulate was, the Court concluded, entirely unclear whether agency use of this "bubble" concept had been authorized; it could be read in either way, and the history of the statute was inconclusive. Courts in some national systems might react to this conceded legislative failure by disapproving the agency's action—saying, for example, that the agency's authority was not sufficiently clear to uphold its action. Or it might be expected that the Court would simply resolve the disputed question of statutory meaning, so that it could be known for the future whether the "bubble" approach was or was not to be used. The Supreme Court's reaction was different. It decided the case in a way that stressed the range of discretion agencies may be recognized to have. All the Justices writing on the matter agreed that the power to construe the statute lay *in the agency*, and the courts were required to accept the reading of the statute the agency had chosen, so long as it lay within the bounds of linguistic possibility, purpose, and reason (as this reading did).[49] Implicit in this judgment was the proposition that if, at some future point, the agency changed to another reading of the statute that also met these tests, that reading too would have to be accepted. One has, thus, not simply the adoption of rules pursuant to statute, but an unquestioned delegation to the agency of authority to determine, within bounds, the meaning of the statute itself.[50]

---

48. Industrial Union Dept., AFL-CIO v. American Petroleum Institute, 448 U.S. 607 (1980) (the Benzene case); see also American Textile Mfr. Inst. v. Donovan, 452 U.S. 490 (1981) (the Cotton Dust case). Most of the Justices writing opinions in these two cases simply interpreted the statutes to resolve the question left open; Justice Rehnquist in both, joined by Chief Justice Burger in the second, would have found the statutes invalid under the delegation doctrine, for their failure to resolve the political issue noted in the text. American commentators generally agree that—despite such important gaps—contemporary federal statutes like the Occupational Safety and Health Act at issue here are far more detailed than those creating earlier agencies, such as the Federal Communications Commission, that were routinely approved.

49. See the discussion of statutory interpretation on pp. 249-61.

50. Chevron, U.S.A., Inc. v. Natural Resources Defense Council, Inc., 467 U.S. 837 (1984); the case is discussed more fully on pp. 259-61.

The procedures required for rulemaking are statutory in nature—few suggestions are to be found in decided cases that any particular procedure is required.[51] These statutory forms are discussed in a following section. Here it may be remarked preliminarily that in addition to legally binding rules, sometimes described as "legislative rules," agencies generate a vast number of policies, interpretations, and guides of a less formal character. These emanations, advisory only in a technical sense, have not been thought to present constitutional issues.

Fundamental rights

The principal occasions for invoking the Constitution against administrative actions or the statutes empowering them arise when citizens claim violation of fundamental rights under either the Bill of Rights or the Fourteenth Amendment. The Bill of Rights, the first ten amendments to the Constitution, applies directly only to the federal government. It was adopted immediately following the adoption of the Constitution, in part to fulfill promises made to secure its ratification, and defines the fundamental freedoms of Americans from governmental action.

The amendments most often invoked in the administrative context are the First (freedom of speech), Fourth (freedom from unreasonable searches and seizures), and Fifth (privilege against required self-incrimination; protection of property from uncompensated "taking"; no one to be "deprived of life, liberty or property without due process of law"). The Fourteenth Amendment, ratified in 1868, extends to the states the obligation to afford "due process of law," and adds an additional obligation—born of the Civil War struggles to end black slavery but having a much larger contemporary significance—to assure all the "equal protection of the laws." A series of cases in the third quarter of this century obliterated, for our purposes, any difference between the Bill of Rights and the Fourteenth Amendment by finding that the Fourteenth Amendment "incorporated" most important elements of the first ten amendments and made them applicable to the states. Each of the Bill of Rights guarantees invoked in administrative contexts has been judicially deter-

---

51. Bi-Metallic Investment Co. v. State Bd. of Equalization of Colorado, 239 U.S. 441. The few statements that do occur are in the form of statements that, in any event, no more elaborate procedures than have been statutorily provided could be required. Vermont Yankee Nuclear Power Corp. v. Natural Resources Defense Council, Inc., 435 U.S. 519 (1978).

mined to be "incorporated" in the "due process" requirement of the Fourteenth Amendment, without variation as to substantive content.[52]

Aware from the foregoing that the words "due process of law" have been made to do yeoman service in our constitutional tradition, carrying water between state and federal camps, the reader should know that the dominant constitutional controversy of the first third of this century also concerned these words—a controversy whose echoes still reverberate sharply. The question was whether "due process of law" might have a substantive (legislative) as well as a procedural (administrative-judicial) reference—whether the clause permitted federal courts to say that certain sorts of legislation were forbidden to the states because they "deprived" citizens of protected liberties.

The best-known, now notorious, example of this reasoning was a 1905 case in which New York legislation regulating the working hours of bakers was found to be unconstitutional because the public benefit of the legislation was not, in judicial estimation, rationally related to the adverse impact of depriving the bakers of their liberty to contract for employment under whatever terms they found advantageous.[53] Such willingness closely to reexamine legislative judgments about the desirability of social or economic programs could be, and was, used by conservative judges to retard the emergence of social welfare legislation. After years of sharp criticism, this approach was repudiated as to "economic regulation" in the late 1930s;[54] today, state (or federal) legislative measures imposing regulatory constraints on economic activity for any public welfare purpose

---

52. See the discussion at pp. 34-35, below.

The Court has also found ways to incorporate the Fourteenth Amendment's guarantee of "equal protection of the laws" in the federal (Fifth Amendment) "due process" requirement. Thus, the citizen now enjoys a guarantee of equal protection of the laws against the federal government as well as the states. Perhaps it should be added that the "equal protection" guarantee has proved to be, generally, a substantive one—forbidding, for example, measures that attach negative legal consequences to the race of a citizen—with no uniquely "administrative" application. Consequently, it will not be much discussed here.

53. Lochner v. New York, 198 U.S. 45 (1905).

54. This repudiation is attributed both to the internal inconsistency of the substantive due process idea and to the perceived need for more creative government regulation in response to the depression. The Court suggested that "neither property rights nor contract rights are absolute. . . . Equally fundamental with the private right is that of the public to regulate it in the common interest." Nebia v. New York, 291 U.S. 502 (1934). It also exhibited more deference for the legislatures' substantive policy choices, seeing economic regulation not so much as intrusions on human freedom as a reasonable way to combat the pressures of evil created by mental imperfections or unequal bargaining power. West Coast Hotel Co. v. Parrish, 300 U.S. 379 (1937). See G. Gunther, Constitutional Law 453-67 (11th ed. 1985); L. Tribe, American Constitutional Law 442-55 (1978).

could hardly be questioned on this ground. "Revulsion" is not too strong a word to use in characterizing current judicial and (in general) scholarly attitudes to the former practice and its results.[55]

The problem of "substantive due process" has remained vital in two ways. First, there is the question why, if state legislative judgments about regulatory issues must be respected when they conflict with arguable economic rights (the right to contract, for example), those judgments aren't equally to be respected when they collide with individual liberties of another description (the right to equal protection of the laws, for example).

In fact the courts will not accept a regulatory rationale for action that appears to effect racial discrimination unless an extremely strong showing of justification is made. The asserted legislative rationale receives "strict scrutiny" from the courts in such cases.[56] Second, a number of critics assert that some recent judicial decisions protecting non-economic individual liberties involve judicial imposition of personal value judgments to defeat democratically representative legislative choices, in just the manner of the early "substantive due process" cases. A prominent example is the Supreme Court's decision sharply limiting, and in many respects prohibiting, state regulation of a woman's choice whether or not to have an abortion.[57] For our purposes, the important point to recognize is that efforts to use the Due Process Clause outside the procedural context will entail this history and its remnants of attitude and continuing controversy.

It may be appropriate here to give a few words to each of the most common issues of fundamental rights that arise in an administrative context. As might be imagined, debates over whether the rights are applicable most often involve tension among competing values each worthy

---

55. See, in addition to the materials of the previous note, Ferguson v. Skrupa, 372 U.S. 726 (1963); G. Gunther, Foreword: In Search of an Evolving Doctrine on a Changing Court: A Model for a Newer Equal Protection, 86 Harv. L. Rev. 1 (1972); C. Sunstein, Lochner's Legacy, 87 Colum. L. Rev. 873 (1987).

56. The Supreme Court reserved the possibility of making such a distinction in the famous "footnote form" of its decision in United States v. Carolene Products Co., 304 U.S. 144 (1938). Much ink has been spilled in the years following about the justification for the resulting double standard. See, e.g., Gunther, note 55, above; J.H. Ely, Democracy and Distrust, A Theory of Judicial Review (1980); L. Lusky, Footnote Redux, A Carolene Products Reminiscence, 82 Colum. L. Rev. 1093 (1982); B. Ackerman, Beyond Carolene Products, 98 Harv. L. Rev. 713 (1985).

57. Roe v. Wade, 410 U.S. 113 (1973); see notes 17-18, above. On Roe, see J. Ely, The Wages of Crying Wolf: A Comment on Roe v. Wade, 82 Yale L.J. 920 (1973); M. Perry, Abortion, the Public Morals, and the Police Power: The Ethical Function of Substantive Due Process, 23 U.C.L.A. L. Rev. 689 (1976); R. Epstein, Substantive Due Process by Any Other Name: The Abortion Cases, 1973 Sup. Ct. Rev. 159.

of some recognition. The effort of the following pages is to identify in a summary way those tensions and any characteristic analytic or didactic framework used to resolve them or express their resolution.

Speech/consumer protection

The First Amendment provides that "Congress shall make no law abridging the Freedom of Speech." While it is generally accepted that the prohibition was intended primarily for the protection of political expression, the difficulty of distinguishing what may be political from what is not and the perceived general value in our society of free expression has produced much broader readings.[58] Judicial readings forbid, for example, censorship grounded in sexual offensiveness equally with censorship grounded in political repression. Courts have also limited the private use of the civil remedies of libel, slander and invasion of privacy to protect personal reputation almost as sharply as they have limited the states' use of criminal libel laws to punish dissidents.[59] These readings restrain both prospective and reactive government response to speech activity, but especially the former. Censorship or other forms of "prior restraint" of speech not yet publicly uttered is precluded, whatever may be the provocation of past conduct. At one time the Supreme Court identified "commercial speech" (as at one time it identified pornography) as being outside the ambit of "speech" whose freedom from federal (and, later, state) interference was assured by the First Amendment.[60] In later years, the widespread use of advertisements for political purposes, the emergence of corporate participation in public affairs, and the realization that the business of successful book and newspaper publishers is readily described as "commercial speech" have undercut that simple analysis.

Regulators often seek to control behavior that could be called speech—for example, a merchant's (allegedly) fraudulent advertising or an employer's (allegedly) coercive speech to employees seeking to organize a labor union. The remedies they use may appear to regulate speech: denying an advertiser use of the mails, requiring it to publish a corrective announcement, or simply ordering it to refrain from like conduct in the future; directing an employer to issue a corrective notice, or to cease from addressing his employees in a particular way. Often enough, the assertion that the advertisement communicates important ideas is, from a common-

58. V. Blasi, The Checking Value in First Amendment Theory, 1977 Am. B.F. Res. J. 521; F. Schauer, Free Speech: A Philosophical Inquiry (1982); T. Emerson, The System of Freedom of Expression (1970).

59. New York Times Co. v. Sullivan, 376 U.S. 254 (1964).

60. Valentine v. Christensen, 316 U.S. 52 (1942).

sense perspective, farcical;[61] none doubt that consumer fraud and the suppression by economic coercion of worker organization are both forms of conduct government may seek to suppress. Yet the strength of the impulse toward protection of speech reflected in current First Amendment law, the presence (at least in contemplation) of genuine issues of characterization as between idea-communication and illegal conduct, and the current absence of a sharply defined analytic framework make these issues unexpectedly troublesome.[62]

Inspection/unreasonable search

The Fourth Amendment is concerned with physical searches of "houses, persons or effects," and forbids "unreasonable searches and seizures." A second sentence specifies certain procedures for the issuance of search warrants—official papers authorizing searches to be made, even in the face of physical resistance—and states that no warrant shall issue except upon a showing of "probable cause" to a judicial official, and that the warrant must "particularly describe" the place to be searched and the material being sought. The amendment has its historical origins in the behavior of British colonial governors and troops during the pre-Revolutionary period, as they sought out political opponents of the regime, tax resisters and the like. As may be imagined, the principal reference of this provision is criminal law enforcement, and a surprisingly large proportion of the Supreme Court's jurisprudence is consumed by such issues as when a search may proceed in the absence of a warrant[63] and what consequences the unlawfulness of a search has, once the trial

---

61. As when an advertiser preys on readers' insecurities, claiming that a zinc dietary supplement has the potential to double the size of the male sexual organ.

62. See Virginia State Board of Pharmacy v. Virginia Citizens Consumer Council, 425 U.S. 748 (1976); N. Redish, The Value of Free Speech, 130 Pa. L. Rev. 591 (1982); V. Blasi, The Pathological Perspective in the First Amendment, 85 Colum. L. Rev. 449 (1985); Forbes, Commercial Speech and First Amendment Theory, 74 NW.U. L. Rev. 372 (1979).

63. The presumption in favor of searches being done pursuant to warrants is strong, but not irrebuttable. Terry v. Ohio, 392 U.S. 1 (1968). While the question when it is practicable to obtain a warrant is often difficult, in general some substantial justification for not procuring one must be present, and the Court has a high opinion of the capacity of police officers to maintain premises in a searchable state while seeking a warrant. Thus, a search for weapons on the person of an arrested individual, in his room or in the passenger compartment of his car would be permitted, to avoid the threat of assault; but the opening of a locked car trunk or the general search of a house in which an arrest was made would not be.

is reached, for the admissibility of any evidence it uncovered.[64] The Fourth Amendment's application to administrative matters has arisen in two related contexts—inspection by government officials of regulated premises; and formal agency requisitions from private persons, generally those regulated, of documentary materials thought relevant to some regulatory purpose. Both these activities are central to the success of regulatory activity; information is the life's blood of the regulatory process.

The suggestion that the Fourth Amendment might require a search warrant before, say, a city health inspector could demand entrance to a factory or home to search for evidence of rat infestation was initially rejected. Unlike the criminal searcher, the inspector was seeking improvements in community health, not convictions; if he had to show some particular reason for suspecting each house he wanted to inspect, his searches would be less effective than if he made them randomly through the community, or according to some general plan. In the late 1960's, however, the opposite view was taken,[65] and it has since been confirmed several times.[66] The only exception is for industries so pervasively regulated—like stores selling firearms or nuclear power plants—that the state could demand unfettered inspection as a condition of its permission to be in the business at all.[67] Thus, for the last two decades, inspections have been regarded as "searches" for constitutional purposes; the Fourth Amendment commands not only that they be performed reasonably (say, during business hours) but also that the person being inspected may insist upon a warrant.

This rather neat analysis has given rise to both practical and theoretical difficulties. In practice, to be sure, most businesses subject to inspection

---

64. Currently, such evidence must generally be excluded, as a practical means of discouraging the police from a species of unlawful conduct that has few if any other significant discouragements. The Court is nibbling at the fringes of that rule, however—recognizing, for example, that the fruits of a search which proves to have been unlawful but which was made in "good faith" belief in its lawfulness may be admitted—and there is some thought that the Court may be prepared to reexamine this issue.

65. Camara v. Municipal Court, 387 U.S. 523 (1967); See v. City of Seattle, 387 U.S. 541 (1967); these cases made no distinction between searches of factories and searches of homes.

66. Marshall v. Barlow's Inc., 436 U.S. 307 (1978).

67. Donovan v. Dewey, 452 U.S. 594 (1981). The idea that there are some businesses ("closely regulated") the pursuit of which the state may condition as it chooses, and others that (by implication) it may regulate only in limited ways—that it need not respect the Fourth Amendment's warrant requirement for one sort but must for the others—is only one of the many curious remnants of the "substantive due process" idea discussed above at notes 53-57. A recent Supreme Court decision applying this reasoning to an automobile junk yard suggests a broad view of what constitutes a "closely regulated" business. New York v. Burger, 107 S. Ct. 2636 (1987).

appear not to insist upon warrants—doubtless to promote good will or to recognize that inspections are mutually beneficial in many cases, in response to effective coercion[68] in others. Yet other businesses do insist upon (and then resist) warrants; doing so can impose substantial costs and uncertainties upon regulators, and in this way may encourage regulators with limited resources to direct their efforts to more compliant subjects. The criminal connection and noncooperative attitude suggested by the Fourth Amendment may also have contributed, on both sides, to the confrontational (as distinct from cooperative) tone one scholar noted in comparing American to Swedish administration of workplace safety laws.[69]

The theoretical problem arises from the particularity of the amendment's description of the warrant process, with its focus on suspicions already held and particular evidence of crime being sought. To make its conclusion about the applicability of the Fourth Amendment at all workable, the Supreme Court has had to redefine "probable cause" in the administrative context to include random or patterned inspections. The requirement that warrants "particularly" describe what is being searched for, too, has had to be ignored, save as the inspection must be for matters within the inspector's regulatory ken. One may see these distortions as a natural product of the effort to adapt language written two centuries ago, with particular problems in view, to the differing issues of the modern era.

Formal demands for information present other issues. It is not that hard to see the connection between the law-backed visit of an inspector to business premises, demanding that doors be opened for him, and the criminal process forcible "search and seizure" of effects to which the Fourth Amendment was primarily addressed. The connection between searches and seizures and a demand that citizens or other regulated entities provide specified information or documentation to the regulator is somewhat more remote.[70] Here, the only risk to privacy lies in the

---

68. If, for example, the business is awaiting some official action that will not be forthcoming absent the inspection. Wyman v. James, 400 U.S. 309 (1971).

69. S. Kelman, Regulating America, Regulating Sweden: A Comparative Study of Occupational Safety and Health Regulations (1981); see also E. Bardach and R.A. Kagan, Going By The Book: The Problem of Regulatory Unreasonableness (Temple University Press, Philadelphia 1982).

70. The Court first applied the Fourth Amendment's instruction on searches and seizures to the required disclosure of documents in its somewhat mystical decision in Boyd v. United States, 116 U.S. 616 (1886), which merged Fourth and Fifth Amendment considerations in a manner later decisions have found difficult to explain. See United States v. Doe, 465 U.S. 605 (1984); McKennan, The Constitutional Protection of Private Papers: The Role of a Hierarchical Fourth Amendment, 53 Ind. L.J. 55 (1977).

requested disclosure itself. While that risk may be substantial, it does not present issues of violence or of intrusion into living quarters by agents of the state.

Agencies commonly are granted the authority to demand information of persons subject to their jurisdiction, either generally (as in the requirements that citizens file tax returns and that regulated corporations produce financial reports) or in particular cases. In the former case, the instrument of production is characterized as a "required record or report," and the controls over its legitimacy are more statutory than constitutional.[71] Compliance with a "required report" may be directly enforced by the agency, prior to any judicial control.

Where information is particularly sought from one or a small number of individuals, on the other hand, the instrument of production (usually called a subpoena) is generally thought to require judicial participation in its enforcement. The courts reach this conclusion for constitutional reasons, by analogy to the Fourth Amendment's requirement for a magistrate's review of a proposed search warrant before it acquires legal force. While a subpoena does not grant permission for forcible entry to another's premises on any construction, its particularity and individuality (requiring a specific person to provide identified documentation) suggest a degree of exposure to adverse legal consequences warranting that protection. As with inspection warrants, the standards for issuance and enforcement of subpoenas are in fact highly permissive; yet the fact that they cannot acquire legal force before a judge has been persuaded that those standards have been met creates potentials for delay that are readily open to manipulation. While the Supreme Court has occasionally seemed open to the possibility that the Fourth Amendment does not require prior judicial approval of subpoenas for them to be legally binding,[72] the focused nature of the subpoena inquiry and its corresponding potential for intrusion into personal privacy makes it likely that the court will maintain the current position.

---

71. The Fifth Amendment's privilege against self-incrimination, discussed in the following subsection, is available only to individuals, not corporations or other associations. Similarly, the Fourth Amendment's prohibition of unreasonable searches and seizures does little to prevent the government from requiring organizations to report information of arguable regulatory importance. United States v. Morton Salt Co., 338 U.S. 632 (1950). The Paperwork Reduction Act, 44 U.S.C. §§ 3501-3520, briefly discussed at p. 71, note 72, serves as a statutory control of a general character, requiring agencies to clear proposed information requirements with the Office of Management and Budget, a presidential agency. See pp. 76-77.

72. Compare See v. City of Seattle, 387 U.S. 541 (1967) with Zurcher v. The Stanford Daily, 436 U.S. 547 (1978); see Note, The Argument for Agency Self-Enforcement of Discovery Orders, 83 Colum. L. Rev. 215 (1983).

Information/incrimination

In addition to providing a judicial check on the reasonableness of administrative information demands, the Bill of Rights establishes a form of testimonial privilege that may occasionally be invoked to support a refusal to cooperate with such demands. The Fifth Amendment includes among its provisions an assurance that no "person" shall be required to incriminate himself. Thus, when a "person" can point to a crime and believably assert that his response to some demand for information might serve as a link in a chain of evidence tending to convict him of that crime, he will be excused from responding. As a general matter, this privilege has been a "strong" one in our political history; fear of police coercion in criminal interrogations initially marked understanding of its scope. The widespread use of the privilege by witnesses at congressional and administrative hearings during the anti-Communist hysteria of the early 1950's, and the political demagoguery consequently associated with opposition to its use, have assured a broad reading of the amendment in other investigative contexts as well. The Supreme Court has used it, for example, as the basis for a series of important decisions about warnings policemen must give suspects before interrogation.[73] It has strongly resisted efforts to punish invocation of the privilege, as by making any claim of the privilege a ground for removal from a public job.[74]

Perhaps because of the power to frustrate much regulatory activity, however, the use of this privilege in ordinary administrative contexts is limited. In the first place, it is not available in any respect to corporations or other artificial persons,[75] and as an extension of this cannot be claimed even by a natural person about corporate documents or information (of which she may be custodian) that would have the tendency to incriminate not only the corporation but also herself.[76] Note that distinguishing real from artificial persons in this way is highly unusual. No such distinction is made concerning freedom of speech, or the protection of property from

---

73. Miranda v. Arizona, 384 U.S. 436 (1966).

74. Gardner v. Broderick, 392 U.S. 273 (1968). A public employee could, however, be fired for refusing to answer questions directly and narrowly relating to the performance of his duties.

75. Such as partnerships, unions or unincorporated associations. Hale v. Henkel, 201 U.S. 43 (1906); Bellis v. United States, 417 U.S. 85 (1974).

76. Braswell v. United States, 108 S. Ct. 2284 (1988); the government is not permitted, however, to make any use of the fact of production against the individual. See also United States v. Doe, 465 U.S. 605 (1984). Also, the privilege is available only for testimonial acts. It does not preclude the government from requiring the target of investigation from signing a letter directing foreign banks with which he may have accounts to cooperate with the investigation. Doe v. United States, 108 S. Ct. 2341 (1988).

unreasonable inspection by the state, or the Fifth Amendment's guarantees of fair procedure and "just compensation" when property is taken for public use, shortly to be discussed. Nonetheless, it is reasoned that the protection against self-incrimination seeks to avoid the overbearing of an individual's will by the state, an interest in personal integrity that— unlike interests in expression, property and fair procedure—real and artificial persons do not share. One may understand, also, that the most feared types of official coercion, as physical torture, are unlikely to occur in the regulatory context.

Even real persons face numerous obstacles to using the privilege in the regulatory context. First, they may assert it only by affirmatively claiming it. For example, if a taxpayer's sources of income were unlawful, she could not use the privilege to excuse her failure to file an income tax return, but would have to file the return indicating a privilege claim on the line where earned income is to be reported. This is a more conspicuous gesture than most would wish to make. Second, the claim can be made only for "testimonial" communications; it is unavailable, for example, as a basis for resisting the taking of a fingerprint or other physical evidence. Third, it can be made only on the basis of potential incrimination, not merely a tendency to bring about undesired regulatory consequences. Finally, the circumstances in which a claim can be made are highly limited: the papers must both belong to the claimant and be in her possession. Thus, if my papers are subpoenaed from my accountant or my bank, the privilege is not available, for it is not I who am required to produce them; and if my accountant's papers are sought from me, the fact that they incriminate me is also irrelevant—only if I can establish that the very fact of producing the papers in response to the subpoena is a testimonial act that might incriminate me, might a claim be made.[77] In a hearing process, where oral statements are sought, the application of the privilege is more obvious. Here the risk is that the claimant will be thought to have waived it by earlier answers indicating cooperation with the relevant line of the inquiry.

"Due process of law" as procedure

Introductory

The fundamental right having greatest relevance to administrative law is expressed in both the Fifth and Fourteenth Amendments, the assurance that no person (here, including artificial persons) may be "deprived of

---

77. United States v. Doe, 465 U.S. 605 (1984).

life, liberty, or property without due process of law." In their procedural aspect, these eleven words are the source of all fundamental claims about fair procedure in our legal system. We have already seen a little about the evolving understanding of these words, in the text above at notes 10 to 14. Here it may be appropriate to give more attention to issues of doctrinal structure.[78]

While the text of the due process clause is extremely general, the fact that it is (uniquely) expressed twice in the Constitution strongly suggests an understanding that its words state a central proposition about the requirements of legal order. Historically, the clause reflects the Magna Carta of Great Britain, both its expression of principles of legality and its particular assurance that all would receive the ordinary processes (procedures) of law. They also echo that country's seventeenth century struggles for political and legal regularity, and the American colonies' strong insistence during the pre-Revolutionary period on observance of regular legal order. The requirement that government function in accordance with law is, in itself, ample basis for understanding the stress given these words.

The problems that have arisen under the clause come from the further perception—steadfastly held since its adoption—that in at least some of the contexts in which government acts, the clause also limits the procedural regimes that the legislature (or the courts or the executive) can choose to employ. Thus, it is not always sufficient for the government to act in accordance with such law as there may be. In some circumstances, citizens may be entitled to have the government observe or offer certain procedures, *whether or not those procedures have been statutorily provided for.* A statute denying those (unspecified) procedural protections would be unconstitutional. If, for example, a state were to enact a statute assigning all ordinary common law litigation to a non-judicial body, or permitting an administrative agency to revoke a professional license without providing a rather full opportunity to be heard on the matter, federal courts would surely find those statutes void, as threatening deprivation of life, liberty or property without due process of law.

Thus, the struggle over "substantive due process," already recounted,[79] circumscribed rather than eliminated the problem of judicial subjectivity in ascertaining the demands of the Constitution. If "due process" refers only or chiefly to procedural subjects, it still communi-

---

78. An excellent general treatment of the due process problem, though more theoretical/prescriptive than analytical in its later pages, is J. Mashaw, Due Process in the Administrative State (Yale University 1985); see also T. Rakoff, Brock v. Roadway Express, Inc., and the New Law of Regulatory Due Process, 1987 Sup. Ct. Rev. 157.

79. See pp. 24-25.

cates very little about what process is "due," and in what circumstances. Courts not willing simply to accept legislative judgments on that subject are required to go outside the document to find their norms.

This problem first became apparent in the years following the "substantive due process" struggle, first as part of a major constitutional controversy over the problem of "incorporation." This controversy required the Supreme Court to decide which of the liberties in the Bill of Rights were so fundamental as to restrict the actions of state governments as well as the federal government. Liberties held to be fundamental in this sense were said to have been "incorporated" by the Fourteenth Amendment's requirement that the states observe "due process of law." In substantial part, these disputes concerned the meaning of the Fourteenth Amendment's guarantee of "due process of law" in the context of criminal trials. The federal Bill of Rights contains a number of relatively detailed provisions on the subject of required procedure in criminal cases.

The battle in the incorporation cases, vigorously joined in the late 1940s[80] and lasting until the mid-1960s, was precisely over styles of interpretation. Those arguing for incorporation, in the end largely successful,[81] saw it as a means for containing judicial subjectivity. They believed that the provisions of the Bill of Rights that were to be incorporated had quite definite content, as they were already the subjects of a substantial jurisprudence about their meaning in application to the federal government. The opponents of incorporation were Justices who thought the Fourteenth Amendment's guarantee of "due process" in criminal trials did not entail a list of specific procedures mirroring the Bill of Rights, but only an assurance of those liberties "indispensable to the dignity and happiness of a free man"[82]—a catalog to be identified by reference to the Justices'

---

80. Adamson v. California, 332 U.S. 46 (1947).

81. For a decade and a half after *Adamson*, the Court adhered to the "fundamental fairness" approach, reading into the Fourteenth Amendment only what that standard was said to require. The Court rejected the argument that the whole Bill of Rights had been incorporated. During the 1960's, however, while never explicitly abandoning this analysis, it began to incorporate more and more individual rights under the rubric of due process. At this point, most of the guarantees of the Bill of Rights have been held to apply to the states equally as to the federal government. What searches are unreasonable, that is, does not vary whether federal or state officials are doing the searching. See, e.g., Duncan v. Louisiana, 391 U.S. 145 (1968). The limited exceptions to incorporation, such as the right of one accused of *federal* crime to be indicted only by a grand jury, do not have wide significance.

82. Adamson v. California, note 80, above (Frankfurter, J., concurring). Justice Cardozo had earlier struck a similar theme, describing those protections that constituted "the very essence of a scheme of ordered liberty." Palko v. Connecticut, 302 U.S. 319 (1937).

own informed sense of what constituted the needs of civilization. Pro-incorporationists found this as objectionable as the subjectivity that had underlain the "substantive due process" imbroglio. Importing the provisions of the Bill of Rights, and only those provisions, appeared to offer sufficient certainty of outcome, a freedom from judicial fiat.[83]

No such easy solution was at hand for procedural claims concerning administrative and civil judicial actions, however, since for such proceedings the Bill of Rights was no more detailed than the Fourteenth Amendment. In either case, only the requirement that "due process" be observed was available in the constitutional text. Moreover, both the jurisprudence of fair procedure and the available techniques for resolving questions that might arise were quite undeveloped.[84] Nineteenth century cases, largely challenges to tax assessment procedures, had developed the proposition that determinations turning on individualized facts about the taxpayer or his property required an opportunity for hearing that had some (albeit informal) trial-like characteristics—there must be some opportunity for oral presentation of evidence and argument by the taxpayer before a final determination is made, the Court said, but if such an opportunity was afforded it was permissive about the details.[85]

The constitutional inquiry had two arguably separate elements: whether any procedures at all were "due"; and, if so, just what those procedures were to be. As regulation became more and more prevalent, dispute over the necessity for some form of oral hearing repeatedly arose in varying circumstances. Despite much debate over the question just what procedures that right to hearing entailed, however, little judicial development occurred.[86] The question whether any procedures at all were

---

83. Of course, only relatively so; whether the Sixth Amendment's guarantee of the assistance of counsel in criminal cases, for example, required the federal government or the states to provide defense counsel for persons too poor to afford their own receives no definitive answer in the text, and was finally resolved by the Court only during this period. Gideon v. Wainwright, 372 U.S. 335 (1963). To be sure, incorporation tended to assure the states that the standards to which their criminal justice systems would be subjected were the same as those applicable to the federal government; but as the "rights of civilized persons" alternative almost invariably permitted more state choice, this was not an assurance they especially wanted.

84. See generally, J. Mashaw, Due Process in the Administrative State, note 78, above.

85. Londoner v. Denver, 210 U.S. 373 (1908). An important case early in the 20th century distinguished from these holdings the situation in which an essentially legislative judgment was to be made, turning on propositions of more general fact. Bi-Metallic Investment Co. v. State Bd. of Equalization of Colorado, 239 U.S. 441 (1915). The cases are more fully discussed on pp. 133-36.

86. A third type of question also arose, whether there were constitutional limits (and if so what) on the issues that could be assigned to an administrative

constitutionally "due" became trapped in a sterile classification of "rights" and "privileges." Deprivation of a "right" was said to require an oral hearing where deprivation of a "privilege" did not. Many important relationships with administrative government, such as licenses or public employment (but not all, and not according to a discernible pattern), fit into the "privilege" category. On the second question, the detailed provisions made for trial-like procedures by enactment of the federal Administrative Procedure Act in 1946 pretermitted for a while the necessity of defining constitutional content for those hearing rights at the federal level. A Supreme Court decision made a few years after its adoption went so far as to suggest that the arrangements it made were what the Constitution required.[87]

The political investigations of the 1950s provided numerous occasions for consideration of due process issues in both judicial and administrative settings, at the same time as the struggles over "incorporation" were giving emphasis to the problems of and need for exact definition of procedural rights (albeit, there, in a criminal context). Efforts to deprive government workers of their jobs, based on rumors generated by faceless informers, underscored the importance of fair and open procedures to maintaining public trust in government. These loyalty and security hearings also brought into question the (previously) easy conclusion that office-holders, possessors of a mere "privilege," had no claim to procedural

---

agency for resolution, as distinct from a court. These questions reflected "due process" concerns—whether fair procedures would be available at the agency level—but tended to be presented and discussed in terms of separation of powers (what is necessarily for the judicial power). Their importance subsided almost to the disappearing point once the courts became convinced that, through the adoption of regularized procedures, agencies had become reliable triers of fact. Crowell v. Benson, 285 U.S. 22 (1932); V. Rosenblum, The Administrative Law Judge in the Administrative Process, in Subcommittee on Social Security, House Committee on Ways and Means, 94th Cong., 1st Sess., Report on Recent Studies Relevant to Disability Hearings and Appeals Crisis 171-245 (Comm. Print 1975); H. Monaghan, Marbury and the Administrative State, 83 Colum. L. Rev. 1 (1983). Their remaining influence is to be seen in a judicial disposition to make independent factual findings on constitutional issues of the deepest significance (for example, determinations important to freedom of speech issues) and in the Supreme Court's recent refusal to permit Congress to assign extensive judicial authority in bankruptcy matters to judge-like officials not formally within the judicial branch. See the text at notes 34-35, above.

87. Wong Yang Sung v. McGrath, 339 U.S. 33 (1950). This suggestion has been silently abandoned, however. The Court upheld the constitutionality of a subsequent statute explicitly adopting the procedure it had suggested might be invalid, Marcello v. Bonds, 349 U.S. 302 (1955); its recent decisions on the question what process may be "due" ignore the APA as a source of possible learning.

protections. And they emphasized the value, in an administrative context, of procedural protections long associated with Anglo-American criminal trials: the right to have the assistance of counsel; the right to know one's accuser and the evidence against one; the right to confront and cross-examine that person; the right to have decision based solely upon a record generated in open proceedings; as well as the right to present argument and evidence on one's own behalf.

Yet, for each case that seemed to demand a detailed procedural prescription, another plainly required flexibility. A legislative investigation of alleged communistic activities could not be undertaken without respecting witness' claims to procedural safeguards[88]; but the Court would not burden a legislative investigation into civil rights issues with rigid procedural requirements, although the investigation's conclusions might harm the reputation of witnesses before it in some parts of the country.[89] An aeronautic engineer could not be threatened with loss of access to military secrets on which his profession depended, on the basis of anonymous accusations about his loyalty, without the opportunity to confront the information and his accuser;[90] but a cook on a military installation threatened with loss of access to the installation (and hence that particular job), apparently on the basis of undisclosed concerns about her security status, had in all the circumstances no similar claim.[91] The Court during this period seemed to agree on little, save the proposition that what the Due Process Clause required could only be determined on the basis of all the circumstances of a given case—a view not far distant from "the very essence of a scheme of ordered liberty."[92]

---

88. Watkins v. United States, 354 U.S. 178 (1957).
89. Hannah v. Larche, 363 U.S. 420 (1960).
90. Greene v. McElroy, 360 U.S. 474 (1959).
91. Cafeteria Workers v. McElroy, 367 U.S. 886 (1961).
92. See note 82 and the accompanying text, above. A widely cited formulation was that of Justice Felix Frankfurter in Joint Anti-Fascist Refugee Committee v. McGrath, 341 U.S. 123 (1951): " . . . 'Due process,' unlike some legal rules, is not a technical conception with a fixed content unrelated to time, place and circumstances. Expressing as it does in its ultimate analysis respect enforced by law for that feeling of just treatment which has been evolved through centuries of Anglo-American constitutional history and civilization, 'due process' cannot be imprisoned within the treacherous limits of any formula. Representing a profound attitude of fairness between man and man, and more particularly between the individual and government, 'due process' is compounded of history, reason, the past course of decisions, and stout confidence in the strength of the democratic faith which we profess. Due process is not a mechanical instrument. It is not a yardstick. It is a process. It is a delicate process of adjustment inescapably involving the exercise of judgment by those whom the Constitution entrusted with the unfolding of the process."

Goldberg v. Kelly

The last twenty years have witnessed an enormous outpouring of "due process" litigation, and a strong effort to establish workable structures for analysis, both of the question *whether* process is "due" (formerly answered by reference to the "right/privilege" distinction) and of the question *what* process is required. An approach that appears to have been influenced by the incorporation idea—seeking concrete standards with which to anchor judicial subjectivity—first found expression in *Goldberg v. Kelly*,[93] a case arising out of a state-administered welfare program. *Goldberg* appeared to generate, not a method for analysis, but a highly detailed list of required procedures.

The case appeared to require decision of only a limited point: New York was seeking to terminate the enrollment of Kelly and others in its welfare program, and conceded that before finally terminating their enrollment it was required by federal statute to provide a full viva voce hearing before a hearing officer. At issue in the case was only its effort to suspend payments pending that full and formal hearing. For this limited purpose New York employed a more informal process. It was willing to give persons like Mrs. Kelly opportunities to confer with responsible bureaucrats and to submit written views before suspension, but it gave no "hearing" in the judicial sense before the suspension was put into effect. This was insufficient for the Court, and its opinion is worth stating at some length; it conveys premises of analysis that still shape American "due process" reasoning.

The first proposition, in fact conceded by the state, was that the welfare recipients' claim to continued benefits was within the ambit of the Due Process Clause. The "right"-"privilege" dialectic had been under critical assault for years, particularly with reference to the growing dependence-in-fact by citizens on the sorts of relationship with modern government that tended to be characterized as a "privilege." These critics argued that if the purposes of the Due Process Clause (and the Bill of Rights generally) in protecting citizens from governmental arbitrariness were to be served, relationships so important to life in the modern state had to be brought within the clause's reach.[94] The Court now clearly signalled that this argument had prevailed.

Next was the question how (if at all) analysis would be shaped by the fact that the case dealt with interim suspension of welfare payments rather than termination. What was to be the timing of the hearing the state

---

93. 397 U.S. 254 (1970).
94. H. Jones, The Rule of Law and the Welfare State, 58 Colum. L. Rev. 143 (1958); C. Reich, The New Property, 73 Yale L.J. 733 (1964).

conceded had to be provided? This was a question that had its own history, marked by understanding that the burden of the interim period could be a substantial one on either side. Government emergency actions (the seizure of contaminated foods, the closure of a bank) were generally tolerated, and the Court several times had remarked that where only property interests were involved, the required hearing need only occur before the government's action became final.[95] Yet, the tremendous need facing a person dependent on welfare and erroneously deprived of it, even for an interim period, now persuaded the Goldberg Court that it should regard the suspension as in itself a deprivation. Thus, suspension commanded due process protections just as the ultimate termination of welfare eligibility would. Balanced against the welfare recipient's need, as the Court then saw it, was "only" the financial cost of administration— a consideration the Court dismissed at that time, but that has proved more persuasive since.

The final problem: just what procedures had to be employed. The state conceded the need for *some* procedure: it provided notice, an opportunity to discuss the matter with a welfare official, a decision, the chance to seek review of that decision by a senior welfare official, and the right to submit written materials at that point. It did not, however, provide a hearing before an impartial judicial officer, the right to an attorney's help, the right to present evidence and argument orally, the chance to examine all materials that would be relied on or to confront and cross-examine adverse witnesses, a decision limited to the record thus made and explained in an opinion. The Court now held that due process required all of these.

The Court's basis for this elaborate holding has never been clear. Various prior cases were cited for the different ingredients provided for— the naval engineer's case (but not the cook's), for example, on the question of cross-examination—but without attention to context. The Court asserted that it was respecting the interim character of the administrative decision to suspend, by requiring less in the way of procedure than would be appropriate for a final termination of benefits. Yet, overall, the collection of procedures it required was atypically demanding even of *final* government administrative determinations on issues of great importance. A survey of forty federal programs made a few years after Goldberg, for example, found only one other program (also welfare-oriented) in which

---

95. Phillips v. Commissioner, 283 U.S. 589 (1931); see also N. Am. Cold Storage Co. v. Chicago, 211 U.S. 306 (1908); Fahey v. Mallonee, 332 U.S. 245 (1947). In the field of criminal procedure, of course, suspects are often deprived of their liberty for interim periods following procedures far less formal than criminal trial; that analogy has had surprisingly little use in the administrative context.

all the *Goldberg* rights were respected. For the substantial majority, fewer than half were provided; only notice, the assurance of some degree of impartiality, and an explanation of the basis of decision were observed with any degree of universality.[96]

Goldberg was a signal that the trend of detailed specification characterizing the preceding decades' work in criminal procedure had spilled over to the civil side. The "hearing first" aspect of its holding spread rapidly through a variety of civil judicial remedies—for example, sharply curtailing the use of summary procedures for lien or attachment that creditors had used for many years to protect their security when payments ceased. The case and many following it were products of a "law and poverty" movement that had taken root in the wake of the civil rights movement's success. The government was subsidizing the law offices that produced these challenges to the sufficiency of its procedures, and for a brief while it appeared that that subsidy too might be found constitutionally required. Since it had found in criminal cases that indigent defendants had a right to have counsel appointed to defend them, perhaps the Court would expand the *Goldberg* language about the right to assistance of counsel to require the state to provide free counsel for persons unable to afford legal services.[97] Commentators spoke, without apparent irony, of a "due process revolution" having occurred. Looking back today, one can see enduring contributions of *Goldberg*, but also a quick realization of the need to moderate the rigor of its demands, and an effort—not wholly successful—to build an analytic structure to replace its style of confident dictat.

Threshold issues

If the language of the Due Process Clause does not say *what* procedures must be accorded, it might seem to say *whether* a procedural claim can be made, what the threshold is for invoking its protections. It is when the state seeks to "deprive" a person of "life, liberty or property" that process is due. Those elements were brought forward, and made an explicit part of analysis, in two cases involving the unexplained and summary refusal of two state colleges to renew the employment contracts of two instructors.[98] Analysis there focused on the content of "life, liberty, or property." If the teachers had been dropped in retaliation for political positions (as was suspected but not at this point established) they had

---

96. P. Verkuil, A Study of Informal Adjudication Procedures, 43 U. Chi. 739 (1976).

97. See Boddie v. Connecticut, 401 U.S. 371 (1971).

98. Board of Regents of State Colleges v. Roth, 408 U.S. 564 (1972); Perry v. Sindermann, 408 U.S. 593 (1972).

been deprived of liberty.[99] If the teachers had a "property" interest in continued employment, then they could not be dropped without a hearing on the question of cause, at which they could challenge the state's evidence and attempt to contradict it by presentations of their own.

"Property"/"not property" might not seem much of an improvement over "right"/"privilege," and has been criticized on that ground. The Court was explicit, however, that what is to be regarded as property must be broadly understood—in just the terms, basically, of the writings about dependence-in-fact relationships with modern government that had spurred the abandonment of "right"/"privilege." One has property, from the perspective of the Due Process Clause, if state or federal law creates an entitlement to a continuing relationship absent some reason to alter it.

Kelly had "property" in this constitutional sense. She had an established eligibility for continuing welfare payments. Thus, she had a claim to due process before she could be deprived of it. Whether the two teachers had "property" would depend in each instance on whether persons in their position, under state law, held some form of tenure or rather served "at will," without any state law claim or expectation to continuation. The expectation need not be based on a statute. An established custom of treating instructors who had taught for X years as having tenure could be shown, for example. Yet some law-based relationship or expectation of continuation had to be shown before a federal court would say that process was "due."

This question remains at the threshold of due process inquiries, but its application has been checkered in three respects. The first is what is described in the literature as the "positivist trap," an aspect of the criticism of the "property"/"not property" distinction. Since whether one has an entitlement depends on the prescriptions of state law, legislatures may be able to define important relationships—ones on which citizens in fact come to depend—in ways that preclude the conclusion that an "entitlement" is present.[100] Even if an entitlement *is* present, a further difficulty can arise when state law not only describes a relationship between a citizen and government but also prescribes the procedures by which that relationship can be ended or altered: how can a court separate the (positive law) "entitlement" from its accompanying procedures? Mustn't the citizen be prepared to accept the "bitter with the sweet"?

---

99. In fact, no procedure could compensate for such an offense; here the operation of the Due Process Clause, directly reminiscent of the substantive due process cases, would have been simply to identify the act as unlawful. Ultimately both cases were settled in a manner that appeared to concede that the discharges *had* been politically motivated.

100. O'Bannon v. Town Court Nursing Center, 447 U.S. 773 (1980).

This issue was presented when a civil servant, enjoying tenure under statutes specifically identifying the procedures to be followed for removal, challenged the constitutionality of an aspect of those procedures. While a majority of the Court asserted that the procedures must in fact meet an independent judicial test, the opposing position was strongly stated.[101] It was not until recently that the Court forcefully repudiated the "bitter with the sweet" reasoning, in a similar case.[102]

The second problem in application of the threshold inquiry is probably best described in terms of the idea of "deprivation." The Court has reached a series of almost inexplicable results concerning the application of the Due Process Clause as a result of grievous harm done to citizens, apparently turning on the issue of "deprivation." For example, an early case established (as might be imagined) that a state could not post a picture of a person naming them as an habitual drunkard without following appropriate procedures; the posting made it unlawful for that person to be served alcoholic beverages in a bar.[103] Yet when a city circulated the photograph of a person recently arrested (but not convicted) for petty theft under the heading "Active Shoplifters," causing enormous damage to his reputation, the failure first to provide a hearing was not objectionable.[104] Another case established that school officials could not suspend a student for ten days without first giving him some kind of hearing; attendance at public school was said to be an "entitlement" of students within the Due Process Clause.[105] Yet a teacher who severely caned a student, requiring a hospital stay of several days but not formally excluding him from school, had not deprived her student of liberty or property without due process of law.[106]

The cases in which liability was denied were cases in which the challenged official acts did not change the legal aura of the victim's personality. It was still lawful to shop, or to come to school if health permitted. Perhaps more importantly, in these cases (and others) state law appeared to provide a post-event remedy, in the form of ordinary civil actions for the torts of defamation or assault. To find "due process" violations in such matters threatened to rework the arrangements of federalism, by creating broadscale federal supervision of state officials about behavior whose control had previously been left to the states.[107] These consider-

---

101. Arnett v. Kennedy, 416 U.S. 134 (1974).
102. Cleveland Board of Education v. Loudermill, 470 U.S. 532 (1985).
103. Wisconsin v. Constantineau, 400 U.S. 433 (1971).
104. Paul v. Davis, 424 U.S. 693 (1976).
105. Goss v. Lopez, 419 U.S. 565 (1975).
106. Ingraham v. Wright, 430 U.S. 651 (1977).
107. Both of the cases in which liability was rejected involved suits brought under the Civil Rights Act, 42 U.S.C. § 1983. This statute, discussed on pp. 276-

ations appear to explain the results in a technical sense. Yet it seems fair to characterize the justice of the opposing results in these cases as deeply questionable.

The third aspect of the threshold inquiry concerns potential entitlements for which a citizen is applying, and has not yet been determined to qualify. Does the statutory judgment that every citizen possessing characteristics A, B and C *shall receive* stated benefits or be recognized as enjoying a stated legal relationship with the state (say, a driver's license) create an "entitlement" so that "due process" constrains the application procedures the state can choose? These are settings in which it is clear that, once qualified, the citizen could not be deprived of her "entitlement" without due process. Yet the Supreme Court has had no occasion to say directly whether the same judgment applies at the application stage. Some Justices apparently believe that it does not.[108] On the one hand, it can be said that the law is always more solicitous of established relationships than expectations. However, the "entitlement" analysis suffers some embarrassment in this argument. The claim of the citizen seems the same whether he has wrongly been denied access to an entitlement he has not yet enjoyed or has been terminated in one previously recognized.

The procedures due

Once over the threshold, and assuming the positivist trap has been at least provisionally avoided, the problem remains how the Justices can define procedures, other than those legislatively chosen, that are constitutionally due. The principal contemporary case on that question, *Mathews v. Eldridge*, arose in a context much like *Goldberg* but produced quite a different result. Where *Goldberg* had listed the procedures to be followed ex cathedra, *Mathews* attempted to define the judicial inquiry to be undertaken in any case in which a question about constitutionally required procedures might arise. The inquiry was said by the Court to involve analysis of three factors:

First, the private interest that will be affected by the official action; second, the risk of an erroneous deprivation of such interest through

---

78, makes state officials civilly liable for the consequences of any act performed under color of state law that deprives citizens of federal rights—including, of course, rights under the Due Process Clause of the federal Constitution. Federal redress for *some* actions by state officials is an essential safeguard of citizen liberties—for example, in the area of civil rights. The possibility of constitutionalizing nearly all torts committed by state officials presents much larger difficulties.

108. See, for example, the opinion of Chief Justice Rehnquist in Walters v. National Association of Radiation Survivors, 105 S. Ct. 3180 (1985).

the procedures used, and the probable value, if any, of additional
or substitute procedural safeguards; and finally, the Government's
interest, including the function involved and the fiscal and administrative burdens that the additional or substitute procedural requirement would entail.[109]

Eldridge had been receiving disability benefits under a federally supported scheme. Responsible officials came to believe, on the basis of
information he had provided and physicians' reports, that he was no
longer disabled. They then notified him that they intended to terminate
his benefits. Only written procedures were available before the termination was made provisionally effective. Eldridge was entitled to a full
oral hearing at a later date, and would have received full benefits for the
interim period if he prevailed. His argument, like Kelly's in *Goldberg v.
Kelly*, was that even suspending payments to him pending the full hearing
was a deprivation of a property interest that could not be effected without
the use of the procedures specified in *Goldberg*.

Using the three factors it had identified, the Court majority first found
the private interest here less significant than in *Goldberg*. A person who
is arguably disabled but provisionally denied disability benefits, it said,
is more likely to be able to find other "potential sources of temporary
income" than a person who is arguably impoverished but provisionally
denied welfare assistance. Second, the Court found the risk of error in
using written procedures for the initial judgment to be low, and unlikely
to be significantly reduced by adding oral or confrontational procedures
of the *Goldberg* variety. It is reasoned that disputes over eligibility for
disability insurance typically concern one's medical condition rather than
honesty in reporting one's need; the latter would be more typical in the
welfare context. Medical condition could be decided, at least provisionally,
on the basis of documentary submissions. The Court was impressed that
during the preliminary process Eldridge had full access to the agency's
files, and the opportunity to submit in writing any further material he
wished. Finally, the Court now attached more importance than the *Goldberg* Court had to the government's claims for efficiency. In particular,
the Court assumed (as the *Goldberg* Court had not) that "resources available for any particular program of social welfare are not unlimited." Thus
additional administrative costs for suspension hearings and payments
while those hearings were awaiting resolution to persons ultimately found
undeserving of benefits would subtract from the amounts available to
pay benefits for those undoubtedly eligible to participate in the program.
The Court also gave some weight to the "good-faith judgments" of the

---

109. Mathews v. Eldridge, 424 U.S. 319 (1976).

plan administrators concerning what appropriate consideration of the claims of applicants would entail.

Mathews v. Eldridge thus reorients the inquiry in a number of important respects. First, it emphasizes the variability of procedural requirements. Rather than create a standard list of procedures that, en gross, constitute the procedure that is "due," the opinion emphasizes that each setting or program invites its own assessment. About the only *general* statement that can be made is that persons holding interests protected by the Due Process Clause are entitled to "some kind of hearing." Just what the elements of that hearing might be, however, depends on the concrete circumstances of the particular program at issue. Second, that assessment is to be made both concretely, and in a holistic manner. It is not a matter of approving this or that particular element of a procedural matrix in isolation, but of assessing the suitability of the ensemble in context.

Third, and particularly important in its implications for litigation seeking procedural change, the assessment is to be made at the level of program operation, rather than in terms of the particular needs of the particular litigants involved in the matter before the Court. Cases that are pressed to appellate courts often are characterized by individual facts that make an unusually strong appeal for proceduralization. Indeed, one can often say that they are chosen for that appeal by the lawyers, when the lawsuit is supported by one of the many organizations that seek to use the courts to help establish their view of sound social policy.[110] *Goldberg* was such a case, and the Court's opinion drew strongly on the plight of the particular individuals threatened with loss of welfare in justifying its conclusions. In *Mathews*, the Court requires judges confronted by such cases to look past the particular facts of the individuals before them to the general operation of the program. This instruction seems more likely to preserve than to endanger existing procedural arrangements. Finally, and to similar effect, the second of the stated tests places on the party challenging the existing procedures the burden not only of demonstrating their insufficiency, but also of showing that some specific substitute or

---

110. Much not-for-profit or non-commercial litigation in America is organized by "public interest" lawyers and law firms. The importance of suits initiated by such organizations is especially great in constitutional and administrative law areas. Public interest groups can use their access to procedural review even at times when they have better direct influence in the legislature. In administrative law, these groups tend to excuse their litigation rights to stimulate regulatory implementation and enforcement, block new plants or projects or otherwise influence agency policy. See A. Chayes, The Role of the Judge in Public Law Litigation, 89 Harv. L. Rev. 1281 (1976); O. Fiss, The Supreme Court, 1978 Term - Forward: The Forms of Justice, 93 Harv. L. Rev. 1 (1979); R. Stewart, The Discontents of Legalism: Interest Groups Relations in Administrative Regulation, 1985 Wisc. L. Rev. 655-59.

additional procedure will work a concrete improvement justifying its additional cost. Thus, it is inadequate merely to criticize. The litigant claiming procedural insufficiency must be prepared with a substitute program that can itself be justified.

The *Mathews* approach may be more successful if it is viewed as a set of instructions to attorneys involved in litigation concerning procedural issues, than if it is seen in judicial perspective. One knows what the elements of demonstration on a procedural "due process" claim are, and the probable effect of the approach is to discourage litigation drawing its motive force from the narrow (even if compelling) circumstances of a particular individual's position. Yet deep problems for judicial inquiry are suggested by the absence of fixed doctrine about the content of "due process" and by very breadth of the inquiry required to establish its demands in a particular context—the insistence that courts assess the operation of an entire procedural scheme across the full range of its functioning.[111] The judge has few reference points to begin with, and must decide on the basis of facts likely to be peculiarly inaccessible to litigation techniques. A not-at-all-surprising result is to encourage judges to accept resolution of procedural issues by legislatures or others better placed to make these complex yet general assessments.

Two examples may illustrate the problems judges face. The first arose when one of the federal circuit courts of appeal had to decide a dispute about the procedures to be followed in determining certain low-value claims under the national medical insurance scheme. Initially, the court ruled with confidence that access to *some* kind of oral procedure was required under *some* circumstances, for no reported case had ever approved a completely written procedure for a setting in which process was "due." Yet this reference point arose outside the *Mathews* decision as such; and when the case returned to the court at a later stage, it became clear that the *Mathews* inquiry did not answer for the court just how tightly access to an oral procedure could be controlled and just how informal that procedure could be. For example, would provision for discussions over the telephone suffice? The detailed outcome of the lawsuit seemed much more likely to be the product of negotiations between the litigants than to be the result of judicial decree.[112]

---

111. Two recent decisions revealing these difficulties are FDIC v. Mallen, 108 S. Ct. 1790 (1988) and Brock v. Roadway Express, 107 S. Ct. 1740 (1987); see T. Rakoff, note 78 above.

112. Gray Panthers v. Schweiker, 652 F.2d 146 (D.C. Cir. 1980), reconsidered after remand 716 F.2d 23 (D.C. Cir. 1983). This litigation is a good example of the programmatic litigation often found in American practice, note 110, above. The Gray Panthers organization is a privately funded foundation dedicated to representing the interests of the aged, as its members understand them to be. No

The second example is a recent Supreme Court decision involving a statute that, by very severely restricting the fees that could be paid, had the effect of denying veterans access to attorneys in prosecuting claims under veterans benefits statutes. Although the Court has not always been closely attentive to the *Mathews* formulation, in this case it was. It relied on statistics about the general run of veterans' claims to establish that their need for attorneys' assistance was not high. Most veterans prevailed; veterans' organizations were available to provide substitute representation that seemed effective; and in the few cases in which lawyers had appeared, presumably without fee, veterans were not notably more successful than the general run.[113] Yet these statistics cloaked what several of the Justices regarded as a real need for lawyers' assistance in a smaller group of much more complex cases. This was a focus the attorneys for the veterans groups[114] had not developed. Some of the Justices thought that in a well-developed case the *Mathews* inquiry might demonstrate that attorneys' help *was* constitutionally required in that sub-group of cases; others would have decided that, like the element of orality, access to an attorney was a necessary element of the process "due," one that could never be denied. What was apparent to both groups of Justices (together, a majority of the Court) was that the *Mathews* inquiry in this case was distorted by the great number of "easy cases," for which the desired procedural change would make little difference.

It follows from the preceding discussion that one cannot expect to list the elements of "required procedures" under American law. In the case involving a ten-day suspension from public school, a chance to tell the school principal (someone other than the complaining teacher) one's own side of the story was sufficient.[115] Suspension of welfare payments may still be held to require all the elements specified in the *Goldberg* case, and actual termination of those payments, somewhat more. Nonetheless, an analysis made by the late Judge Henry Friendly in his well-regarded article, "Some Kind of Hearing,"[116] generated a list that remains highly influential, as to both content and relative priority:

1. An unbiased tribunal.

---

one individual with a $75 claim for medical insurance would be likely to take the matter to the courts, or to have the resources for the appeals and remands of lengthy litigation, no matter how strongly she believed the claim had been wrongly denied, using faulty procedures. A group such as Gray Panthers, by contrast, in some sense exists just to take such actions.

113. Walters v. National Association of Radiation Survivors, 473 U.S. 305 (1985).

114. See note 110, above.

115. Goss v. Lopez, note 105, above.

116. 123 U. Pa. L. Rev. 1267, 1278 et seq. (1975).

2. Notice of the proposed action and the grounds asserted for it.

3. Opportunity to present reasons why the proposed action should not be taken.

4. The right to present evidence, including the right to call witnesses.

5. The right to know opposing evidence.

6. The right to cross-examine adverse witnesses.

7. A decision based exclusively on the evidence presented.

8. Opportunity to be represented by counsel.

9. Requirement that the tribunal prepare a record of the evidence presented.

10. Requirement that the tribunal prepare written findings of fact and reasons for its decision.

Again, it must be stressed that these are simply the kinds of procedures that might be claimed in a "due process" argument, roughly in order of their perceived importance, and not a list of procedures that will in fact be required.

Note, too, that one item missing from Judge Friendly's list is any claim to have the responsibility for presenting the government's information separated from the responsibility for deciding the dispute. Despite the usual preference of American jurisprudence for having opposing lawyers present a dispute to a neutral and wholly arbitral judge, adversary procedures, as such, are not required in the administrative setting. As lawyers from civilian jurisdictions may understand more easily than some of their American brethren, administrative law judges may be made responsible for directing the inquiry into a disputed matter, and presenting the government's information, without compromising in a constitutional sense their capacity to serve as an "unbiased tribunal" for decision of the dispute.[117]

"Due process of law" as substance: the expropriation problem

We remarked above that use of the "due process" clause is generally limited to matters of procedure, that indeed a major constitutional crisis arose in the first part of this century when judges attempted to use that

---

117. Mathews v. Eldridge, 424 U.S. 319 (1976); Richardson v. Perales, 402 U.S. 389 (1971). The Court *has* suggested that an administrative law judge with such responsibilities has a duty of diligent inquiry on behalf of the claimant. Heckler v. Campbell, 461 U.S. 488 (1983).

clause as a basis for judging the acceptability of the substantive content of statutory regulation.[118] In the field of economic regulation, "substantive due process" has been firmly rejected. The one possible exception to this observation, of occasional interest to lawyers concerned with regulation, arises from another aspect of the Fifth and (by incorporation)[119] Fourteenth Amendments. Immediately following the injunction that no person "be deprived of life, liberty, or property, without due process of law," the Fifth Amendment adds "nor shall private property be taken for public use, without just compensation." Regulation imposing extremely severe constraints on private property for public benefit might be characterized as involving a "taking," for which compensation must be paid, rather than merely a failure to observe necessary procedures.

Even a quite severe regulation of private property will not be considered to be a taking, if the court can discern a public purpose in the measure and finds no "undue interference in . . . investment-backed expectations." What purposes are "public" and what interferences are "undue" are, however, subject to dispute—as witness a 1987 decision by the Supreme Court involving a requirement that underground coal mines leave 50% of the coal in place as support for the surface, which might otherwise subside. The coal mine operators had earlier purchased both the right to underground minerals *and* the right to support of the surface from the owners of the surface of the land. Only five Justices concluded that this regulation had a "public" purpose distinct from aiding the particular owners of surface rights against the mine operators, and that the interference with the mine operators' ownership of the coal was not "undue"; four would have reached the opposite conclusion.[120] If a "taking" *has* occurred, then the state can be required to pay "just compensation" for what has been taken—even if the taking is only temporary because, ultimately, the regulatory action is found to be beyond its authority.[121]

---

118. See pp. 53-57.

119. See pp. 34-35.

120. Keystone Bituminous Coal Ass'n v. De Benedictis, 107 S. Ct. 1232 (1987); compare Nollan v. California Coastal Commission, 107 S. Ct. 3141 (1987) (*no* public purpose in requiring land owners to donate a public access to a beach adjacent to their property, as a condition to permitting them to build residences on the property).

121. First English Evangelical Lutheran Church v. County of Los Angeles, California, 107 S. Ct. 2378 (1987).

$\equiv 3$
THE MACHINERY OF GOVERNMENT

The discussion of separation of powers in chapter 2[1] introduced the three chief authorities of the federal government: Congress, the President, and the Supreme Court. These are the only federal actors whose functions are definitely set out in the federal Constitution. While there are references to the possibility of other courts and to the "departments" and their heads (the inevitable bureaucracy), all legislative power given the federal government is placed in the two houses of an elected Congress; all executive power, in an elected President; and all judicial power, in a Supreme Court whose members are appointed to lifelong terms with the approval of the upper house of Congress, the Senate.

Congress

The Congress has two chambers, the Senate and the House of Representatives. The Senate is comprised of 100 Senators, two elected from each state. Each Senator is elected by the entire voting population of the state and serves a six-year term, with elections occurring every two years so that one third of the Senate stands for election each two years. Unless a special election is required to fill an unexpired term, only one of a state's two Senate positions is involved in any Senate election, and in one of every three Senate elections neither is. The House of Representatives comprises 435 Representatives, or Congressmen, allocated among the states according to population, but with each state having at least one. Each member stands for election every two years. In states with more than one Representative, each represents a unique geographical subdistrict of the state defined by state legislation. These districts are generally redefined every ten years, when the results of the national census are known, in order to assure compliance with the constitutional requirement that each district contain populations as nearly equal as possible.[2] The shape (as distinct from the size) of the districts is often determined by

---

1. See pp. 12-18.
2. Reynolds v. Sims, 377 U.S. 533 (1964).

51

political principles, as might be expected, and lively legal disputes continue whether this is acceptable and, to the extent not, whether a workable judicial remedy can be devised.[3]

It can be seen that the design of the Congress serves a number of national political ends (as well as creating national bodies suitable for generating legislation). Both Senators and Representatives, perhaps especially the former, are directly identified with particular states. Indeed originally Senators were elected by the state legislatures rather than directly by the voting population. While popular election of Senators was introduced by the 17th Amendment in 1913, they remain important statewide officials and often reach prominence through the state political apparatus.[4] Thus, they are likely to be strong representatives in the national legislature of state political interests. Also, their six-year terms encourage a degree of independence of momentary political winds. The drafters of the Constitution saw them as (and they have often been) a conservative check on the activities of the more populous and political House of Representatives.

Members of the House, in turn, are never more than two years from the need to be reelected,[5] a fact which strongly encourages responsiveness to their constituencies. House members typically maintain important staff offices in their districts, and frequently serve for their constituents the functions that Ombudsmen have in other systems, assisting them in their difficulties with the federal bureaucracy.[6] The closeness of the Represen-

---

3. The process of creating a representative district to serve a particular political end—say, concentrating voters favoring the Democratic party—is known as "Gerrymandering." A political boundary created with the inescapable purpose of excluding black voters was found invalid in Gomillon v. Lightfoot, 364 U.S. 339 (1960). Not until 1986 did the Supreme Court hold the courts open more generally to cases involving apparent discrimination along political lines. Davis v. Bandemer, 106 S. Ct. 2797 (1986).

4. Changes in the political process within states, however, have made Senators less often the product of state political structures. State party organizations have declined in importance as the effect of money, media, and celebrity have increased. Senators and Members of the House are more likely to develop independent constituencies based on their constituents' support of national initiatives, rather than state interests. Kaden, Politics, Money, and State Sovereignty, 79 Colum. L. Rev. 847 (1979).

5. In fact, incumbent congressmen are almost always re-elected, for reasons of pre-existing popularity and relatively easy access to fundraising. The incumbents' advantage is especially pronounced in the House, where 91% were re-elected in 1980. In the Senate, 77% were re-elected in 1970, but just 55% in 1980, when the Republicans took control of the Senate. 1986, similarly, was a bad year for Senatorial incumbents, when Democrats regained the advantage.

6. Senators also do personal service for constituents. But because they represent an entire state and need run for re-election only each sixth year, constituent

tatives to the people is reflected in the constitutional requirement that fiscal legislation—tax and budget—originate there. Otherwise, proposed legislation may first be enacted in either House.

Legislation and appropriations

The principal work of Congress concerns the enactment of legislation, including the annual national budget. Although the President and the agencies of government are often *in fact* the source of proposed legislation, as a formal matter all legislation is introduced by Senators or Representatives whatever its actual source. The source of a legislative proposal has no legal (as distinct from political) significance. Legislation on any subject may be introduced in either the Senate or the House (although the House must be the first to enact legislation on fiscal subjects), and will typically be referred to one or more committees for investigation and report. The committees of the House and of the Senate, discussed in somewhat greater detail below, are small bodies composed of Representatives or Senators (with professional staff) and are specialized according to subject matter. Their membership is divided between Democrats and Republicans in roughly the proportion that those two parties hold seats in the relevant part of Congress. They meet under the chairmanship of a member of the majority party. The committee will generally act first through a subcommittee. It may (but need not) hold public hearings on proposed legislation.

When public hearings are held, the persons appearing may include other legislators interested in the proposal, government officials responsible for activities in the area under inquiry, experts, and representatives of interested industries or public groups. Typically witnesses give a brief oral statement summarizing a longer written submission, and members of the committee or its staff may then address questions to them. Following the hearings, drafting revisions may be made in "mark-up" sessions of the committee, often held publicly and with the active participation of private lobbyists who work with committee members and their staffs to effect their particular point of view.[7] If the subcommittee can

---

service—at least on the retail level—is traditionally a smaller part of the Senators' function.

7. There are few legal constraints on the work of lobbyists, who may be retained by trade and business groups as well as by civil rights and environmental proponents. Occasionally lobbyists do evoke political criticism and controversy. In general, however, the lobbyist's function in attempting to persuade or even pressure congressmen politically is seen as legitimate. Bribes, of course, are illegal; but campaign contributions are legal—even if coming from organizations that also lobby. The size of contributions are regulated, although one can donate

agree on support of a particular proposal for legislation, it will bring that before the full committee, where further hearings and change may occur. The committee may, in turn, send the proposal to the floor of the chamber it represents; there, it is subject to formal debate, amendment, and vote.[8] As may appear, the committees are the dominant influence on the process. Even seemingly popular proposals for legislation are often defeated there by powerful members.

If a bill is passed, it is then sent to the other chamber, where it usually undergoes the same process. As may be apparent, it may never emerge from that chamber, or emerge in very different form. In the first case, the bill is defeated.

In the second, two methods of resolving the dispute are possible. First, the chamber that originally enacted the legislation may be satisfied to adopt the second chamber's version; then no further work is required. If it is not willing to accede, however, each chamber then appoints representatives to a special "conference committee" whose work it is to meet and work out a suitable compromise measure that can be recommended to both chambers. This work, like other committee work, is generally done in public session, and lobbyists often seek to work with committee members to obtain what their clients regard as the most satisfactory outcomes. To become law, a bill must be enacted in identical form by each of the two chambers during the two-year period that marks the term of office of Representatives.[9] This requirement of bicameralism is an important element of the constitutional scheme.

The final, and necessary, step in the process of enactment is the presentment of the bill to the President for his signature. If he signs it, it becomes law. He may, however, refuse to sign the legislation and return it to Congress with a veto message. In that event, it does not become law unless Congress is able to override his veto by a two-thirds vote of the members of each chamber.[10] Notice that the President's authority at

---

unlimited amounts to political action committees, which in turn can contribute to candidates. 2 U.S.C. §§ 262-270. Agents of foreign governments, including their political lobbyists but not their diplomats, must register and comply with lobbying regulations and with the Attorney General, subject to criminal penalties. 18 U.S.C. § 2386.

8. In the House of Representatives, but not in the Senate, the terms of the debate and amendment process are set by a special committee, the House Rules Committee, which creates a "rule" for each proposed legislative act.

9. At the end of the two-year period, all legislation not finally enacted lapses— even if it had cleared all but the final hurdle. Of course it may be reintroduced, but without any formal claim to shortened procedure.

10. Ordinarily, a veto requires a positive act; a bill becomes law ten business days after passage unless specifically vetoed. If Congress adjourns during the ten-day period, so that a veto message cannot be received, it does not become

this point is strictly negative—he can only veto, not alter, the enacted bill; and the veto applies to the entire legislation. The President cannot select a portion only for veto. This restriction has particular significance in the appropriations process shortly to be described, since it binds the President to Congress' choices about spending priorities.[11]

In the regulatory context, three different types of legislation may be required before an agency can act. Most obvious is the substantive legislation that empowers the agency and creates standards for it to administer in its assigned field. This need be enacted but once, and has continuous legal force until revised. The second and third types of legislation concern the agency's necessary expenditure of public funds to perform its work. The general dimensions of the agency's program, from a fiscal perspective, are established by a law that establishes a maximum amount "authorized" to be expended for agency programs. Authorization to expend funds is usually given permanently, but in some cases agencies are required to return to Congress each several years, or even annually, for fresh authorization. This can be considered a device by which Congress prompts itself to review agency functioning to determine whether its continuance is in the public interest. The third type of legislation, the annual appropriation, is the device by which Congress establishes the actual level of agency functioning for the coming year by setting the fiscal resources to be made available. Agencies are permitted to expend funds from the public treasury only pursuant to an appropriation.[12] For smaller agencies, appropriations may be, and often are, simply a statement of the total amount of money the agency may spend for its programs in the coming fiscal year, without further specification.

For larger programs, funds may be allocated for specific aspects of agency functioning, controlling in this way not only the overall level of agency effort but also its internal allocation. It will be evident that this annual process has great significance for the agency, and permits both Congress and, as will be seen, the President a high degree of oversight and control of agency functioning.

The appropriations process is a complicated one, and in a work of this character the main point is to establish it as a significant control of

law unless the President signs it. A refusal to sign during this period is called a Pocket Veto.

11. For a fuller description of the legislative process see E. Redman, The Dance of Legislation (1973); W. Eskridge and P. Frickey, Cases and Materials on Legislation (West 1988).

12. Art. I, § 9 Cl. 7. The Treasury is not the only possible source of funds; agencies are occasionally authorized to collect fees from those they regulate and to apply those fees to the expenses of their programs. To the extent this is done, it frees agencies from the discipline of the budgetary process.

agency action, one that reflects both national priorities and contemporary political forces more systematically and with more accuracy and timeliness than judicial or other legal controls. Of the process itself, it seems sufficient here to add only the following details. Although occurring annually, appropriations are legislative in form, and so must pass through each of the steps outlined above. With limited exceptions, agencies first make their requests for appropriations to the President's Office of Management and Budget, discussed below.[13] Whether or not the language of the appropriation bill will go into program details, the agency must be prepared at this point, and in legislative discussions, to give full and detailed justifications for every aspect of its proposed programs. After OMB review is complete, the President draws up and sends to Congress a proposed consolidated national budget. In generating that proposal, he will necessarily determine the relative priority to be given the agency's work within the national government and, if the agency budget is detailed, his ideas about the priorities it should follow.

Following legislative reforms made in 1974,[14] Congress is in the meantime developing its own budgetary proposals with the assistance of another agency, the Congressional Budget Office. Appropriations proposals for a given agency go at various stages before several different committees, of which the most important are specialized "appropriations committees" in the House and the Senate, committees which over the years develop extremely powerful relationships with the agencies that annually depend on them for funding of their programs.[15] Since 1974, new "budget" committees have steadily gained influence at the expense of the appropriations committees, and even the substantive committees. While debates over general spending levels and major programs such as the defense budget are common in the two chambers, agency budgets are a small part of overall national expenditures.[16] These budgets are not often the subject of debate outside the relevant committees or (if the House and Senate have appropriated different amounts in their respective bills) the conference committee.

The work of the committees and congressional staff

Oversight relations are perhaps the most important relationships administrative agencies have with Congress. These are relationships that

---

13. See pp. 76-78.
14. Congressional Budget and Impoundment Control Act of 1974, P.L. 97-258, 96 Stat. 877, 31 U.S.C. §§ 1400 ff.
15. See the works cited in note 41, p. 20.
16. In 1985, for example, the EPA regulatory budget was about $660 million; the Securities and Exchange Commission, about $106 million; the Federal Trade Commission, about $32 million. In comparison, that year's defense budget was $294.67 billion, and the total national budget for the year was $1,074.1 billion.

arise outside the usual legislative context, and even the annual process of securing necessary appropriations. Each agency will have an oversight relationship with at least one committee in each of the Senate and the House of Representatives. In this relationship congressional investigations and hearings into the agency's conduct of business may occur quite independently of any proposal that may exist for legislative change. Committee members expect to be informed of important proposals within the agency and feel free to conduct hearings or to seek in other less formal ways to influence it. Interactions are frequent and generally treated with seriousness on the agency side.[17] Generally the professional staff of the respective oversight committees will be as well informed respecting the functioning of an agency as any persons in official Washington outside the agency itself. Aggressive oversight is more common in connection with agency planning or proposals for rulemaking—the adoption of subordinate legislation—than it is respecting the decision of formal agency proceedings of an adjudicatory character, since political pressures in the latter context can give rise to "fairness" claims by those who may seem to be their target.[18]

In addition to these formal and continuing relationships with committees and their staffs, agencies are in frequent contact with individual Senators and Representatives respecting matters of particular interest to their constituents. It is normal for a person frustrated with or concerned about an agency's action to write about it to his Senator or Representative, and for her staff then to pass the question on to the agency. Usually this comes in the form of an inquiry or more-or-less standard request to learn the status of a given matter, have it expedited, etc.[19] It is not unknown, however, for the Senator or Representative to state a view on the desirable outcome of the matter, and these interventions can be influential. As already remarked,[20] Representatives in particular view this form of constituency service as a major aspect of their role, seeing it as a way of generating community support for reelection; some scholars believe that its tendency is to eclipse the directly legislative function that is the only responsibility specified for Senators and Representatives in the Consti-

---

17. Evidence of its effect does not often appear. But see Home Box Office, Inc. v. Federal Communications Commission, 567 F.2d 9 (D.C. Cir.), cert. denied 434 U.S. 829 (1977); SEC v. Wheeling-Pittsburgh Steel Corp., 648 F.2d 118 (3d Cir. 1981); Sierra Club v. Costle, 657 F.2d 298 (D.C. Cir. 1981).

18. Pillsbury Co. v. Federal Trade Commission, 354 F.2d 952 (5th Cir. 1966).

19. See A. Sofaer, The Change-of-Status Adjudication: A Case Study of the Informal Agency Process. 1 J. Leg. Stud. 349 (1972) and J. Mashaw et al., Social Security Hearings and Appeals (1978). Both studies suggest that Congress members often will act to speed agency action on matters which concern their constituents, but usually stop short of acting as advocates.

20. See text at note 41, p. 20.

tution.[21] Be that as it may, responding to such interventions occupies a good deal of agency time, and is regarded as an activity of some importance to the agency's future well-being.

Congressional agencies—the General Accounting Office and the Congressional Budget Office

All this oversight activity has resulted in an enormous growth in congressional staff, both on committees and in the personal offices of individual Senators and Representatives.[22] In addition, two major agencies operating, in effect, as delegates of Congress serve a continuing, professional oversight function. Although this function is not often highly visible to the public, it has a considerable impact on administrative functioning.[23] The Congressional Budget Office, already mentioned,[24] is responsible for the congressional side of the annual appropriations process. In that capacity, it shares with the appropriations committee a continuing relationship with agencies respecting their need for funding. Since 1922, agencies have had to satisfy a presidential office (now the Office of Management and Budget)[25] about the relative importance of their needs for financial support and the contributions of particular programs to national policy. Since creation of the Congressional Budget Office in 1974, they have also had to justify their claims on the national budget to this body, which acts as a professional financial analyst on behalf of the two houses of Congress.[26]

The General Accounting Office is a large agency, of more than 4,000 professional employees, whose responsibility, in the first instance, is retrospective analysis of agency functioning to audit the correctness of agency expenditures; and, more broadly, to search out fraud, waste, and

---

21. Ibid.
22. See note 40, p. 19.
23. The two agencies to be discussed are not the only congressional agencies, although they are perhaps the most prominent. The Library of Congress performs research and analysis functions in addition to serving its nominal function. The Office of Technology Assessment assists committees and members to identify and plan for the social and physical consequences of policy choices affecting the uses of technologies—a function not unlike the "impact analyses" conducted by the executive branch. See pp. 70-76.
24. See p. 56.
25. The OMB is discussed at pp. 76-78.
26. See W. Wander, F. Hebert and G. Copeland, Congressional Budgeting: Politics, Process and Power (1984) and A. Schick, The First Five Years of Congressional Budgeting, in R. Penner, The Congressional Budget Process After Five Years 3 (1981). The Budget Office's principal function, however, is to make broadscale assessments of the budget and its impact.

mismanagement in federal agency functioning. The GAO performs particular studies of agency functioning at the request of relevant committees, Senators or Representatives; as important, it has a continuing presence at agencies in its audit function. This work results in reports to Congress of its findings—reports accompanied by agency responses and, frequently, offers of "corrective measures" that mark a substantial contribution of GAO oversight to the control of agency functioning. In addition, GAO disapproval of the correctness or lawfulness of a proposed expenditure of agency funds, in an opinion of its head, the Comptroller General, generates legal consequences for the relevant agency staff that will make them very reluctant to spend those funds.[27] And in certain contexts, the GAO has been authorized to intervene in governmental contract disputes. This last activity is thought by some to raise significant "separation of powers" problems.[28] However that dispute is resolved, it seems apparent that the GAO will remain as a major agency for congressional oversight and control of administrative agency action.[29]

President

The President of the United States is its chief executive officer, and the only executive officer whose existence and function is specified in the Constitution. Article II of the Constitution principally discusses the (rather complicated) mechanism for his election each four years, and says very little even about his authority: "the executive Power shall be vested" in him; he is to be "Commander in Chief" of the armed forces; "may require the Opinion, in writing, of the principal Officer in each of the executive Departments, upon any subject relating to the Duties of their

27. General sources on the GAO include F. Moghen, The GAO: The Quest for Accountability in American Government (1979) and E. Kloman, Cases in Accountability: The Work of the GAO (1979).

28. Ameron, Inc. v. United States Army Corps of Engineers, 787 F.2d 875, reaffirmed on rehearing 809 F.2d 979 (3d Cir.1986). The position of the Comptroller General is somewhat anomalous. He is appointed by the President to a single fifteen-year term, but this appointment is expected to be made from a list of three candidates given him by the leadership of the Senate and the House of Representatives and once the Comptroller General *is* appointed, removal requires congressional rather than presidential action. See pp. 63-68. Confusion about his place in government and his proper roles marked the Supreme Court's decision in a case involving Congress' effort to control the national deficit, Bowsher v. Synar, 106 S. Ct. 3181 (1986). See Strauss, Formal and Functional Approaches to Separation of Powers Questions—A Foolish Inconsistency? 72 Cornell L. Rev. 488 (1987).

29. F. Mosher, The GAO, The Quest for Accountability in American Government (1979).

respective Offices"; he may pardon offenses. With the advice and consent of two thirds of the Senators present, "he shall have the Power . . . to make treaties"; and with the advice and consent of a majority of Senators he appoints major federal officers, including judges. Congress can place appointment of less important officers "in the President alone, in the Courts of Law, or in the Heads of Departments." Finally, "he shall take Care that the Laws be faithfully executed."

Earlier discussion of the problem of separation of powers[30] suggested some of the history of these arrangements and their difficulty. In particular, that discussion suggested the continuing tension between the view of the President as politically responsible for all acts of government, and the view of the other officers of government, who operate pursuant to statutory authority, as legally responsible for all decisions respecting their particular programs.[31] That tension can be seen in the language just quoted: "the executive power," unspecified, is in the President. Yet "Duties" are in the principal officers of the (also unspecified) "executive Departments." The only stated relationship between these officers and the President (with his personal staff) is that he can require their "Opinion, in writing" on those matters. Is he capable of acting on that opinion? Or, does the Constitution's provision that "he shall take Care that the laws *be* faithfully executed" (that is, be executed *by someone else*), suggest that he is merely to exercise oversight?

The laws establishing the governmental apparatus distinguish sharply between the office of the President, on the one hand, and the operating divisions of government on the other. The latter take many forms—cabinet departments headed by Secretaries, executive agencies headed by Administrators, independent regulatory commissions headed by collegial bodies, even government corporations. Here, a unifying characteristic should be stressed. It is typically in these bodies, *not* the President, that Congress places the legal authority to act when it enacts regulatory programs. Whatever the President may be able to say to the Secretary of Agriculture or to the Chairman of the Securities and Exchange Commission about matters pending before them, in form it is the Secretary or the Commission that acts. It is to the Department and the Commission that Congress appropriates the resources necessary to act. The President and his personal staff are rarely authorized to act in ways that may directly affect a member of the public, and the resources of the presidency itself

---

30. See pp. 12-18.

31. A well-regarded history of the formation of the presidency is Thach, The Creation of the Presidency 1775-1789 (1923). As he shows, the framers sought at the same time to choose for a strong executive and against monarchy—a compromise which has created continuing instability in the American view of the office.

are quite limited.[32] The following paragraphs suggest the ways in which those resources may be used to oversee or control administrative action.

Political and administrative authority

If a law fixes an absolute duty on an official, that is to say one as to which he has no discretion, it has been settled since the earliest days[33] that his compliance with that duty may be enforced by law, and the President has no authority to interfere. This is the very least that might be expected of a commitment to legality—that the President as well as the official is bound by the law's specification of duty. Administrative regimes of any interest, however, confer substantial discretion. The law fixes not an absolute duty but a range of circumstances within which the official is empowered to act. Whether, or the extent to which, the President is entitled to control that exercise of discretion directly or through his staff is, and remains, the more interesting question. While there has been no definitive resolution of that issue as a constitutional matter, the statutory frameworks generally assume no more than persuasion on his part, and at least as a formal matter that is respected. A regulation governing the amount of sulfur dioxide that may be released into the atmosphere by electric power generating stations, and the measures to be taken by the stations in compliance, is issued by the Administrator of the Environmental Protection Agency, albeit after intense and private consultations with the President and his staff.[34]

The early cases tended to take the existence of discretion as a signal that the President's acts could not be controlled by law, at least within the ambit of that discretion. Thus an early case, central to the theory of judicial review of executive action, contrasted "cases in which the executive professes a constitutional or legal discretion" with those "where a specific duty is assigned by law, and individual rights depend upon the performance of that duty," and denied any claim to reach the former:

---

32. The President and a few hundred political appointees are at the apex of an enormous bureaucracy whose members enjoy tenure in their jobs, are subject to the constraints of statutes whose history and provisions they know in detail, and often have strong views of the public good in the field in which they work. President Truman is reported to have described his authority as the power "to bring people in and try to persuade them to do what they ought to do without persuasion. That's what I spend most of my time doing. That's what the powers of the President amount to."

33. Marbury v. Madison, 5 U.S. (1 Cranch) 137 (1803); Kendall v. United States, 37 U.S. (12 Pet.) 524 (1838).

34. Sierra Club v. Costle, 657 F.2d 298 (1981); B. Ackerman and W. Hassler, Clean Coal, Dirty Air (Yale 1981); J. Quarles, Cleaning up America (1976).

The province of the court is, solely, to decide on the rights of individuals, not to enquire how the executive, or executive officers, perform duties in which they have a discretion. Questions, in their nature political, or which are, by the constitution and laws, submitted to the executive, can never be made in this court.[35]

Over time, however, it has become clear that "discretion" may refer to at least two differing phenomena. First, it refers to political areas that reasons of state may require be left essentially devoid of law. Second, it connotes administrative settings in which much specification is provided and regularity of official behavior is deeply desired, although acts of judgment are also called for. An example of the first, in fact the example stressed in the case, is the conduct of foreign relations. In this political arena, where one might say there is "no law to apply,"[36] an executive officer is "to conform precisely to the will of the President. He is the mere organ by whom that will is communicated."[37] An example of the second sort of discretion is the case mentioned above, concerning pollution controls for electric utilities. One might not say that "individual rights depend" upon the EPA Administrator's exercise of his statutory responsibilities, and he enjoys substantial discretion in that exercise. Yet there he functions within the atmosphere of law, subject to more-or-less clear statutory limits on what he may do. Using the word "discretion," a contemporary analyst would have no difficulty concluding that a court could review the Administrator's action to see whether his discretion had been abused.[38]

This essay is concerned only with the second, administrative, form of discretion.[39] While, as already indicated, the President often enjoys much scope to influence decisions of this character, few argue today that the officers empowered to make them must "conform precisely to the will of the President" or that such officers are "the mere organ by whom that will is communicated." Both they and he, in the first instance, must

---

35. Marbury v. Madison, 5 U.S. (1 Cranch) 137 (1803); see Monaghan, *Marbury and the Administrative State*, 83 Colum. L. Rev. 1 (1983).

36. Citizens to Preserve Overton Park, Inc. v. Volpe, 401 U.S. 402 (1971).

37. Marbury, note 35, above.

38. This distinction is reflected in the federal Administrative Procedure Act's provisions for judicial review, which in seemingly conflicting passages state that judicial review is to be denied to the extent agency action is committed by law to agency discretion, 5 U.S.C. § 701(a)(2), but that agency action may be reviewed for abuse of discretion, 5 U.S.C. § 706(2)(a). See the discussion on pp.221-23 and 261-69.

39. Thus, problems arising from (for example) most actions of the CIA are not of interest here; but its personnel actions may be controlled to some extent. Webster v. Doe, 108 S. Ct. ____(1988)

comply with such legal constraints as do exist: specifications of expenditures to be made,[40] procedures to be followed, investigations to be undertaken, factors to be considered (or excluded from view). Formal legal authority to act rests with the officer, not the President. Yet self-evidently the President is better placed than the official in respects that argue for his substantial participation. Only the President bears any direct political responsibility for the work of administration. Although, to be sure, the President will not often suffer political loss because of this or that detail of official action (as against, for example, his commitment to national defense), he is the only official accountable in any degree.[41] The President is well placed, as the heads of individual agencies are not, to reconcile the sometimes conflicting instructions of national statutes, to set national priorities in executing the laws as a whole, and to coordinate the work of government.[42] Each of these capacities permits him to bring to bear a perspective on decision that an agency could not enjoy. The primary commitment of the Constitution to a unitary executive[43] suggests a legal basis for giving that perspective force.

Appointments and removals

Short of formally displacing an officer's decision—an authority recent Presidents have rarely sought to assert—the most obvious way for the President to control the character of administration is by appointing officials sympathetic to his policies, reasoning with them as they act, and disciplining those who do not respond to his suggestions for carrying them out. Specific provision is made in the Constitution respecting the President's appointment of government officers. None is made about his participation in their removal (or other forms of discipline).[44] Both ap-

---

40. Under the Congressional Budget and Impoundment Control Act of 1974, note 14, above, this is both an affirmative and negative obligation. Never able to expend moneys that have not been appropriated, the executive is also restrained in withholding from payment (or impounding) moneys that have been appropriated; to refuse to expend money for a purpose to which it was dedicated is to refuse faithfully to execute the law. See K. Dam, The American Fiscal Constitution, 44 U. Chi. L. Rev. 271 (1977).

41. J. Mashaw, Prodelegation: Why Administrators Should Make Political Decisions, 5 J. Law, Ec. & Org. 81; Chevron, U.S.A., Inc. v. Natural Resources Defense Council, Inc., 467 U.S. 837 (1984).

42. The importance of this function is suggested by the observation in ABA Comm'n On Law And The Economy, Federal Regulation: Roads to Reform 70 (1979), that there exist "sixteen federal agencies, within and outside the executive branch, each created and governed by its own separate statute, with responsibilities that directly affect the price and supply of energy."

43. See p. 14.

44. The Constitution does specify the possibility of impeachment, for the

pointment and removal have been the subject of congressional efforts at regulation, and of disputes and litigation that continue to the current day.

The appointments clause of the Constitution is straightforward in placing the principal appointments in government in the hands of the President, acting under the check of required consent by the Senate. Congress can place the appointment of "inferior officers" in the President acting alone, in the courts, or in departmental heads. Without much difficulty these provisions have been taken to authorize creation of a merit-based competitive civil service system under which the great majority of government officials serve in protected tenure. Political principles may not be applied to their appointment, and they are free as well from removal on political grounds.[45]

More difficult, but never yet found unconstitutional, are laws that restrict the President's choice even among appointments that seem irreducibly his to make, because they concern major federal office. At one end of a range of possibilities are reasonable qualifications for a position, for example that the Attorney General must be a lawyer. Also easily justified is a requirement that appointees possess qualities that may contribute to the acceptance or character of agency decision, as when Congress provides for a measure of bipartisanship by limiting to a bare majority the number of appointees to a collegial regulatory commission who may belong to the same political party. Not as readily justified are provisions that tightly restrict the President's nominating choices, and give Congress a role in the selection of particular individuals. A notable example of this sort of arrangement is the provision governing appointment of the head of the General Accounting Office, the Comptroller General of the United States.[46] The President is expected to appoint one of three persons on a list provided him by the leadership of the House and Senate. Here, the restrictions on the President's nominating seem to reflect a congressional effort to displace the President's authority with its own. Strikingly, and with evident significance from a separation of powers perspective, Congress and its constituents are missing from the constitutional list of officials other than the President to whom appointments authority for "Officers of the United States" may be delegated.

President as well as other officers. This is a highly formal and cumbersome procedure, requiring grave offenses and action by both houses of Congress. No one supposes that it is the only means available to remove officers who are neither elected to a definite term, like the President, nor appointed to serve during "good behavior," as judges are.

45. United States v. Perkins, 116 U.S. 483 (1886). See also the recent decision upholding statutory provisions for appointment of special prosecutors by the courts, on the Attorney General's request. Morrison v. Olson, 108 S. Ct. _____ (1988)

46. See pp. 58-59 and note 28 above.

A congressional effort directly to control the appointment of "Officers" *was* found unconstitutional in recent litigation concerning the Federal Election Commission, a body intended to investigate practices in federal elections and to set and enforce rules respecting them. As Congress established the Commission, some of the commissioners were to be presidential appointees *not* requiring senatorial confirmation. Others were to be directly appointed by the leadership of the Senate and of the House. The evident purpose was to achieve a political balance, a mutuality of control, in matters of great political sensitivity. Nonetheless, the Supreme Court concluded, the Commission's responsibility was to enforce the federal election laws. Therefore, it must be headed by "Officers." Congress could not appoint them.[47] Here, as in the example of the Comptroller General just discussed, Congress had not only weakened presidential authority, but also sought to expand its own, in ways finding no support in the constitutional text.

A more limited, but still highly disputed question is presented by the Open Market Committee of the Federal Reserve Board. The Federal Reserve Board is an independent commission with enormous power over the national economy through its control of banking and the nation's money supply. It is composed entirely of presidential appointees, whose fourteen-year terms and other arrangements give them a degree of freedom unusual even among the independent commissions. The Board's Open Market Committee makes and secures the implementation of decisions respecting operations in the money markets. The Committee's membership is drawn both from Board members and from members selected by the federal reserve banks, essentially private institutions. Here, Congress is not directly involved in the displacement of presidential appointment, and the body in question might be regarded as subordinate. Yet committee members could readily be characterized as "Officers," and the legality of placing designation of those who will exercise such substantial authority in private hands has not been established.[48]

Once an "Officer" has been appointed, how much freedom must the President enjoy to remove him? Unless important government officials serve at the President's pleasure, he may have to conduct the most important affairs of state through persons in whom he lacks confidence. At a less dramatic level, the threat of dismissal, while not the only disciplinary measure that might be imagined, would evidently be a major contributor to presidential control over administrative action. Again, as is typical of issues of this character, definitive answers are possible only at

47. Buckley v. Valeo, 424 U.S. 1, 121 (1976).
48. Carter v. Carter Coal Co., 298 U.S. 238 (1936); A.L.A. Schechter Poultry Corp. v. United States, 295 U.S. 495 (1935).

the outer limits. Where restrictions on the President's ability to employ such threats contribute to legality and are independent of congressional/presidential competition for power over the apparatus of government, they present no difficulties. Thus, again, civil service constraints on the removal of federal employees raise no significant constitutional concerns, even as to employees exercising substantial authority over the implementation of policy under particular statutes. On the other hand, constitutional difficulties *are* presented by arrangements that threaten substantial congressional displacement of the President's intended unitary responsibility for the execution of the laws. Thus, in two cases in which Congress sought to require its own active participation before a presidential appointee/officer could be removed from office, one decided as recently as July of 1986, the Supreme Court has found a constitutional offense.[49]

The case just decided concerned the Comptroller General of the GAO, who can be removed before the conclusion of his term of office (fifteen years) only by congressionally initiated action based upon the existence of "cause." As has been suggested, most of the Comptroller's functions do not involve or affect the public; GAO's internal investigations of government practice, resembling legislative hearings and having no legally binding result, would not be considered law-implementation required to be performed within the President's sphere.[50] Under recent legislation intended to control the federal budget deficits, however, the Comptroller was given responsibilities that *could* be considered to implement law in the full public sense. A majority of the Court, assuming him to be an "Officer" by appointment,[51] and so a proper recipient of such responsibilities in other respects, found that Congress' retention of control over his removal made the provision improper.[52]

Unlike the "appointments" issue, no constitutional text speaks directly to the ordinary question of removal from office.[53] When the first

---

49. Myers v. United States, 272 U.S. 52 (1926); Bowsher v. Synar, 106 S.Ct. 3181 (1986); see P. Strauss, Formal and Functional Approaches to Separation of Powers Questions—A Foolish Inconsistency? 72 Cornell L. Rev. 488 (1987).

50. See Buckley v. Valeo, note 47, above.

51. See the text at note 46, above.

52. A concurring Justice (Stevens) reasoned instead that the Comptroller General was *not* an "Officer" but a congressional official, and for this reason could not be given the authority to act in the manner provided. Two dissenters took positions differing from both positions, and from each other, that would not be profitable to examine here. See P. Strauss, note 49, above. The conceptual confusion on the Court should be ample warning of the need for caution in relying on the necessarily simplified descriptions of the text. See also Morrison v. Olson, 108 S. Ct. _____(1988).

53. On the special issue of impeachment, see note 44, above.

provisions for the shape of the government were made by the first Congress, meeting in the shadow of the constitutional convention, Congress' right to participate in removals as well as appointments was hotly debated. The view that the principal officers of the government should serve at the pleasure of the President prevailed by the narrowest of margins. A major constitutional crisis following the Civil War, the attempted impeachment of President Andrew Johnson, arose from a statute in which Congress converted the tenure of all departmental heads (cabinet secretaries) from service at pleasure, to removability only with the Senate's concurrence. The impeachment following President Johnson's attempt to remove the Secretary of War failed by only one vote. Thus, it may be that the "Decision of 1789," as the first arrangements have been called, involved a question much closer than this century's decisions have asserted. Congressional efforts to participate in removal, however, have been rare. The problems congressional participation in officers' tenure would pose for the President's control of administration are clear enough. On this point, the cases seem to have come to rest.

The intermediate case arises when Congress sets a determinate term of office for a high-level official, and limits removal during that term to "cause," without seeking itself to participate in any determination of that issue. This is the arrangement typical for the "independent regulatory commission," a collegial body generally having five to seven members, each of whom serves a term so calculated that the term of only one member expires each year. When a new President enters office, then, he will find the leadership of the commissions principally in the hands of appointees of his predecessor. In ordinary course, it will be years before his own appointees can assume control. Although rarely given political as distinct from administrative responsibility,[54] such bodies are responsible for a good deal of law-implementation, and thus are well within reach of the President's unitary "executive power."

This problem came before the Supreme Court in the 1930's, during President Franklin Roosevelt's administration. Shortly after his election in 1932, he dismissed a Republican commissioner of the Federal Trade Commission, whose term would otherwise have lasted until 1938. President Roosevelt did not assert any "cause" for this removal, but simply claimed the right to fill important governmental positions with persons whose political views resembled his own. The Supreme Court found,

---

54. An exception may be the United States Nuclear Regulatory Commission, which in its functions concerning import and export of nuclear materials has responsibilities and must consider information that ordinarily would be in the province of political actors such as the Department of State.

without apparent difficulty, that the President could be required to observe the "cause" restriction for removing such an officer.[55]

As ought not be surprising, since the occasions for such litigation rarely arise, many questions respecting the President's ability to discipline governmental officers through removal remain open. Since the Tenure in Office Act involved in the Johnson impeachment, an act since said by the Court to have been unconstitutional,[56] Congress has not tried to impose a similar limitation on officers exercising more political than administrative authority—such as, for example, the Secretary of State. The Court had insisted in the case just mentioned that Federal Trade Commissioners did not exercise "executive" authority. While that is counter-factual when law-implementation is considered,[57] the Court's assertion suggests the distinction we earlier observed between political and administrative authority,[58] with "executive" used here in the former sense. Thus, the case does not suggest that the Congress could impose similar controls over the terms of office of officials responsible for "questions, in their nature political" officials who are "to conform precisely to the will of the President."[59]

More importantly, even for those officers who *can* be given fixed terms of office, from which they are to be removed only for "cause," no case has decided what "cause" might be. Should it include insubordination, that would give the President a substantial lever with which to move them. The issue would then become, explicitly, what directions the President is entitled to give "officers" in fulfilling his obligation to see that all laws are faithfully executed. Those laws include, of course, the laws entrusted to the administration of the independent commissions. Strong arguments have been made that "cause" must be construed in light of that obligation,[60] and a recent Supreme Court decision involving the appointment and removal of special prosecutors appears to have adopted these arguments.[61]

---

55. Humphrey's Executor (Rathbun) v. United States, 295 U.S. 602 (1935).
56. Myers v. United States, 272 U.S. 52 (1926).
57. Today, it would be conceded that virtually everything the Federal Trade Commission does involves carrying out the law, in the sense that would require its chief officers to be appointed by the President (as they are) with senatorial consent. See Buckley v. Valeo, note 47, above.
58. See pp. 61-63.
59. Marbury v. Madison, see notes 35 and 37, above. In his dissent from the recent opinion involving the Comptroller General, note 49 above, Justice White is careful to reserve this point.
60. G. Miller, Independent Agencies, 1986 Sup. Ct. Rev. 41 (1987); H. Bruff, Presidential Power and Administrative Rulemaking, 88 Yale L.J. 451 (1979); P. Strauss, The Place of Agencies in Government: Separation of Powers and the Fourth Branch, 84 Colum. L. Rev. 573 (1984).
61. Morrison v. Olson, 108 S. Ct. _____(1988).

The White House staff

Evidently the President's controls cannot be strictly personal; his influence—which is dominantly political rather than legal[62]—must be achieved through the intervention of others. His personal staff, numbering about 100, and a considerably larger bureaucracy directly attached to the White House act for him in this respect, both in sifting and organizing the problems requiring his attention and in communicating what are said to be his wishes. Any realist understands, of course, that much done or said in the President's name has never crossed his desk. This realization is a cautionary signal for arguments about the President's directory authority in administrative matters—the direction being given is too likely to reflect the understandings and desires of a relatively junior bureaucrat, rather than the President himself.[63] Of course this, too, is understood by those to whom such statements are made, and the result can be an elaborate and deeply political exercise.

The organization of the White House staff is, as one would suppose, relatively fluid and organized around the problems of politics and state as much as the problems of administration which are the concern of this volume. From time to time, the staff of the Vice President,[64] of the Council of Economic Advisors[65] and of White House Counsel[66] have become in-

---

62. Beginning with his position as head of the nation with its symbolic values, and also of a major political party, able to command its resources of reward and punishment and associated with its programs; the President also strongly influences, where he does not directly command, the central administrative apparatus of government responsible for goods all agencies require, from budgetary submissions and authorization of high-level bureaucratic positions to legal services and office space and equipment; and the President (and the forces under his command) can be a powerful ally in struggles against Congress and for public regard.

63. The position is well stated by an articulate former Cabinet Officer, William T. Coleman, Jr., in his dissent from the ABA study "Roads to Reform" (See note 42 above), pp. 156-61; compare the response of Judge Henry Friendly, id. at 163-64, who had earlier taken the same position, but abandoned it in the face of a burgeoning federal bureaucracy.

64. Vice Presidents, however, rarely wield great governmental power or influence. The significance of the office is that it is often occupied by leading national political figures, and that the office holder becomes President upon the death or resignation of the President, which has happened five times in this century. The Vice President has no defined constitutional role in government and is chief of no governmental agency. The Vice President does preside over the Senate and can cast tie-breaking votes. But his power is generally political rather than administrative.

65. The Council of Economic Advisors analyzes the national economy, advises the President on economic policy and appraises the economic programs of the Federal Government. It also prepares the President's annual economic report to

volved in regulatory issues. In the early days of the Reagan administration, for example, a Task Force on Regulatory Reform was established under the aegis of the Vice President, to coordinate the administration's effort to reduce what it saw as the often negative impact of federal regulation on the national economy. A similar function had been served during President Carter's administration by a group operating within the Domestic Council, an umbrella organization concerned with domestic issues that was headed, interestingly, by the EPA Administrator. Over the years, by far the largest role has been played by the Office of Management and Budget; the work of this office, in effect the President's professional staff, is discussed below.[67]

"Opinion, in writing"

Before turning to that, however, it is useful to turn to the principal constitutional basis for the White House staff's functioning in relationship to the administrative decisions of the rest of government, the provision that the President may require the written opinion of the head of any executive department on a matter within her sphere of competence. Recall that the implication of this provision, an implication that is at least formally observed, is that decision of administrative matters lies with the official to whom it is delegated by law, not the President or his staff. Yet consultation is proper, and is expected to occur in advance of that decision.[68] In the past, such consultations were informal, not readily observed and

---

Congress, a widely used statistical reference work. The Council consists of three members, one of whom the President designates as chair (usually a distinguished academical economist).

66. The White House Counsel acts as the President's personal attorney and aide. His office is small, about 10 lawyers, and should not be confused with that of the Attorney General. The Attorney General, who also gives legal advice to the President, is the head of the Justice Department, which manages the civil and criminal legal affairs of the entire federal government. Several thousand attorneys, including United States attorneys in each federal judicial district, are employed by the Justice Department—along with the Federal Bureau of Investigation, the Immigration and Naturalization Service, the Bureau of Prisons, and several other important offices.

67. See pp. 76-78.

68. One wants to distinguish here between consultation on issues of policy, and consultations about the outcome of particular controversies having a judicial character. The latter would generally be rejected as improper, on analogy to the inappropriateness of any official contacting a judge about the merits of some matter before him for decision. Professional Air Traffic Controllers Organization v. Federal Labor Relations Authority, 685 F.2d 547 (D.C. Cir. 1982). The former, however, are generally accepted. Sierra Club v. Costle, 657 F.2d 298 (D.C. Cir. 1981); W. Cary, Politics and the Regulatory Agencies (1967).

according to no particular form. Certainly, much informal and formless consultation persists. The past two decades, however, have witnessed the development of more formal techniques for analysis and reporting having considerable prominence, and influence. These are the techniques of policy analysis, which examine proposed actions and alternatives to determine their projected costs and benefits. The expectation is that decisions will then be taken in light of those projections.

Central management of such analysis was in fact first required by legislation, when the National Environmental Policy Act of 1969 established a regime of "Environmental Impact Statements" to be administered by a presidential office, the Council on Environmental Quality.[69] Agencies proposing to act in a manner that might have a significant environmental impact were required to undertake a form of analysis of both that impact and means of avoiding or controlling it. An agency was to conduct its analysis under the general guidance of the Council, but responsibility for both the analysis and the ultimate decision in the matter remained in the agency's hands.[70] In the years since, Congress has found the device useful in at least two other contexts: first, agencies are required to engage in forward thinking about the possibly harsher impact of complex regulation on small rather than large business;[71] second, they are to analyze the necessity and impact of their demands for reporting of data by citizens and other regulated entities.[72] The analyses are to be made under the central supervision of the Small Business Administration and the Office of Management and Budget, respectively.

The President has imposed similar requirements non-legislatively on the executive agencies,[73] relying on his "Opinion, in writing" authority. Each President since President Nixon has required these agencies to submit economic impact analyses of proposed regulations having a potential

---

69. 42 U.S.C. §§ 4331-4335. Consistent with the usual arrangements for presidential offices, the authority of the Council is strictly internal to government. It was given authority to oversee and coordinate the activities of governmental agencies in making the required analyses, rather than authority to reach decisions on disputed issues of policy affecting the environment and the interests of the public directly.

70. As an obligation of the agencies involved, the impact analysis procedure came to be regarded as judicially enforceable by affected citizens, industries, or interest groups, a development that since has contributed much to litigation about administrative action. For an overall appraisal of its effectiveness as a mechanism of bureaucratic control, see S. Taylor, Making Bureaucracies Think (Stanford 1984).

71. Regulatory Flexibility Act, 5 U.S.C. §§ 601-612. See P. Verkuil, A Critical Guide to the Regulatory Flexibility Act, 1982 Duke L.J. 213.

72. Paperwork Reduction Act of 1980, 44 U.S.C. § 3507(c).

73. Independent regulatory commissions have been excused from any formal requirement. See p. 76, below.

for significant effect on the national economy for White House review before final decisions on the proposals are reached. Each President has elaborated upon the work of his predecessor, extending both the reach and the scope of the requirement. President Reagan's regime is embodied in Executive Order 12291, adopted very shortly after his accession to office.[74]

For each proposed regulation, Executive Order 12291 requires an executive agency first to assess its probable impact upon the national economy, largely (for these purposes) in terms of additional costs required to be borne by corporations or others subject to the regulation. Before announcing even its proposal to the public, it must submit its assessment to the Office of Management and Budget. If it has concluded that the impact will be "major" (for example, that it will impose new costs in excess of $100,000,000 annually), the submission must include the draft of an economic impact analysis that considers in detail the projected costs and benefits of the proposal and possible alternatives. Publication of the proposal is to await OMB clearance, the timeliness of which can usually be assured only by political means,[75] and must then be accompanied by the analysis. Final action on the proposal requires a second, final economic impact analysis, which again must be cleared with OMB. "To the extent permitted by law," *all* rules, whether or not "major," must meet stringent criteria of economic justification: on the whole, their potential benefits outweigh potential costs; their objectives maximize net benefits and the means chosen to achieve them minimize net social costs; and the agency's overall program, including this rule, must reflect regulatory priorities that "maximiz[e] the aggregate net benefits to society." The qualification is an important one; OMB cannot override legislative specifications.[76]

At the beginning of his second term, President Reagan issued a second Executive Order, No. 12498,[77] that underscores the last of these objectives and strongly reflects a vision of the President in a central and coordinating role. As reflected in the appropriations process discussed above,[78] agencies have long been required to do advance fiscal planning, which then receives national coordination through the work of the OMB and CBO. The setting of regulatory priorities had never been required even at an

---

74. 46 Fed. Reg. 13193 (Feb. 17, 1981).

75. In Environmental Defense Fund v. Thomas, 627 F. Supp. 556 (D.D.C. 1986), a court held that OMB could not delay analyses past deadlines set by statute; but such deadlines rarely apply.

76. Ibid.; see C. Sunstein, Cost-Benefit Analysis and the Separation of Powers, 23 Ariz. L. Rev. 1267 (1981).

77. 50 Fed. Reg. 1036 (Jan. 4, 1985).

78. See pp. 55-56.

agency level, however, except to the extent it may have been implicit in the budgetary process. National coordination of projected governmental administration of regulatory programs had never been attempted. Executive Order 12498 seeks to impose such a regime. Annually, agencies are to submit to the OMB a draft regulatory agenda for the coming year. When made final, that agenda becomes the exclusive work the agency may do absent special justification. The agenda is itself to be drawn up and justified in cost-beneficial terms. Once OMB has the drafts of agenda from all agencies, it may seek to create a national agenda. This process seems necessarily to envision denying to some agencies what they would prefer to do, in the name of a national program or other failures of justification to "the President."

It may be useful to note some questions about these orders, and the ways in which they illustrate themes about administrative government already established. First, what is the legality of an "executive order" purporting to bind the actions of discrete legal entities, when "all legislative power" vested by the Constitution is placed in Congress? Second, and relatedly, note the reappearance here of the problem of the President's authority to direct decision of matters committed to agency judgment. Third, what is the impact of these measures outside government—their visibility, accessibility to comment or input, even susceptibility to judicial enforcement? And fourth, what is the application of these orders to independent commissions such as the Federal Trade Commission?

As may be suggested by the high numbers attached to the Executive Orders we have just been discussing, such orders have long been an established mode for the President's formal effectuation of policy. Among those his office entitles him to command, they have the force of law. The President's position, which presumably would be sustained, is that he requires no legislative authorization to announce such measures or to give them that force. Note that this conclusion, if correct, can be related to the problem of "for cause" dismissal discussed a few pages earlier. If the President, by virtue of office, can give a binding directive to a commissioner of the Federal Trade Commission, disobedience would warrant dismissal even if the commissioner ordinarily could expect to be protected from removal. Executive Orders have been used to establish government-wide regimes for the control of sensitive information, for assuring the loyalty and security reliability of government employees and of government contractors, for establishing nondiscrimination programs within government and with government contractors, and for many like purposes.

While occasional doubt has been expressed about the application of Executive Orders to government contractors or their employees,[79] cer-

---

79. Chrysler Corp. v. Brown, 441 U.S. 281 (1979).

tainly their acceptance within government reflects a proposition already encountered: that the limitations of separation of powers, such as they are, apply to government in its dealings with other branches and with the citizenry at large, and do not proscribe useful internal arrangements.[80] The case of government contracting, and the disposition of other government resources,[81] can be regarded as an intermediate one. While private citizens are affected, they are affected through the government's decisions in the course of control over the disposition of its own resources, and in a relationship voluntary on their part.

The contrasting case is that in which the President seeks to use an Executive Order to effect a change in the legal status of an ordinary citizen or corporation not in the course of a business relationship with the government. When President Truman, during the Korean War, sought to use an executive order to seize the steel mills in order to avoid a strike and the resultant disruption of war material production, he was sharply rebuked by the Supreme Court for an act unauthorized by law.[82] That rebuke was marked by stern language—although language generally regarded by American scholars as overbroad—about the impropriety of the President's attempting to act as a legislator. No one, however, appears to have believed that that rebuke rendered invalid the nation's loyalty and security clearance regime, founded in an executive order, or any of the many other useful regimes of internal, property, and contract management executive orders had established. The intended unitary character of the Presidency requires some means for his giving appropriate instructions to the government as a whole, and that is the office of the executive order.

There remains the problem of the potentially directory character of the two executive orders we are considering here. Viewed simply as a requirement for use of specified analytic tools, Executive Orders 12291 and 12498 fit comfortably in the established tradition. One can even claim that they enhance the effective authority of high-level officials within the directly responsible agencies, by promoting the early surfacing of proposals and alternatives, at a time when those officials can readily take command. Before the executive orders were in place, one often heard that the civil service staff of government agencies tended to compromise disagreements among themselves *before* going to the politically more visible chief officers of their agencies with their proposals. While from one perspective such practices make efficient use of limited resources, from another they sharply restrict the effective command that high-level officers enjoy over their agencies. Measures such as the Reagan executive

80. Compare p.59, above, where a similar point is made concerning the GAO.
81. United States v. Midwest Oil Co., 236 U.S. 459 (1915).
82. Youngstown Sheet and Tube Co. v. Sawyer, 343 U.S. 579 (1952).

orders tend to force the staff to show its hand at an earlier point, enhancing upper-level control.

The structure of the process also gives OMB, and through it the President, substantial control over the particular outcomes of proceedings: first, through the assertion that, "to the extent permitted by law," stated decisional principles must be applied; second, by requiring the agency to secure OMB approval of its analyses before going forward, and thus enhancing OMB's already considerable political authority. Suppose that the law empowers the Administrator of the Environmental Protection Agency to decide a matter, and permits but does not require him to make that decision employing analyses such as Executive Order 12291 commands. Does the Administrator's use of those analyses, not by his own choice but because the President requires it, in itself contravene the delegation to *the Administrator* of the authority to make this decision?

That question remains open, although the better argument appears to support the President's authority so to structure decision to national priorities or policies, within the bounds of law,[83] because the application of judgment to the particular circumstances of the matter remains the agency's. Yet the agency's application of judgment may also be subverted if, under the cover of a requirement of analyses, OMB is actually dictating particular outcomes. At the moment, the factual basis for such a claim is a matter of substantial (and understandably political) controversy in the United States.[84] While few assert that OMB could lawfully dictate a precise decision, when the law places authority for that decision in the hands of someone other than the President,[85] its political influence over outcomes is greatly enhanced by these measures.

The Executive Orders are public documents, as are the analyses, draft and final, prepared under them. Their public character raises questions about involvement by interested persons outside government: are these merely tools of bureaucratic management, which the public may be able to watch but not affect, or are there means for becoming involved in this process? The orders themselves encourage public participation at the agency and even presidential level; and they attempt to preclude subsequent judicial involvement or enforcement. Thus, regulatory agenda are published, and when published contain within them both an indication

---

83. See C. Sunstein, Cost-Benefit Analysis and the Separation of Powers, 23 Ariz. L. Rev. 1267 (1981); C. Sunstein & P. Strauss, The Role of the President and OMB in Informal Rulemaking, 38 Ad. L. Rev. 181 (1986).

84. C. DeMuth and D. Ginsburg, White House Review Of Agency Rulemaking, 99 Harv. L. Rev. 1075 (1986); A. Morrison, OMB Interference With Agency Rulemaking: The Wrong Way To Write A Regulation, 99 Harv. L. Rev. 1059 (1986).

85. C. Sunstein, Cost-Benefit Analysis and the Separation of Powers, 23 Ariz. L. Rev. 1267 (1981). See Environmental Defense Fund v. Thomas, note 75, above.

of the agency's projected work for the coming year and the name of a person within the responsible agency who can be contacted respecting its progress, to make comments, or the like. Draft regulatory impact analyses are also published, when the agency makes its proposals for rulemaking public, and the public is encouraged to comment upon them. In addition to approaching the agency about such matters, it is possible to approach the OMB; both for political and for legal reasons, OMB's position has been that it discourages such contacts. The orders' attempt to exclude both judicial enforcement of the economic impact analysis requirement and judicial review of its adequacy draws on what some regard as the disruptions introduced by the development of judicial review of compliance with the National Environmental Policy Act.[86] These provisions, untested in litigation, seem likely to prove successful. Both the analysis and any "record" that may have accompanied its creation, however, are likely to be considered part of the record on review of any subsequent rule. These matters are further developed below, in connection with the problem of the rulemaking record.[87]

Finally, what of the "independent regulatory commissions" like the Federal Trade Commission? A strictly legal analysis suggests that these executive orders, grounded in the "Opinions, in writing" clause, could be extended to the head of any agency made responsible for carrying out federal law. Since the independent commissions meet this definition, the executive orders could be applied to them.[88] The executive orders have not been directly applied to the independent commissions, however, for essentially political reasons. Achieving congressional acceptance of these regimes has proved somewhat difficult even for those agencies which Congress has placed "close" to the presidency by making their chief officers individuals who hold office at the pleasure of the President. Extending their reach to the independent agencies would create a political storm, however justified the legal position. To date no President has believed the possible gains of such a step outweigh its costs.

The Office of Management and Budget

The Office of Management and Budget is the professional arm of the Presidency, corresponding in many ways to the Congressional General Accounting Office.[89] Indeed, the two offices were created in the same

---

86. See p. 71.
87. See pp. 159-74.
88. P. Strauss & C. Sunstein, The Role of the President and OMB in Informal Rulemaking, 38 Ad. L. Rev. 181 (1986); G. Miller, Independent Agencies, 1986 Sup. Ct. Rev. 41.
89. See pp. 58-59.

statute, in 1921, which for the first time directed the President to present a unified national budget.[90] The Bureau of the Budget, predecessor to the OMB, was responsible for the coordination to produce that budget; GAO was responsible for audits to assure that the constraints of the budget had in fact been honored. Originally placed in the Department of the Treasury, the Bureau of the Budget was moved to the White House proper in 1939; it was redesignated the Office of Management and Budget, in recognition of its expanding functions and size, in 1970. Its present staff consists largely of professional bureaucrats with civil service tenure; it operates under the leadership of a Director and a limited number of other political appointees serving at the pleasure of the President.

OMB's primary responsibility remains the coordination for the President of the annual budget process. That role carries with it a good deal of oversight of agency activity, as OMB's budget examiners (its professional staff) are expected to become closely familiar with the work of the agencies to which they are assigned, and are in a position to demand justification of agency decisions with budgetary implications. Although it is possible to make appeals to the President (or, informally, to relevant congressional actors), OMB annually sets the resources an agency can expect to be made available for its future work. That gives it enormous practical power over the course of governmental administration.

Some other OMB functions have already been encountered: under a recent statute, OMB coordinates information demands made on the public by government agencies;[91] and under Executive Orders 12291 and 12498, it oversees economic impact analyses and regulatory agenda.[92] In addition, it serves a number of coordinative functions: mediating interagency disputes; overseeing studies or other efforts that involve the work of more than one agency; and coordinating the President's legislative program. This last function has two elements: legislative proposals are not to be made by individual agencies, but must be cleared with OMB for consistency with the President's program; and when agencies are asked by congressional committees to respond to legislative proposals, by testimony or in written form, that response must also be cleared. This process is less demanding for the independent regulatory commissions than for the rest of executive government, but all but a few participate; it serves as a major centralizing feature of the national government. OMB, it will be apparent, is a major power center for the President in his administration of domestic government, even though its work is not widely to known to lawyers or the general public.[93]

---

90. Previously, each agency made its own requests to Congress.
91. See text at note 72, above, and pp. 184-85.
92. See pp. 72-73.
93. An account of the functioning of the President's office prepared for Pres-

Federal judiciary

Article III of the federal Constitution specifies that the "judicial power of the United States shall be vested in one Supreme Court, and in such inferior courts as the Congress may from time to time ordain and establish." The judges of any such "Article III court" are appointed by the President, with senatorial consent, to an indefinite term ("during good behavior") and compensation protected against reprisal. The reach of the judicial power is defined with some precision; for the purposes of this essay it is enough to know that it reaches any "case" arising under federal law, a category that easily includes any case involving issues of national administration or the application of the federal constitution to state or local administration.[94] Cases raising only questions of state or local law come into federal courts only if the parties reside in differing states— the so-called "diversity jurisdiction," meant to protect against regionalist bias in judgment. Under the principles of federalism, the legal questions in such cases are finally resolved in accordance with the law of the relevant state.

The most important question of constitutional structure concerning the relationship between the courts and administrative agencies is what is the necessary role of courts—what issues *must* be decided by Article III judges rather than agency officials serving in less protected tenure. This may seem the obverse of the question just considered respecting the President and the agencies, whether the President's constitutional position permits him to displace agency decision.[95] The question will be

---

ident Carter, emphasizing the OMB, can be found in H. Heclo, A Government of Strangers (Brookings 1977); see also L. Berman, The Office of Management and Budget and the Presidency, 1921-1979 (Princeton University 1979); F. Mosher, A Tale of Two Agencies (LSU 1984); note 84, above.

94. The question, what constitutes a "case," raises interesting problems in constitutional law. One can say in summary that there must be a real dispute, between parties having real and opposing interests, respecting which a court is in a position to give final and effective relief. A proceeding for declaratory judgment by a manufacturer whose present activities are directly threatened by a statute or regulation it asserts to be unlawful would be a "case," since the courts will consider that by declaring the validity or invalidity of the statute or regulation they give effective relief against its enforcement. A proceeding brought by a citizen who believes that another's possible future plans would be unlawful would lack these elements of reality. See the discussion of standing, pp. 223-36.

95. The analogy in that setting would be if it were argued that a certain decision was required to be made by the President, and the creation of an agency authorized to make it consequently interfered with his necessary role. Such an argument underlay the objections to the special prosecutor's office, which makes prosecutorial decisions beyond the President's immediate control. It was rejected. Morrison v. Olson, 108 S. Ct. _____(1988).

taken up in greater detail within.[96] Here it seems sufficient to remark that the question has at least two aspects: first, whether there is a necessary review relationship between the judiciary and the products of administrative action, a level of control constitutionally required as a condition of placing decisions directly affecting the rights of citizens in a government body; second, whether there are types of proceedings, or issues within proceedings, that must be assigned to the courts for independent decision—that are required to receive judicial judgment, not merely judicial oversight.

American law has not given precise answers to either question, although the areas of dispute can be located with some confidence. The law does permit tremendous scope for agency adjudication. Partly these results are a function of Congress' general authority to create the arrangements of government; its power to create "exceptions" to the Supreme Court's appellate jurisdiction gives it substantial control over the judicial review function, including the authority substantially to exclude it, and Congress has often successfully assigned to agencies tasks that strongly resemble the inherently judicial. Outside the criminal law, only limited types of proceedings or issues to which the government is one party must be the subject of judicial rather than administrative judgment; an example of an issue requiring judicial determination would be the facts on which certain claims to constitutional liberties depend. Administrative adjudication of the remainder, subject only to the possibility of judicial review, is permitted. While the courts have hesitated on occasion in describing judicial review of agency action as constitutionally required,[97] other indications are that a necessary review relationship exists in matters directly affecting a citizen's entitlements.[98] The uncertainty about both issues exists in good part because the margins so correspond to the common sense of legislators creating statutory schemes that they have not often been tried.

Examples may make the problems clearer. A citizen charged with federal crime would expect a judicial trial, with use of a jury if she chose, as a matter of constitutional right. Yet Congress can place decision whether to levy substantial "civil penalties" for violation of agency regulations or statutes governing workplace safety in the hands of the administrative agency generally responsible for regulation of the workplace,

---

96. See pp. 241-43; R. Fallon, Of Legislative Courts, Administrative Agencies, and Article III, 101 Harv. L. Rev. 916 (1988).

97. Thomas v. Union Carbide Agricultural Products Co., 105 S. Ct. 3325 (1985); Johnson v. Robinson, 415 U.S. 361 (1974).

98. Goldberg v. Kelly, 397 U.S. 254 (1970); Crowell v. Benson, 285 U.S. 22 (1932).

subject only to a somewhat permissive regime of judicial review.[99] The differences between imprisonment and fine give a formal, but not wholly satisfactory, explanation.

Two citizens with a contractual dispute whose resolution is governed by state common law would ordinarily expect to have that dispute resolved by a court—a state court most frequently, but a federal court if jurisdictional requisites were met. When the contractual obligation is asserted in response to a claim founded in federal regulatory law and voluntarily brought before an agency rather than a court, Congress can permit a regulatory agency to decide the matter as part of an integrated dispute, subject to limited judicial review.[100] Congress cannot, however, create a body of "bankruptcy judges" who, without Article III tenure protections, are broadly empowered to resolve disputes against the interests of citizens who in no sense chose that forum, who seem in most functional respects to be operating as courts, and whose judgments are subject only to limited review.[101] The difference between these two situations is more readily expressed in the subjective terms of perception of threat to overall judicial function, than in clear principle.

Finally, Congress can assign to an administrative agency the final resolution of an application for government benefits. But Congress cannot keep from the courts final resolution of a dispute about the constitutional fairness of the procedures designed by Congress to that end.[102] Judicial suggestions of what constitutes the irreducible function of judicial review vary from the profound[103] to the perfunctory.[104] The generally accepted doctrinal test for necessary judicial role—whether Congress has so restricted judicial involvement as to threaten the core functions of the court[105]—is so indefinite as to be virtually unmanageable.

---

99. Atlas Roofing Co. v. Occupational Safety and Health Review Comm'n, 430 U.S. 442 (1977); note that if the action to determine a civil penalty were initiated in court, a jury trial would be required on the issue of liability. Tull v. United States, 107 S. Ct. 1831 (1987).

100. Commodity Futures Trading Commission v. Schor, 106 S. Ct. 3245 (1986).

101. Northern Pipeline Construction Co. v. Marathon Pipe Line Co., 458 U.S. 50 (1982).

102. Johnson v. Robison, 415 U.S. 361 (1974); Walters v. National Association of Radiation Survivors, 473 U.S. 305 (1985).

103. Goldberg v. Kelly, 397 U.S. 254 (1970).

104. Thomas v. Union Carbide Agricultural Products Co., 105 S. Ct. 3325 (1985).

105. H. Hart, The Power of Congress to Limit the Jurisdiction of Federal Courts: An Exercise in Dialectic, 66 Harv. L. Rev. 1362 (1953); G. Gunther, Congressional Power to Curtail Federal Court Jurisdiction: An Opinionated Guide to the Ongoing Debate, 36 Stanford L. Rev. 895 (1984); CFTC v. Schor, 106 S. Ct. 3245 (1986).

The Supreme Court

The Supreme Court is a panel of nine Justices and performs all of its functions en banc—that is, with the whole tribunal sitting. For our purposes, its functions are wholly appellate;[106] under Article III, its "appellate Jurisdiction, both as to Law and Fact, [is] with such exceptions and under such regulations as Congress shall make." This revisory power of Congress has raised some interesting problems of separation of powers, threatening effective reprisal against an over-ambitious Court. Its most important use for our purposes, however, has been to make the Court's review function largely a discretionary one. Virtually all cases coming before the Court, including all ordinary review of federal administrative action or of the compliance of state or local agencies with federal constitutional requirements, are first presented to it by a "petition for a writ of certiorari." This pleading seeks to persuade the Court to review a lower court judgment. To be effective it must show reasons of legal importance for review—for example, that the Circuit Courts of Appeal for differing parts of the country have reached conflicting results on the legal question presented—rather than reasons to believe the lower court ruled in error, as such. The other side is then able to respond showing reasons why review is unimportant, for example that the decision below, whether correct or incorrect, raises no question of general significance but depends on its special facts.[107] If four Justices agree, one less than a majority, the petition will be granted. The Supreme Court generally grants fewer than 5% of these petitions in any given year, according full review to about 160 cases out of a pool of over 4000.[108]

Ordinarily, if a petition for certiorari is granted, the case will be fully briefed on the questions the petitioner presented to the Court,[109] an oral argument (ordinarily an hour or less in its entirety) will be held, and after a period of time—invariably by July of the term of Court in which the case was argued—a more or less elaborate written opinion will be

---

106. A very limited group of controversies, chiefly concerning the states or foreign states, can originate in the Supreme Court.

107. On this subject and others of importance to Supreme Court practice, consult R. Stern and E. Gressman, Supreme Court Practice (BNA 6th ed. 1986).

108. In the 1985-86 term of Court, the Supreme Court disposed of 4289 cases, 159 by written opinion, 131 by per curiam or memorandum decision (generally without full briefing or oral argument), and 3999 by refusing review. If one excludes from these figures cases brought in forma pauperis, generally by state or federal prisoners, the figures are 2107 disposed of, 244 by written opinion or memorandum decision and 1863 by refusing review. 100 Harv. L. Rev. 308 (1986).

109. Occasionally, the Court limits the questions from those addressed to it by the petitioner.

issued.[110] Under the precedential system followed by the courts, this opinion constitutes binding authority on all questions necessary to be resolved, for all courts *and agencies*. Frequently enough these opinions contain statements on matters not strictly necessary to decision ("dicta"). By encouraging the Court to view its function as deciding important legal issues, rather than resolving important controversies, the certiorari selection process contributes substantially to this practice. While not binding in the same formal sense, these dicta give strong indications of the Court's view on the legal matters addressed, and are likely to be followed by judges and agency officials in other proceedings. It is important to understand, however, that the denial of a petition for certiorari has no similar impact: it is not explained, and is made without oral argument or elaborate briefing; while it terminates the litigation, it has no precedential force whatever. A denial of certiorari cannot even be regarded as having determined that the question presented to the Court is one that, in another case, would not warrant the Court's full review.

Note that one implication of these limits on the Supreme Court's annual body of opinions is that its control over particular programs or issues is highly attenuated. "In 1924, the Court reviewed about one in ten decisions of the courts of appeals. . . . [I]n the 1984 Term the Court was able to review only 0.56% of court of appeals decisions. . . . [T]hese courts of error, at least for practical purposes, have become the final expositors of federal law in their geographical region in all but a miniscule number of cases."[111] If a court of appeals judge participates each year in about 125 cases with signed opinions, writing the opinion in one third of those, Supreme Court review of one in ten would put her in direct intellectual contact with the Court several times over the course of a year; review of one in 200 suggests that even her panel votes will not be reviewed as often as once a year, and her opinions, on average, will come under scrutiny only two or three times in a decade.[112] The steepness of this pyramid should be kept in mind in the pages following.

---

110. In cases where the appropriate outcome is obvious—for example, where the lower court's judgment needs to be reconsidered in light of a subsequent Supreme Court decision on point—the petition may be granted and action summarily taken without these steps.

111. T. Baker & D. McFarland, The Need for a New National Court, 100 Harv. L. Rev. 1400, 1405-06 (1987).

112. See P. Strauss, One Hundred Fifty Cases Per Year: Some Implications of the Supreme Court's Limited Resources for Judicial Review of Agency Action, 87 Colum. L. Rev. 1093 (1987). R. Posner, The Federal Courts: Crisis and Reform, 69 (1985), reports 5572 signed opinions for the courts of appeals in 1983. Assuming them to have been evenly distributed among 45 panels of three means approximately 125 opinions per panel, 42 per judge. Given the participation of senior judges and other factors, the actual numbers are lower.

The circuit courts of appeal

With the exceptions discussed on pages 85-86, the jurisdiction of the inferior federal courts is organized along geographic rather than subject-matter lines. That is, these courts are courts of general (federal) jurisdiction, who hear all matters within the Article III federal judicial power that arise within their geographical area. Subject to specific, contrary jurisdictional provisions, that means that all disputes about federal administrative law can be heard either in the federal courts of Washington, D.C. or in the federal courts of the location where the person seeking review is, or where the dispute arose. For these purposes, the country is divided into 12 geographic "circuits." Within the circuits, two levels of court are created—a trial court, known as a United States District Court, and an intermediate appellate court, a United States Court of Appeal.

The twelve circuits vary considerably in size[113] and in geographical extent,[114] but the jurisdiction and practice of the courts of appeal that preside over them is generally similar. Ordinarily, its judges—there are 156 nationwide—sit in rotating panels of three to hear appeals, moving among the commercial and legal centers of their circuit to hear argument. A circuit court of appeals hears all appeals from United States district courts sitting within its circuit, and also any review cases that can be brought directly from a federal agency to a court of appeals and that arise within the circuit. The allocation of review cases between those that come directly to the courts of appeal from the agencies, and those that originate in district court, is further discussed below;[115] here it may be enough to say that the direct review cases are always provided for by special statute, and generally concern formal proceedings before the larger federal agencies.

In contrast with the Supreme Court, appeals come to the circuit courts—whether direct from a federal agency, or from a district court—as a matter of party right. All cases are briefed, but as a measure of docket control a significant proportion are identified as presenting no question difficult enough to warrant oral argument, and are decided

---

113. The First Circuit, comprising the New England states of Maine, New Hampshire, Massachusetts and Rhode Island, plus Puerto Rico has five circuit judges; the Ninth, embracing Hawaii, Alaska, California, Oregon, Washington, Idaho, Montana, Nevada and Arizona, has 28.

114. The District of Columbia circuit embraces only the 70 square miles and roughly 800,000 residents of the nation's capital; the Ninth Circuit, note 113, above, includes the nation's largest and third largest states by area and its largest by population.

115. See pp. 211-15.

simply on the basis of the briefs. Similarly, whether or not oral argument is held, in some cases the court will either forego writing an opinion or direct that its opinion not be published; when this is done, the court's action decides the case, but cannot be said to have any precedential effect for future, similar cases arising within the same circuit. Since the judges sit in small panels, it can happen that one panel will reach a different conclusion on a legal question than did another in the same circuit; this can lead to the convening of all the judges of the circuit to decide, en banc, the question subject to this disagreement. For a large and geographically extended circuit, it will be evident, this can present major administrative difficulties, but other means of attaining a uniform understanding of law within the circuit are not apparent.

The geographic arrangement of the circuits means that the precedential effect of their decisions is limited to those states within the particular circuit reaching the decision. For a national agency, responsible for administering national regulation, this can mean that different understandings of the law apply in different parts of the country—one interpretation in Iowa, another in Florida, California, or New York. In one respect this can be viewed as an opportunity: if the Commissioner of Internal Revenue does not accept the construction given to the Tax Code by the Second Circuit, he ordinarily could not expect to obtain Supreme Court review (because of the absence of any conflict). The Second Circuit's ruling does not prevent him, however, from continuing to use the construction he prefers in cases likely to arise in other circuits, where he may prevail. In another respect, of course, it is destructive of the uniformity of national administration to have the same statute or rule understood differently in different parts of the country; and it is destructive to some understandings of legality to have an administrator continue to apply an interpretation of his authority that one court has found unlawful and that he has not brought before a higher court for review. Thus, real problems for administrative justice in the United States can be thought to arise from the stringent limitations on the capacity of the Supreme Court to accept and resolve such conflicts when they arise (or, even, when they would be threatened by an administrator's refusal to acquiesce in the first negative judgment he receives).

In the particular case of administrative law, the special stature of the United States Court of Appeals for the District of Columbia Circuit helps to control the problem of inter-circuit disagreement. While this court is not, in general, given exclusive jurisdiction over judicial review of federal agency decisions, its location in Washington, D.C. gives it possible jurisdiction over almost all, and its special experience with administrative matters often leads counsel to choose it. While less than one half of one percent of the nation's population lives there, a significant proportion of all federal administrative law cases are brought there, especially those of likely national significance. Other circuit courts, in turn, may give special weight to the views of the D.C. Circuit because of the greater frequency with which it considers such issues, even though in a formal sense they are free to apply their own judgment.[116]

The district courts

The United States is divided into 93 judicial districts, ranging between one and four in each state, with each district containing a number of federal district judges. At this writing, 563 district judges are authorized for the nation as a whole. In all but a few cases a single judge presides over any district court proceeding; although juries of civilians are used for fact-finding in many district court trials, they are not used in administrative review proceedings, so that the judge almost invariably sits alone. District court jurisdiction over administrative matters can arise in either of two ways: a statute may specifically provide for it, as is the case for review of agency decisions under the federal Freedom of Information statute; or litigants may simply be able to invoke the district court's general jurisdiction over "federal questions." As the product of a trial court, the district court's judgments have little impact beyond the case being decided. The manner in which review proceeds is treated in chapters 7 and 8.

Special courts

For a group of specialist issues and/or tribunals, federal judicial jurisdiction *is* organized along national and subject matter rather than geographical lines. The United States Court of Appeals for the Federal Circuit, corresponding to the circuit courts of appeal, is the appellate court for these tribunals and issues. Trial courts include the Claims Court (monetary actions against the United States, chiefly those arising out of alleged contracts or torts), the Tax Court, the Patent Court, and the Court of International Trade. Some of these courts, for example the Tax Court, provide specialist review of administrative decisions; others, a specialized

---

116. This expertise has had other consequences in the D.C. Circuit's relationship with the Supreme Court. Since Supreme Court review is so limited, the D.C. Circuit has on occasion been able to build up a substantial body of law through its own precedent-setting process, only to find some years later that the Supreme Court has a different view. A. Scalia, Vermont Yankee: The APA, the D.C. Circuit, and the Supreme Court, 1978 Sup. Ct. Rev. 345. The sharpness with which some of these reversals have been expressed in Supreme Court opinions presumably diminishes the influence of the D.C. Circuit among the other courts of appeal.

setting for initial trial of issues (which, as in the Claims Court, may also concern the propriety of government conduct).[117] Perhaps especially noteworthy here is the use of the Federal Circuit to achieve national uniformity below the Supreme Court, even as to some matters within the jurisdiction of the ordinary district courts. If patent issues arise in district court litigation—say, in the course of a proceeding under the anti-trust laws— a decision against the validity of the patent entitles the party supporting the patent to appeal to the Federal Circuit, rather than to the geographical circuit to which his appeal would ordinarily be referred. In this way, the patent supporter is assured a single decision on the validity or not of the invention, which will then have national effect.

The political leadership of administration

The units of government, outside the Presidency, assume a diversity of forms. Each form is the product of legislative specification. For persons seeking to understand administrative law, four are of principal importance: the cabinet department, the bureau or administration within a department, the independent agency within the executive branch, and the independent regulatory commission.[118] The paragraphs following sketch the characteristics and possible interrelationships of each. Bear in mind, however, that they share important features in common: all are at root the creatures of statute, rather than the Constitution or presidential specification;[119] their political leadership, composed of persons subject to presidential appointment, is thin in relationship to the size of the agency as a whole; with limited exceptions, all fall under the same set of statutes for the internal management of government (the civil service laws, etc.); all reflect the same principles of internal organization, generally hierarchical but with provision also for specialist offices housing lawyers, economist/planners, fiscal specialists, secretariat, etc.

---

117. General descriptions may be found in S. Dornette and R. Cross, Federal Judiciary Almanac (1984) and F. Klein, Federal and State Court Systems—A Guide (1977).

118. Other possibilities, which do not ordinarily possess significant regulatory authority, include corporation-like forms responsible for providing services to the public—the generation and distribution of electric power (Tennessee Valley Authority; Bonneville Power Authority), the provision of postal service (United States Post Office), or of passenger or freight railroad services (AMTRAK, Conrail).

119. Congress has occasionally given the President provisional authority to reorganize existing governmental functions into new or altered governmental writs.

Most important for our purposes, the public procedures agencies employ do not vary with the type of government organization employed. While some variations do occur from agency to agency, these are a function of specific programs. The general procedures—and the expectations of government structure and performance that flow from them—are uniformly provided for by an Administrative Procedure Act and associated statutes that pay no heed to issues of agency form.

Cabinet departments

The departments were the original, and remain the most important, elements of executive government outside the Presidency itself. Early drafts of the Constitution specified a number of departments each exercising a particular responsibility—over foreign affairs, the army, internal commerce, marine matters, and so on. They were to be headed by Secretaries appointed by the President who would sit with him in a council, or cabinet, to oversee the conduct of government. With the choice to emphasize the unitary character and responsibility of the presidency, and to leave future Congresses substantial flexibility in establishing the detailed structure of the national government,[120] these provisions disappeared. Contemplation that there would be such departments remained, however, in the provisions made for appointments and for the President's receipt of "opinions, in writing" from their principal officers.[121] The first Congress promptly established Departments of State, Treasury, War, and Navy, and the office of the Attorney General, headed by prominent individuals who in fact did quickly come to be regarded by the President as a "cabinet" with which to consult on important matters. The central offices of these departments were miniscule. They enjoyed only limited control over employees, often acting weeks or months away, in the communications circumstances of the time.[122]

Today's departments number 13: Agriculture, Commerce, Defense, Education, Energy, Health and Human Services, Housing and Urban Development, Interior, Justice, Labor, Transportation, Treasury, and State. Each represents a bureaucracy of substantial size, headed by a Secretary[123] appointed with senatorial confirmation to serve at the pleasure of the President. Other political appointees generally include an Under-Secretary or Deputy Secretary responsible for general administra-

---

120. See pp. 13-14.
121. See pp. 70-73.
122. L. White, The Federalists: A Study in Administrative History (MacMillan 1948), recounts the available information.
123. Or, in the case of the Justice Department, the Attorney General.

tion, a General Counsel, and assistant secretaries with responsibilities for administration or for overseeing the administration of particular programs. Even the assistant secretaries, however, may be one step removed from direct responsibility for particular legislative regimes.

An example may give concrete shape to these generalizations. The Department of Agriculture had 106,000 employees and spent more than $55,000,000,000 in fiscal 1985. Its organizational chart shows 29 different offices, services, or administrations, each placed under the responsibility of one of seven assistant secretaries. For example, the Department's Assistant Secretary for Marketing and Inspection Services had responsibility for its programs on agricultural cooperatives, transportation, agricultural marketing, animal and plant health inspection, grain inspection, food safety and inspection, and the regulation of meat packers and stockyards—a highly diverse group of subjects and regulatory challenges. The other assistant secretaries enjoyed similarly diverse responsibilities. One must expect, then, that while the Secretary and his assistants can give general policy guidance and shape within their department, the detailed understanding and actual implementation of programs occurs within its bureaus, at some remove from the political appointees.

While these pages naturally stress regulatory themes, it is appropriate to remark that the greatest part of departmental responsibilities—for some departments, virtually all—lies in administering programs for spending or other activities that one would not ordinarily consider "regulation." Thus, a great proportion of the Department of Agriculture's budget is expended on transfer payments to farmers; similarly, the Departments of Transportation and of Housing and Urban Development administer a variety of programs for supporting facilities, such as road construction or housing projects, that rarely appear in judicial or even administrative settings.[124] The Departments of State and Defense have responsibilities that can hardly be conceived in those terms. Even in these, however, particular bureaus or offices exist with responsibilities that do invoke our concerns.

Departmental bureaus

Like the departments within which they function, the "offices," "administrations" and "bureaus" of government tend to be organized

---

124. The central case defining scope of review of administrative decision, however, Citizens to Preserve Overton Park v. Volpe, 401 U.S. 402 (1971), extensively discussed on pp. 164-69 and 261-67, arose in just such a context: the decision by the Secretary of Transportation (through the Federal Highway Administration) to subsidize Tennessee's construction of a major highway, even though it traversed valuable urban parklands.

along standard hierarchical lines, within which bureaucratic structure and routine play important roles. An interesting book by the political scientist Herbert Kaufman, The Administrative Behavior of Federal Bureau Chiefs,[125] analyzed the functioning of the heads of six sub-units of the sort just described, each responsible for the implementation of one or more massive government programs. The six units studied were the Animal and Plant Health Inspection Service and Forest Service (both of the Department of Agriculture), the Food and Drug Administration and Social Security Administration (both of the Department of Health and Human Services), and the Customs Service and Internal Revenue Service (both of the Treasury Department). They are merely representative of a general phenomenon; others of equal prominence performing major regulatory functions would include the Occupational Safety and Health Administration in the Department of Labor, the Federal Aviation Administration in the Department of Transportation, or the Federal Energy Regulatory Commission in the Energy Department. These bodies, even in their leadership, are largely apolitical, and their work is less subject to political swings than their presence in a political department might otherwise suggest:

> [B]eing a Chief [of such a bureau] is gratifying only for those who derive pleasure from accomplishments on a small scale and from the chance that some . . . may lead to larger benefits in the future. The chiefs . . . certainly do calculate and negotiate to accomplish all they can. But they make their marks in inches, not miles, and only as others allow.[126]

Often the statutes that create them, even while placing them in political departments, contain special measures safeguarding against political influence: decisions of the Internal Revenue Service respecting the selection of individual taxpayers for investigation are shielded from political direction, for example, and the Federal Energy Regulatory Commission, although made part of the Department of Energy, is in form an independent regulatory commission whose relationships with the Secretary of the Department are highly formal.

Independent executive agencies

Occasionally Congress has created an office at the responsibility level common to departmental administrations or bureaus, but placed it out-

---

125. Brookings, 1983.
126. At 174. Book-length studies of bureau functioning, tending to confirm their bureaucratic character, can be found in an earlier work of Kaufman's, The Forest Ranger (Resources for the Future 1960) and in J. Mashaw, Bureaucratic Justice (Yale 1983), a study of the Social Security Administration.

side the departmental structure—independent in the sense that no Secretary commands it, but nonetheless headed by a single administrator
who serves at the President's pleasure and thus is clearly placed within
his sphere of influence. The most prominent contemporary example of
this arrangement is the Environmental Protection Agency (EPA), whose
13,788 employees and $4.6 billion annual budget are devoted to generating
and enforcing standards for pollution control and supporting facilities for
the alleviation of pollution that may already be occurring. Because EPA
is in some sense (despite its several programs) a single-purpose agency,
because its functions seem susceptible to technocratic rather than political
management, because its independent status gives efforts to control its
decisions fairly high visibility, and because those decisions often have a
major impact on industry and the quality of life, it has been a focal point
for arguments about political controls over administration.[127] Indeed, the
regime of economic impact statements discussed above[128] came about
substantially in reaction to EPA's work, and perceptions of its impact on
the economy.

Internally, the EPA is shaped along lines similar to a department. Some
offices, such as that of the General Counsel, are responsible for providing
services to the agency as a whole; others have operating responsibilities
for particular programs: the Clean Air Act, water pollution, noise pollution, etc. The highest level officials are political appointees who serve
at the President's pleasure, but virtually all agency staff, including many
with important responsibilities for decision, are permanent government
employees. What distinguishes it from a department in the traditional
sense is, perhaps, as simple as size; but there is also a sense in which
its work is more uniformly regulatory in character. One can believe that
Congress, by avoiding the more traditional departmental structure, has
encouraged a level of visibility for the agency's work that will reduce to
some degree political influence over it.[129] At the same time, as an agency
in the executive branch, the EPA is unequivocally subject to the various

---

127. See, for example, Sierra Club v. Costle, discussed on pp. 171-74. A useful
short book giving an account of the EPA's curious position, and clearly favoring
technocratic rather than political controls, is B. Ackerman and W. Hassler, Clean
Coal/Dirty Air (Yale 1981).

128. See pp. 71-73.

129. For a now somewhat dated account of the EPA's struggles with the White
House in its early years, see J. Quarles, Cleaning Up America (1976). A bitter
dispute between Congress and the White House over EPA administration during
the Reagan administration led to the resignation of its then administrator, Anne
Gorsuch; her replacement, William Ruckleshaus, was appointed in circumstances
that made plain that direct White House control over EPA decisionmaking was
unlikely.

presidential controls of budget formation, required analyses, and legislative discipline discussed above.

Independent regulatory commissions

The independent regulatory commission, already briefly introduced,[130] is the form Congress employs in creating offices of law-administration at the greatest distance from presidential control. The responsibilities of such agencies (often called simply "independent agencies") invariably have a high component of regulation, although regulating is not all they do[131] and it is already apparent that they are not the only governmental bodies that regulate. The first such commission, the Interstate Commerce Commission, was created in 1887 to regulate railroad rates. The half-century following saw the creation of only a few others, notably the Federal Reserve Board (banking and monetary supply) and the Federal Trade Commission (trade practices and advertising). Beginning with the New Deal and President Roosevelt in 1932, however, the device was much more frequently employed. Prominent independent commissions today, whose areas of activity are generally apparent from their names, include the Securities and Exchange Commission, the National Labor Relations Board, the Federal Maritime Commission, the Federal Communications Commission, the Consumer Product Safety Commission, the Commodity Futures Trading Commission, the Federal Energy Regulatory Commission (in the Department of Energy), the Occupational Safety and Health Review Commission (in the Department of Labor), the Federal Elections Commission, the Equal Employment Opportunity Commission, and the Nuclear Regulatory Commission.

The commission form, as previously remarked, employs a collegial body at its head. Members are appointed by the President with senatorial consent to fixed terms, generally of five or seven years, with one term expiring each year; usually, the President must observe limited constraints of bipartisanship in making appointments, and can discharge a member before the end of her term of office only for "cause." The chairman, who often enjoys special executive authority within the commission, is presidentially designated, usually to serve in that capacity only at the President's pleasure. Thus the chief officer of the agency is, to a degree, responsible to the President in the ordinary mode. Other agency officials

---

130. See p. 15.
131. The Nuclear Regulatory Commission, for example, awards and oversees the performance of contracts for research into issues of safety in the operation of nuclear power plants.

are appointed by the commission, or by the chairman; while there may be informal consultation with the White House, it does not control the subordinate political positions as it would in a department or at an independent executive agency like the EPA. In hierarchical structure, in the internal allocation of responsibilities, as in the procedures it follows in carrying out its work, an independent regulatory commission is essentially indistinguishable from any other form of governmental agency.

The decision to use the "independent regulatory commission" format is often said to reflect a faith in the possibility of expert, as distinct from political, judgment on matters of public importance. No clear pattern is observable, however, in the assignments of responsibility Congress has made: both the independent Federal Trade Commission and the Department of Justice are responsible for aspects of anti-trust policy; both the independent Federal Reserve Board and the Treasury Department's Controller of the Currency have important responsibilities for banking regulation (along with a number of other agencies); the Department of Health and Human Welfare's Food and Drug Administration, the executive Environmental Protection Agency and the independent Nuclear Regulatory Commission all have responsibilities for assessing and controlling the possibly harmful activities of high-technology industries. The preceding description should suggest that elements of independence are present in the operative bureaus even of cabinet departments. Similarly, the leadership of the independent regulatory commissions, although protected from the possibility of presidential removal without formal "cause," has significant exposure to the realities of presidential guidance on important policy issues. Indeed, it would be surprising if conscientious governmental officials did not desire such guidance, at least where it could be given in a manner consistent with their own ultimate responsibility for decision. Thus, the undoubted differences in political leadership ought not to overwhelm a larger sense of similarity; in particular, such differences as exist reach few of the concerns of administrative law.

The civil service

Discussion thus far, so far as it has concerned the individuals responsible for government actions, has centered on the roughly 700 persons, from a civilian work force of 2.9 million, whom the President appoints with the advice and consent of the Senate, and the like number he is able to appoint personally. The miniscule size of this group makes plain that the expert staff of all federal agencies, to a level that may reach as high as bureau head, is professional rather than political in character. Its tenure and conditions of employment are governed by the civil service laws, which in turn are administered by a somewhat complex arrangement of bureaucratic agencies. The Office of Personnel Management, an independent agency within the executive branch like the EPA, is responsible for policy and enforcement aspects of personnel policy: it establishes compensation levels, authorizes agencies to use the high-grade positions often necessary to attract and hold strong talent, administers the competitive examinations for entry into the civil service and other government-wide controls such as conflict of interest regulation. The Merit Systems Protection Board, an independent regulatory commission of three members, sits in judgment on proceedings brought to discipline individual members of the civil service and other adjudicatory matters under the civil service laws.

Employees subject to the civil service laws obtain their jobs through a competitive process. Once they have successfully completed a probationary period, they become permanent employees removable only for cause or because of general reductions in force; even reassignment to another position can be a matter which the employee (if dissatisfied with the reassignment) can require to be made the subject of formal proceedings. The interest the employee holds in her job is regarded as an "entitlement" for purposes of the due process analysis discussed above,[132] so that—in formal terms at least—the procedures the government must supply for these purposes are subject to constitutional constraints, not merely a matter of statutory provenance.[133] (Indeed, in recent years the courts have found that the First Amendment's protections of free speech prevent political removals of some government workers *not* within civil service laws, if party affiliation or political confidence is not an appropriate requirement for the effective performance of the office in question.)[134] While some positions even of an ordinary character are omitted from these tenure protections, notably those of lawyers, all positions are subject to elaborate regulations of "grade," appointment and promotion practice, and other matters intended to prevent political manipulation of the bureaucracy's work. The genesis of these measures lay, first, in perceptions that such manipulation often served corrupt, or at least highly personal, ends; and, second, in political struggles between a party system domi-

132. See pp. 32-48.
133. Arnett v. Kennedy, 416 U.S. 134 (1974); Cleveland Board of Education v. Loudermill, 470 U.S. 532 (1985).
134. See Elrod v. Burns, 427 U.S. 347 (1976); Branti v. Finkel, 445 U.S. 507 (1980); Jimenez Fuentes v. Gaztambide, 803 F.2d 1 (1st Cir. 1986).

nated by Congress and local political machines, and reformers seeking more stable, central direction in the interests of a complex and integrated national economy.[135]

To the extent such measures succeed, of course, they diminish pro tanto the capacity of new political leadership to reshape the work of the bureaucracy, in what most would regard as entirely appropriate ways. An entrenched civil service, serving far longer than any particular administration, may easily be able to find ways to serve its own agenda rather than that of its political leadership.[136] In 1978, responding to this problem, Congress subdivided the civil service, redefining its highest levels as a "Senior Executive Service." The political leadership of executive government now enjoys more (but not complete) authority over the service of these officials, who exercise important policy-making or implementing functions, than it has over the ordinary civil service. They can be rewarded with bonuses, reassigned, and in other ways given incentives relating directly to their programmatic responsibilities. Whether these changes have succeeded in reintroducing a measure of political control over agenda, without reintroducing the abuses that generated the civil service laws, is not yet clear. In any event, it should be clear that the ends of political control and of a protected civil service are in unavoidable tension.

Administrative adjudicators — the corps controversy

Respecting one group of civil servants, those who serve as "judges" in hearing administrative adjudications, maximum protection from po-

---

135. The story of the emergence of the civil service system, alongside the regulatory state, is well told in S. Skowronek, Building a New American State: The Expansion of National Administrative Capacities, 1877-1920 (Cambridge Univ. 1982).

136. Political scientists are fond of describing the "iron triangle" that faces a new President and his political appointees in attempting to put programs in place: permanent agency staff, permanent congressional committee staff (with whom the agency staff has every incentive to develop and nurture a long-term relationship), and the functionaries of private industries or groups most interested, over the long term, in the matters subject to the agency's jurisdiction. H. Merry, Five Branch Government: The Full Measure of Constitutional Checks and Balances (University of Illinois 1980). See also H. Heclo, A Government of Strangers, Executive Politics in Washington (Brookings 1977), a work whose analysis was influential in promoting the changes next described in the text.

litical pressures is desirable. The courts have generally tolerated the assignment of adjudications in agency matters, in the first instance, to the agencies themselves.[137] The arguments for an "independent" judiciary (that in this respect underlie separation of powers concerns) have led to creation of "administrative law judges" as an unusually well-insulated cadre of civil servants responsible for most formal adjudication within executive government.[138] Administrative law judges are paid at the level of the senior executive service, but—although formally located within the particular agencies they serve—are virtually beyond agency control. Appointments must be made on a competitive basis, from the top few names on a list supplied by civil service authorities. Once made, appointments are permanent (without probationary period). Within the agency structure, administrative law judges must be free of supervision or direction from agency employees responsible for the cases that may come before them; neither salary nor assignments nor any disciplinary measure can be controlled from within the agency, but (if adverse) must be the subject of formal proceedings before the Merit Systems Protection Board.[139] Any conversations administrative law judges may have with agency employees concerning the outcomes of formal proceedings they are hearing must be on the record—that is, there may be no private consultations.[140]

---

137. See pp. 12-18 and 78-86.

138. The pattern next described in the text is not invariable. Immigration matters, for example, are heard by Immigration Law Judges in the Department of Justice who enjoy some, but not all, of the protections of administrative law judges; the members of a Department of Labor review board hearing appeals from the decisions of departmental administrative law judges in benefits matters serve in unprotected tenure. Neither arrangement was found to violate principles of due process. Marcello v. Bonds, 349 U.S. 302 (1955); Kalaris v. Donovan, 697 F.2d 376 (D.C. Cir. 1983), cert. denied 462 U.S. 1119 (1983). These are, however, exceptional arrangements, and even within them the influence of the values reflected in the text would presumably work to prevent direct efforts at political control of outcomes. Any such efforts would be regarded as offending the procedural rights of the particular persons involved in the proceedings in which they occurred.

139. In recent years, this restriction has engendered bitter feuds and even litigation within the Department of Health and Human Welfare, over measures which departmental officials defend as seeking to impose only standards of productivity and competence and the Department's more than 800 administrative law judges perceive as a direct threat to their independence of decision. See Nash v. Califano, 613 F.2d 10 (2d Cir. 1980); Association of Administrative Law Judges v. Heckler, 594 F. Supp. 1132 (D.D.C. 1984); Gellhorn, Byse, Strauss, Rakoff, and Schotland, Administrative Law, Cases and Comments (Foundation Press 1986), pp. 862-79.

140. These arrangements are, of course, no guarantee of quality in the pool

Agency structures for adjudication are generally the same, whether they arise in a cabinet department, an independent executive agency like EPA, or an independent regulatory commission. The administrative law judges all serve in a separate office, which may be located for bureaucratic purposes within the agency secretariat but which is independent of policy guidance from any other part of the agency;[141] there will usually be a chief administrative law judge responsible for administrative matters. Proceedings are assigned at random, as they arise, and remain with the administrative law judge to whom they are assigned until the proceeding is completed, unless she is disqualified or leaves office, or (in rare cases) the agency directs that it be sent up without decision. In smaller agencies, her opinion may be reviewed directly by the agency head or commission itself. Frequently, however, provision is made for a judicial officer or review board to serve that function, and direct involvement of the agency head itself occurs only on a discretionary basis, analogous to the Supreme Court's certiorari practice.[142] Whichever organization is followed, conversations about the matters pending before the administrative law judges follow the common judicial protocols: they occur only in public, before all parties. If the head of an agency, reviewing an administrative law judge's decision, wishes help in understanding some aspect of the decision or of a complex record on which it is based, he must seek that assistance formally.[143]

It might not seem a very far step to creation of a system of administrative law courts located outside the agencies whose disputes they considered, and such proposals have often been voiced. A number of states use a central board of hearing examiners for all their administrative disputes. At the federal level, resistance to this measure has been based on the varying tasks administrative law judges face in differing agencies, and the belief that the current legal regime protects their independence to a degree that would not be much improved by such a change. Those administrative law judges the readers of this essay are most likely to encounter are highly specialized and relatively few in number, serving in the major federal regulatory agencies; yet the great bulk of adminis-

---

of applicants, and the selection process and working conditions have been thought by many to discourage a high level.

141. See Nash v. Califano, note 139, above. While it appears conceded that productivity failures would be an appropriate basis for discipline, the practical difficulties of establishing them in a formal Merit Systems Protection Board proceeding has meant that, in practice, such controls have little effect. See Social Security Administration v. Goodman, 58 P&F, Ad. L.2d 780 (MSPB 1984).

142. See pp. 81-82.

143. An important reason for this restriction is suggested by the unique role of the administrative law judges' report on judicial review. See p. 246.

trative law judges serve in the Department of Health and Human Services or the Department of Labor, resolving high-volume, small-scale questions such as eligibility for welfare or disability benefits.[144] A central agency might not be able to maintain the expertise in regulatory issues individual agencies can now encourage; in practice, its work would tend to be swamped by the demands of its mass-justice clientele. Locating hearing outside the agency, it is also feared, might tend to defuse agency responsibility for and control of policy even if (as is usually conceded) review of any decision by a central panel administrative law judge could be had within the agency itself.

State and local government

This essay is principally concerned with national administrative law. An effort to describe the machinery of state and local government is beyond the reasonable dimensions of this essay, and the writer's competence. Nonetheless, the reader may find the following very summary comments helpful.

State governments are generally organized under a written constitution along lines similar to the federal: a chief executive (governor) is generally responsible for overseeing the work of departments or agencies, which are principally staffed by a professional civil service; a legislative body, bicameral in all cases but one (Nebraska), enacts laws; an independent judiciary of trial and appellate courts, often organized into three tiers like the federal, handles ordinary litigation including the review of agency action. In the regulatory context litigation may begin within an agency before a figure like an administrative law judge, possibly assigned from a central panel, and continue through agency review before it reaches the courts.

Important differences between state and federal governments include a larger range of elected officials. For example, some or all of many states' judges are elected, generally to lengthy terms. A state's chief financial officer may be elected. In a sizable minority of states, the members of its public utility commission, responsible for setting rates for energy and communications services, are elected; and almost all states elect their attorney general, who—as chief enforcer of state law—is a powerful figure from the administrative law perspective.[145] State constitutions tend

---

144. In 1983, 812 ALJs served in the Social Security Administration, 233 in labor-related agencies, 89 in regulatory bodies, and 42 elsewhere in executive government.

145. This fracturing of political responsibility for the work of government has

to be both more detailed than the federal, more readily amended, and less important an element of public life.

Much of American economic regulation is accomplished at the state level. Entry into and conduct of many professions, including the legal profession, are controlled by state agencies, as are many businesses (hospitals, insurance, much banking, retail delivery of utility services, etc.). The states commonly have local laws respecting labor practices, health, safety and environmental protection, and the like that are close counterparts of the national schemes administered by the federal government. They also administer many public services, notably welfare and education. And the general law applicable to citizens, both civil and criminal, is administered in their courts.

The subdivisions of state government—counties, cities, towns, villages—each tend to reflect the same patterns of organization, operating under written charters, although the powers of these authorities all are subordinate to state law. They do not have an independent political existence, as the states do in the federal scheme.[146] One might expect to find a mayor or city manager or county executive at the head of executive government; a council or board of aldermen or county manager; even town or city courts, generally for initial decision of minor matters that can be appealed into the state judicial system. Local agencies administer welfare in the first instance, are responsible for public protection (police, fire, sanitation, health and safety inspections), administer land use and building controls, and license some types of business.

While federal and state authorities have historically been distinct, the last half-century has witnessed the beginnings of a merger that could signal a major change in the political organization of American government. When national welfare laws were first enacted during the New Deal, they were enacted in a form encouraging state participation: if the states would meet legislative conditions, they would receive substantial federal subsidies; under the unemployment laws, for example, an otherwise payable federal tax would be greatly reduced. Thus encouraged, the states adopted these laws—producing a need for supervision to assure that the conditions of the federal statute continued to be met. The supervision has become more rigorous over the years, as conditions have multiplied and public awareness and participation have increased.[147] The more than 800 administrative law judges of the Department of Health

---

been criticized as substituting "policy balkanization . . . for policy coordination." Pierce, Shapiro & Verkuil, at 116.

146. Some state constitutions provide "home rule" or "charters" for larger population centers, creating to that extent a federal model; neither the sharing of authority nor the safeguards for continued existence of these arrangements match the arrangements at the federal-state level.

147. See NWRO v. Finch, 429 F.2d 725 (D.C. Cir. 1970).

and Human Services spend the great bulk of their time redetermining issues of welfare eligibility that have already encountered several levels of administrative review at the state level; and the Secretary of the department is authorized to suspend federal payments entirely to any state he finds to be in systemic violation of the federal scheme. Understandably, given both its political and its human consequences, this sanction has rarely been invoked.

The idea that federal programs might be implemented by state officials acting under the supervision of federal officials has spread. States obtain federal funds for road projects that meet federal standards and the Secretary of Transportation's approval; similarly conditioned subsidies may be had for education, housing, and other worthy purposes, under the approval of other departments. States may regulate the transportation of hazardous waste through their territory more stringently than general national standards would require (through the Secretary of Transportation), again with his approval; they may regulate medical uses of radioactive materials under the supervision of the federal Nuclear Regulatory Commission. Probably the most striking of these arrangements from the perspective of administrative law are to be found in the field of environmental regulation. The enforcement of federal standards to protect common resources, such as air and water, is placed in a federal agency—the Environmental Protection Agency. States are commanded to develop state implementation plans that will meet the federal agency's approval. Any state that fails to do so suffers federal implementation, which commonly will mean defeating important state regulatory bodies.

It will be apparent that the political independence of the states is at some risk in these programs. As the states have come to rely on federal funding for their programs, the reach and firmness of the conditions on the basis of which they can obtain it has increased.[148] When state and federal officials share responsibility for implementation of a given regulatory program, power and responsibility may be hidden and diffused. Recent years have seen a surge in constitutional litigation over the limits of federal control of state activities.[149] While that is not a central subject for this inquiry, the interested reader should see this problem of administrative federalism as one that will mark the American scene for years to come.[150]

---

148. See A. Rosenthal, Conditional Federal Spending and Constitution, 39 Stan. L. Rev. 1103 (1987).

149. The most recent decision is Garcia v. San Antonio Metropolitan Transit Authority, 469 U.S. 568 (1985).

150. A. Rapaczynski, From Sovereignty to Process: The Jurisprudence of Federalism After *Garcia*, 1985 Sup. Ct. Rev. 341; L. Kaden, Politics, Money, and State Sovereignty: The Judicial Role, 79 Colum. L. Rev. 847 (1979).

Enforcement officials

Law enforcement activities in the United States, at all levels, are commonly divided between the functions of investigation and apprehension, on the one hand, and prosecution or presentation on the other—one might say, between the world of the inspector or the policeman, and the world of the lawyer-prosecutor. In the realm of criminal law, which includes certain (generally aggravated) administrative violations, investigation and apprehension is the responsibility of the police force. Such forces can be found at every level of government. Numerically the overwhelming number are local, but at the federal level, the Border Patrol, Alcohol and Tobacco Bureau, and Federal Bureau of Investigation are among those readily identified as serving this function. The bringing of criminal actions (or other litigation) to court is the function of a public attorney—often called a district attorney at the local level, a state Attorney General, or, at the federal level, a United States Attorney attached to a particular United States District Court and functioning under the general supervision of the Attorney General of the United States.[151]

Administrative enforcement, in the first instance, is commonly in the hands of agency officials rather than a separate agency dedicated solely to investigation and apprehension. In 1978, these included more than 100,000 persons working as inspectors for one or another local, state, or federal agency; local inspectors might visit restaurants or construction sites, federal inspectors, slaughterhouses or nuclear power plants. In each instance these inspectors seek to determine compliance with the regulations of their particular agency. Other means of investigation are of course employed, notably office review of reports filed by companies subject to regulation, and of other information. Determining to open a proceeding and presenting the agency's position in that proceeding will usually be the responsibility of another agency official, in this case an attorney functioning under the supervision of an agency principal attorney, whose title may be general counsel, solicitor, executive legal director, or the like.

---

151. One might consider the United States Attorney's offices to be the field offices of the United States Department of Justice, although historically they came into existence a century before it did and they often act with considerable independence of the Department; U.S. Attorneys are themselves appointed by the President with senatorial consent, and frequently are important figures in their home communities. The Department of Justice itself (that is, the Washington office) most often does not become involved in litigation until an appeal is sought or made.

At the federal level, the role of the Attorney General as the chief legal officer of the national government becomes important for agencies when disputes about their work pass beyond the agencies' own jurisdiction. A dispute between two agencies respecting the meaning of a legal provision that affects the work of both may be settled—at least so far as they are concerned[152]—by a formal Opinion of the Attorney General, drafted in his Office of Legal Counsel. Where the dispute is between the agencies and a citizen, agencies are required in varying degrees to rely on the legal resources of the Department of Justice (and its willingness to employ them) for representation in court. Unless explicitly authorized by statute, as the independent regulatory commissions generally are, no agency can initiate litigation in a United States District Court. Even so simple a matter as seeking enforcement of an agency subpoena must be done through the Department or the relevant United States Attorney. This confronts the agency with views about relative priority in the use of government litigating resources that may be very different from its own. If the case is lost, it may be appealed only with the Department's permission, in this case centrally granted through its Office of the Solicitor General.

Even when the agency is brought to court by a citizen rather than vice versa, as in petitions for judicial review, the agency may not be fully in command of its own defense. Unless statutes explicitly provide otherwise, the final form of the government's argument will be determined in the Department. While on the whole this occurs professionally rather than politically (in the Civil Division of the Department of Justice, for example, rather than the Attorney General's personal office), it nonetheless marks a loss of control, a need to satisfy other officials even before reaching court of the soundness of one's position.

The Department's control is near complete, even over the independent commissions, when the Supreme Court is reached. A petition for certiorari may not be filed without the permission of the Solicitor General.[153] With rare exceptions, he determines the final form of any papers to be presented to the court; he controls the assignment of (and most frequently makes) any oral argument. Although the Solicitor General is a political appointee, most Presidents have realized that the government's continuous dealings with the Supreme Court make it advisable to select this official for professional attainment, and his office works at high levels of professionalism. If the Solicitor General and the agency cannot reach

---

152. Once the agencies have received advice from the Attorney General, they may lack the means to generate valid litigation that would test its correctness; but if the issue later arises in a proper dispute, say between a citizen and an agency, the Attorney General's prior expression of view would have only persuasive authority for a court.

153. United States v. Providence Journal Co., 108 S. Ct. 1502 (1988).

agreement on appropriate position, his brief will often inform the Court of that fact and the agency's position. Even so, the loss of initiative and control can appear substantial; perhaps more to the point for private attorneys, the independence of the Solicitor General in determining the government's position in litigation suggests that a conference with him about pending litigation may often prove fruitful.

$\equiv 4$
THE SCOPE OF ADMINISTRATIVE LAW

General statutory measures that purport to deal with "administrative law" define the scope of their application in terms of three concerns: the procedures employed by "agencies" in effecting "agency action"; judicial (and, to a lesser extent, political) review of those actions; and special procedures relating to the handling and release of information in the government's possession.[1] Neither a court nor a legislature nor an elected chief executive can be an "agency" under these statutes, although the relationship of courts, legislatures and chief executives with agencies is very much a matter of administrative law concern. Otherwise the concept includes virtually every administrative unit[2] exercising public authority. "Agency action" is also embracively defined. While the provisions of administrative procedure legislation generally deal with the relatively formal procedures of adjudication and rulemaking, as discussed below, federal "agency action" includes any grant, denial, or failure to act upon "the application or petition of, and beneficial to, a person";[3] under the most recent draft of model state administrative procedure legislation,[4] "agency action" includes "an agency's performance of, or failure to perform, any . . . duty, function, or activity, discretionary or otherwise."[5] Again, the category is virtually as broad as the field of public administration; only traditional criminal law proceedings, traditional civil litigation, and political acts in the strict sense, those indisputably beyond the control of law, are excluded.

---

1. Federal Administrative Procedure Act, 5 U.S.C. § 551(1, 13); Revised Model State Administrative Procedure Act § 1-102(1, 2).
2. The unit may be a subdivision of some other body that might also be regarded, for some purposes, as an administrative agency: for example, the Forest Service (which manages national forests) is an "agency" under the federal Administrative Procedure Act, along with the Department of Agriculture in which it is placed. Whatever the internal political relationship between the Chief Forester of the Forest Service and the Secretary of Agriculture, the Forest Service has legal responsibility for administration of the national forests.
3. 5 U.S.C. § 551(11(C), 13).
4. See pp. 187-89.
5. Revised Model State Administrative Procedure Act § 1-102(2)(iii) (1981).

103

It should not be surprising to find the domain of "administrative law" in the legal system so broadly defined. Scholars developed the concept toward the beginning of this century, as public administration grew. As unruly as the developments it sought to capture, it was a grab-bag for all government actions affecting private persons that did not fit comfortably any of the existing structures of legal analysis—either those of the criminal law or of the ordinary civil law as administered by courts. The scholarly view of administrative law has grown, with government, to embrace almost all subjects that can be connected with public administration. Although criminal trials are excluded, many assert that it embraces the exercise of discretion by police officers and prosecutors. Although it excludes an action initiated by the government in federal court to collect a simple debt, it would include that action if begun within an executive body and later brought before courts for enforcement or review. One might have said at the outset that it was sub-constitutional in character, concerned with statutory and customary arrangements of government; yet as the preceding pages make plain, constitutional issues respecting governmental structure and conduct are now important concerns.

In the American framework, a focus on procedural issues provides an analytic structure for generalizing about the central tasks of administrative law: assuring the control as well as the effectiveness of government. Such a focus is needed despite the recognition that generalizations are made problematic by the diversity of agencies and agency actions, and the close relationship between the substance of any particular agency's responsibility and the procedures it will employ. Talking from the perspective of "administrative law" about the work of the federal Securities and Exchange Commission (or of the Forest Service, or of a state public utilities commission, or a local building inspector) focuses on its procedures, rather than its particular substantive responsibility for implementing a certain part of federal (or state or local) policy. One assumes, initially, that all agencies employ certain paradigmatic procedures to accomplish their ends and that these agencies have paradigmatic relationships with overseers such as courts who review the end product of these procedures. These paradigmatic procedures and relationships can and do vary to meet the needs of particular situations. Consequently, in dealing with a concrete situation, one must always seek to understand the responsibilities and procedures of the particular agency whose work is at issue. Nonetheless, analysis usefully begins at the paradigms, which are expressed in procedural forms that are not directly a function of the particular agency whose work is under examination.

These paradigms are the focus of the following chapters. It would be wrong to anticipate them here in any detail. The remaining paragraphs of this chapter examine a variety of substantive responsibilities commonly given administrative agencies. For purposes of initial comprehension it may be useful to have the following sketchy models in mind:

Formal adjudication: A proceeding strongly resembling a civil trial, conducted "on the record" before an administrative law judge or agency to determine a particular dispute. Formal adjudications are generally characterized by a strict separation of functions within an agency, so that staff responsible for investigation and presentation of the agency's position do not participate in the decision process. The results of formal adjudication are generally reviewed by courts with relatively close attention to the existence of factual and legal support for the outcome.

Informal adjudication: Procedures for resolution of a particular dispute that do not require "on the record" hearing. If a hearing format is used, it may be quite informal. But "informal adjudication" is used to describe the taking of decisions by bureaucratic routine—for example, a decision to authorize the use of federal money for the construction of a particular road project. Judicial review is relatively permissive, recognizing considerable discretion in the person acting.

Formal rulemaking: A proceeding conducted "on the record" to determine a statute-like norm for future application, for example what proportion of peanuts should be required in a substance to be labeled "peanut butter," or what is a reasonable rate to be charged for utility services. Formal rulemaking differs from formal adjudication in certain structural arrangements; those responsible for developing and presenting the agency's analysis at the hearing, for example, are not required to be separated from the decision process as they are in formal adjudications. The character of the hearing and of subsequent judicial review, however, strongly resembles formal adjudication.

Informal rulemaking: The ordinary procedure for generating statute-like norms for future application. Its public stages are initiated by a notice of the proposed action; the interested public then has an opportunity to file written comments on the proposal. Oral hearings are optional, although encouraged by some statutes, for example, many connected with environmental, health, and safety rules. On adopting a rule, the agency is under some obligation to explain its basis and purpose. Decision is taken bureaucratically, and judicial review is relatively permissive, although with increasing attention to the existence or not of factual support for rules of importance.

A rule once validly adopted has the full force of statutory law on those subject to it.

Interpretation: An informal procedure for generating and announcing agency interpretations of applicable norms. Interpretations may be generated internally or in response to a request; ordinarily no procedure is required (although procedures like those for informal rulemaking are often followed). The interpretations do not formally bind persons outside the agency, although they are likely to be regarded as persuasive by the courts. Decision is taken bureaucratically; judicial review may not be directly available and, when available, is generally deferential.

Inspection: Direct physical view by a qualified government official, sometimes used as a substitute for adjudication procedures (as, for example, in grading agricultural commodities, or examining the skill of applicants for a driver's license) but also employed to determine the existence or not of conditions warranting formal administrative action.

Economic regulation

Much of the work assigned to administrative agencies has its source in judgments that the public needs protection from economic injury; or that public ordering of certain economic activities could otherwise contribute to the public good. From early times, for example, states regulated the rates that could be charged by the owners of private bridges and ferries across important waterways; or provided rules for the liability of an innkeeper or a common carrier to guests or passengers. In recent years, economic analyses of public law have raised significant questions how effective some of this regulation can be,[6] and the result has been, in some quarters, a retrenchment. Following are some of the more important types of economic regulation in the United States today:

Economic concentration.   Ever since the enactment of the federal Sherman Anti-Trust Act in 1890—even earlier in individual states—government has sought to prevent excessive concentration of economic power in private hands. While enforcement of the anti-trust laws is predominantly judicial, the Federal Trade Commission has long had responsibilities both to investigate and report generally on issues of economic con-

---

6. A full and highly regarded analysis, influential in changes at the federal level, may be found in S. Breyer, Regulation and Its Reform (Harvard 1982).

centration, and to regulate corporate mergers in light of their impact on industrial concentration.

Common carrier and public utility regulation. Common carriers (railroads, buses, trucks, taxis, airlines, pipe lines, barge lines, communications satellites) and public utilities (water, electricity, gas, telephone) are frequently state-owned in other systems; in the United States, they are ordinarily private enterprises subject to close regulation. At least two grounds are suggested for the characteristically intense regulation of these enterprises. For many, although not all, the large investments and fixed networks required to provide service suggest that public interest will be best served by a form of monopoly, avoiding wasteful duplication of facilities (with consequent threat to the economic viability of all competitors); however, such measures create a level of economic power over the communities served, and that power must be controlled. For all these enterprises, the public's dependence on the quality and safety of the services being provided suggests other needs for regulation: that service is non-discriminatory, that honest and competent service is provided, that safe practices are maintained, that economic conditions necessary to these ends are assured, and so forth.

This regulation may occur at the national (interstate transportation or utilities), state (local trucking; retail gas, electricity and telephone) or local (water, taxis) level, and overlapping responsibilities assure that some will be subject to regulation from many sources. In the course of building a power station, for example, a utility may have to secure permissions and meet regulatory requirements of federal,[7] state,[8] *and* local[9] authorities. To enter the industry, or to provide a desired service, an applicant may be required to show that the "public convenience and necessity" support new facilities or services; members of the affected public and those already supplying such services may be permitted to oppose the application in proceedings generally having the character of formal adjudication. Those already operating in the industry also face a wide range of regulations, suggested by the ends sketched above: they may be required, generally in formal rulemaking proceedings, to justify any changes in the rates they charge and/or the service levels they provide; statutes or rules may impose extensive record-keeping requirements; periodic inspections may occur to assure compliance with service regulations; and informal rulemakings create a variety of legal standards binding upon the regulated industry and open to enforcement against it.

---

7. Location of hydro-electric or nuclear facilities; interstate sale of power; safety and environmental consequences.
8. Need for additional generating capacity; location; construction of transmission lines; in-state rates.
9. Location of transmission lines; zoning.

Much of the movement for deregulation of the economy can be ascribed to the realization that, in some cases, the economic power of the industries subject to these entry, rate and practice controls is not as great as had been imagined; and that regulation itself enhances the economic power of those already in the industry by protecting them from competitive incentives and pressures. Thus, early federal regulation of air transportation services was very close. The Civil Aeronautics Board (CAB) controlled who could fly, what rates they could charge, what particular communities they could or must serve, and how often. It became apparent that the result was to keep ticket prices artificially high, and service provided equivalently low. Analysis suggested that the airline industry could safely be permitted to become much more competitive; unlike railroad tracks, utility plants or telephone cables, airplanes—the major capital investments of airlines—were fully mobile. When the CAB was abolished, removing all but safety-related restraints on entry and service and most restraints on rates, ticket prices dropped, passenger levels soared, and traffic patterns changed in ways that have provided virtually all communities with a higher frequency of service. Similar analyses suggest equivalent changes for surface transportation industries like trucking and busing, that do not require heavy capital investment in fixed facilities. Even these changes, of course, do not mark a return to *laissez faire* in its pure form; for facilities on which public reliance is high, continuation of regulation to secure honest, reliable and safe practice is only to be expected.

Other forms of market regulation occur quite explicitly for the benefit of the producers involved—for example, price stabilization for agricultural producers. Milk marketing regulation has been a fertile source of administrative law development over the years, as the Department of Agriculture has attempted to control the impact of a number of market forces: that cows produce milk according to an annual rhythm, so that assuring an adequate supply of fresh milk for the fall guarantees a surplus in the spring; that transportation advances permit a national market even for fresh milk, where city-dwellers would prefer a local source of supply; and that land values near the cities would not ordinarily permit dairy farms to remain there. The complicated results, administered under local "milk marketing orders," have produced some stability in the dairy community, but a good deal of administrative law and also the familiar mountain of butter and cheese.

Regulation of the professions. Perhaps nowhere in administrative law has the capacity of economic regulation to enhance the welfare of the regulated at the expense of the public been illustrated as well as in regulation of the professions. Controls over professional practice commonly are administered under state rather than federal law, and typically involve control over entry to the profession, some regulation of professional practice, and discipline for professional misconduct. Entry is generally controlled by educational requirements and examination; professional practice, by regulations adopted by the governing body; and discipline, by formal adjudications conducted before that body. In addition to the learned professions—law, medicine, accounting—such regulation may reach barbers, cosmeticians, plumbers, or welldrillers; "literally hundreds of occupations are subject to the licensing laws in one or more states."[10]

The articulated basis for such regulation is to protect the public from incompetent or even unscrupulous practice of a calling the ordinary consumer could not appraise, while assuring to the qualified practitioner economic conditions conducive to sound practice. Although precise arrangements vary from state to state and even profession to profession, professional regulation is typically administered by a board of part-time state officials drawn predominantly from the group subject to regulation. Such arrangements conduce to self-interest, which often enough is served; recent federal Supreme Court litigation, generally lost by the regulators, revealed practices of rate-setting,[11] suppression of competitive advertising,[12] and other efforts to suppress competition;[13] and academic analyses are almost invariably unflattering.[14] Suspicions run high that the rates at which medical associations charter specialists or the level at which a state's bar examination passage is set are as directly linked to the capacity of the relevant market to support new competition, as to the skills of the fresh applicants. That the public can use protection against unsanitary conditions of hair-cutting is indisputable; placing regulation of barbers in the hands of the barbers conduces to other ends as well.

Regulation of the economic conditions of labor. The labor market's well-known imperfections as an economic market generate a wide variety of regulatory measures. At both the federal and the state level, depending on the involvement of interstate commerce or not, important independent agencies employ formal adjudicatory procedures to control aspects of the conduct of labor relations. Coercive behavior is barred, both in the process

---

10. W. Gellhorn, The Abuse of Occupational Licensing, 44 U. Chi. L. Rev. 6 (1976).

11. Goldfarb v. Virginia State Bar, 421 U.S. 777 (1975).

12. Bates v. State Bar of Arizona, 433 U.S. 350 (1977).

13. Gibson v. Berryhill, 411 U.S. 564 (1973); but see Friedman v. Rogers, 440 U.S. 1 (1979). While willing to find such arrangements may be unfair to individuals directly and adversely affected by them, the Supreme Court has been unwilling to say that the arrangements are in themselves impermissible.

14. E.g., W. Gellhorn, note 10, above; see also G. Liebman, Delegation to Private Parties in American Constitutional Law, 50 Ind. L.J. 650 (1975).

of organizing labor unions and in the conduct of economic negotiations or strikes; employee discharges found to have resulted from employer coercion are corrected, with the employer required to pay back wages as well as offer reinstatement. Other regulators oversee the conduct of union affairs to assure democratic practice within the labor movement; the administrative stages of these proceedings are highly informal, with only limited controls available to interested individuals.[15]

Other forms of regulation, taken at the national level through the executive Department of Labor, protect within limits the economic position of the individual employee. Since the New Deal, federal law has sought to control minimum wages and working hours in most workplaces large enough to affect interstate commerce. These provisions are directly enforceable in court, either privately or in a suit by the responsible administrator. Over the years a significant practice of interpretation has grown up: through widely publicized responses to industry requests for advice, the administrator is able to secure wide compliance without need for formal proceedings. Other laws regulate such disparate matters as the conditions of labor of migrant workers, and the terms and conditions of retirement or pension plans in employment offering that benefit.

Consumer protection. Much regulation at all levels of government is undertaken to protect the economic position of consumers and, through them, the public generally. Most prominent in this respect is the regulation of the nation's banking system, money supply, credit practices, securities and commodities exchanges, and insurance industry. All but the last of these are generally accomplished at the federal level[16] (although with some state participation in the case of banking); for historical reasons, insurance is regulated chiefly by the states. These bodies generate standards by informal rulemaking, control entry through licensing, and frequently enjoy extraordinary summary enforcement authority, thought necessary to maintain public confidence in financial institutions. Much is done informally; while formal proceedings are possible, the very fact of convening such proceedings would have such a negative effect in the relevant financial community that that stage is rarely reached. Those seeking approval either abandon the project, or make the changes suggested to them for securing the agreement of agency staff to their proposed course of action.

---

15. Dunlop v. Bachowski, 421 U.S. 560 (1975).

16. Principal agencies include the Federal Reserve Board (money supply, national banks, credit practices), the Comptroller of the Currency (national banks), the Federal Home Loan Bank Board (savings banks), the Federal Deposit Insurance Corporation, and the Federal Savings and Loan Insurance Corporation, each with responsibility for a different aspect of national banking practice.

This effect is especially prominent in the work of agencies such as the federal Securities and Exchange Commission (SEC), which not only seek to control the operation of sensitive financial markets—in this case, dealings in corporate stock—but also to assure that consumers acting in those markets have access to complete and accurate information about the securities offered for sale there. Corporations must be sure that there will be no controversy about the prospectuses and other papers they draw up in attempted compliance with SEC regulations. What is wanted is the SEC staff's assurance that "no action" will be sought in response to a given filing, not a formal hearing to resolve some controversy; suggested changes will quickly be made to gain that assurance. As in the case of the SEC, the aim of much consumer protection regulation is informative, to assure full and honest disclosure of the terms on which credit will be given or a corporate security issued, or of the economic condition of a corporation seeking fresh capital or additional debt. Other regulatory forms with a similar end would include, at the federal level, the regulation of labels on clothing by the Federal Trade Commission, or of food and drink by the Food and Drug Administration. At the state and local level, one finds disclosure requirements in connection with real estate developments, and control over the honesty of weights and measures, and even restaurant menus.

Allocation of artificial or public goods. Certain kinds of economic activity may face inevitable constraints, that are not likely to be or cannot be reflected in a market absent regulatory structure. Only so many radio stations can be squeezed into the broadcast spectrum, and their transmission must be controlled even then to avoid mutual interference over much of the listening area; only so many airplanes can take off from a given airport during a desirable morning hour. A stream can accept only so much effluent before the available oxygen is consumed. Up to the applicable limit, each of these activities is safe and acceptable; beyond it, it is not.

While a variety of techniques could be imagined for the required rationing—contemporary economists tend to favor auctions—regulation is often employed. Applicants for radio or television licenses must apply to the Federal Communications Commission for a license to operate the desired broadcast facility, under conditions that will control interference. They must establish in formal adjudications that they will meet service standards in the public interest. Competition for the license requires the Commission to choose between the competitors. The fee for the license is a tiny fraction of the value that may thus be conferred. Similarly, factories putting effluent in streams must have a permit to do so, based on available pollution control technology and subject to agency monitoring and enforcement; but use of the stream need not be directly paid for. For distribution of airport slots, as for the government's sale of rights to harvest its timber or explore for oil on its lands, a competitive bidding system is employed, with apparent success.

Health and safety regulation

Regulation to protect the citizenry from the harms of a technologically advanced society is sometimes thought a more recent development than regulation to remedy the deficiencies of the economic marketplace. Indeed, this has been the predominant character of the great expansion of federal government regulation in the past two decades. Redress for injuries occasioned by hazard was long thought the domain of ordinary tort law. Yet the federal government was regulating the safety of steam boilers by the middle of the 19th century and railroad safety by the century's end. At the same time, the states were substituting administrative schemes of workmen's compensation for court actions to deal with injuries suffered in the workplace. Pure food and drug legislation and regulation of unhealthful working conditions emerged, first in the states and then in the federal government, at about the same time as railroad rate regulation became prominent. The importance of modern times lies more in the enhancement of our capacities both to generate and to detect risk, and in the increasing use of regulation as a substitute for tort liability, than in innovation in the character of the harms the state seeks to prevent.

More appropriately viewed as innovative is the widespread use of informal rulemaking as a major tool in recent federal regulation of health and safety matters. When the Environmental Protection Agency (EPA) sets Clean Air Act standards to govern emissions of sulfur dioxide by electric power stations or the Occupational Safety and Health Administration (OSHA) establishes the permitted levels of cotton dust in the atmosphere of a textile mill, it employs a slightly modified form of informal rulemaking to do so. The resulting standards may have an enormous impact on the affected industry, requiring first installation and then maintenance of highly complex environmental control machinery. Economic regulators, by contrast, used informal rulemaking only occasionally, and then to establish standards of conduct that rarely required a large investment to meet. The paradigmatic proceeding for them was the application for license, invocation of a sanction, or generation of a rate— in each case a formal proceeding decided "on the record" and determining the outcome of a particular controversy involving, even in ratemaking, a limited number of specially interested parties. The first important federal regulator of health issues, the Food and Drug Administration, fit the same mold: ordinarily, it determined applications for permission to market particular drugs, or proceeded against specific items asserted to have been mislabeled; when it did make rules, as in determining what percentage of peanuts had to be in a substance to be labeled "peanut butter," it was required to employ formal rulemaking procedures. OSHA and EPA (along with other health and safety regulators, such as the Nuclear Regulatory Commission or the Department of Transportation's National Highway Traffic Safety Administration) are, in procedural terms, significantly freer in adopting norms to carry out their responsibilities.

The range of regulatory activity involved in control of health and safety issues is, of course, far broader than the simple setting of norms. Among the other responsibilities of the EPA,[17] for example, are:

- Bureaucratic oversight, describable as informal adjudication, of state implementation of state-administered federal environmental controls;

- Permitting (licensing) of industrial discharges presenting pollution hazards, requiring formal adjudication if opposed;

- Inspection of operating facilities; and enforcement through the courts (or formal adjudication) of sanctions for violations of statutory or agency standards;

- Certification of industrial and agricultural chemicals for safety in use;

- Identification and control of sites used for the disposal of hazardous wastes, including clean-up activities and administrative and judicial enforcement of fiscal responsibility against former users.

Probably the dominant intellectual issue presented in this field today, one with significant political and moral overtones, concerns the assessment of risk. One deals here with activities whose capacity for harm may be latent, not emerging for a decade or more. The threat of harm may be indirect—that is, it may be easier to point to an increase in cancer resulting from an activity, than to identify a particular episode or even a particular source as the exact cause of any one individual's harm. And the results of a failure of regulation, however unlikely, may be catastrophic, as the incident at Chernobyl so graphically illustrated. No amount of regulation of an activity permitted to continue can completely eliminate risk; and many if not all risks require a difficult comparison with others which they displace. The small but real risk of a second Chernobyl, if a nuclear reactor is built, must be compared to the deaths

---

17. See pp. 89-91.

and damage that would result from generating the same electricity in a conventional coal-fired utility, the enhanced risks of international disruption from using oil, the availability of alternative technologies, and the social impacts and risks of foregoing the electricity altogether. Identifying a socially acceptable level of risk, finding reliable means for identifying and comparing the risks presented by alternative activities, and determining the level of confidence one can have in the regulatory system's ability to control them—all appear to be central tasks of the political system.

Our legal system is only beginning to come to grips with these matters. Congress has not adopted any consistent attitude to socially acceptable risk, as three measures dealing with the potential of chemicals to cause cancer will attest: smoking remains lawful (although increasingly the subject of strident mandatory warnings about its health effects, national restraints on advertising, and local restraints on smoking in public places); carcinogenic chemicals used in the workplace are subject to OSHA's development of rules under a statutory direction to adopt those standards "which most adequately assure[ ], to the extent feasible, on the basis of the best available evidence, that no employee will suffer material impairment of health or functional capacity";[18] the Food and Drug Administration's responsibility is to prohibit further use of any food additive for which there is an indication, however slight, that the additive is carcinogenic to laboratory animals and might therefore be carcinogenic to humans.[19] Similar contrasts can be found in the levels of risk Congress has found acceptable in providing for regulation of other hazards.[20]

One can understand, in political terms, Congress' reluctance to be consistent; smoking is widespread, and the public is easily alarmed about the risk of cancer from food. Yet even in stating a general standard for occupational health protection, Congress hedged its bets with the words

18. Occupational Safety and Health Act § 6(b)(5), 29 U.S.C. § 655(b)(5) (1982).

19. 21 U.S.C. § 342 (1982). When this stringent standard resulted in an order banning the further use of saccharin, a popular sugar substitute, because of laboratory evidence of bladder cancer in rats given massive doses of the chemical, Congress responded by calling for further study, and temporarily exempting saccharin from the law. The general standard remains in place—although recently there have been signs that the Food and Drug Administration, whose proceedings it governs, may have found ways to avoid such stringent mandates for risks it regards as de minimis. See Young v. Community Nutrition Inst., 106 S. Ct. 2360 (1986).

20. In the field of transportation, for example, automobiles, airplanes and the transportation of nuclear materials are treated with varying stringency; the small but catastrophic risks of nuclear power engender a different legislative response than the chronic health risks associated with burning coal, or the geopolitical risks of burning oil, in generating electric power.

"to the extent feasible," a formula that essentially put definition of the acceptable level of risk in the hands of an agency (OSHA) and the courts. This political irresponsibility, as he saw it, led one Justice of the Supreme Court to insist that an unlawful delegation had occurred.[21] While increasing use of environmental impact statements[22] and other like means for structuring bureaucratic policy analysis suggest some reason to hope for more consistency in the future, the limits of our knowledge and depths of our fears about today's complex technology and its by-products suggest that the political difficulties will endure—and with them, the disposition to use administrators rather than legislation.

In addition to programs directly concerned with human health, a variety of regulatory programs, largely in the Department of Agriculture, seek to assure the soundness of the national food supply. These vary from programs (also to be found at the state level) for identifying agricultural pests and quarantining affected farmlands or produce, to programs for the inspection and grading of produce, to programs for market control, as earlier discussed.[23] Although the impact of these programs can often be substantial—a farmer's entire orchard may be destroyed if found to be infected with citrus canker—determinations are generally made by inspectors, and formal adjudication even at the agency level is a rarity.

Social security, health and welfare

The federal Department of Health and Human Services encompasses most national programs involving personal financial benefits—social security and other benefits for the elderly; disability insurance for persons unable to participate in the work-force; welfare for impoverished parents with dependent children; medical insurance for the elderly and the im-

---

21. Industrial Union Department, AFL-CIO v. American Petroleum Institute, 448 U.S. 607 (1980) (Justice Rehnquist, concurring). No majority could agree on a reading of the statute's qualification about feasibility. Four of the Court's nine Justices agreed with OSHA that it required any protection that would reduce the risk of cancer and was both technologically and economically "achievable"; three would have required an initial determination by the Secretary that "a significant risk of material health impairment" existed under the existing industrial practice or standard; the eighth would have insisted that the expenditures necessary to achieve a given health standard not be "wholly disproportionate to the expected health and safety benefits."
22. See p. 71.
23. See pp. 88 and 108.

poverished—but some such programs exist in other departments: the Department of Labor, for example, administers the federal workmen's compensation programs applicable to certain employees; the Department of Agriculture, the food stamp program for subsidized foodstuffs for the poor; the Veterans' Administration, benefits for those who have served in the armed forces. Individual states administer unemployment compensation under loose federal supervision, and a variety of local welfare programs.

These programs involve the distribution of benefits to or on behalf of individuals rather than the regulation of conduct, and the typical problem is one of individual eligibility for commencing or continuing to receive benefits. Generalization is difficult—the Medicare/Medicaid program, for example, is administered in the first instance by private insurance carriers under contract with the federal government; the social security program by a federal bureaucracy; and federal welfare assistance by a state bureaucracy under federal supervision. One can say, however, that the process begins—fittingly for the minor dimensions of any individual case—with bureaucratic routine. For federal welfare assistance and other state-administered schemes, this may pass through several levels of review. If dissatisfied, the applicant or recipient may demand an on-the-record hearing;[24] in most federal programs this hearing is conducted before a federal administrative law judge and is subject to administrative review. Under recent constructions of the Due Process Clause of the federal constitution, as discussed above,[25] a procedurally quite elaborate hearing is mandatory for persons being deprived of benefits they had already been receiving, in some cases before the payment of benefits may even be suspended. Although the great bulk of cases never pass the bureaucratic stages, such hearings keep more than 800 administrative law judges occupied in the Department of Health and Human Services alone; judicial review of the work of these administrative law judges and the departmental appeals council that oversees their work constitutes a significant proportion of the work of the United States district courts.[26]

These programs present other kinds of issues, as well. To ease bureaucratic administration, the responsible agencies adopt rules substituting general standards for individual judgment, raising standard issues

24. The availability of hearings under the medical insurance programs is restricted, as a function of the amount in dispute. See Gray Panthers v. Schweiker, 652 F.2d 146 (D.C. Cir. 1980).

25. Pp. 32-48, above.

26. The Judicial Conference of the United States reported 30,000 actions under the Social Security Laws were initiated in 1984, 11.5% of the total caseload. Annual Report of the Directors of the Administrative Office of the United States Courts 133 (1984).

both of authority and of application.[27] Where state agencies exercise important administrative responsibility, federal regulators must have (essentially adjudicatory) procedures for resolving disputes; they are not permitted to support state programs that fail to meet federal standards, and the states, federal government and beneficiary community all have evident stakes in such matters.[28] And questions are presented, as well, about the level of procedural specification required. The food stamp program, for example, involves grocery store owners as well as recipients, and questions of eligibility can arise for either group. The owners are permitted to accept the stamps only in payment for staple foods—not for cash, or for electric light bulbs; administrative sanctions against misbehaving store owners result from procedures strikingly less formal than would be available to a recipient believed no longer to be eligible to continue receiving the stamps.

Perhaps the issues they illustrate most sharply, however, concern the problems of achieving coherence in administering a vast national program. Professor Jerry Mashaw's series of books grounded in studies of the administration of federal disability insurance[29] illustrate two dimensions of this problem: first, the question *whose* coherence is to be achieved; second, the conflicting models available for achieving it. The first of these questions concerns the appropriate relationship between political top administration and permanent civil service staff. How seriously, for example, the problem of welfare cheating is viewed, and how stringent measures are taken to pursue it, will often be a function of political administration. Securing the implementation of a new policy in this regard against the more constant outlook of the permanent staff presents well-known difficulties. The second question assumes agreed ends, but notes at least three differing and conflicting means for achieving them: a bureaucratic model stressing the tools and discipline of internal management, such as staff manuals, hierarchical structure and an effort to build morale; a professional model building on the commitments to helpfulness of the doctors and caseworkers most directly responsible for program administration; and a model of individual right, stressing the claims and dignity of the persons who participate in the program. The bureaucrat will regard as successful a program that generates few gross errors, and

---

27. Heckler v. Campbell, 461 U.S. 458 (1983).

28. National Welfare Rights Organization v. Finch, 429 F.2d 725 (D.C. Cir. 1970).

29. Bureaucratic Justice: Managing Social Security Disability Claims (Yale Univ. 1983); Due Process in the Administrative State (Yale Univ. 1985); Social Security Hearings and Appeals: A Study of the Social Security Administration Hearing System (with Goetz, Goodman, Schwartz, Verkuil and Carrow) (Lexington 1978).

is as likely to err for as against a claimant in marginal cases. The professional will value a program that leaves ample room for her exercise of the professional judgment on which questions of eligibility turn, trusting her professional commitments to produce appropriately favorable results. The individual may prefer a program that maximizes his personal participation and opportunity to advance the merits of his particular claim. Each is attractive to a point, and none is readily reconciled with the others.

A third dimension of the problem of national coherence, already suggested above,[30] is brought about by the geographical arrangement of the national courts and the Supreme Court's limited capacity to oversee their results. The Secretary of Health and Human Services administers a national program, and the departmental Appeals Council that reviews administrative law judge decisions is also a single body, bringing a uniform approach to its work. Yet that work is reviewed in 93 different judicial districts, then twelve disparate circuit courts of appeal—each of which understandably believes that the Secretary has the obligation to follow its view in cases arising within its jurisdictional catchment area. One court may be very tolerant of administrative judgment; another, particularly sensitive to the Department's handling of asserted mental disability; a third, more concerned about its findings respecting the availability of work in the national economy for persons never likely to be more than marginal contributors. When the Secretary responded to this situation by announcing that she might choose to regard some court decisions as binding only in the case actually decided, and not as precedent governing future decisions in other cases, this "non-acquiescence" produced a major confrontation with the courts. While the particular point on which she had disagreed with the courts—in the event, not a few courts but most of them—was resolved (against her) by legislation, the general problem is one that can be expected to recur.[31]

State goods

The great bulk of early administration in the United States concerned public goods, the land and to a lesser extent the mails. As an expanding nation on an unpeopled[32] land mass, the United States regarded its real

---

30. See pp. 82-84.
31. See P. Strauss, One Hundred Fifty Cases Per Year: Some Implications of the Supreme Court's Limited Resources for Judicial Review of Agency Action, 87 Colum. L. Rev. 1093, 1110-16 (1987).
32. Of course, it was peopled by the Indians; yet they were more or less

property as a resource to be exploited for growth. Under a variety of programs, veterans of its wars, persons who would farm its surface, persons who would mine its minerals, and railroads that would traverse it were given the chance to qualify for ownership. A sizable bureaucracy grew up to conduct and keep records of surveys, and to process the variety of claims made under these laws. While most of these programs have been quiescent since the beginning of this century,[33] others have replaced them, and the Departments of Interior and Agriculture in particular expend a good deal of their effort in these directions.[34] Prominent actors include the National Park Service (regulation of national parks and persons providing services within them); the National Forest Service (regulation of the national forests and their users—campers, resort owners, miners, and livestock grazers as well as timber harvesters);[35] the Bureau of Land Management (regulation like the Forest Service on the remainder of the public lands, particularly administration of programs for livestock grazing and mineral leasing (coal and oil)); and the Bureau of Reclamation (development of western water resources, and management of resulting irrigation districts). Access to these programs is often governed by auction, or even lottery, so that disputes at this stage most often concern issues of eligibility. The permissions granted, a coal mining lease in a national forest or a concession in a national park, are often conditional, and supervision of those conditions requires administrative actions of the kind readily anticipatable from the circumstances.

An interesting and distinctive characteristic of some of these administrative schemes is the use of advisory committees of interested private citizens to assist in the formulation and application of policy at the local level. How grazing rights are distributed in the arid West, for example, in relation to timbering and other activities on the public lands is a matter of deep import to the local economy. An administrative unit of the Department of Interior's Bureau of Land Management may encompass hundreds of

---

uniformly regarded as nomadic interlopers to be confined (or displaced) to designated "reservations," not owners in the western sense. However land came from the Indians or other nations (France, Spain, Mexico, Great Britain, Russia) to the United States, it came immediately into public ownership. Even today, upwards of one third of the nation's land mass is federally owned.

33. It remains possible for an enterprising person to "locate" a mining claim on most public lands; upon proving the discovery there of a "valuable mineral" and some (but not much) work to develop it, one can force the sale of the tract at turn-of-the-century prices.

34. The situation is not much changed since a presidential commission issued a major body of studies in the late 1960's, under the general rubric One Third of the Nation's Lands.

35. A dated but still valuable account of Forest Service responsibilities and administration is given in H. Kaufman, The Forest Ranger (Resources for the Future 1960).

square miles of federal land, with private holdings interspersed, and a handful of federal officials to oversee its operation. By coopting a local advisory committee of ranchers, sheepherders, lumbermen, and others interested in the use of the land to assist in the annual provision for its use, the Bureau can attain substantial adherence to its policies without having to expend major efforts in enforcement.[36]

Problems of apportioning what economists describe as the "commons"—air, water, the broadcast spectrum, the power to be captured from free-flowing water—generally have not been treated as the disposition of public property, like land, but as issues of allocation, and accomplished by the devices of economic or health and safety regulation. Increasingly, however, voices are heard to suggest that sale or lease on condition is the more appropriate means here as well.[37]

The government acts as a proprietor, also, in administering its business relations—notably (but not exclusively) through the General Services Administration, which acts as provisioner for the whole of government, and the Department of Defense, purchaser of all supplies for the armed services. These relationships give rise to a rich body of issues of public administration. The government may wish to advance various public policies through its award of contracts.[38] Questions arise concerning the eligibility of bidders and the propriety of awards; and disputes arising during contract administration, often enough on matters of urgency for the national interest, must be resolved. Occasionally sanctions such as debarment from future bidding will be thought appropriate for contractor misbehavior. Similar situations arise when the government seeks to purchase not goods but services— research on a virulent disease for the National Institutes of Health, or on a problem of administrative law for the Administrative Conference of the United States. "Government contracts" is a specialty, neither administrative law nor contract law, but partaking of some of the characteristics of each.

---

36. L. Laitala, BLM Advisory Boards Past, Present, and Future (BLM 1975); and see G. Libecap, Locking up the Range 81 (Ballinger 1981).

37. E.g., B. Ackerman and R. Stewart, Reforming Environmental Law, 37 Stan. L. Rev. 1333 (1985).

38. Notable examples, each achieved by presidential executive order well in advance of a statutory provision, were contracts conditioned on non-discrimination in employment, first on racial and then on sexual bases. Other government contracting policies have favored industries employing the handicapped or owned by members of a racial minority. By statute, government contractors must pay an administratively determined "prevailing wage" for their area.

State employment

One might expect arguments based on the government's position as proprietor to apply with special vigor to public employment. That is, the public employee has no "right" to a public job, is "simply" in an employment relationship with the government, and must accept its terms as he would have to accept the terms on which he might be offered private employment. Nonetheless, that argument has been emphatically rejected, as suggested in previous discussion of the evolution of our understandings of "due process of law."[39] States need not provide for a tenured civil service,[40] but when they do, their regulation of its terms and conditions must meet constitutional standards that appear to require a rather formal, on-the-record adjudication process. The civil service mechanism is briefly discussed above.[41]

Land

Earlier discussion also briefly touched the constitutional relationship between the problem of "due process," very much a part of administrative law, and the regime of expropriation or taking of private property for public use.[42] The latter is not generally regarded as a part of "administrative law"; judicial rather than administrative tribunals are employed to determine such issues as "fair value" and whether property has been lawfully taken for public use. Controls over the development of land remaining in private ownership, on the other hand, generally are administrative in character. The most pervasive such controls are zoning ordinances, local provisions governing such issues as density, use, and even aesthetics adopted and administered by a community body that often is elective in character. Land use controls can also be found at the federal and state level, ranging from the protection of historical landmarks or districts, to the location of large industrial sites such as electric utilities or pipelines, to the control of activities creating some hazard to the community, such as surface mining or the disposal of hazardous waste. These

---

39. See pp. 41-42.
40. This is the orthodox position; to a degree, Supreme Court cases providing constitutional protection against politically motivated discharge from apolitical office, text at note 134, p. 93, might be thought to require state recognition of civil service status.
41. See pp. 92-94.
42. See pp. 48-49.

are, in effect, particular instances of economic regulation, and health and safety regulation, and the procedures commonly employed are typical of those settings.

Taxes and excises

The collection of taxes and other excises has long been an important ground of administration; in the earliest days of the republic, the assessment and collection of taxes and duties were the principal administrative functions the national government performed, and histories of early administrative practice give much attention to them.[43] Taxation remains important, obviously enough; while, with the natural specialization of the modern legal profession, tax practitioners tend not to present themselves as "administrative lawyers," tax practice and procedures are in fact readily understood in administrative law terms. At the federal level, most tax and excise issues are within the jurisdiction of elements of the Treasury Department—the Internal Revenue Service for taxes, the Customs Service for import duties (and some other regulations of international commerce), and the Bureau of Alcohol, Tobacco and Firearms for the special taxes, and associated controls, on those commodities. These agencies flesh out applicable statutory controls by regulation; issue periodic interpretations of the laws subject to their jurisdiction; prescribe the forms on which taxes are to be reported; collect and process those forms; conduct necessary investigations; and initiate proceedings. In tax administration, these proceedings, if contested, are generally conducted in the ordinary courts or before specialized tribunals such as the Tax Court or the Court of International Trade, rather than within the Department as such; but before any such trial occurs, audits or other proceedings within the Department give ample opportunity for administrative resolutions to be reached.

Tax investigations form the backdrop against which much of the law respecting agency investigations, briefly discussed above,[44] has been made. Our tax system is one of voluntary reporting, enforced by regular disclosures by third parties (that is, employers report wages to the government, corporations report dividends, etc.) and by occasional investigations after the fact. It does not seem excessively cynical to speculate that the needs of such a system have significantly contributed to the

---

43. L. White, The Federalists: A Study in Administrative History (MacMillan 1948).
44. See pp. 31-32.

unwillingness of American courts to entertain generalized pleas of self-incrimination as excusing the obligation to file reports, or to extend the protections of the self-incrimination claim to the provision of any documents that are not both personal and in the personal possession of the individual making the claim. So also for the relatively permissive standards of relevance that attend enforcement of administrative requests for information (subpoenas and the like) in the course of an investigation, the legality of requirements for record-keeping, the broad scope permitted searches in support of customs regulation, and so forth. A substantial proportion of the general law on these subjects, particularly those relating to documentary production, in fact has its origin in tax administration.

Public services

Much of the effort of American civil bureaucracy is expended in administering programs for support of public services such as education, housing, research, and road construction. The federal Departments of Education, Housing and Urban Development, and Transportation annually oversee the distribution of billions of dollars for these purposes, either as grants to approved state programs or in the form of guaranteed loans to individuals. Federally contracted research, seeking cancer cures and energy technology development as well as strategic defense initiatives, provides major support for both public and private universities as well as important elements of the business community. At the state and local level, the institutions that provide these services must be operated, suggesting a rich harvest of possible controversy over both planning and operations.

A hypothetical housing development may serve to suggest the range of problems that can arise. (Examples could be given, with equal ease and richness, concerning public schools or other services.) If the project is to be financed with federal support, there will first be the matter of satisfying the various conditions attached to such support—for example, that adequate provision be made for the handicapped or (depending on the program) for the aged or other purposes. Disputes over such issues are resolved internally by bureaucratic means, which a court would be disposed to describe as "informal adjudication"; a member of one of the groups within the protective purposes of the federal conditions would be able to obtain review in court of any decision that allegedly did not meet them.[45] (What a state's remedies would be if, in its view, the project

---

45. Citizens to Preserve Overton Park, Inc. v. Volpe, 401 U.S. 402 (1971).

were being wrongfully withheld or excessively conditioned is far less certain.) In addition, if the project is significant, the federal agency will be required to issue an "environmental impact statement" before approving it, first in draft for public comment and then in final form. This provides a substantial opportunity for still broader public participation, as by those concerned about its impact on wildlife in a nearby marsh. Compliance with this requirement, too, is subject to federal enforcement although generally only as a procedural matter.[46] Once made, the grant is subject to continuing federal oversight and possible administrative enforcement, through agency proceedings, for adherence to its conditions; violation of some conditions (e.g., non-discrimination in employment) may threaten not only the particular project, but all similar federal funding.[47]

Those constructing and undertaking the project will likely face constraints of state and local law on such issues as siting, requiring public procedures of greater or lesser formality. Once in operation, such questions will arise as eligibility for access, conditions of tenancy (notably, the rent to be paid), and discipline for tenants who are thought to have violated the terms of their eligibility or tenancy. The usual situation for public housing is that there are many more eligible applicants than spaces; applications (like welfare generally) are handled in a bureaucratic process, and the interesting and difficult question has been whether disappointed but eligible applicants are entitled to any kind of regularity in the process of selection among those eligible.[48] The conditions of tenancy—rent,

---

46. That is, the courts will usually ask only whether the environmental analysis required by the National Environmental Policy Act, 42 U.S.C. § 4334, has been made, not whether the results of that analysis force a particular decision. Strycker's Bay Neighborhood Council v. Karlen, 444 U.S. 223 (1980). On occasion, however, the analysis will reveal matters that do bring other federal laws into play—for example, that the proposed site is the habitat of a species protected under the federal Endangered Species Act—and then those laws will control whether and under what conditions the project may go forward. See TVA v. Hill, 437 U.S. 153 (1978).

47. The threatened loss of federal funding as a means of enforcement of federal programs has proved particularly controversial in education. In one well publicized case, the Supreme Court held that financial grants to a particular program in a private college did not allow the Department of Education to demand compliance with statutes prohibiting sex discrimination in all aspects of the college's behavior. In other words, the assistance and the conditions that went with it were deemed program specific rather than institutional under the statute there at issue. Grove City College v. Bell, 465 U.S. 558 (1984). The Court's statutory construction thus limited the pull of these strings attached to federal financial assistance; yet the case and the publicity it generated demonstrate the persuasiveness and power of those strings. See also A. Rosenthal, note 148, p. 99; R. Katzmann, Institutional Disability: The Saga of Transportation Policy for the Disabled (Brookings 1986).

48. Since an applicant for a scarce resource could not easily be described as

maximum earnings a tenant can have without forfeiting her place to a more needy person, rules of conduct—are the product of rulemaking rather than adjudication, and so subject only to statutory constraints on their formation.[49] The conditions of eligibility are also, however, a matter of continuing interest to the grantor, and the terms of a federal grant or guaranteed loan may well require the grantee to justify any proposed change to the supporting agency. Tenants' efforts to participate in and force formality upon these proceedings, which otherwise would likely be resolved through negotiation or informal adjudication, have generally proved unavailing although strong arguments have been made to support their interest.[50] Tenants in place, finally, are within the ambit of "due process" entitlement, and can therefore require relatively formal adjudicatory procedures to be employed in removing or disciplining them—procedures which may take place in an administrative "housing court," or in the municipal judicial system.

Custodial institutions

Custodial institutions directed by the state, prisons in particular but also mental hospitals and residential schools for the mentally retarded,

---

having an "entitlement" to it, the conventional due process analysis, pp. 40-43, would not regard her as having any constitutional claim to procedures. (There might, of course, be enforceable statutory provisions.) Nonetheless, the involvement of the state in the distribution of these resources and the apparent ease with which at least some principles of fairness in distribution might be observed has produced strong arguments for constraint. Holmes v. New York City Housing Authority, 398 F.2d 262 (2d Cir. 1968); K. Davis, Administrative Law Treatise § 7.26 (2d ed. 1979).

49. See pp. 133-36.

50. Tenants in public housing have sued in federal courts under a number of theories. While federal agency decisions to increase rents have traditionally been held to be unreviewable by courts, Langevin v. Chenango Court, Inc., 447 F.2d 296 (2d Cir. 1971), a recent Supreme Court case permits tenants to sue local housing authorities if rent increases violate federally imposed rent guidelines. Wright v. Roanoke Redevelopment and Housing Authority, 107 S. Ct. 766 (1987). The pervasive issues are the competence of the judiciary to review what seems to be managerial actions such as determination of rents and whether courts or administrators have final responsibility to enforce tenants' rights.

In a case where nursing home residents protested the de-certification of the home (meaning the residents would have to move), the Court held it was enough that the home itself had been given procedural protection before the final decision. The large number of patients had no individual interests that would permit a due process claim in federal court. O'Bannon v. Town Court Nursing Center, 447 U.S. 773 (1980).

can be regarded as administrative agencies whose decisions have a particular consequence for the values of "liberty." At the federal level, a sizable prison system is administered by the Bureau of Prisons of the Department of Justice. As a general matter, however, custodial institutions are state institutions, and the statutory law governing commitment to them is state law. As public institutions, federal or state, custodial institutions present all the standard faces of administrative law—formulating policy, contracting, engaging civil servants, etc.—but it is in their relationships with the individuals placed in their care that the sharpest questions are raised. The question of commitment, indeed, is so momentous as to be placed in the hands of the courts—universally so for criminal conviction, and generally, in conjunction with medical examiners, in the case of involuntary commitments for mental illness or retardation;[51] no one doubts that the greatest care must be taken at this stage.[52] Issues that arise in the course of a commitment once made, however, and many questions associated with release are dealt with from the perspective of administrative law.

Thus, analysis of what procedures a prison warden must follow in transferring an inmate in his charge to another facility presents a question of administrative due process;[53] so also, what form of hearing is required before prison discipline can be imposed is a question to be settled according to the norms of administrative, rather than criminal, procedure, and the discipline results from a hearing within the prison system, not before the courts.[54] As public servants in close and sometimes brutal contact with private citizens (in this case, prisoners), state wardens and prison guards have been the frequent objects of suits seeking monetary damages for allegedly unlawful acts under § 1983 of the federal Civil Rights Act,[55] suits that have been successful to what outside observers may regard as a surprising degree.[56] And at the end of imprisonment, an inmate's chances for early, probationary release turn not only on

---

51. S. Brakel, The Mentally Disabled and the Law (Am. Bar. Foundn, 3d ed. 1985).

52. In the case of mental retardation, commitment is generally at the request of a family, often while the person being committed is still a child. More informal procedures are common in these cases, relying on the family's discretion, but even here the need for explicitly judicial supervision of ostensibly medical judgments is recognized. Parham v. J.R., 442 U.S. 584 (1979).

53. Meachum v. Fano, 427 U.S. 215 (1976).

54. Walpole v. Hill, 105 S. Ct. 2768 (1985).

55. See pp. 276-78.

56. See H. Monaghan, State Law Wrongs, State Law Remedies, and the Fourteenth Amendment, 86 Colum. L. Rev. 979 (1986). Recent Supreme Court decisions undercut these developments. Hudson v. Palmer, 468 U.S. 517 (1984); Parratt v. Taylor, 451 U.S. 527 (1981).

internal, administrative judgments about "good behavior," but more importantly on the judgment of an administrative tribunal, the parole board, respecting his prospects for law-abiding behavior on return to the community. To what extent those bodies are subject to the constraints of regularity, relying as heavily as they must on judgment and on information informally obtained, has been a matter of significant dispute.[57]

Corresponding issues can arise in the context of mental health care and the habilitation of the mentally retarded. For a period in the 1970's, lawsuits seeking to enforce principles of acceptable care and planning were a common feature of American jurisprudence; and these suits against public authority seeking to compel the performance of an asserted duty are readily characterized in administrative law terms. In a number of these cases, the public administration of the programs in question was revealed to be so deficient as to cause the judges hearing them, in effect, to place the programs in judicial receivership.[58] Doubts about the capacity and legitimacy of judges to assume the burden of administering state institutions contributed to more recent Supreme Court judgments discouraging quite such adventurous oversight;[59] yet the facts that these are state institutions, whose acts have major consequences for the liberty and well-being of those assigned to them, promises the continued availability of administrative law remedies in some settings.

Immigration, deportation

"Liberty" is also central, but encounters opposing state interests of unusual force, in the administration of the alienage laws, those governing the lawfulness of aliens' presence on American soil. Although some bureaucratic processing associated with these laws (issuance of visas) occurs in the Department of State, their administration is generally committed to the Immigration and Naturalization Service, a constituent element of the Department of Justice; this function is wholly federal in character. Hearings on such issues as visa extension, qualification for permanent residence status, exclusion, political asylum and deportation—varying in

---

57. See Superintendent, Mass. Corr. Institution, Walpole v. Hill, 105 S. Ct. 2768 (1985); Morrissey v. Brauer, 408 U.S 471 (1972) (revoking parole); Pickens v. United States Board of Parole, 507 F.2d 1107 (D.C. Cir. 1974).

58. D.& S. Rothman, The Willowbrook Wars (1984); Special Project: The Remedial Process in Institutional Reform Litigation, 78 Col. L. Rev. 788 (1978); A. Chayes, The Role of the Judge in Public Law Litigation, 89 Harv. L. Rev. 1281 (1976).

59. E.g., Pennhurst State School & Hospital v. Halderman, 465 U.S. 89 (1984).

the degree of formality attached with the perceived balance between the individual liberty claims and the state interests understood to be in-volved—occur informally, in less important cases, before regional officials of the Service; and in more important cases, before immigration law judges of the Department of Justice.[60]

Immigration law is a highly developed and complex speciality, inap-propriate to summarize here.[61] What may be remarked is that it is almost entirely the creature of statute: the courts "have long recognized the power to expel or exclude aliens as a fundamental sovereign attribute exercised by the Government's political departments largely immune from judicial control";[62] and because of "Congress' plenary authority to reg-ulate aliens, . . . some congressional rules, validly applicable to aliens, 'would be unacceptable if applied to citizens.' "[63] An alien whose pres-ence in the United States has no color of lawfulness (as distinct from one whose presence is colorably lawful, yet who is subject to deportation, as for violation of a condition of her admission) has little claim on either agency or courts for relief. The writ of habeas corpus,[64] not frequently employed to secure review of administrative action generally has a sig-nificant utility to that end in the immigration context.

International commerce

Regulation of international commerce is, presumably, an area of sub-stantial interest to foreign readers. It is, regrettably for this enterprise, far outside the reporter's usual ambit, and he can only point to materials that seem likely to prove likely bibliographic starting points.[65] Such reg-ulation is a strictly federal responsibility that (customs and related func-tions aside) is generally centered in the International Trade Administration of the Department of Commerce. Licenses that may be required for the export of certain sensitive technology are obtained there through an applications process made less-than-usually "judicial" in character by the

---

60. See note 138, p. 95.
61. Gordon & Rosenfield, Immigration Law and Procedure (1987).
62. Fiallo v. Bell, 430 U.S. 787 (1977).
63. Hotel & Restaurant Employees Union v. Attorney General, 804 F.2d 1256, 1259 (D.C. Cir. 1986), quoting Mathews v. Diaz, 426 U.S. 67 (1976).
64. See note 20, p. 214.
65. National Chamber Foundation, Federal Regulation of International Busi-ness: An Annotated Source Book (1981); Johnston, Law and Practice of United States Regulation of International Trade (Oceana 1987); R. Sturm, Customs Laws and Administration (Oceana 1982).

frequent involvement of state-classified information in the decisions to be made.[66] Administration of the anti-dumping and countervailing duty laws intended to protect American industry against discriminatory practices abroad is more formally dealt with, in part by the independent United States International Trade Commission. The Court of International Trade, a specialized court that is one of the trial-level constituents of the Court of Appeals for the Federal Circuit, reviews these matters, and has general authority in judicial actions arising under federal laws, such as the customs statutes, governing import transactions.[67]

State enterprise

State enterprise is more common in the United States than many would at first believe. Public entities commonly provide services that might equally (and often are) supplied by private enterprise in education, postal service, transportation, and the provision of public utilities; less prominently, in some manufacturing capacities associated with state needs—cement, in South Dakota; mineral water in New York State.[68] The conduct of such enterprises, however, is not ordinarily a particular concern of administrative law. Except that the public character of the enterprise invites application of the Due Process Clause to some activities—drivers for a municipal bus line may be civil servants; tenured professors at a state university have a constitutional entitlement to "fair procedure" before they are disciplined that tenured professors at a private university do not enjoy—such enterprises operate under regimes not very different from those of their private counterparts. Rates of municipal and private electric utilities, public and private bus-lines are each subject to close control, along similar lines and following similar procedures for justification and public participation. For external purposes, they tend to be regarded as distinct from the state. Over the years an attempted differentiation between "proprietary" and "governmental" activities, while never secure, has expressed this determination of the legal system

---

66. See U. Va. Center for Law and National Security, Technology Control, Competition, and National Security: Conflict and Consensus (1987); Practising Law Institute, Coping with U.S. Export Controls (1986). Cf. In the Matter of Edlow International Co., 3 N.R.C. 563 (1976).

67. See D. Serko, Import Practise: Customs and International Trade Law (PLI 1985).

68. Reeves, Inc. v. Stake, 447 U.S. 429 (1980); New York v. United States, 326 U.S. 572 (1946).

to recognize no special socialist character of public enterprise when it occurs.

The principal federal "enterprises" are the Postal Service, the Communications Satellite Corporation (Comsat), two railroad enterprises,[69] and two major regional power suppliers, the Tennessee Valley Authority and the Bonneville Power Authority; one might also include the superstructure of the national banking system, which since 1911 (and several times previously in the nation's history) has been a mixture of private enterprise and public authority. While some of these, notably the reserve banks and the two power authorities, are major actors in the national economy, one is hard-put to identify particular notions of administrative law that apply to their activities. For most purposes they are treated as legal entities independent of government, albeit entities whose legal authority to act depends on their statutory charter much as a corporation's would depend on the provisions of its certificate of incorporation. While they may sue and be sued, the lawfulness of their behavior or internal operations is not generally conceptualized in administrative law terms; in particular, they are not regarded as agencies, nor their behavior as "agency action," for the purposes of general administrative procedure legislation.

Other matters

Any such discussion as the preceding must be partial, and even in its incompleteness risk overwhelming the reader with unwanted detail. A sense that the administrative lawyer brings limited tools to an unruly and diverse universe of public actors may be sufficient. Nonetheless, reviewing what has been said, it seems appropriate to mention here one additional variety of administrative action that occasionally appears— emergency economic measures such as price controls. These present the administrative lawyer with, in a sense, her largest challenge: economy-wide, generally invoked at a time of national crisis, typically with only the broadest of legislative instructions, to be administered by a bureaucracy assembled for the purpose under conditions of urgency, without historical experience or practice, following procedures that the necessities of smoothly administering so large a program require to be highly in-

---

69. Passenger services are provided, nationwide, by Amtrak; most railroads in the northeastern part of the country are operated by Conrail, a consolidated facility formed by the government from a number of previously private carriers. Both were formed in response to private business failures.

formal. Public acceptance of such regimes is doubtless connected with the emergency itself, a widely shared sense of need that permits much to be tolerated that over the longer run and in ordinary circumstances would not be accepted. But other contributors to a sense of regularity and control ought also be noted.

General price controls first made a successful appearance in World War II and were again invoked, for brief periods, in later years. The instructions given the administrator were highly general—in the Emergency Price Control Act of 1942, to issue regulations fixing those prices that "in his judgment will be fair and equitable and effectuate" the generally described purposes of price control legislation in a war-time economy; in the Economic Stabilization Act of 1970, "to issue such orders and regulations as he may deem appropriate to stabilize prices, rents, wages and salaries at levels not less than those prevailing on May 25, 1970 . . . making . . . such adjustments as may be necessary to prevent gross inequities." Out of these instructions, the administrators in each instance constructed both rules governing general prices—set according to the objective circumstances of markets on specified dates—and bureaucratic mechanisms for securing, first, informal advice, second, possible exemption from these rules, and, third, enforcement against apparent violators. These mechanisms generated an enormous volume of business for the administering agencies: 1,340,955 landlord petitions for upward adjustment of rents had been received by the World War II Office of Price Administration as of its seventeenth quarterly report, for the period ending March 31, 1946, and 130,000 actions seeking rent reductions had been initiated within the agency during that quarter alone; the 90-day price freeze during 1970 produced 6,000 requests for exception, 50,000 complaints of violation, and 750,000 requests for advice.[70] The regularity and sense of systemic openness to private need these mechanisms produced—a result certainly not inevitable on the face of the statutes creating these regimes—is generally credited with persuading the courts to sustain them;[71] and the ready availability of informal means of advice and adjustment appears in fact to have settled most controversies. In the 1970 price and wage freeze, for example, only 214 cases proved serious enough

---

70. R. Kagan, Regulatory Justice: Implementing a Wage-Price Freeze (Russell Sage 1978) is an invaluable book-length study of the 1970 episode, particularly revealing in its treatment of the informal processes by which the regime was principally administered.

71. See Yakus v. United States, 321 U.S. 414 (1944); Bowles v. Willingham, 321 U.S. 503 (1944); Lichter v. United States, 334 U.S. 742 (1948); Amalgamated Meatcutters & Butcher Workmen v. Connally, 337 F. Supp. 737 (D.D.C. 1971); and the observations of Prof. Kenneth C. Davis, 1 Ad. Law Treatise 207-8 (2d ed. 1978).

cases to be considered at the highest levels for possible judicial enforcement action; and only eight lawsuits were in fact brought. These regimes thus illustrate the power of informal advice-giving and dispute resolution in administration; that judicial remedies or judicial enforcement may be available need not imply that it is often invoked.[72]

---

72. The creation of such systems has often, although not invariably, called forth an "emergency court of appeals," composed of judges on temporary assignment from the regular courts but enjoying a national jurisdiction over judicial proceedings arising from the regime, with the end of further encouraging national uniformity of administration and prompt resolution of disputes.

5
THE PROCEDURAL FORMS OF ADMINISTRATIVE ACTION

The wide variety of regulatory activity just described follows procedural forms created, in the first instance, by the concrete statutes, regulations, and/or body of custom attached to each activity. The enormous variation in that activity makes generalization difficult.[1] Generalization about administrative procedures nonetheless gains impetus from constitutional provisions enforcing fair procedures and from general-purpose administrative procedure statutes. More importantly, it arises from the imperatives of a system of law. If a generalized framework of analysis applicable to the behavior of the thousands of diverse instruments of government did not exist, surely judges and lawyers would be obliged to invent it to assure the possibility of control and avoid unsustainable specialization. This chapter briefly describes this general framework, beginning with its sources. The reader must remain aware that the analytical elements of the framework are abstractions, whose application in any particular setting might be procrustean but for the fact that it will in any event depend as well on the concrete circumstances of that setting and the actors involved. Only the federal system is described in any detail, with a brief introduction to two principal sources of structure for state administrative law, indicating the applicability of similar concepts in those proceedings.

The sources of structure for federal administrative procedure

Constitution

Judicial interpretations of the federal Constitution could be said to create a framework of three basic procedure-types within which proce-

---

1. See, e.g., on the genesis of the Administrative Procedure Act and the difficulties then encountered, the reminiscences of two highly influential American administrative law scholars, K.C. Davis and W. Gellhorn, Present at the Creation: Regulatory Reform Before 1946, 38 Ad. L. Rev. 507 (1986).

dural claims can be analyzed—rulemaking, investigation, and adjudi-cation. These correspond, roughly, to the three characteristic "powers" of government in separation of powers analysis, legislative, executive, and judicial. As we saw in chapter 2, pp. 23-49, constitutionally based procedural forms constrain investigation and adjudication in some cir-cumstances. Thus, the Fourth Amendment's prohibition of "unreason-able" searches and seizures, the same Amendment's general requirement that the government obtain a warrant for search, and the Fifth Amend-ment's protection against required self-incrimination, each limit the gov-ernment's ability to compel cooperation with investigations. Where the government seeks immediately to deprive particular individuals of life, liberty, or property, the Fifth Amendment's Due Process Clause requires *some* elements of an adjudicatory hearing, although the precise elements of that hearing will vary with the situation.[2] But the courts to date have generally refused to find procedures for rulemaking constitutionally re-quired; where government generates a rule of conduct for future appli-cation rather than determines its application to particular circumstances, citizens' "rights are protected in the only way that they can be in a complex society, by their [political] power, immediate or remote, over those who make the rule."[3]

This constitutional distinction between adjudication and rulemaking found strong expression in two cases decided by the Supreme Court in this context around the turn of the century; they warrant brief discussion for their continuing influence. The first, *Londoner* v. *Denver,*[4] concerned a special assessment or tax to be levied against properties benefited by the paving of a road. A series of decisions had to be made by public au-thorities: to pave the road, to determine the total costs of doing so and the proportion (if not all) to be recouped from benefited landowners; and, finally, to decide exactly what sum was to be collected from each affected piece of property. Responsible authorities, ultimately the elected city council, had decided to pave the road; a board then determined the total

---

2. See pp. 44-48.

3. Bi-Metallic Investment Co. v. Colorado, 239 U.S. 441 (1915). The distinction remains vital today; save as specific statutes provide otherwise, ordinary agency rulemaking may be done without resort to oral procedure. Indeed, the Court has never found that any participant in a rulemaking has a claim that some particular "process" is constitutionally "due"; it is sometimes asserted that the statutory requirements generally applicable to federal rulemaking, public notice of possible action with an opportunity to provide written commentary on it, would be found constitutionally required if the question ever arose. Compare Minnesota State Board for Community Colleges v. Knight, 465 U.S. 271 (1984) with Burr v. New Rochelle Municipal Housing Authority, 479 F.2d 1165 (2d Cir. 1973).

4. 210 U.S. 373 (1908).

cost and proposed an allocation along lines suggested by each piece of property's frontage on the road; landowners then had a chance to file written objections with the city council before it acted on the proposal. The second case, *Bi-Metallic Investment Co.* v. *Colorado*,[5] concerned the valuations assessed against all properties in the same city, on the basis of which the annual real estate tax would be calculated. A state agency (responsible for assuring that all valuations in the state were comparable) had decided that the valuations of city property should be increased by 40%, in order to equalize them with valuations in the remainder of the state. It was assumed that not even an opportunity to file written objections to this decision had been given.

In the first case, the Supreme Court found the procedures given to be constitutionally insufficient. "[A]t some stage of the proceedings before the tax becomes irrevocably fixed," it wrote, "the taxpayer [must] have an opportunity to be heard," and "a hearing in its very essence demands that he who is entitled to it shall have the right to support his allegations by argument however brief and, if need be, by proof, however informal." The opportunity to file written objections did not suffice. In the second case, no such requirement applied; rather than fix the assessments to be made on particular, individual pieces of property, the order in question in the second case applied generally. "Where a rule of conduct applies to more than a few people it is impractical that every one should have a direct voice in its adoption. . . . There must be a limit to individual argument . . . if government is to go on."

The suggestion that the decisive question concerns the number of persons affected is misleading: the *Londoner* result should be the same if 10,000 different parcels were to be assessed, but in each case on individual grounds. The *Bi-Metallic* result, too, ought not change if the change in general valuation affected a small village rather than a large city. The difference is between the application of a norm to particular circumstances, for which hearing will be required if life, liberty, or property is to be adversely affected, and the generation of the norm itself. However many adjudications there might be, they were to be decided "in each case upon individual grounds"; but the reassessment was a more general result. Over the latter process, the Supreme Court remarked in the language already quoted and still influential, citizen's "rights are protected in the only way that they can be in a complex society, by their power, immediate or remote, over those who make the rule."

While the Constitution suggests a tri-partite division of procedure-types, and contains procedural specifications applicable to two of them, we must be careful not to conclude that those specifications are universally

5. 239 U.S. 441 (1915), quoted at note 3, above.

applicable within the relevant field. Some inspections must be permitted irrespective whether a warrant has been obtained;[6] some information must be provided without regard to prior judicial enforcement of a subpoena.[7] Similarly, much "adjudication" is not governed by the Due Process Clause, since it threatens no one with a deprivation of "life, liberty or property." Thus, an applicant for a license to build a nuclear power station faces "adjudication" of its qualifications, but denial of the license application is not a constitutional deprivation. And while revocation of such a license, once granted, *would* be a deprivation that entitled the license-holder to "due process," that conclusion would not assist a neighbor interested to have the facility closed. While procedural claims may also be important to the neighbor, she is not threatened with deprivation by official action. Any procedural issues about hearings for the applicant or the neighbor are strictly statutory in nature. As to rulemaking, as we have seen, the Constitution says nothing at all. Plainly one must look past the constitutional text for a general framework of analysis.

The Administrative Procedure Act

For the national government, much of the framework is provided by the federal Administrative Procedure Act. This statute was enacted with broad bipartisan support in 1946, following almost a decade of study and debate whose principal themes, paradoxically, illustrated the great difficulty in formulating apt generalizations;[8] its basic procedures have been little changed since. As previously seen,[9] the statute applies to a broadly defined range of "agency action," addressing in separate chapters internal agency procedures and structural arrangements, and judicial review. It was enacted as a statute of general application, so that a "subsequent

---

6. See p. 28.

7. See p. 30.

8. A brief and informal account of the Act's genesis in detailed studies during 1940-41 of the actual functioning of forty different federal agencies is given in K.C. Davis and W. Gellhorn, note 1, above. In it, Gellhorn recounts the frustration of one member of the responsible committee that no generalizations seemed available; Gellhorn, seeking to mollify, suggested that perhaps open hearings should always be required—and soon discovered that for banking regulation, an open hearing would be the worst thing you could do for a bank under suspicion; if not insolvent when the hearings were announced, it soon would be. See also the several studies performed by the Attorney General's Committee on Administrative Procedure, culminating in its Final Report, Sen. Doc. 8, 77th Cong., 1st Sess. (1941); more recently, see The Administrative Procedure Act, A Fortieth Anniversary Symposium, 72 Va. L. Rev. 215 (1986).

9. See p. 103.

statute [does not] supersede or modify [it], except to the extent that it does so expressly."[10] Here we discuss the provisions on internal procedures and structural arrangements, 5 U.S.C. §§ 551-59, leaving to a subsequent point[11] consideration of the provisions on judicial review, 5 U.S.C. §§ 701-6.

While the analysis below follows the tripartite division of procedural function just suggested, the Administrative Procedure Act generally appears to contemplate a world of only two procedural functions, adjudication and rulemaking. Its definitional provisions, 5 U.S.C. § 551, characterize the products of "agency action" as either a "rule" or an "order." Rules are defined as agency statements of "general or particular[12] applicability and future effect designed to implement, interpret, or prescribe law or policy or describing [agency structural or procedural arrangements]," specifically including ratemaking. An "order," the end product of "adjudication," is defined as an agency's "final disposition . . . of . . . [any] matter other than rulemaking."

One reason for this failure to identify investigation as a separate procedure-type is that the Act's central concern is with formal proceedings, the sort that produce a "final disposition." Detailed provision for preliminary stages could seem to invite premature disputes about secondary issues, at the cost of substantial delay to the public's business. Conclusions reached in the course of an investigation do not mark "final disposition." Correspondingly, such limited provisions as the APA does have about internal procedures characteristic of investigations appear under the heading "ancillary matters." Yet, the decision either not to open an investigation or to close one is itself a final disposition—one subject, as will be seen, to limited judicial review[13]—and such a decision therefore falls within the APA's definition of "adjudication"; in this sense, the definition somewhat misleadingly includes decisions characteristic of executive as well as judicial action.

In addition to its specifications of agency procedure and of the general terms of judicial review, the APA embraces two other subjects. Section 3, 5 U.S.C. § 552, addresses public information about agency rules, opinions, orders, records and proceedings. Originally Section 552 was limited to requiring the publication of information about agency decisions and

---

10. APA Section 12, 5 U.S.C. § 559.

11. Pp. 211-69.

12. The reference to a statement of "particular applicability and future effect" is troubling from the perspective of the constitutional distinction developed at pp. 134-136, above. In practice, "rules" that can be described in this way, for example rate schedules, are formulated through procedures of substantial formality.

13. See pp. 151-152 and 221-22.

internal structure, to avoid the problem of "secret law." It has since become the provision most extensively amended since adoption of the APA. It now contains the Freedom of Information Act, requiring agencies to permit public access to virtually all agency documentation. The FOIA is considered below.[14] Section 11 of the APA, now distributed among several parts of 5 U.S.C.,[15] creates the office of administrative law judge, and provides for holders of that office the structural protections against political interference already noted.[16]

Other statutes

A number of statutes in addition to the APA provide general structure for one or another aspect of administrative procedure or its control. The Judiciary Code, 28 U.S.C., and the judicial rules of procedure adopted pursuant to it contain many provisions governing the relationship of agencies to the courts: enforcement procedures for subpoenas; provisions respecting jurisdiction and venue for judicial review; the delegation of litigating responsibility to the Department of Justice and its officers.[17] The National Environmental Policy Act and Regulatory Flexibility Act impose generally applicable analytic requirements for important rulemakings;[18] the Paperwork Reduction Act of 1980,[19] uniform procedures governing information-gathering activities; the Federal Advisory Committee Act[20] and Government in the Sunshine Act,[21] control over the openness of activities by multi-member bodies in the generation of policy.

In addition, the statutes of individual agencies often, some believe increasingly, contain procedural specifications beyond those to be found in the APA. This has proved particularly important in the context of rulemaking. As that activity has emerged as central to health and safety regulation in particular, but also in other fields, Congress has repeatedly provided for procedures that differ (usually in the direction of somewhat greater formality) from those shortly to be described. To some extent,

---

14. See pp. 195-200.
15. E.g., 5 U.S.C. §§ 1305, 3105, 3344, 5372, 7521. Title 5 of the U. S. Code is denominated the Code of Government Organization and Employees; it is, however, integrated with the other titles of the Code. In American practice no particular significance is attached to the code title within which a provision appears; it serves principally as an organizational device.
16. See pp. 94-97.
17. See pp. 100-102.
18. See pp. 70-76.
19. See text at note 183, below.
20. See p. 204.
21. See pp. 200-202.

these formulations represent indirect means of accomplishing substantive ends. It is widely believed, for example, that Congress' recent requirements of increasing procedural rigor for rulemaking by the Federal Trade Commission reflect distaste for its aggressiveness as a regulator. Similarly, some think that the provision of somewhat formal rulemaking procedures for the new Occupational Health and Safety Administration was an accommodation to industry for a regulatory regime that could not be openly opposed. Yet the new formulations also embody procedural judgments that are widely regarded as both important and susceptible of general application. Section 307(d) of the Clean Air Act amendments of 1977, which sets rulemaking procedures for the Environmental Protection Agency under that statute, is perhaps the most important example. Its provisions governing the formation of the official record of rulemaking proceedings have since been widely accepted as apt for most such proceedings.[22]

The courts

Judicial decisions are also an important source of structure for agency procedures. The courts are highly influential in at least three ways: first, through their interpretation of relevant constitutional requirements, addressed above;[23] second, through their interpretation of statutory procedural requirements such as the APA; and third, through the atmosphere created by the manner in which they exercise their review functions. Thus, Supreme Court interpretation of the APA's provisions on party standing to seek judicial review has greatly extended the range of agency behavior agency officials will foresee as subject to possible review (and therefore treat with care); less directly, it has required agency officials to admit as participants in agency proceedings persons they might otherwise have excluded. Similarly, the courts of appeal have interpreted the "notice," "comment," and explanatory statement provisions of the APA's informal rulemaking procedure in ways that add significant procedural detail to what appears simply on the face of the statute or in what one can learn of its drafting history.[24] And judicial development of the "hard look" doctrine of judicial review,[25] which generates relatively intense over-

---

22. In 1982, the Senate unanimously passed a bill that would have made these provisions generally applicable to all agency rulemaking, S. 1080, but for political reasons unconnected to this matter the bill was never brought to a vote in the House of Representatives.

23. See pp. 23-49.

24. See pp. 164-69.

25. See pp. 267-69.

sight of agency policy decisions, has effectively required agencies to exercise a level of procedural care the APA itself would not lead one to expect.

The stated limit on judicial specification of agency procedures is that it may not occur independently of statute. Courts act long after agencies have made their procedural choices, and the Supreme Court has been explicit in rejecting after-the-fact judicial formulation of a common law of required procedure to supplement the APA. The congressional formulations are those "upon which opposing social and political forces have come to rest," and judicial displacement would not only dishonor the legislative judgment but also, more importantly, force agencies to anticipate possible new requirements by excessive formalization.[26]

Political oversight

One does not ordinarily think of political oversight as generating or even much shaping public procedures within the agencies. Yet the recent presidential initiatives on rulemaking[27] must be seen in that light. The requirement of regulatory impact analysis has generated additional documents on which public comment is invited; provision, first, for a periodic calendar of federal rulemaking activity and, now, for a regulatory agenda can bring agency rulemaking into public view at an earlier stage and consequently expand the range of participation. As a general matter, internal bureaucratic structures have had to be reshaped to accommodate these requirements, resulting both in tighter coordination within the agency and greater prominence, generally, to the policy planning function.

The agencies

Each agency itself, of course, enjoys substantial freedom to shape the procedures it employs. Detailed provisions will usually be found in an early chapter of the agency's volume of the Code of Federal Regulations— an annually revised compendium organized along the lines of the United States Code, and at least ten times as large. Any attorney involved with a particular agency or proceeding will pay careful attention to that chapter.

---

26. Vermont Yankee Nuclear Power Corp. v. Natural Resources Defense Council, Inc., 435 U.S. 519 (1978). The case is discussed on pp. 174-76.
27. See pp. 70-76.

Adjudication

As will shortly appear, the bulk of federal activity describable as adjudication occurs under procedures that are *not* generalized, but are particular to the agency involved. Nonetheless, it is sensible to begin with the provisions on adjudication of the federal Administrative Procedure Act.

As earlier noted,[28] the APA defines "adjudication" very broadly, as the "agency process for the formulation of" any "final disposition, whether affirmative, negative, injunctive, or declaratory in form, of an agency in a matter other than rule making but including licensing."[29] Thus, the Secretary of Transportation's decision to award the state of Tennessee $12 million for the construction of a certain road would constitute "adjudication," as would the Nuclear Regulatory Commission's decision to assess a $2 million penalty against an electric utility for rule violations in running a nuclear power station, or the Federal Communication Commission's decision to grant Joseph Green the license he seeks to engage in amateur radio broadcasting. Yet these are evidently very different sorts of proceedings, not merely in their economic importance, but also in the moral claim they make for procedural specification. These differences are reflected in the APA's provisions about adjudication.

Informal agency adjudications

Perhaps the most striking aspect of the APA's provisions on adjudication is their essential failure to specify *any* procedure for informal adjudications. The APA section on adjudications, 5 U.S.C. § 554, applies only to formal adjudications, those "required by statute to be determined on the record after opportunity for an agency hearing," with six stated and generally uncontroversial exceptions.[30] The tendency of the courts is to find that most statutory references to "hearing" require such a deter-

---

28. See p. 137, above.
29. 5 U.S.C. § 551(7, 6).
30. The exceptions concern matters for which judicial trial is nonetheless required or for which the agency is acting for a court, ordinary civil service matters, certification of worker representatives, matters implicating military or foreign affairs functions, and "proceedings in which decisions rest solely on inspections, tests, or elections." Thus, the grading or inspection of agricultural products, or flight certification of airline pilots need not occur following APA procedures, even though one anticipates a certain formality in the performance of these functions. See pp. 183-84, below.

mination, because of the values seen to lie in the APA's adjudicatory procedures.[31]

Yet informal adjudications constitute the great bulk of government actions meeting the statutory definition of "adjudication," perhaps as much as 95% of those actions; and, as we shall see, they are fully subject to judicial review. Such adjudications, *not* required to be determined on the record after hearing, are not subject to the provisions of either § 554 or other sections that build upon Section 554.[32] The only APA provision that might apply is 5 U.S.C. § 555(e), on "ancillary matters". It requires prompt notice of the denial of any written application, petition or other request "made in connection with any agency proceeding...accompanied by a brief statement of the grounds for denial." This general failure of procedural specification reflects, in part, the demands of informality. Beyond that, and perhaps more importantly, one senses the enormous difficulty the drafters would have faced in devising and stating general procedural provisions to govern matters that, in 1946, made no substantial claim for procedural detail.

One consequence of the subsequent due process explosion was to make the claim for procedural specification substantial in many contexts. In 1976, not long after the Supreme Court's decision in *Goldberg* v. *Kelly*,[33] Professor Paul Verkuil published a study of informal adjudication procedures used in forty-two different federal programs to reach final conclusions.[34] Many if not all of these programs could deprive persons of "entitlements" and therefore invoke the federal Due Process Clause. Looked at through the lens of Judge Friendly's ten possible procedural

---

31. Seacoast Anti-Pollution League v. Costle, 572 F.2d 872, cert. denied 439 U.S. 824 (1978); but see United States Lines v. FMC, 584 F.2d 519 (D.C. Cir. 1978); compare the quite different situation respecting formal rulemaking, pp. 158-59.

32. A separate question is presented by adjudications required to be determined on the record, not "by statute" but by the Constitution. An early decision held that the APA's provisions—notably the requirement that an administrative law judge be employed—applied in these cases as well. Wong Yang Sung v. McGrath, 339 U.S. 33 (1950). The specific holding was almost immediately reversed by Congress, see Marcello v. Bonds, 349 U.S. 302 (1955), and with the subsequent flowering of due process analysis the general holding appears to have been overruled sub silentio. As a matter of historical interpretation, it is doubtful that Congress, with its eye fixed on the large-scale proceedings suggested by statutory provisions for on-the-record hearings, wished to provide uniform procedures for all proceedings a court might later find required to be conducted "on the record" under the Due Process Clause.

33. Discussed at pp. 38-40.

34. A Study of Informal Adjudication Procedures, 43 U. Chi. L. Rev. 739 (1976). The study included 17 grant programs (e.g., food stamps), 12 licensing programs (e.g., drug approvals), 5 inspection programs (e.g., meat grading), 6 planning programs (e.g., urban development), and 2 characterized as "other."

elements of a fair hearing,[35] these programs presented a picture of remarkable diversity. Only two programs (both grant programs in the welfare field) provided all ten elements; two others provided none. Only three of the ten elements—notice, a statement of reasons, and impartial decision-maker—were assured by substantially all programs; twenty-seven of the fortytwo programs provided four[36] or fewer of the elements and only nine provided as many as eight of them. While the due process explosion itself doubtless has changed these results where the clause applies, the diversity otherwise endures.

Formal agency adjudications

The unifying characteristic of hearings identified by statute as requiring determination "on the record after opportunity for an agency hearing" is that the matter at issue has an importance warranting substantial procedural detail. Section 554 and two associated sections specifying procedures for formal hearings, 5 U.S.C. §§ 556-57, delineate the procedures to be followed in such cases with some elaborateness. Even within this group of cases, however, one can find a good deal of diversity of claim. An applicant for a license, for example, will most often succeed or fail on the basis of technical criteria requiring evaluation by a specialized staff; and while a statute may provide for on-the-record determination of the application, the applicant apparently lacks a Due Process Clause "entitlement" to such procedures.[37] Where a sanction is to be applied, on the other hand, the judgment to be reached may be less technical and more moral; and, in any event, the private party's procedural claims are rendered stronger by the threatened penalty and any "entitlement" it may enjoy to a continued relationship with the agency during good behavior. These variations are reflected in the procedural provisions made, resulting not in one model of "formal adjudication" but perhaps three.

---

35. See pp. 47-48.

36. The fourth most common element, recognized in just half the programs, was an opportunity for oral presentation of argument.

37. As noted at p. 43, the Supreme Court has recently stressed that the bearing of the Due Process Clause on applications has not yet been decided. The indications are that if required to be decided, it would be decided against the due process claim. At the least, the balancing approach of Mathews v. Eldridge, discussed in the text at pp. 43-46, would find less private interest in obtaining a license not yet in hand, than in maintaining one already granted and on the basis of which investments may have been made.

On-the-record adjudication

The central model is described by Sections 554, 556 and 557. The hearing is to be conducted under procedures that, although simplified, strongly resemble those characteristic of an American trial.[38] Parties are to have full notice of the hearing, the authority under which it is to be held, and the issues to be resolved. Participants include the agency and others directly affected, together with other interested persons as intervenors; intervention may be granted—indeed, has been required by judges to be granted[39]—much more freely than would be the case in judicial proceedings, "so far as the orderly conduct of public business permits."[40] The parties are entitled to appear by attorneys, and participate in all stages, before and during the hearing; they control the presentation of evidence, and are entitled "to conduct such cross-examination as may be required for a full and true disclosure of the facts"; the agency may receive any matter as evidence,[41] excluding only the "irrelevant, immaterial, or unduly repetitious." The burden of proof, except as otherwise provided by statute, is placed in each case on the party seeking a given outcome. An opportunity for settlement discussions must be provided when circumstances permit.

When a hearing is in fact held, its on-the-record character is protected in a variety of ways:

The hearing must be held before the agency itself (that is, the agency head(s)), one or more members of a multi-member agency or, in the usual case, an administrative law judge.[42] The presiding em-

---

38. A notable exception occurs in the procedure employed in determining issues respecting welfare benefits, discussed on pp. 115-18. While the hearing, when obtained, occurs before an administrative law judge, she directs the inquiry and marshals the data known to the government as well as decides the outcome; no separate attorney or representative for the government side appears.

39. National Welfare Rights Organization v. Finch, 429 F.2d 725 (D.C. Cir. 1970), United Church of Christ v. FCC, 359 F.2d 994 (1966); see pp. 149-54.

40. 5 U.S.C. § 555(b).

41. That is, administrative proceedings are not governed by the formal rules of evidence applicable in the courts. In particular, the rule excluding indirect, or "hearsay," evidence from judicial trials does not apply. The rule is thought to protect lay juries from the problem of determining how much credence to give one person's account of what he claims to have heard another say; it tends to force testimony directly by witnesses to the underlying transaction. Agency hearings do not use lay fact-finders; and the nature of the disputes to be resolved often gives eye-witness testimony secondary importance. Even in court application, in fact, the hearsay rule has so many exceptions as to render it almost ineffectual.

42. The special position of the administrative law judge is discussed on pp. 94-97.

ployee's participation is subject to challenge in cases of personal bias or other disqualification, as a judge's would be.

The presiding employee may communicate with "a person or a party on a fact in issue"[43] only on the record,[44] and agency personnel responsible for investigative or prosecuting functions are excluded from any participation except as public witnesses or counsel.

The presiding employee is then the individual responsible for drawing up the official report of the proceeding, whether an actual, initial decision of the matter or merely a recommendation to the agency how it ought to decide the matter.

The record on which decision is based and review will occur is limited to testimony and exhibits in the proceeding, together with any papers filed. If the agency takes "official notice" of facts that do not appear on the record—matters, for example, it believes it "knows" on the basis of acquired expertise—any party is entitled, "on timely request, to an opportunity to show the contrary."[45]

---

43. This is the formula of § 554(d). A 1976 amendment, 5 U.S.C. § 557(d), somewhat complicates matters by using a different formula in forbidding "ex parte communication." Section 557(d) applies only to conversations between agency decisonmakers and persons "outside the agency"; it forbids any off-the-record communication "relevant to the merits of the proceeding." Is it, then, statutorily acceptable for an administrative law judge to communicate privately with agency personnel (i.e., not "outside the agency") on questions of policy or interpretation that are "relevant to the merits of the proceeding" but do not concern "a fact in issue"? Most lawyers would fervently condemn any such consultation as unfair and unlawful; the writer is not aware of any efforts by agency personnel to exploit this apparent distinction between fact-based and policy-based internal conversations. The distinction can be understood as a recognition of the frequency with which innocent internal conversations about policy occur, that may appear to bear on on-the-record agency business for which one or another of the conversers is responsible. It is not an invitation to pointed, surreptitious conversation about the business at hand, then, but a recognition of agencies' need for protection against secondary disputes over their on-going pursuit of policy ends.

44. The sanctions against interested parties found to have attempted off-the-record influence can be severe. Thus, 5 U.S.C. § 556(d) permits the agency, if "consistent with the interests of justice" to "consider a violation . . . sufficient grounds for a decision adverse to a party" who has "knowingly" committed or caused such a violation.

45. 5 U.S.C. § 556(e). The courts, on occasion, have been fierce in protecting participants from agencies' claims of untested expert knowledge. Seacoast Anti-Pollution League v. Costle, 572 F.2d 872 (1st Cir. 1978); Wirtz v. Baldor Electric Co., 337 F.2d 518 (D.C. Cir. 1963). Generally, however, the "material" facts subject to the rule of official notice are only those facts particular to the proceeding at issue, and not facts of a more general character—facts such as a legislature might

Where the hearing does not occur before the agency itself, and it almost never does, the presiding employee will render an initial decision or, very occasionally, recommend a decision to the agency which will itself make the initial decision. Whichever may occur, the parties are entitled to submit proposed findings and conclusions; and the maker of the decision or recommendation must rule in writing on these proposals, stating "findings and conclusions, and the reasons or basis therefor, on all material issues of fact, law, or discretion presented on the record."[46] This statement becomes a part of the record of the proceeding, a matter of some importance to later judicial review.[47] An initial decision will, unless reviewed by the agency or its delegate, become the decision of the agency itself.

Review within the agency is easily obtained, although there is a good deal of variation from agency to agency in the structures within which it occurs. In most of the traditional regulatory agencies, appeals are heard by the agency head or, for some multi-member commissions, by a panel of commissioners smaller than the whole body. In the larger agencies and cabinet departments, however, provision is often made for a specialized appellate body to exercise some or all review functions—for example, the Judicial Officer of the Department of Agriculture; the Appeals Council of the Department of Health and Human Services, for welfare and disability assistance issues; the Atomic Safety and Licensing Appeals Board of the Nuclear Regulatory Commission. The APA does not assure the members of these tribunals the protected status of ALJ's,[48] although in practice they operate independently of political direction (as the on-the-record requirement itself virtually demands). Where such a body is provided for, the agency head may have reserved power to review its decisions in turn, but ordinarily does so only as a matter of discretion in important cases, on analogy to the Supreme Court's certiorari function.[49]

When review is sought, the parties are entitled to make and brief any exceptions they may have to the initial decision of the ALJ (or intermediate

---

be expected to find. Indeed, the corresponding rule of evidence in federal courts, Rule 201 of the Federal Rules of Evidence, governs *only* judicial notice of "adjudicative" facts, those bearing on the immediate parties to the dispute; for "legislative" facts such as a judge might wish to know to resolve a dispute of policy— for example, whether segregated education generally disadvantages black children—the judge may consult any source he regards as pertinent, independent of the parties. See Administrative Law: Cases and Comments, pp. 795-861.

46. 5 U.S.C. § 557(c)(A).
47. See pp. 244-49.
48. Kalaris v. Donovan, 697 F.2d 376 (D.C. Cir. 1983), cert. den. 462 U.S. 1119 (1983); cf. pp. 94-97.
49. That function is briefly discussed on pp. 81-82.

decision of a review tribunal). The agency then "has all the powers which it would have in making the initial decision"—that is, it may decide the case as if *it* had heard the witnesses itself rather than act as a reviewing tribunal.[50] Determinations made by the administrative law judge, even on so delicate an issue as witness credibility, are regarded merely as an element of the record on the basis of which the agency acts and against which the acceptability of its result will be measured. The agency must, however—like its ALJ—fully explain both its findings and its responses to party positions advanced to it, and in practice this restrains its freedom to reshape the ALJ's decision.

These findings requirements have some of the faults of formula; no court would take seriously an obligation to respond to every contention, however trivial, the parties may throw up in a proceeding. But they also serve important functions in the allocation of responsibility between an agency and its staff, and between the agency and the courts. By fixing the basis for the agency's action, that explanation limits the arguments that agency lawyers (or others) can make to support the agency's result on judicial review. They may use only the reasons the agency assigns publicly for its decision, not others that might be imagined. This gives some assurance that those ostensibly responsible for a decision will actually be responsible for it.[51] At the same time, moreover, findings protect

---

50. On judicial review of an agency decision, then, the court is obliged to treat the agency's decision as having been made in direct relation to the facts rather than as the act of a reviewing tribunal; and this has occasional significance for outcome. See the general discussion of judicial review of agency factual determinations on pp. 244-49.

51. The point is stated guardedly, because the opinions are themselves the product of a bureaucratic staff, which the ostensibly responsible but busy agency heads may have little real time to consider. An extreme example of this is related by Derthick and Quirk, Why the Regulators Chose to Deregulate, in R. Noll, Ed., Regulatory Policy and the Social Sciences 215 (Univ. of California 1986), as a partial explanation of the dissatisfaction that led to disestablishment of the Civil Aeronautics Board:

Late in 1969, [a CAB attorney] had been assigned to write the board's decision [choosing the recipient of an airline route among several competitors] with no instructions whatever except the name of the winning airline. . . . [I]t was up to him to contrive the board's reasons for the decision. And after he was done, the board did not change a word of what he had written. It came to him as vivid proof of what many in the CAB knew or sensed: the board's alleged rationales for route awards were not the real rationales, but were artifices designed to give the gloss of legal reasoning to awards made privately by the board on other grounds. Not that there was anything corrupt about these other grounds. . . . Roughly, the board acted in a commonsensical way to make sure that every carrier got a reasonable share of new route authority and that none was exposed to financial hazard. Not everyone was disillusioned . . . [; s]ome very intelligent people found the exercise to be fun "much in the way that

the agency from judicial second-guessing, by focusing attention on its reasoning and responsibility, rather than the outcome as such.

License applications

Less formal models for on-the-record hearings are stated in "exceptions" to the general provisions of Sections 554, 556 and 557; as might be anticipated, these exceptions are made for circumstances in which the moral claim to hearing is not so large as in the ordinary case, and where fewer formal barriers to use of the agency's expertise may correspondingly be appropriate. Thus, applicants for licenses, money or benefits (as well as participants in formal rulemaking)[52] may be limited to proceeding on the basis of written submissions, unless they can specifically show that the denial of oral trial-like hearings would be prejudicial;[53] in other cases subject to the on-the-record requirement, oral hearings are a matter of course. Separation of functions constraints are less rigorously required for license applications (and formal rulemaking) as well: administrative law judges or agency members may consult off the record with agency staff;[54] and responsible members of staff, rather than the administrative law judge, may be permitted to draw up the recommended decision.[55]

The relative freedom thus provided is readily enough understood. Licensing, like ratemaking and other formal rulemaking, can be highly technical in character, putting a premium on the fullest participation of expert staff; few agencies have the richness of resources to permit hiring duplicate staffs (even if it were wise), one for day-to-day functions and the other to advise decisionmakers. At the same time staff participation in this activity often lacks the qualities of moral commitment, of side-taking, that recurrently characterize ordinary litigation and especially prosecution and its administrative analogs. Indeed, from the perspective of the license applicant and the agency staff, the hearing stage, if ever reached, may seem a formality. Much can be accomplished in negotiations between an applicant and those within the agency most expert in the

---

doing crossword puzzles is fun."
One need not believe that quite the same situation obtains for other boards, that have not been disestablished out of the realization they serve no useful function; but suspicions about the reality of a board's professed reasons have underlain a good deal of judicial worrying about political controls. See, for example, the discussion on pp. 169-74 and 256-66.

52. See pp. 158-59.
53. 5 U.S.C. § 556(d).
54. 5 U.S.C. § 554(d)(A).
55. 5 U.S.C. § 557(b)(1).

criteria to be satisfied, that would be clumsy to do a formal setting. The license applicant, while having the greatest concrete interest in the outcome of the proceedings, may seem for this reason to have a comparatively low interest in formality.

The situation is different when licensing is opposed by persons outside the agency, who lack any continuing or detailed relationship with it, and who may tend to distrust its performance of public function—to fear that agency staff will have taken sides with the applicant and against their interest. For them, the formality and forced openness and objectivity of a trial-like process is central. Where such opposition arises, the statutory possibilities of diminished formality are in fact rarely availed of. Lawyerly, judicial, and even administrative attitudes about the importance of oral proceedings and separated functions are so strong that the provisions are, in effect, disbelieved.[56]

License sanctions

The third of the APA's adjudicatory models applies to proceedings for the withdrawal, suspension, revocation or annulment of a license already obtained, a setting in which both the license-holder's stakes and the risks of prosecutorial commitment on the part of agency staff are especially high. Special written notice "of the facts or conduct which may warrant the action" is required and, unless willfulness is present or public protection requires otherwise, the licensee must be given an "opportunity to demonstrate or achieve compliance with all lawful requirements."[57] This is less a variation of procedure than of substance, underscoring the economic importance of licenses already granted to their holders by protecting tenure from too-casual interference by agency staff. As the judgment it reflects appears not to be a controversial one, it has not often been the subject of litigation. Yet the contrast with the lesser formality provided for initial licensing is revealing and instructive.

Participation claims of the protected public

Aside from the continuing effort to give content to the Due Process Clause, discussed at some length above,[58] probably the most interesting developments concerning adjudication have to do with the participation in agency proceedings (or agency-forcing proceedings) of members of

---

56. See American Telephone and Telegraph Co., 60 F.C.C. 1 (1976); Seacoast Anti-Pollution League v. Costle, 572 F.2d 872, cert. denied, 439 U.S. 824 (1978).
57. 5 U.S.C. § 558(c).
58. See pp. 32-48.

the public or groups on whose behalf regulation is supposed to occur. Private activities on behalf of law enforcement can occur in two different ways. The first is to authorize citizens themselves to use the courts for direct private enforcement of regulatory provisions against businesses that might also be (but have not been) proceeded against by an agency for their alleged violations. Such authority was early conferred by antitrust statutes, which enabled citizens to seek judicial redress of harm they personally suffered; similar authority is created under the civil rights statutes. It can readily be viewed as statutory creation of a new form of tort remedy for private wrongs.[59] In the field of environmental protection, some statutes have authorized the same mechanism to vindicate the rights of the community at large; citizens may sue to redress alleged regulatory violations, independent of personal harm as such, when the agency has not acted despite notice of the allegedly illegal activity.[60] These statutes may provide incentives, such as compensation for attorney's fees and other costs, for successful plaintiffs.

The second means by which members of the public or groups participate in law enforcement is indirect, seeking a remedy either within the agency, as a party in its proceedings, or against it, in an action to force desired agency behavior. Authority to initiate or participate in agency proceedings may have its source in explicit statutory language. The Interstate Commerce Act, for example, authorizes shippers and others to begin proceedings to have a rate charged by a common carrier declared unlawful; the Atomic Energy Act grants party status in proceedings to

---

59. In recent years the Supreme Court has generally discouraged federal courts from inferring private rights of action for regulatory violations, although it has recognized the appropriateness of doing so in certain settings—notably, under the civil rights laws and the statutes regulating trader behavior in security and commodity markets. This development is discussed on pp. 281-83. The discouragement arises in part from considerations of federalism; the legal systems of the states, rather than the federal courts, have general responsibility for the development of the common law of torts, and the Justices appear to believe that the practice of inferring civil remedies from federal regulatory statutes will threaten that allocation of responsibility. M. Field, Sources of Law: The Scope of Federal Common Law, 99 Harv. L. Rev. 881 (1986). Another line of reasoning, which has appeared in a number of contexts recently (see, e.g., Block v. Community Nutrition Institute, 467 U.S. 340 (1984), see notes 73 below, 47 on p. 221, and 52 on p. 283), is that federal regulatory schemes reflect complex and balanced congressional judgments, which could be disrupted by judicial enlargement of the remedies explicitly provided for. Tort remedies against the government itself, or against public servants, raise separate questions dealt with on pp. 274-83.

60. See, e.g., Gwaltney of Smithfield v. Chesapeake Bay Fndn., 108 S. Ct. 376 (1987). Full treatment of the subject, including practical guidance for persons wishing to bring such actions, appears in J. Miller, Environmental Law Institute, Citizen Suits: Private Enforcement of Federal Pollution Control Laws (Wiley 1987).

license nuclear power reactors to citizens of the area where the plant is to be located. The more interesting problems, however, have arisen where the statute appears to leave the agency in control over the institution or conduct of proceedings, and outsiders have sought nonetheless to force its hand.

Two cases illustrate the problems involved in forcing an agency to conduct proceedings it had not chosen to initiate. In the first, a union member lost a federally supervised election under circumstances he believed should have led the Department of Labor, responsible for supervising the election, to set it aside.[61] When he complained to the Secretary of Labor, the Secretary investigated and indicated, without stating his reasons, that he would not proceed; the statute—doubtless to protect the winners of such elections from frivolous or harassing actions—was explicit that the Secretary's enforcement authority was exclusive. The union member nonetheless persuaded the courts to require the Secretary to reconsider his decision and to indicate his reasons for declining to proceed. The Court recognized the risk that permitting such suits would interfere with the executive's ability to deploy its limited resources in accordance with public, rather than private, priorities. Nonetheless, it found that the statute in question was unusually explicit in detailing the factors the Secretary was to consider in deciding whether or not to proceed, and "demonstrate[d] a deep concern with the interest of individual union members, as well as the general public, in the integrity of union elections." A statement of reasons would not only satisfy that concern, but also permit a court to assure that the relevant factors (and only the relevant factors) had been considered by the Secretary in reaching his judgment.

The second case arose in unusual facts: prisoners sentenced to be executed by an injection of lethal drugs had petitioned the federal Food and Drug Administration to act against this unapproved use of the drugs, and the FDA had refused to act, indicating its reasons.[62] All nine Justices agreed that the agency's decision should not be disturbed, but only one reached that conclusion on the ground that the decision had been properly justified. For the others, the decisive consideration was that "an agency's decision not to prosecute or enforce . . . is a decision generally committed to an agency's absolute discretion." The union election case was distinguished on the ground that the statute there indicated a purpose to circumscribe the agency's exercise of enforcement power; that indication was missing in the present case. The one Justice who reached the merits rejected the majority's presumption that administrative (as distinct from

---

61. Dunlop v. Bachowski, 421 U.S. 560 (1975).
62. Heckler v. Chaney, 470 U.S. 821 (1985).

prosecutorial)[63] decisions not to act are unreviewable, as inconsistent with "a firmly entrenched body of lower court case law that holds reviewable various agency refusals to act. . . . The problem of agency refusal to act is one of the pressing problems of the modern administrative state, given the enormous powers, for both good and ill, that agency inaction, like agency action, holds over citizens."[64]

Both because the Administrative Procedure Act specifically makes agency *inaction* reviewable as "agency action," and because more appealing facts may often encourage courts to find that the language or history of a specific statute overcomes any general "presumption of unreviewability" of inaction, one should not expect the latter decision invariably to control.[65] At most it reflects a changing mood, of which there are some other indications,[66] away from litigation as a means for shaping public interest issues. Over a decade ago, observing cases more like the first than the second of the two just summarized, a leading scholar wrote that judges were beginning "to assume the ultimate protection of the collective social interests which administrative schemes were designed to secure."[67] Skepticism of that possibility, one may believe, underlies the current withdrawal.

A somewhat different question is presented when an agency has in fact initiated a proceeding, and the issue is whether and to what extent it is required to recognize as a participant in that proceeding a private litigant asserting some interest in the outcome, who has no clear statutory

---

63. The foreign reader will perhaps be surprised to learn that American (criminal) prosecutors enjoy an essentially unchecked discretion whether or not to enforce the criminal laws in particular cases. It is from the premise of that unreviewable discretion that American analysis proceeds.

64. Justice Thurgood Marshall, the author of this opinion, cited 24 lower court cases decided between 1970 and 1983 in support of his proposition, and relied heavily on a well-regarded scholarly analysis of the general problem: R. Stewart and C. Sunstein, Public Programs and Private Rights, 95 Harv. L. Rev. 1195 (1982). See also R. Stewart, The Reformation of American Administrative Law, 88 Harv. L. Rev. 1669, 1754-56 (1975); C. Sunstein, Reviewing Agency Inaction after Heckler v. Chaney, 52 U. Chi. L. Rev. 653 (1985). The author of the majority opinion, Justice Rehnquist, had been the sole dissenter from the union election case.

65. See, e.g., Center for Auto Safety v. Dole, 828 F.2d 799, revised on rehearing 846 F.2d 1532 (D.C. Cir. 1987, 1988). Among the examples cited by Justice Marshall: litigation to force the Department of Housing and Urban Development to enforce the required removal of lead-based paints (poisonous to small children) from federally supported housing; to require the Environmental Protection Agency to take action against a pesticide, DDT, with demonstrated (and extraordinary) adverse ecological effects; to require the Department of Health, Education and Welfare to enforce certain provisions of the civil rights laws.

66. See, e.g., p. 154, below.

67. R. Stewart, note 64, above, 88 Harv. L. Rev. at 1756.

right of intervention. The cases that led to the scholarly observation just quoted included a substantial number of this character. The APA itself encourages agencies to permit "interested persons" to appear "so far as the orderly conduct of public business permits." This formulation[68] suggests the agency will be the principal determiner of the issue, but during the last two decades the courts have often overridden agency judgments limiting participation, in order to facilitate representation of a wider range of interests in agency proceedings.

An influential, early such decision arose in a proceeding before the Federal Communications Commission to renew the license of a southern radio station that allegedly failed to serve the interests of black members of its community. The FCC limited the participation of a church group claiming to be representative of black radio listeners. They were permitted to submit views but not admitted as a party. Thus, they lacked the right to adduce evidence, to examine witnesses, and otherwise to control the course of the proceedings. The Commission's evident concern was that "the orderly conduct of public business" would be threatened by according that much control over the proceeding to an outside group interested in issues the Commission itself was responsible to protect. The reviewing court of appeals required that the listener group be admitted to formal party status, interjecting its own sense of what the public interest called for:

> The theory that the Commission can always effectively represent the listener interests in a renewal proceeding without the aid and participation of legitimate listener representatives fulfilling the role of private attorneys general is one of those assumptions we collectively try to work with as long as they are reasonably adequate. When it becomes clear, as it does to us now, that it is no longer a valid assumption which stands up under the realities of actual experience, neither we nor the Commission can continue to rely on it.[69]

Strikingly, the author of this opinion was no radical, but Judge Warren E. Burger, who was shortly to become Chief Justice of the United States Supreme Court on the basis of his strong reputation as a cautious and conservative judge.

Underlying this decision, others like it,[70] and a tremendous volume of "public interest" litigation and generally approving literature, was a

---

68. Still-useful discussion appears in D. Shapiro, Some Thoughts on Intervention Before Courts, Agencies, and Arbitrators, 81 Harv. L. Rev. 721 (1968).

69. Office of Communication of the United Church of Christ v. FCC, 359 F.2d 994 (D.C. Cir. 1966).

70. E.g., National Welfare Rights Organization v. Finch, 429 F.2d 725 (D.C. Cir. 1970).

belief, as one scholar characterized it, that expanded participation in agency proceedings would

> be an effective and workable means of assuring improved agency decisions. Advocates of extended access believe that an enlarged system of formal proceedings can, by securing adequate consideration of the interests of all affected persons, yield outcomes that better serve society as a whole. . . . Such participation . . . is valuable in itself because it gives citizens a sense of involvement in the process of government, and increases confidence in the fairness of government decisions. . . . The judges' incipient transformation of administrative law into a scheme of interest representation is responding to powerful needs that have been neglected by other branches of government.[71]

As the President, in particular, has asserted stronger political controls over regulatory action, and as national politics have become more skeptical about regulation as a whole, some judges have begun to sound less confident about the value of regarding agency adjudication, and particularly the judicial role in overseeing it, through this political lens. In a number of recent opinions, the Supreme Court has referred explicitly to the political responsibilities of Congress and the President, in contrast to its own.[72] One recent unanimous opinion for the Court (including Chief Justice Burger) seemed to go out of its way to dampen participatory claims. Discussing consumer participation in the Department of Agriculture's regulation of milk marketing, the Court noted that the Act in question provided explicitly for the participation of milk handlers and producers in this "complex scheme" of regulation, but did not mention consumers. "[T]he omission of such a provision is sufficient reason to believe that Congress intended to foreclose consumer participation in the regulatory process."[73] The consumers group had not sought to participate in the administrative proceeding,[74] rendering this passage simple dictum; yet the attitude it suggests is quite different from that which informed the earlier cases. While it is unlikely that the idea of public interest representation will disappear from the American lexicon—in part, because so many statutes are explicit in permitting it—the courts seem less likely to be its aggressive promoters.

---

71. R. Stewart, note 64 above, 88 Harv. L. Rev. at 1760-62.

72. Chevron, U.S.A., Inc. v. Natural Resources Defense Council, Inc. 467 U.S. 837 (1984). The passage is quoted at note 48, p. 256.

73. Block v. Community Nutrition Institute, 467 U.S. 340, 346-47 (1984).

74. The case involved only the question of their standing to obtain review of the outcome, see p. 221.

Rulemaking

Rulemaking, like adjudication, embraces a broad range of possibilities, from the setting of rates for public utilities, to the creation of binding norms to govern private conduct, to the publication of non-binding statements of policy or guidelines to shape understanding and compliance efforts. The APA's definition of "rule" includes the product of each of these activities. Its definition in 5 U.S.C. § 553 of rulemaking procedure—identified by one leading scholar as "one of the great inventions of modern government"[75]—reflects this diversity by providing three different models of rulemaking procedure: a publication model, a notice and comment model, and a formal hearing model. One or another of these models applies to all rulemaking unless military or foreign affairs functions are involved, or matters relating to the government's proprietary functions.[76]

The APA models

Notice and comment rulemaking

Again it seems useful to start with the central model, which in the case of rulemaking is that of notice and comment (or, as it is often called, "informal") rulemaking. This is the procedure generally referred to as rulemaking. It is the procedure most affected by the recent presidential initiatives requiring cost-benefit analysis and central coordination,[77] and the procedure from which recent legislative and judicial innovations, discussed at some length below,[78] have arisen. And it is the minimum procedure statutorily required for adoption of a rule in the strong sense—that is, for adoption of a rule which if valid will have the force and effect of a statute. Such rules, often described as "substantive" or "legislative"

---

75. K.C. Davis, in Present at the Creation, note 1, above, 38 Ad. L. Rev. at 520.

76. The exemption of proprietary functions from rulemaking procedures has been sharply criticized insofar as it bears on matters having an impact on persons outside government—as rules governing "public property, loans, grants, benefits or contracts," 5 U.S.C. § 553(a)(2), easily may. Most if not all agencies have responded to these criticisms by providing by rule that APA rulemaking procedures are to be followed in these cases, despite the formal statutory exception. Where such rules exist, they may be judicially enforced; that is, a rule adopted without following the APA procedures will be denied legal effect by a reviewing court.

77. See pp. 70-76.

78. See pp. 159-74 and 267-69.

rules, are the bulk of the provisions published in the Code of Federal Regulations. The Supreme Court has indicated, with increasing intensity in recent years,[79] that Congress must have delegated explicit statutory authority to an agency for it to adopt legislative rules; however, the delegation itself may be in rather general terms.[80]

Statutory notice and comment rulemaking procedures begin with the publication of notice of a proposal for rulemaking in the Federal Register, a daily magazine of the federal government used for a broad range of official notification and publication purposes. Of course, this publication may occur at a very late stage in the bureaucratic development of the proposal within the agency itself.[81] It begins a period defined by the notice, but generally 30 to 60 days in length, during which any interested person may submit written comments—"data, views or arguments"— to the responsible agency for its consideration. The agency's obligation, "after consideration of the relevant matter presented," is then to publish with any rule it may decide to adopt "a concise general statement of [its] basis and purpose."[82] The agency may provide more elaborate opportunities for public participation if it chooses. Two rounds of notice are sometimes given for important rules; oral hearings (generally of a legislative rather than judicial character) and opportunities for responsive comment are often provided.

Overall, the striking characteristic of the procedure as statutorily specified is its informality. What must be contained in the notice is loosely defined.[83] The notice itself need not appear until late in the rule's development. If public participation is limited to a single round, commenters of necessity will be able only to put forward direct views, not responses or challenges to the data, views or arguments of others who may join in the proceedings. The defined record, initial decision, and bureaucratic separation of staff from decisionmakers that characterize formal adjudi-

---

79. Chrysler Corp. v. Brown, 441 U.S. 281 (1979).

80. National Petroleum Refiners Assn v. Federal Trade Comm., 482 F.2d 672 (D.C. Cir. 1973), cert. denied, 415 U.S. 951 (1974).

81. For example, under the presidential executive orders discussed on pp. 70-76, the agency will already have established this task as part of its "regulatory agenda" and cleared with the Office of Management and Budget any necessary draft cost-benefit impact analysis; it will have drafted, as well, any other impact analysis document that may be required.

82. 5 U.S.C. § 553(c).

83. "(1) A statement of the time, place, and nature of the public rule making proceedings; (2) reference to the legal authority under which the rule is proposed; and (3) either the terms or substance of the proposed rule or a description of the subjects and issues involved." 5 U.S.C. § 553(b). Note that this does not, in terms, require even that the text of the proposed rule, or data the agency believes it has to support its proposed action, be revealed.

cation are completely absent. Finally, the agency's obligation to explain its ultimate conclusions is stated far more permissively than for the case of adjudication. The contemporary reality of important rulemaking proceedings is in fact more formal and open than these spare provisions would suggest, as developed below;[84] yet it seems appropriate to begin with a statement simply of the statutory framework.

Publication rulemaking

When an agency adopts "interpretative rules, general statements of policy, or rules of agency organization, procedure, or practice,"[85] notice and comment procedures need not be followed unless specified by a particular statute. These and similar instruments, such as staff manuals, may be thought of as statements that announce an agency's positions or procedures on matters within its competence but that are not legally binding upon the outside world. The underlying statute remains the source of any legal obligation and the agency's views, if well-informed, will be regarded only as constructions entitled to weight by a court or other authority that may later be required to reach a conclusion on the legal question involved.[86] Of course, the agency's views may well have an impact on the positions the agency itself will be able to take, or the burden of explanation it will face should it attempt to vary its view.

Interpretive rules and other like formulations comprise a volume of text and regulatory activity enormously greater than the body of legislative rules. Examples include the Internal Revenue Service's opinions about the meaning of the tax laws, the Nuclear Regulatory Commission's "regulatory standards" informing applicants for nuclear power plant licenses how they may be able to satisfy Commission staff that they have met the technical specifications for licensing, and the Department of the Interior's staff manuals on procedures to be followed in carrying out its various regulatory responsibilities. The dimensions of each are many times greater than the agency's body of legislative rules.

Although not formally binding, these opinions may carry great weight in the practical world. They shape behavior that never reaches the courts, and influence decisionmakers with formal responsibility for decision, such as the courts, with the persuasiveness of their origin in an expert and responsible agency. Agencies issue these interpretations and opinions precisely to shape external behavior, reducing to that extent the need for regulatory enforcement. For this reason, it is widely recommended that

---

84. See pp. 159-74.

85. 5 U.S.C. § 553(b)(A).

86. Pacific Gas & Electric Co. v. Federal Power Comm., 506 F.2d 33 (1974); Skidmore v. Swift & Co., 323 U.S. 134 (1944); see also pp. 249-61.

notice and comment procedures be followed here also, even if the procedures are not required. While that is sometimes done, however, all that is necessary for an interpretive rule or like formulation to achieve the formal status that may entitle it to deference, is that the agency's position must be published—a step one would imagine the agency taking in any event if it wished its position to have influence, by providing some assurance of visibility.

These requirements are specified, not in 5 U.S.C. § 553, but in Section 552(a)(1 and 2). Important matters are to appear in the Federal Register. Statements of agency policy or interpretations not published there, along with final agency opinions in adjudications and "administrative staff manuals and instructions to staff that affect a member of the public," must be published by the agency itself and indexed by the agency in a published document. No member of the public may be adversely affected by an agency interpretation, policy, opinion or manual that has not been published in one or the other manner. In addition to publishing its interpretations and policies, each agency must afford "an interested person the right to petition for the issuance, amendment, or repeal of a rule,"[87] including in this instance interpretive rules and the like.

Formal rulemaking

Individual statutes occasionally require rules "to be made on the record after opportunity for an agency hearing."[88] When this is the case, the comment stage and "concise general statement of . . . basis and purpose" of informal rulemaking are replaced by a hearing comparable to that provided for initial licensing.[89] On the record constraints are applicable, with relatively elaborate provision for "party"[90] participation in evidentiary matters and argumentation. The agency's conclusions must be fully and responsively explained; and neither oral process nor the observance of separation of functions within the agency decisional structure is as rigorously insisted upon as would be the case in ordinary on-the-record adjudication.

Proceedings to fix permitted rates for a public utility or common carrier are by far the commonest setting for formal rulemaking. For the utility

---

87. 5 U.S.C. § 553(e).
88. 5 U.S.C. § 553(c).
89. See pp. 148-49.
90. The ideas of rulemaking (a procedure for the formulation of general norms) and "parties" are not easily reconciled. As a general matter any person who wishes to is permitted to participate in any rulemaking. At least some formal rulemakings, however—those setting rates for public utilities, for example—require the participation of particular entities, as well as permitting the participation of all.

or carrier facing the possibility of being denied a reasonable return on its investment, the claim to formal hearing has a constitutional dimension.[91] Formal rulemaking proceedings are, however, notoriously inconvenient and difficult to manage, given the frequent diffuseness of the issues presented and the large number of parties that may wish to participate.[92] Consequently, courts are reluctant to find that statutes require rules to be formally made. In sharp distinction from the practice where the question arises concerning statutory provision for adjudicatory hearings,[93] the courts virtually require a formula including the words "on the record" to appear before they will conclude that the informal rulemaking procedures of Section 553 will not suffice.[94]

The continuing problem of the rulemaking record

Against the spare provisions of the Administrative Procedure Act, consider both the tremendous importance of rulemaking as an activity in contemporary regulation, and the rich internal—one might even say political—life of government in reaching decisions of magnitude. Since the explosion of environmental, health and safety regulation in the late 1960s and early 1970s, rulemaking has become the pre-eminent administrative activity in the United States. Whether the petro-chemical industry will be required to take special precautions (and which precautions) in its uses of benzene, to name only one of the many chemicals it handles with implications for the health of workers and the public generally; what controls coal-fired electric power plants must employ to prevent emission of soot, heat, or chemicals possibly harmful to the environment; what technology fish-processors shall use to avoid the threat of botulism poisoning from imperfectly smoked fish—each of these decisions raises highly complex questions of physical science, technology, human health, economics, and political will. These questions will engage whoever has the responsibility and opportunity to participate in their resolution and their resolution will affect a wide range of interests in the community.

One can imagine, then, widespread dissatisfactions with a procedure whose public aspects, slight to begin with, occur so late in policy development. One can imagine, as well, persistent efforts to secure earlier

---

91. ICC v. Louisville & Nashville R. Co., 227 U.S. 88 (1913).
92. R. Hamilton, Procedures for the Adoption of Rules of General Applicability: The Need for Procedural Innovation in Administrative Rulemaking, 60 Calif. L. Rev. 1276 (1972).
93. See note 31, above.
94. United States v. Florida East Coast Railway Co., 410 U.S. 224 (1973).

and more influential roles than the public procedure suggests. At the same time—in view of the high stakes for the community as a whole—one could understand a certain insistence on regularity and visibility, particularly when rulemaking comes before the courts for their necessarily retrospective assessment of its outcome.

These developments were emphasized by a growing awareness of the imperfections in the analogy first drawn by Justice Holmes in *Bi-Metallic Investment Co.*[95] between rulemaking and legislative action. Recall his statement there that the procedural claims of citizens in respect of legislation are strictly political ones—"their rights are protected in the only way that they can be in a complex society, by their power, immediate or remote, over those who make the rule." This position, together with the judiciary's profound unwillingness to examine the factual justification for statutes following the "substantive due process" crisis of the 1930's,[96] produced extremely permissive standards of judicial review of rulemaking. When agency rules were challenged on judicial review—and it did not become clear until 1969 that such challenges could often be made in advance of government-initiated enforcement proceedings[97]—judges presumed their validity just as they would presume the validity of a statute. A challenger would be required to show (on the basis of a record freshly made in court) that the agency's judgment had been arbitrary and capricious in the strongest sense, that no facts could be adduced to support the rule it had adopted.[98]

Yet an agency is not an elective body. The ties between federal administrative agencies and the electorate are limited to the periodic election of the American President, a connection that at times has seemed so frail as to escape even the description "remote,"[99] and to the possibilities inherent in legislative revision and oversight of agency authority. What, then, was the warrant for according such respect to the products of agency rulemaking, which could "affect the person or property of individuals, sometimes to the point of ruin"?[100]

These themes will be presented in the following pages from a perspective familiar to administrative lawyers—what is and must be in the

95. See pp. 134-36.
96. See pp. 24-25.
97. Abbott Laboratories v. Gardner, 387 U.S. 136 (1967); the case is discussed on pp. 216-23.
98. Pacific States Box & Basket Co. v. White, 296 U.S. 176 (1935).
99. On the recent strengthening of this connection, see pp. 70-76; Chevron, U.S.A., Inc. v. Natural Resources Defense Council, Inc., 467 U.S. 837 (1984); J. Mashaw, Prodelegation: Why Administrators Should Make Political Decisions, 1 J. Law, Ec. & Org. 81.
100. Bi-Metallic Investment Co., note 95, above.

"record" of informal rulemaking assembled for purposes of judicial review? That is, how much is or ought to be known about the process by which the agency actually developed its rule, and the information on which it is premised?

This is hardly the only perspective possible. It is a peculiarly "legal" perspective. Even for lawyers, its focus on judicial review creates a risk of misunderstanding (or, worse, poorly structuring) the bureaucratic stages that precede it. Finally, a focus on the problem of the record is made somewhat more difficult by our not yet having encountered extended treatment of the subject of judicial review.[101] Yet presenting the themes in this way should help the reader understand developments that, over the past fifteen years, have been the most striking of any in our administrative law.

Bureaucratic structures of rulemaking and rulemaking decision

Rulemaking is characterized by *institutional* processes for consideration and decision of controversial matters. In this respect it is sharply distinct from adjudication, in which decision is taken by specified individuals. These institutional processes complicate the process of defining a "record" of decision if they do not deny the possibility altogether.

In adjudication, one imagines that the whole issue is placed before a discrete individual at a certain time. The adjudicator considers identifiable matters, argument and data, more-or-less formally placed before her and reaches an individual decision. Although difficulties can be introduced when the adjudicator takes judicial notice of some matter the parties have not placed before her,[102] that practice is constrained; on the whole, everyone knows (without having to rely on the judge to state) what is the basis on which a decision is taken and may be defended. Additionally, the decider is committedly neutral and will not talk to any contender outside the presence of the others, or participate in the rough-and-tumble of political discourse.

The characteristic rulemaking decision, like that of most organizations other than courts when faced with important problems, is institutional. That is, the taking of decisions is not focused on a particular judge-like individual or group of individuals, but occurs within and across the ordinary operating staff of the agency. Responsibilities may be divided within the agency in accordance with interest or expertise in particular aspects of a given problem, perhaps under the supervision of an ad hoc

---

101. See, in this respect, pp. 239-69, especially 267-69.
102. See note 45, above.

working group. Over time piecemeal decisions are taken across the desks of numerous members of agency staff. As they gradually accumulate, only what remains controversial rises through the agency hierarchy. The data that produced resolution of a given aspect may be entirely within the knowledge of a particular employee—his "expertise"—and does not travel with that resolution to later stages. Similarly, controversy may be eliminated or shaped by informal conversations among agency staff whose ordinary roles bear on the particular controversy (but who have no responsibility for the rule as a whole); once those conversations have occurred, traces of the controversy or the basis for its resolution may disappear. The resolution becomes part of what the agency "knows." Even when controversy rises to the level of the agency heads, they may suggest new inquiries or additional approaches that they hope will permit staff to resolve the matter, rather than decide it themselves. That approach often succeeds.

The rulemaking process as a whole also lacks the characteristic isolation of traditional adjudication from other aspects of an agency's work. Those working on the rule continue their work on other aspects of the agency's business. They are encouraged to bring whatever they learn to bear; may and do speak with whoever seems relevant to the matters before them; and feel no need either to inform other "parties" of these conversations or to permit their participation in them in any way.[103]

To speak of a "record" in this context, then, is highly artificial—at least if we are imagining a collection of data all of which was exposed to the interested public for its response and challenge, placed before a single decisionmaker at a given point in time, and uniquely made the basis for her decision. There will have been no *single* decisionmaker. Much that has been relied upon will not have been collected, certainly will not have been presented to the individual or collegial body formally identified by statute as responsible for the adoption of a rule. On the other hand, documents will have been submitted to the agency as comments on the rulemaking, and the APA requires that they be attended to. Major studies may have been commissioned, or other large bodies of data may exist, on which the agency or members of its staff have drawn for decision of one or another aspect of the proceeding. Memoranda will have been written within the agency as decision went forward, indicating resolutions

---

103. A full and still useful description of a characteristic rulemaking process, as seen from inside an important administrative agency, appears in W. Pedersen, Formal Records and Informal Rulemaking, 85 Yale L.J. 38 (1975). While the rulemaking processes of the Environmental Protection Agency have since been changed by statute—in good part as a result of Pedersen's analysis—most agencies continue to make rules today under the statutory procedures that governed the EPA when he wrote.

reached, controversies remaining and, in a healthy bureaucracy, the contending positions on those controversies. Meetings may have occurred within the agency or with outsiders, private interests or other government officials, where views are expressed and data provided that could be, and sometimes are, recorded. All of these, if public, could be described as a "record," at least in the sense of their being a body of data bearing on the agency's rulemaking decision, against which its rationality and lawfulness could be tested.

The impact of open government legislation

Passage of the Freedom of Information Act[104] and (later, and to a lesser extent) the Government in the Sunshine Act[105] sharply altered rulemaking practice, by bringing much of the internal documentation of agency rulemaking, and some of its decisionmaking, into public view. This enormously increased the public and professional sense of what might constitute the "record" of rulemakings.

Without this legislation, persons outside the agency were essentially limited to what the agency chose to report in its statement of basis and purpose as the factual grounding for its decision. Internal documents, even factual studies, were not public documents, and courts did not require them to be revealed. The traditional process of rulemaking review briefly described above[106] put few demands on the agency. It might have to supply the file of comments that it had received in the rulemaking; but generally was free simply to show what it knew that could be regarded as supporting its conclusions. Inquiry into its actual decisionmaking process would not be undertaken.

The Freedom of Information Act, first adopted in 1967 and vastly strengthened in 1974, opened agency rulemaking up to public view. While not intended as a record-enhancing statute as such,[107] it permitted participants in rulemaking to request the release of all documents that the agency was considering in connection with a rulemaking proceeding. It quickly became a mandatory element of competent professional practice to file a request "for all documents the agency regards as bearing upon its proposed rulemaking . . . ," a request sufficiently definite to have to be honored. Not all parts of all documents had to be revealed; in partic-

---

104. 5 U.S.C. § 552, discussed on pp. 195-200.
105. 5 U.S.C. § 552(b), discussed on pp. 200-202.
106. See p. 160.
107. The statute makes government records available on demand to "any person," and the courts have in fact resisted litigant efforts to tie FOIA requests to judicial review of agency action. National Labor Relations Board v. Sears, Roebuck & Co., 421 U.S. 132 (1975).

ular, predecisional advice given by agency staff to their superiors could usually be withheld as privileged.[108] Yet even in staff memoranda only advice could be withheld. Factual assertions—data and technical analysis—are not privileged, and the agency's obligation under the FOIA is to edit privileged material out of a document and honor the remainder of the request. Thus agencies could be forced to reveal their factual basis for action. Often enough they would provide the advice portion of memoranda as well, rather than go through the trouble of redaction. Anticipating the requests, they began to organize, and to make available at the outset of rulemakings, data that inevitably would have to be disclosed at some later stage.

The Government in the Sunshine Act, adopted in 1976, made explicit the FOIA's latent judgment about openness in rulemaking. Under this statute, multi-member commissions are required to hold their meetings on advance notice, in public view.[109] The act's limited exemptions, quite intentionally, do not permit an agency to close any part of a discussion of ordinary rulemaking. Unlike the FOIA, that is, the Sunshine Act recognizes no privilege whatsoever for predecisional consultations with staff about policymaking; only discussions about decision in on-the-record adjudication are protected in that way. To be sure, the Sunshine Act mechanism does not apply to agencies like EPA or OSHA, that function with a single individual at their head; only the multi-member commissions are affected. Yet this can be seen as a technical judgment about the difficulty of constructing a "Sunshine" mechanism for a strictly hierarchical decision process lacking collegial elements, or as a result of the President's greater ability to protect agencies attached to the executive branch as distinct from the independent agencies.[110] As a comment on rulemaking, its message is clear.

The "paper hearing"

Three related elements of the APA's notice and comment rulemaking procedure permitted judicial interpretation that would draw agency rulemaking away from the simple legislative analogy: what constituted "notice"; what, an effective opportunity for "comment"; and what, an adequate "statement of basis and purpose," however "general" and "concise." The mood of the legislature in 1946 on enacting these provisions, no one could doubt, was highly permissive. Yet the widespread

---

108. See the discussion of the act's fifth exemption at pp. 197–98.

109. In public view, but *not* with public participation. Like FOIA, the Sunshine Act's focus is on openness, not additional external controls or decision procedures.

110. See p. 76.

use and enormous impact of rulemaking resulting from environmental, health, and safety legislation was not foreseen at that time. When it occurred, these were the obvious pressure points.

The last of them, the findings requirement, was the first to respond to the new circumstances. Faced with the first rules adopted to regulate automobile safety under the National Traffic and Motor Vehicle Safety Act—rules that, as the reader knows, would contribute tremendously to reshaping the automobile market—the D.C. Circuit cautioned "against an overly literal reading of the statutory terms 'concise' and 'general.' These adjectives must be accommodated to the realities of judicial scrutiny. . . . We do not expect the agency to discuss every item of fact or opinion included in the submissions made to it . . . [but we do expect that the statement] will enable us to see what major issues of policy were ventilated by the informal proceedings and why the agency reacted to them as it did."[111]

Generally—Citizens to Preserve Overton Park, Inc. v. Volpe. The attitude underlying this opinion, that judges were entitled to see and understand what had occurred at the agency level, received major impetus in a 1971 Supreme Court opinion that focused particular attention on the problem of the record. *Citizens to Preserve Overton Park, Inc. v. Volpe*[112] challenged the decision of the federal Secretary of Transportation to provide federal financing for a portion of highway that would inevitably interfere with an important urban park, despite recent federal legislation intended to protect park lands against such uses. In the APA's terms, the Secretary's decision would be characterized as informal adjudication, not rulemaking. Nonetheless, it shared the institutional characteristics of rulemaking. The decision had been reached through a coordinated, informal bureaucratic process, after a number of opportunities for public comment but without any procedure resembling a trial. The Secretary did not issue an opinion explaining his judgment at the time he granted permission to go forward with the project. He attempted to explain it only when review was sought by a group of citizens opposing the project.[113]

The Supreme Court strongly endorsed review of that judgment, describing its appropriate elements in a manner to be examined later in this

---

111. Automotive Parts & Accessories v. Boyd, 407 F.2d 330, 338 (D.C. Cir. 1968). For a trenchant critique of the impact of this judicial attitude on the agency's performance two decades later, see J. Mashaw and D. Harfst, Regulation and Legal Culture: The Case of Motor Vehicle Safety, 4 Yale J. Reg. 257 (1987).

112. 401 U.S. 402 (1971). This case is also discussed on pp. 261-67.

113. See the discussions of standing on pp. 225-28 and of public participation on pp. 149-54.

essay.[114] It made two observations of particular moment to the present discussion. First, it said that judicial review, while "narrow" (to avoid the substitution of judicial for agency judgment) was to be "thorough," "probing," and "careful" in examining the Secretary's declared basis for his decision against the materials before him. Second, and relatedly, the Court indicated that this review was to occur on the basis of "the record" compiled in the agency in the course of the decisional process.

The call for "thorough," "probing" and "careful" review only reinforced the attitudes already emerging in cases like the D.C. Circuit's review of the automobile safety rules. If this was the judicial responsibility, how much more important that the statement of basis and purpose "enable us to see what major issues of policy were ventilated by the informal proceedings and why the agency reacted to them as it did"![115]

The Court's confident reference to the administrative "record" is surprising in light of the structural realities of the decision process, one much like that just described for informal rulemaking. Except as the FOIA would eventually compel them to learn it, agencies did not have the habit of identifying in this way all the materials brought to bear on an accumulating decision as it passed through the various levels of bureaucratic review. In all likelihood the reference was encouraged by a misunderstanding on the part of the attorney who had argued the case for the government, a young lawyer accustomed to the judicial model of litigation.[116] Nonetheless, the reference was made and—among lawyers and

---

114. See pp. 261-67.

115. Note 111, above. Paradoxically, one of the holdings of the Overton Park case was that formal findings were *not* required; however, the Court continued, judicial review must occur in the described manner whether or not such findings had been made. The absence of findings thus would warrant calling the Secretary to court to explain what his reasoning had been—an examination of mental processes courts are otherwise disposed to avoid. See pp. 265-66. Predictably, administrators, too, wish to avoid having to subject themselves to the costs in time and indignity of submitting to hostile examination about their reasoning process; and, thus, the case is a strong incentive to the making of findings even though, in formal terms, it denies any obligation to do so.

For rulemaking, moreover, an obligation of written findings is imposed by statute. It has proved natural to interpret that obligation in light of the review functions the Supreme Court described.

116. The government's brief referred repeatedly to "the administrative record" as if a defined set of papers existed. After the Supreme Court had remanded the case for further proceedings, it quickly became apparent that no such collection existed. Definition of the materials before the various agency personnel sharing responsibility for the decision consumed weeks of litigation effort. Because a major highway project was being suspended during the litigation, the case had been argued and briefed in the Supreme Court on an unusually condensed schedule—one usually reserved for the most important affairs of state—and this haste doubtless contributed to the government's failure.

judges equally used to that model—was easily accepted. Together with the FOIA as a new statutory tool for discovering what materials had been considered by the agency in developing a rule, the reference served to focus new attention on the problem of defining an agency's data base.

The special case of technological rulemaking. Once one began to know what material was being considered by an agency (in addition to the outside comments that long had been a matter of public record), the natural instinct to wish to be able to respond to that material—to confront it, challenge it, contradict it—quickly took shape. The impulse was perhaps especially strong for rules setting industrial standards to protect the health and safety of workers and/or the public. Many of the issues to be resolved appeared to involve factual disputes, albeit disputes about such general questions as the impact of breathing various concentrations of a given substance on human health.

The instinct found expression in a 1973 proceeding involving an EPA rulemaking to set standards for the control of concrete dust.[117] After the rule had been adopted but before it had been judicially reviewed, the EPA (prompted by a recent court of appeals decision in another case)[118] put new information about the methodology it had employed to reach its conclusions in the record for review. With its information about the agency's data thus enlarged, one of the participants in the rulemaking now persuaded the court to send the rule back to the agency, to allow the filing of new comments critical of the agency's methodology. When the agency appeared to ignore those comments, the court not only insisted that they be responded to, but gave forceful new content to the statutory provisions for "notice" and "comment" by suggesting an obligation to reveal agency data from the outset: "it is not consonant with the purpose of a rule-making proceeding to promulgate rules on the basis of inadequate data, or on data that . . . [are] known only to the agency."

Four years later, a similar view was expressed by another court of appeals in reviewing a Food and Drug Administration rule governing the preparation of smoked fish:

> Although we recognize that an agency may resort to its own expertise . . . we do not believe that when the pertinent research material is readily available . . . there is any reason to conceal the scientific data relied upon from the interested parties. . . . If the failure to notify interested persons of [the material relied on] actually prevented the presentation of relevant comment, the agency may be held not to have considered all "the relevant factors." . . . One cannot

---

117. Portland Cement Assn v. Ruckleshaus, 486 F.2d 375 (D.C. Cir. 1973), cert. denied, 417 U.S. 921 (1974).

118. Kennecott Copper Corp. v. EPA, 462 F.2d 846 (D.C. Cir. 1972).

ask for comment on a scientific paper without allowing the participants to read the paper.[119]

Thus, "notice" is to include not only the information described in the statute,[120] but also any data of which the agency is aware that bears on its proposed rule. "Comment" requires an opportunity to challenge that data, in addition to the chance to supply fresh data, argument or views. And the statement of basis and purpose must be full enough to show the agency's reasoning in some detail, including its response to important comments that have been made.

This understanding of rulemaking process came to be described as a "paper hearing" procedure. It was widely accepted, characterized by one scholarly proponent as a "requirement of reasoned elaboration" that "combines many of the advantages of a trial-type adversary process (excepting oral testimony and cross-examination) while avoiding undue delay and cost."[121] This assessment was echoed by at least one thoughtful bureaucrat, who found the intensity of judicial involvement, and the expectations it created, "a great tonic" to the integrity of the rulemaking process within the agency, giving "those who care about well-documented and well-reasoned decisionmaking a lever with which to move those who do not."[122] Most thoughtful observers would concede that the problems of fact-finding in these portentious matters, typically complicated by issues of modelling, scientific judgment, and projection,[123] require a public procedure of some fullness and visibility.

---

119. United States v. Nova Scotia Food Products Corp., 568 F.2d 240 (2d Cir. 1977).

120. Note 83, above.

121. R. Stewart, The Development of Administrative and Quasi-Constitutional Law in Judicial Review of Environmental Decisionmaking: Lessons from the Clean Air Act, 62 Iowa L. Rev. 713, 731 (1977).

122. W. Pedersen, Formal Records and Informal Rulemaking, 85 Yale L.J. 38, 60 (1975).

123. Modelling involves the use of computer models or other analytic devices to predict the outcome of complex interactions—for example, the economic impact of a proposed regulation—and is highly dependent on the assumptions of the model as well as the accuracy of the data employed in it. Scientific judgment issues arise in assessing the outcomes of processes that cannot be directly tested, for example the impact on steel used in a nuclear power plant of being exposed to high levels of radiation for forty years. Projection involves the transplanting of data developed in one sphere to another, as when scientists use the results of experiments on mice employing relatively high doses of a chemical to estimate carcinogenicity in humans at low dosage rates. On the general problem, see B. Ackerman, Reconstructing American Law (1984), and Administrative Law: Cases and Comments 834-61; a highly regarded decision illustrating these problems is Sierra Club v. Costle, 657 F.2d 298 (D.C. Cir. 1981), discussed at pp. 172-74 and 268-69, below.

The development of the "paper hearing" has posed, nonetheless, a number of related difficulties. Several are taken up in the pages immediately following, but here two general issues can be posed. The first is that fullness and visibility have necessary costs. Proceedings become more elaborate and correspondingly more time consuming—to the point, recent scholarship has suggested, of paralysis.[124] The second difficulty lies in finding a procedure that does not impose the lawyer's and judge's instinctive view of the decision process as focused on a neutral, detached individual or group uniquely responsible for decision, rather than as the product of institutional functioning. This is the mischief in references to "a trial-type adversary process"—encouraging the belief that there ought to be one group responsible for presentation and challenge and another for decision, a belief that denies decision mechanisms far more common than the judicial in the world as a whole.

"Ex parte contacts"

The problems of regarding rulemaking as an "adversary process" were underscored by a case involving the Federal Communications Commission, *Home Box Office, Inc.* v. *FCC*.[125] The rule in question regulated the programs that could be shown by companies competing with regular television broadcasters over cable antenna systems. Here there were no particular difficulties about fact-finding, but the monetary implications of the rule were substantial. Many different groups had a financial or viewing interest in the rule and had participated not only by filing comments, but also by approaching FCC commissioners and staff informally to voice their views. An inquiry by the court produced "a document over 60 pages long which revealed, albeit imprecisely, widespread ex parte communications involving virtually every party [to the rulemaking]."

Was this wrong behavior? While the court was horrified, none of the participants appear to have treated it guiltily, one going so far as to boast of its success in bringing congressional pressure to bear. As we have seen, the "ex parte communication" limitation is one characteristic of on-the-record proceedings, in particular of adjudication; all the statutory provisions concerning it are pointed in that direction.[126] Informal rulemaking, on the other hand, encourages contact and interaction; it imposes no structures of separation on agency decisionmaking, and no obligation of mutual disclosure among the participants.

---

124. See J. Mashaw and D. Harfst, note 111, above; D. Costle, Brave New Chemical: The Future Regulatory History of Phlogiston, 33 Ad. L. Rev. 195 (1981); and note 145, below.

125. 567 F.2d 9, cert. denied, 434 U.S. 829 (1977).

126. See notes 43-44, above.

For the Home Box Office court, however, the recent discovery of the rulemaking "record" and the development of the "paper hearing" pointed in another direction:

Even the possibility that there is here one administrative record for the public and this court and another for the Commission and those "in the know" is intolerable. . . . [I]mplicit in the decision to treat the promulgation of rules as a "final" event in an ongoing process of administration is an assumption that an act of reasoned judgment has occurred, an assumption which further contemplates the existence of a body of material . . . with reference to which such judgment was exercised. Against this matter, "the full administrative record that was before [an agency official] at the time he made his decision,"[127] . . . it is the obligation of this court to test the actions of the Commission for arbitrariness or inconsistency with delegated authority. . . . As a practical matter, Overton Park's mandate means that the public record must reflect what representations were made to an agency so that relevant information supporting or refuting those representations may be brought to the attention of the reviewing courts by persons participating in agency proceedings. This course is obviously foreclosed if communications are made to the agency in secret and the agency itself does not disclose the information presented.

The opinion continued in this vein for some pages, adding the thought that the "paper hearing" requirements for the disclosure of materials in agency files were important, also, for their promotion of "adversarial discussion among the parties." Explicitly, then, in this court's view, the opportunity to comment had become not only a chance to contribute argument, data or views to which attention must be paid, but also the occasion for challenging and testing what others had contributed.[128]

---

127. The quotation is from Citizens to Preserve Overton Park, Inc. v. Volpe, note 112, above.

128. The court's reaction could be understood as one of the periodic reactions to suspicion about the reality of an agency's professed findings. See note 51, above. The difficulty of the court's position as a matter of statutory construction of 5 U.S.C. § 553, however, should be evident. The agency is required to provide for only one opportunity for comment; if most or all comments are filed on the final day, one commenter's submission cannot include responses to what others may be saying. Here, again, the court evidently had the elegant rituals of judicial filings in mind. Of course it is also true that (unlike judicial proceedings) the time deadlines for filing rulemaking comments are not jurisdictional. One may file comments, responsive or otherwise, at any time, and the agency is free to consider them. What the designated time period for comments assures is that timely comments *will* be paid attention to. Later comments need not be disregarded.

This opinion excited a good deal of concern for its tendency to convert rulemaking into a species of adjudication. Later decisions have limited its impact. In particular, they have receded from the suggestions that private discussions are generally impermissible, and that "adversarial comment" is generally called for, in informal rulemaking.[129] The very large financial stakes that were to be allocated among the participants are said by some to be special facts that support the result in *Home Box Office*, but permit distinguishing other cases where they are absent.[130] The public record of rulemaking, then, need not be exhaustive of what the agency may know or have heard; nor need there have been an opportunity for each participant to respond to every item that appears there. But the "paper hearing" idea continues to require that the public record contain all documents that the agency may have received in relation to a rulemaking. There also remains a general expectation, reinforced by a recommendation of the Administrative Conference of the United States,[131] that significant oral communications about pending rulemakings—particularly any data they may convey—will be noted, and a precis placed in the rulemaking record. This is the regime adopted in the special rulemaking provisions governing proceedings under the Clean Air Act, which most commentators expect to be the model for any future reform of federal rulemaking procedures generally.[132]

The impact of increasing political oversight

Recall now the trend to heightened political oversight of agency policymaking, especially rulemaking—a trend given particular force by the presidential executive orders requiring economic impact analyses and annual participation in the setting of a regulatory agenda.[133] Factual analyses prepared by the agency in these processes or submitted to it by other agencies, including the OMB, seem a necessary part of the record

---

129. See, e.g., Action for Children's Television v. FCC, 564 F.2d 458 (D.C. Cir. 1977).

130. This reading is challenged, and the general problem thoughtfully explored, in E. Gellhorn and G. Robinson, Rulemaking "Due Process": An Inconclusive Dialogue, 48 U. Chi. L. Rev. 201 (1981).

131. Recommendation 77-3, published at 1 CFR 305.77-3, relied on "the widespread demand for open government" as well as the needs of judicial review in recommending the creation of a rulemaking file that would include the texts of all written communications and notes of "significant oral communications"; it rejected, however, the idea of an "opportunity of interested persons to reply" as inconsistent with the idea of rulemaking, and "neither practicable nor desirable." On the Administrative Conference, see p. 205-6.

132. Note 22, above.

133. See pp. 70-76.

generated by a "paper hearing." Such analyses would not ordinarily be privileged from disclosure under the FOIA.[134] But an FOIA privilege *would* extend to predecisional discussions about policy choices, the very matter as to which oversight is likely to be the most vigorously exercised and the public's suspicions are likely to be the most aroused. The President's office is chary of having notes made and published of its informal oral discussions with agencies about matters on their plate. Yet judicial review may appear somewhat unrealistic, if undertaken without awareness of the President's input. What implications does the "paper hearing" idea have here?

This issue was important to *Sierra Club* v. *Costle*,[135] a case involving judicial review of a Clean Air Act rulemaking with sharp political over-tones—EPA's rules to govern the emission of sulfur compounds by coal-burning electric power plants. The plants could reduce the amount of sulfur they emitted in several ways: use of low-sulfur coal, pre-treatment (washing) of the coal, the use of either of two available technologies for "scrubbing" the exhaust of the plant, or some combination of these mea-sures. Low-sulfur coal was present in some parts of the country but not others. Scrubbing would demand expensive equipment that if not uni-versally required would eliminate an essential market for higher sulfur coals. And scrubbing would produce still cleaner air with low-sulfur coal than high. For environmentalists seeking pure air, eastern coal interests with high-sulfur reserves, other areas with low-sulfur reserves, and a President concerned about the general economic impact of imposing a costly and generally unproven technology, the stakes were high.[136] The Clean Air Act obliges EPA to maintain a rulemaking file including all information or data on which it intends to rely, and it had docketed notes of a series of meetings, including several held shortly before the rule was announced with the President and/or his staff. Some of these meetings included coal industry officials and a powerful senator from one of the eastern high-sulfur states. One meeting with the President and his staff was not docketed. The rule as adopted had been couched in terms tending to favor the eastern interests.

---

134. See pp. 163-64, above. Like its predecessor under the Carter adminis-tration, Executive Order 12044, although not as strongly, Executive Order 12291 seeks to assure the publication in agency rulemaking files of all factual data that may come to the agency through the oversight process. The executive order makes no such undertaking for policy views.

135. 657 F.2d 298 (D.C. Cir. 1981). The case is also discussed at pp. 268-69.

136. The story of the rulemaking is well told, with an emphasis on the dis-tortions (as the authors see them) introduced by the political process in B. Ack-erman and W. Hassler, Clean Coal/Dirty Air (Yale 1981); a shorter account by the same authors appears as Beyond the New Deal: Coal and the Clean Air Act, 89 Yale L.J. 1466 (1980).

Unlike the court of appeals in *Home Box Office*, even despite the special provisions of the Clean Air Act, this panel sought to respect the non-judicial characteristics of the rulemaking process. Informal oral meetings about pending rulemakings would not be forbidden or made the subject of formal recording requirements.

> [T]he very legitimacy of general policymaking performed by unelected administrators depends in no small part upon the openness, accessibility, and amenability of these officials to the needs and ideas of the public. . . . As judges we are insulated from these pressures . . . but we must refrain from the easy temptation to look askance at all face-to-face lobbying efforts, regardless of the forum in which they occur, merely because we see them as inappropriate in the judicial context.

Stressing the President's exclusive constitutional responsibility for exercise of executive authority[137] and the agency's inability to rely on any factual matter not placed in its docket, the court found that the failure to record notes of one of the meetings with the President presented no difficulty.

> After all, any rule . . . must have the requisite *factual support* in the rulemaking record, and . . . the Administrator may not base the rule . . . on any *"information or data"* which is not in the record, no matter what the source. . . . Of course, it is always possible that undisclosed Presidential prodding may direct an outcome that *is* factually based on the record, but different from the outcome that would have obtained in the absence of Presidential involvement. In such a case, it would be true that the political process did affect the outcome in a way the courts could not police. But we do not believe that Congress intended that the courts convert informal rulemaking into a rarified technocratic process, unaffected by political considerations or the presence of Presidential power.[138]

The court was similarly undisturbed by the possibility of congressional pressure inherent in the meetings with the eastern Senator, absent a demonstration that he had introduced extraneous considerations.[139]

---

137. See pp. 12-18 and 59-77.

138. Similar acceptance of political oversight and its results appears in a recent Supreme Court decision discussed elsewhere in these pages, Chevron, U.S.A., Inc. v. Natural Resources Defense Council, Inc., 467 U.S. 837 (1984). See pp. 257-61. On the court's acceptance of possible divergence between apparent and real reasons, compare notes 51 and 128, above.

139. Such a demonstration had been successfully made in an earlier case, D.C. Federation of Civil Associations v. Volpe, 459 F.2d 1231 (D.C. Cir. 1971),

"Where Congressmen keep their comments focused on the substance of the proposed rule . . . administrative agencies are expected to balance Congressional pressure with the pressures emanating from all other sources."

Forcing the agency's hand in rulemaking

Forcing additional procedures

Rulemaking might be much more formal, at least for important and technologically based matters, but for the 1978 decision of the Supreme Court in *Vermont Yankee Nuclear Power Corp.* v. *Natural Resources Defense Council, Inc.*[140] In the years preceding that decision, scholarly appreciations of the "paper hearing"[141] and court of appeals opinions such as *Home Box Office*[142] had been contributing to the formation of "hybrid" procedures for rulemaking by their approving references to the virtues of the adversary process for truth-testing. Under this hybrid model, acclaimed by at least one scholar as a procedure that could unify rulemaking and adjudication,[143] important issues of fact in rulemaking were seen as requiring oral procedures for their determination, procedures having many of the qualities of trial. This was so even if the facts to be found were of a general or "legislative" character, such as the impact of a given level of radiation on human health. Viva voce examination of scientific experts and the presentation of contending expert points of view often enough occur in trial settings.[144] Proponents of hybrid hearings asserted that requiring such procedures in important contested matters in rulemaking would permit more informed decision. They claimed that truth was more likely to arise from the contending views and from partisan challenges to expert testimony than from a process considering such

cert. denied, 405 U.S. 1030 (1972). There, a congressman had demanded that the Secretary of Transportation move forward to authorize construction of a bridge (the decision challenged in the case), and threatened to hold funds for another, unrelated departmental program hostage in the appropriations process until he did so.

140. 435 U.S. 519. The reader is entitled to know that the author was General Counsel of the Nuclear Regulatory Commission when the case was decided by the court of appeals and briefed to the Supreme Court, so that his view of the case is to some extent, inevitably, that of an advocate.

141. Text pp. 164-69, above.

142. Text pp. 169-71, above.

143. P. Verkuil, The Emerging Concept of Administrative Procedure, 78 Colum. L. Rev. 258 (1978).

144. For example, in disputes over forensic evidence such as blood type or psychological state in criminal trials.

disputes only on the papers. The procedure was legislatively adopted for a few particular statutes enforced by particular agencies, and although doubts were being expressed about the costs in time and effort it imposed[145] the courts of appeals seemed poised to require it more generally.

In the federal court of appeals for the District of Columbia circuit, *Vermont Yankee* seemed to be an example of this. Acting in response to a petition for review filed by a private organization dedicated to seeking environmental protection, the court of appeals ordered the Nuclear Regulatory Commission to reconsider a rule it had adopted, apparently requiring it to use these hybrid procedures. The rule depended upon complex findings about the handling and impact of nuclear waste. The agency had in fact used oral proceedings in the rulemaking, and had revealed its data and permitted participants a degree of influence over the proceedings significantly beyond what Section 553 required. The court, however, believed the procedures the agency had chosen were not "sufficient to ventilate the issues" as fully as their importance required.

In the Supreme Court, this reasoning was rejected in a sharply worded and unanimous opinion that appeared to forbid the courts of appeals to require procedures beyond those of Section 553. The APA, it reasoned, settled "long-continued and hard-fought contentions, and enacts a formula on which opposing social and political forces have come to rest." Its rulemaking provisions "established the maximum procedural requirements which Congress was willing to have the courts impose upon agencies in conducting rulemaking procedures. Agencies are free to grant additional procedural rights in the exercise of their discretion, but reviewing courts are generally not free to impose them if the agencies have not chosen to grant them." Permitting courts to determine what would have been "properly tailored" procedures after the fact, the Court reasoned, would lead agencies to choose excessive formality as the only safe means of avoiding reversal on procedural grounds. Such determination would involve the courts in assessing outcomes by hindsight, a perspective denied the agencies when they make their procedural choices. And,

---

145. The most disciplined study was that done for the Administrative Conference of the United States by Professor Barry Boyer; he studied the Federal Trade Commission's experience with hybrid rulemaking procedures a 1974 statute required for its adoption of certain types of rules, concluding they produced little gain in accuracy, fairness, or acceptability of results but a good deal of additional cost and delay. See Boyer, Report on the Trade Regulation Rulemaking Procedures of the Federal Trade Commission, 1979 ACUS Ann. Rep. 41; 1980 ACUS Ann. Rep. 33; for a recent study, see West, Administrative Rulemaking & Political Process (Greenwood 1985). See also the study by J. Mashaw and D. Harfst, note 111, above.

the Court stressed, the argument for more elaborate procedures rested on a false view of the record of rulemaking: "[I]nformal rulemaking need not be based solely on the transcript of a hearing held before an agency. . . . Thus, the adequacy of the 'record' in [rulemaking] is not correlated directly to the type of procedural devices employed, but rather turns on whether the agency has followed the statutory mandate of the Administrative Procedure Act or other relevant statutes."

Clearly enough, the Supreme Court's *Vermont Yankee* opinion now forbids courts to require *oral* procedures in connection with rulemaking. Correspondingly, the *Home Box Office* idea of "adversarial comment"[146] appears to have been rejected. But what of the other elements of the "paper hearing"—the expanded notions of "notice," "comment," and "statement of basis and purpose" that the courts of appeals had developed? In fact the extent and context of rulemaking has changed enormously since the APA was adopted in 1946, and statutes such as the Freedom of Information Act reflect *new* ideas about the procedural context "upon which opposing social and political forces have come to rest." The Supreme Court's casual assumption about the record in *Overton Park*, as we have seen,[147] was a central factor in the development of the "paper hearing" idea. While the Supreme Court's *Vermont Yankee* opinion underscored the differing nature of records in informal rulemaking and on-the-record adjudication, it did not abandon *Overton Park* review and in later cases the Court has reaffirmed it.[148]

Scholarly opinion is generally dubious about the sweep of *Vermont Yankee*,[149] and most would agree that the paper hearing ideas remain vital. Unlike the oral procedures sought to be imposed in *Vermont Yankee*, these can be attached—however loosely—to the language of the APA itself. Permitting fresh understanding of that language as circumstances change reflects conventional judicial function. The nature of rulemaking, and for that matter of judicial review, has changed since 1946, and the Court ought not to be taken as having ignored those developments.

146. See note 128, above.

147. See note 116, above.

148. Motor Vehicle Manufacturers Assn. v. State Farm Mutual Ins. Co., 463 U.S. 29 (1983), discussed at pp. 263-64.

149. R. Stewart, Vermont Yankee and the Evolution of Administrative Procedure, 91 Harv. L. Rev. 1805 (1978); C. Byse, Vermont Yankee and the Evolution of Administrative Procedure: A Somewhat Different View, 91 Harv. L. Rev. 1823 (1978); A. Scalia, Vermont Yankee: The APA, The D.C. Circuit, And The Supreme Court, 1978, The Supreme Court Review 345; A. Neely, Vermont Yankee Nuclear Power Corp. v. Natural Resources Defense Council, Inc.: Response and Reaction on the Federal Judiciary, 14 U. Balt. L. Rev. 256 (1985).

Requiring rulemaking

If parties cannot force procedures on agencies beyond those reasonably related to the statute, can they force rulemaking to occur at all? Or is the decision to undertake rulemaking, by analogy to the decision to initiate a proceeding,[150] one that is entirely (or at least presumptively) within the agency's discretion? Section 553(e) of the APA requires each agency to permit interested persons "the right to petition for the issuance, amendment, or repeal of a rule." Yet forcing action once the petition has been received might appear a different proposition.

Occasional statutes affirmatively require rulemaking on stated subjects, taking the fact (if not the outcome) of rulemaking proceedings out of agency discretion. If the agency cannot lawfully refuse to adopt a rule, it should not be surprising to find the courts willing to command that rules be developed. This is particularly likely if (as it has done increasingly) Congress sets a statutory "action-forcing" deadline for promulgation of the rule. The problems here lie in fashioning effective relief when the agency remains hesitant or politically unable to act. While the court can command, and the agency may even agree, that a rule is to be promulgated by a certain date, the court cannot itself adopt a rule when the date passes. Personal remedies against the responsible administrator for situations brought about by genuine difficulty of issues, bureaucratic inertia within staff, or political resistance from outside the agency will likely appear unwarranted. In one recent case,[151] a district court found that the delay was attributable to presidential oversight under the executive order requiring economic impact analysis[152] and declared that the executive order could not be enforced in conflict with the statutory deadline; "OMB has no authority to delay regulations subject to the deadline in order to review them under the executive order. . . . [It] may review the regulations only until the time at which OMB review will result in the deadline being missed." Even with this protection, of course, the agency must itself generate the political will to act and be able to determine an appropriate outcome to the proceeding it has been commanded to conduct.[153]

Even where no such specific statutory instruction has been given, there remain two situations in which action might be forced. If an ad-

---

150. See pp. 150-52.
151. Environmental Defense Fund v. Thomas, 627 F.Supp. 566 (D.D.C. 1986), review pending.
152. See pp. 70-76.
153. See, e.g., A. Morrison, OMB Interference with Agency Rulemaking: The Wrong Way to Write a Regulation, 99 Harv. L. Rev. 1059 (1986).

ministrator simply has not implemented a congressional program, its intended beneficiaries may be able to require that he do so.[154] While rulemaking will often be the most natural means for the agency to accomplish this, however, courts may be unwilling to require (as discussed in the immediately following section) that this be the mode employed. Second, denial of a petition for rulemaking might under limited circumstances be found an abuse of agency discretion—if, for example, the agency has made a statement in the course of declining to issue a rule revealing a misunderstanding of its legal authority to act. However the court of appeals authority tending to sustain such review[155] has been placed in some doubt by the Supreme Court's subsequent ruling, that agency judgments about enforcement activity are presumptively unreviewable.[156] Here as there the factors influencing agency judgment—budget, personnel, policy program—are both not well suited to judicial oversight, and peculiarly subject to distortion if they can be commanded by private litigants.

Choice between rulemaking and adjudication

Courts "make law" as a by-product of deciding cases. Legislatures do so by the enactment of statutes. As the preceding pages have illustrated, agencies may create binding norms of conduct using procedural modes resembling each. The fact that agencies often have the power to use either technique leads some to describe them as having a choice in each instance how to proceed—by adjudication or by rulemaking—when considering the adoption of new norms. That view is often artificial ahead of time; often new norms emerge unconsciously from the accidents and structural incentives of a largely uncoordinated bureaucratic process.[157]

---

154. Thus, in Allison v. Block, 723 F.2d 631 (8th Cir. 1983), farmers who had defaulted on federal loans (and so risked losing their farm) persuaded the court to block foreclosure until the Secretary of Agriculture had implemented a statutory provision for a regime of discretionary relief. Executive branch refusal to implement a statute, like the impoundment of appropriated funds, note 40, p. 63, has been identified by even the most conservative of Supreme Court Justices as an appropriate occasion for judicial intervention. Motor Vehicle Manufacturers Assn. v. State Farm Mutual Ins. Co., 463 U.S. 29 (1983) (separate opinion).

155. See WWHT, Inc. v. Federal Communications Commission, 656 F.2d 807 (D.C. Cir. 1981); Natural Resources Defense Council, Inc. v. Securities and Exchange Commission, 606 F.2d 1031 (D.C. Cir. 1979).

156. Heckler v. Chaney, 470 U.S. 821 (1985), discussed at notes 62-64, above.

157. See P. Strauss, Rules, Adjudications, and Other Sources of Law in an Executive Department: Reflections on the Interior Department's Administration of the Mining Law, 74 Colum. L. Rev. 1231 (1974).

Nonetheless, the "choice" characterization provides a framework to think about the differences between the two modes of norm creation and, very occasionally, a basis for insisting that one or the other must be employed.

The general view is that rulemaking is the superior mode for the creation of binding new norms of conduct.[158] Its procedures engage a broader range of the interested community, albeit with less formality, and may be better suited to consideration and determination of the sorts of facts and other issues most likely to arise in the policymaking context.[159] The decision structure within the agency more fully engages both its staff expertise and the political responsibility of its leaders than the highly formal decision structure of adjudication. The product of rulemaking— a direct statement of positive law, accompanied by an explanatory statement—is likely to be more accessible both as text and in its placement in the standard legal materials, than will be a discussion dependent upon the facts of a particular adjudication and buried in an adjudicatory opinion. Finally, rulemaking operates prospectively. In contrast, a norm developed in the course of adjudication ordinarily will be applied to the party before the agency in the proceeding in which it is first announced. That party, then, will not have been precisely aware of the norm before its announcement in the course of that proceeding. "Since [an agency], unlike a court, does have the ability to make new law prospectively through the exercise of its rule-making powers," the Supreme Court remarked in the foundational decision on this issue,[160] "it has less reason to rely upon ad hoc adjudication to formulate new standards."

The case in which these words were uttered may be an excellent example of the difficulty involved in finding the "law" made by a judicial opinion, since the Court went on to say that "the choice made between proceeding by general rule or by individual, ad hoc litigation is one that lies primarily in the informed discretion of the administrative agency." It sustained the use of adjudication rather than rulemaking to elaborate new policy in that case. The officers of a company had applied for approval of its reorganization. The Securities & Exchange Commission (SEC) withheld approval, at first basing its decision on an understanding of then-existing judicial decisions. The Supreme Court narrowly reversed that opinion because the SEC's understanding of the judicial cases was erroneous,[161] and remanded the case for reconsideration in light of a correct

---

158. The classic treatment of this issue appears in D. Shapiro, The Choice of Rulemaking and Adjudication in the Development of Administrative Policy, 78 Harv. L. Rev. 921 (1965).

159. See pp. 161-62.

160. Securities & Exchange Commission v. Chenery Corp. (II), 332 U.S. 194 (1947).

161. SEC v. Chenery Corp., 318 U.S. 80 (1943). This first Chenery decision is

understanding of those cases. The SEC now reached the same result—several years after the application had first been made—on the basis of its own policy determinations.

This "second-chance" reasoning was the new policy that Chenery asserted could not fairly be applied to him, but had to be formulated by rule for prospective application. The Court rejected Chenery's argument. Agencies had to be permitted discretion to use adjudication, since in some cases "problems may arise in a case which the administrative agency could not reasonably foresee, problems which must be solved despite the absence of a general rule." In other cases, the newness, specialized character, or variability of the problem might make rulemaking seem inappropriate. As for the possible unfairness of retroactive application of the new rule to Chenery, that "must be balanced against the mischief of producing a result which is contrary to a statutory design or to legal and equitable principles."[162]

This, then, has been the general rule—that agencies have a broad and essentially unsupervised discretion in deciding between adjudication and rulemaking for the formulation of policy.[163] The retroactivity of applying freshly declared standards has occasionally been rejected on grounds of "unfairness." This has usually occurred in cases in which some new liability was sought to be imposed on individuals for past actions taken in good faith reliance on the policies that were then in effect.[164] Other circumstances in which rulemaking has been required are less easily characterized.

The FTC, for example, was compelled to use rulemaking rather than adjudicate in one case in which the governing statute gave its decisions

---

a frequently cited source for the proposition that agency judgments can be reviewed only on their announced reasoning. In contrast to its function in reviewing a lower court's judicial opinion, the reviewing court cannot consider alternative lines of reasoning that might have been (but were not) employed. See pp. 264-67.

162. Any seeming unfairness to Chenery is mediated by the narrowness of the Supreme Court's *first* reversal. It had been decided by a vote of 4-3, with two Justices not sitting. In the circumstances, one can say that Chenery had fair warning from the outset that the suitability of the proposed reorganization was open to doubt, even under existing judicial standards.

163. For a recent strong statement by the Supreme Court, see National Labor Relations Board v. Bell Aerospace Co., 416 U.S. 267 (1974).

164. See R. Gorman, Basic Text on Labor Law 18-20 (1976) for a general review of the cases. The National Labor Relations Board is the most frequent target of these arguments, both because its policies frequently vary with changes in presidential administrations and because it so rarely uses rulemaking to generate policy in the areas of its responsibility.

unusual force and effect.[165] One ordinary difference between rulemaking and caselaw is that the latter is not formally binding on persons who were not parties to the case in which it arises. Non-parties are always free to argue for the reconsideration of a prior decision or for its inapplicability to their circumstances (although such arguments may be unavailing). The FTC statute permitted the Commission to treat policies resulting from adjudications precisely as if they were rules, not open to reexamination in this way. Other cases seem to suggest that rulemaking may be required to structure the exercise of official discretion under grant programs, discretion that might otherwise be exercised in an arbitrary fashion which cannot be checked.[166]

From time to time the suggestion has been made that the opposite problem can arise, that an agency might employ rulemaking in circumstances that require the use of adjudication. This argument is often made when agencies adopt rules that have the effect of foreclosing what would otherwise be a factual issue to be determined in an adjudicatory hearing required by statute or due process. For example, one issue in individual hearings under the national disability insurance statutes is whether work the applicant is capable of exists in the national economy. (Under the statute, which is intended *not* to be an unemployment statute, the question is strictly one of the physical possibility of the applicant's holding such employment; it is not relevant whether the work is available near the person's home, whether vacancies exist, or whether he would be hired if he applied.) At one point, this question was resolved by having vocational experts testify, based on their understanding of the precise situation of the individual seeking to obtain or retain benefits. The Department of Health and Human Services later adopted a rule that created a grid of factors—age, literacy, degree of impairment, previous work

---

165. Ford Motor Co. v. FTC, 673 F.2d 1008 (9th Cir. 1981), cert. denied, 459 U.S. 999 (1982).

166. Morton v. Ruiz, 415 U.S. 199 (1974) is an example, one that commentators have had substantial difficulty in understanding. Others include some of the series of cases requiring the Secretary of Agriculture to implement a legislative program for discretionary relief of farm foreclosures, one of which was summarized in note 154, above. That case left the choice how to implement the statute to the Secretary's discretion—the orthodox position; but later decisions in other circuit courts required rulemaking on the ground that Congress saw an "urgent need . . . for deferral relief to farmers" and it is "a bit late to begin the accumulation of [case-by-case] decisional guides." Curry v. Block, 738 F.2d 1556, 1563 (8th Cir. 1984). Perhaps the court feared, also, that case-by-case decision might never have to find the circumstances warranting deferral—that the Secretary could use it to continue his apparent policy of refusing to implement the program Congress had created.

experience—and specified how the question of employability was to be resolved for each combination of the grid. Experts no longer needed to testify. For example, under the grid, an unskilled woman of limited prior education and advanced age whose impairments rendered her capable only of light work would be regarded as disabled; but the grid permitted characterizing a somewhat younger woman in the same medical position as disabled only if she were also illiterate or unable to communicate in English. The Supreme Court found no difficulty with this substitution of rule-determined facts for trial. The facts at issue had to do with job availability in the national economy, not the particular applicant. Only if the facts to be determined were unique to the party before the tribunal, "adjudicatory" rather than "legislative" in that sense, would the use of rulemaking be foreclosed.[167] Other results are consistent with this ruling.[168]

Investigation

As earlier remarked,[169] the APA is little concerned with agency investigative procedures. Internal instructions or manuals organizing these activities are within the Act's publication requirements, unless "disclosure could reasonably be expected to risk circumvention of the law."[170] Agency personnel engaged in these activities are to be segregated from its decisional process in on-the-record adjudication. The Act does not itself authorize any investigative act, whether inspection, required report, or subpoena; but it provides that no such act or demand may be "issued, made, or enforced except as authorized by law,"[171] and in the particular case of subpoenas provides briefly for judicial enforcement. Overall, the message conveyed—limited but important—is that investigative procedures are neither implicit nor ordinarily self-enforcing; they must be specially authorized by statute (the APA is not such a statute), and their enforcement as well depends upon the law, which may require invocation of the courts.

---

167. Heckler v. Campbell, 461 U.S. 458 (1983).
168. FPC v. Texaco, Inc., 377 U.S. 33 (1964); Vermont Yankee Nuclear Power Corp. v. Natural Resources Defense Council, Inc., discussed at notes 140-49, above. A different question might be presented when the individual asserts that special facts about his circumstances warrant an exception to the generally applicable rule. But see FCC v. WNCN Listener's Guild, 450 U.S. 582 (1981).
169. See p. 137.
170. 5 U.S.C. § 552(b)(7)(E), as amended by the Anti-Drug Abuse Act of 1986, P.L. 99-570.
171. 5 U.S.C. § 555(c).

Investigative procedures can be classified under three different heads, each of which has had some attention in the preceding pages: physical inspection;[172] required forms and reports;[173] and subpoenas, or compulsory process.[174] Together, they mark the citizen's most common experience with government and employ the bulk of government's regulatory personnel. On the whole, however, they are informal and summary procedures, about which there is ordinarily little controversy.

Inspections

The most visible of the three, perhaps, is inspection, a technique that may be either investigative or, in itself, decisional. Decisions to award motor vehicle licenses, to classify agricultural produce, or to quarantine neighborhoods are made directly on the basis of an inspector's observations, without intervening hearing. The APA's Section 554(a)(3) recognizes this by excluding from the ordinary procedures of adjudication "proceedings in which decisions rest solely on inspections, tests, or elections." The question, *which* decisions may so rest, is surprisingly little developed. One sees dim reflections of it in adjudicatory hearings in which the issue becomes whether an inspector used appropriate technique.[175]

The investigative uses of inspection, on the other hand, have prompted development of a fair amount of constitutional litigation, discussed in the opening pages of this essay.[176] The result has been establishment of a capacity on the part of most persons subject to inspection laws to force inspectors to secure prior judicial approval of any proposed inspection.[177] The confrontational and decidedly adversary attitudes ac-

---

172. See pp. 27-29.

173. See pp. 29-30.

174. See pp. 31-32.

175. See, e.g., People v. Porpora, 154 Cal. Rptr. 400 (Super. L.A. Co. 1979), in which an inspector had determined on sampling the defendant's commercial fish catch that the defendant had kept a larger proportion of a protected fish (Pacific mackerel) than California law permitted. A complaint that "failure . . . to preserve the fish . . . denied [the defendant fisherman] access to evidence that would have enabled him to impeach the reliability of the sampling technique and [its] results" was summarily rejected. Cf. Board of Curators of the University of Missouri v. Horowitz, 435 U.S. 78 (1978) and Regents of University of Michigan v. Ewing, 106 S.Ct. 507 (1985), rejecting due process claims for trial-type hearing made by students who had failed courses in state-run universities.

176. Pp. 27-30; see also Administrative Law: Cases and Comments, pp. 673-701.

177. The protection of prior judicial approval is not available for those engaged

companying some inspections are thought by some to reflect characteristic differences between American approaches to administrative justice and those of other nations.[178]

Inspection can have a dual character, seeking either to identify non-compliance, or to develop means for assuring compliance, with regulatory measures. In this context, much will depend on the attitude the inspectorate brings to its work. Because the constitutional developments are associated with the rights of persons suspected of crime to government regularity in developing evidence against them, they may tend to reinforce if they do not generate a posture in which the goal of inspection is seen as identifying and imposing sanctions for non-compliance, rather than encouraging compliance or otherwise promoting the positive ends of law.[179]

Required forms and reports

If inspections are not the citizen's commonest encounter with regulation, then the filling out of required forms and reports surely is. These are materials required from classes of individuals or corporations; they may be as simple as a customs declaration, or as complex as the Federal Trade Commission's requirements for annual economic reporting by conglomerate corporations.[180] The minimal constitutional constraints bearing on these requirements have already been outlined;[181] it should be stressed that unless the courts can be persuaded the requirement of a report is *solely* for the purpose of acquiring evidence of the filer's criminal conduct,[182] no privilege against filing a report will be recognized. Ordinarily, the generality of such requirements, as with tax forms, is sufficient pro-

---

in "closely regulated enterprise," such as a coal mine or a nuclear power station; another exception, hardly surprising yet perhaps of greater moment here, is the requirement to submit to customs inspection at the border.

178. See p. 29.

179. Wyman v. James, 400 U.S. 309 (1971), is one of the few Supreme Court recognitions of this problem. Welfare caseworkers were to make quarterly inspections of the homes in which dependent children supported by welfare lived. Was this for the detection of welfare fraud, as those demanding the protection of a search warrant insisted, or to help develop programmatic benefits for the child? Some of both, doubtless; and in this case the Court emphasized the helpful side and refused to find a warrant required. For apt criticism, see R. Burt, Forcing Protection on Children and Their Parents: The Impact of Wyman v. James, 69 Mich. L. Rev. 1259 (1971).

180. See FTC Line of Business Report Litigation, 595 F.2d 685 (D.C. Cir.), cert. denied, 439 U.S. 958 (1978).

181. See p. 30.

182. Marchetti v. United States, 390 U.S. 39 (1968).

tection. Accordingly, the failure to file a report may itself be made the basis for a fine or other sanction. In the administrative context, this is an important distinction from a subpoena, which seeks to compel named persons to produce identified documents (or information). Before a sanction can be imposed for non-compliance with a subpoena, as will be developed in the next section, judicial enforcement is generally required.

The principal general control over agency reporting requirements at the federal level is the Paperwork Reduction Act of 1980,[183] a statute remarkable for its explicit recognition of presidential oversight over even the independent regulatory commissions. An agency seeking to adopt a required report must secure approval from the OMB,[184] which is authorized to require coordination with other agencies, or to find that the proposal is not "necessary for the proper performance of the functions of the agency, including whether the information will have practical utility." The OMB process of approval is conducted like an informal rulemaking, and is open to public participation (although statutorily shielded from subsequent judicial review). Even the independent regulatory commissions must participate; they may, however, override an OMB disapproval of their proposed action by a publicly explained majority vote.

Compulsory process

A subpoena, or compulsory process, is a directive to a named individual to produce particular documents or information. It can arise in the course of an established agency adjudication, when it is strongly analogous to discovery demands in civil litigation; or it may be issued in the course of and to support an agency investigation that has not yet developed to the hearing stage. The latter is legally the more interesting use of subpoenas (and probably the more frequent). The courts seem increasingly to be recognizing that when a subpoena is sought in adjudication, the presiding administrative law judge can be relied upon to exercise necessary controls. Correspondingly, they are tending to permit the agency to impose the same sorts of sanctions for non-compliance with agency subpoenas in that context as a district court would impose for non-compliance with discovery demands in a civil trial.[185] But where a

---

183. 44 U.S.C. §§ 3501-20.

184. The OMB is discussed on pp. 76-77.

185. That is, failure to respond may be taken as an admission, or a basis for refusing permission to cross-examine a relevant witness, or the like. Cf. NLRB v. International Medication Systems, Ltd., 640 F.2d 1110 (9th Cir. 1981), cert. denied, 455 U.S. 1017 (1982), stating the more traditional view requiring judicial enforcement, with the more recent Atlantic Richfield Co. v. U.S. Department of

subpoena is used at the investigatory stage, a neutral agency official may be lacking. The demand to produce comes from the investigative, as-it-were prosecutorial side of the agency. Here, subpoenas are not recognized as self-enforcing. Unless its subject has incentives to comply with an information demand,[186] the agency will be required to seek judicial assistance to compel obedience.

The judicial inquiry is not itself likely to be demanding. In general, an agency will be required to show only that the subpoena might produce information bearing on its responsibilities, not that it will. The agency need not demonstrate any "probable cause" to seek the information from the subpoena subject.[187] The relevant questions will be whether the subpoena is issued in pursuit of an authorized objective;[188] whether the evidence sought appears to be germane to a lawful subject of inquiry; whether the subpoena makes demands that are unreasonably vague or burdensome;[189] whether it has been issued in proper form; and whether there exists a privilege—such as the privilege against self-incrimination for individuals[190]—not to reply. A summary procedure is employed in district court to test these issues, and one's impression of the cases is that enforcement is not often refused.

Nonetheless, the procedure can introduce substantial delays and opportunities for agency failure of will, which are doubtless valued by subpoena resisters. The agency is required to bring the enforcement action in court, and that requires it to win the approval and use the resources of the Department of Justice, neither of which is invariably to be had. Once the subpoena has been enforced, appeals are available to the courts of appeal and, by certiorari, to the Supreme Court. (This would not be

---

Energy, 769 F.2d 771 (D.C. Cir. 1984). It is not asserted that agencies could themselves impose more dramatic penalties, such as the power to imprison for contempt.

186. For example, a license applicant or any other person seeking affirmative action from an agency may be compelled to satisfy an information demand, in practical terms, by the need to secure an agency response to its application.

187. Oklahoma Press Publishing Co. v. Walling, 327 U.S. 186 (1946).

188. For obvious reasons, courts have resisted efforts to inquire onto agencies' "real" motive for issuing apparently justified subpoenas; inquiries into the possibility of "bad faith" are generally limited. See pp. 265-66.

189. The corrective for a vague or burdensome subpoena is more likely to be some arrangement for increasing the definiteness or moderating the burden imposed by the subpoena than a complete refusal to enforce. For example, relief might provide for inspection of the material at the information-holder's premises as an alternative to requiring its delivery to the agency. A finding of vagueness or burdensomeness is perhaps more likely when the subject of the subpoena is a third party, not itself subject to regulation by the agency making the information demand.

190. See pp. 31-32.

true for a subpoena issued during the course of a civil trial, because that ruling would be considered interlocutory; but the agency's complaint seeking subpoena enforcement initiates a discrete proceeding so far as the judicial system is concerned, and so an immediate appeal may be taken.) When the order of enforcement becomes final, only the first stage is complete. Any question about compliance, including a proceeding to have the respondent found in contempt of court for failure to produce the demanded materials, requires a second judicial proceeding. This brief, and not exhaustive, description should make apparent that a person who resolutely seeks to block an investigation can tie up the proceedings for long periods, and have the benefit of many different views of the correctness of the demands made.

State administrative law

Under American federalism,[191] each state regulates its own administrative procedure, and generalizations would be hazardous.[192] It may be appropriate, however, briefly to remark on two drafts of model state administrative procedure legislation promulgated by the National Conference of Commissioners on Uniform State Laws.[193] The draft of 1961 has been adopted in whole or in part by more than half the states. A more recent draft of 1981 is not yet widely adopted but possibly points the direction of change in administrative procedure legislation generally.

The 1961 draft is rather brief, comprising sixteen operative sections. While taking some account of the smaller size and greater informality of state government, it is clearly modeled on the federal APA, chiefly addressing informal rulemaking and "contested cases"—on-the-record proceedings that, in this case, include ratemaking as well as licensing and other adjudicatory proceedings required to be decided after an oppor-

---

191. See pp. 7-8.

192. For a recent account, see A. Bonfield, The Federal APA and State Administrative Law, 72 Va. L. Rev. 297 (1986); references to the administrative codes of each of the states may be found in Appendix B to Administrative Law: Cases and Comments.

193. The National Conference is a body supported by state governments generally to study legislative subjects on which uniform state laws may be desirable and recommend draft legislation to that end. This is *not* federal activity, and the Congress is not involved. Adoption or not of the drafts depends on the legislatures of each state, and in the course of adoption any given state may amend the draft considerably. Some drafts—the Uniform Commercial Code, for example—come to be universally adopted, or nearly so; others may find a following in only two or three states.

tunity for hearing. The draft does not require state equivalents of the federal administrative law judges to be presiding officers when the agency itself does not hear (although in practice many states provide for such officials), but in other respects does call for the sharp separation of functions within the agency that characterizes the federal regime in ordinary adjudication.

The 1981 draft, by contrast, is a fully fleshed out code of some 94 sections organized into five articles. Of chief interest here are Articles III, "Rule Making," and IV, "Adjudicative Proceedings." Each elaborates the procedures it governs, in what might be thought an effort to assure both larger participation by the public, and more substantial political and judicial controls.

Thus, while rulemaking retains its "notice and comment" character under Article III, a number of additional procedures or requirements characteristic of executive or judicial developments at the federal level are added:

- Agencies are to maintain a public rulemaking docket of all matters under active consideration for rulemaking, specifically including proposals not yet announced, with an indication who at the agency may be contacted about it.[194]

- Notice of proposed rulemaking must include the text of the proposal.[195]

- The issuance of a regulatory analysis and/or the holding of an oral hearing may be required by the request of political overseers or a substantial number of interested private persons.[196]

- Fresh notice and opportunity to comment is required if the agency decides to adopt a rule whose content might be surprising in light of its initial proposal.[197]

- The agency is required to maintain, and hold open for public inspection, a defined record of the rulemaking, including any written data in its possession which it considers in connection with the rulemaking.[198]

- Agency rulemaking is explicitly made subject to political as well as judicial review, and the agency is required periodically to review the

---

194. § 3-102. Similar federal requirements have been imposed by executive order. See text at note 77, p. 72.
195. § 3-103(3).
196. §§ 3-104, -105.
197. § 3-107.
198. § 3-112.

corpus of its rules, as a whole, to assess their effectiveness and need for change.[199]

Article IV, on adjudicative proceedings, would create a centralized administrative law judge corps[200] and in other respects heighten the detail and formality of the provisions made for formal adjudicative proceedings.[201] The draft's most striking innovations, however, lie in its efforts to provide for generalized informal adjudicatory procedures:

- Adjudicatory procedures defined in the act are required "upon the application of any person" in all matters other than investigative matters, or matters explicitly committed to agency discretion.[202] The procedure for formal adjudication, fully comparable in its elaboration to the federal provisions, is presumptively applicable.

- "Conference adjudicative hearings" are defined for matters presenting no factual disputes, or involving relatively minor sanctions (less than 10 days' suspension from school or public employment; less than $1,000), considerably abbreviating the ordinarily applicable requirements of formal adjudication.[203]

- "Emergency adjudicative proceedings" permit summary action "to prevent or avoid . . . immediate danger," to be followed by ordinary proceedings if sought.[204]

- "Summary adjudicative proceedings" are defined for matters of little public interest and relatively low claim to procedural protection, such as very minor sanctions, the denial of application for public goods such as housing or public employment, or public contracting. An opportunity for informal presentation of views and response to agency position is to be provided if any sanction is involved; for simple denial of an application for public goods, an agency is required only to give notice of its action and any available administrative review.[205]

The result is to make the provision of some form of hearing the rule even for informal agency adjudication, and to place on agencies the requirement of justifying departures from that norm.

---

199. Chapter II, §§ 3-201 to -204. The drafters present a choice between review by the governor, or by a select committee of the legislature, but prefer the former. An apparently successful state venture of this character in California is described in M. Cohen, Regulatory Reform, Assessing the California Plan, 1983 Duke L.J. 231 (1983).

200. § 4-301.

201. Chapter II, §§ 4-201 to -221.

202. § 4-101(a), -102(b).

203. Chapter IV, §§ 4-401 to -403.

204. § 4-501.

205. §§ 4-502 to -506.

6
NON-JUDICIAL CONTROLS OF ADMINISTRATIVE ACTION

Preceding pages have already made apparent that judicial review is merely the most formal and lawyerly of controls that may be brought to bear on administrative action. Judicial review usually occurs after the fact, and in any event is limited to assessing the legality of particular actions rather than the appropriateness, direction, or distribution of policy effort. Thus, it will often be far from the consciousness of important agency officials as they shape their agency's business.[1] Those officials are much more likely to be aware of signals from the network of relationships and controls suggested by the materials of the present chapter, a network many of whose elements have already been encountered.

Political intervention or oversight

The relationships of President and Congress to the business of regulation were examined in the third chapter of this essay, and there is no need to repeat that analysis here.[2] One should have emerged from those pages with the impression that the oversight and appropriations activities of Congress, and the coordinative and consultative activities of the Pres-

---

1. An example may be noted in a book written by my late colleague, William Cary. Author of the major law school teaching materials on corporate law and distinguished both as scholar and practitioner of corporate law, Professor Cary was Chairman of the Securities & Exchange Commission during the Kennedy Administration, 1961-63, and wrote a well-regarded book drawing on his experiences there, Politics and the Regulatory Agencies (1967). Judicial review is not mentioned once in the whole of its discussion of the regulatory efforts of the SEC during his chairmanship. Asked about this by a (then) fledgling teacher of administrative law, he responded that the subject simply was not important in his daily life. The relationships suggested by this chapter of the present essay, it should be added, figure importantly in the pages of Professor Cary's book.

2. In addition to the materials in that chapter, see pp. 140, 163-64, and 171-74.

ident (notably through the device of the required analytic report), give each substantial, and sometimes competing, influence over an agency's course. A look at an agency's structure and allocation of time will confirm that impression. Most agencies have major offices concerned with congressional relations and (outside the independent regulatory commissions) the OMB. Communications from the White House, congressional inquiries and testimony to congressional hearings all consume significant amounts of agency resources, especially at the top. Agency heads may spend hours preparing for (and will personally attend) a congressional oversight hearing or a White House briefing; they will rarely review the briefs to be submitted and argued by their attorneys in judicial review proceedings.

It was earlier remarked[3] that the courts seem increasingly aware and approving of these influences, influences given point by the sharp change in political perspective on regulation that occurred when President Reagan took office in 1981. Thus, the following appears in one recent Supreme Court opinion:

> Judges are not experts in the field and are not part of either political branch of the Government. Courts must, in some cases, reconcile competing political interests, but not on the basis of the judges' personal policy preferences. In contrast, an agency to which Congress has delegated policymaking responsibilities may, within the limits of that delegation, properly rely upon the incumbent administration's views of wise policy to inform its judgments. While agencies are not directly accountable to the people, the Chief Executive is, and it is entirely appropriate for this political branch of the Government to make such policy choices. . . . When a challenge to an agency [decision], fairly conceptualized, really centers on the wisdom of the policy, rather than whether it is a reasonable choice within a gap left open by Congress, the challenge must fail. In such a case, federal judges—who have no constituency—have a duty to respect legitimate policy choices made by those who do.[4]

This general realism about the fact, role, and importance of political oversight does not, however, preclude a negative judicial reaction in some settings in which it becomes apparent that it has occurred. Two settings likely to provoke such a reaction, already encountered, are worthy of mention: when the oversight appears to violate the constraints of on-the-

---

3. See pp. 172-74.
4. Chevron, U.S.A., Inc. v. Natural Resources Defense Council, Inc., 467 U.S. 837 (1984).

record proceedings; and when it introduces into a decision factors that Congress has not made relevant.[5]

In on-the-record proceedings

The reader is now in a position to appreciate the sharp differences in procedure, decision structure, and expected objectivity as between those proceedings (especially formal adjudications) that are required to be decided on the basis of a record, and those that are not.[6] Efforts at covert political influence in formal, on-the-record adjudication would violate explicit statutory prohibitions against ex parte contacts[7] and, if detected, produce an emphatic reversal. Even in an informal adjudication, one court found objectionable the State Department's private transmission to an agency of representations from the French and German governments, that it thought influenced the outcome of the proceedings inconsistently "with the principles of fairness implicit in due process."[8] In an on-the-record proceeding, even overt efforts at political influence may be found to have this inconsistency. Judges, after all, are not themselves ever brought before a congressional committee or White House staffer to answer for the policies they may adopt in their opinions.

An influential case illustrating the last proposition arose when the Chairman of the Federal Trade Commission testified before a Senate oversight committee about the FTC's interpretation of statutory language. The Commission had announced its interpretation in adjudication, in a case the Commission had recently remanded to one of its ALJ's for decision of other matters. The Senate committee chairman subjected the Chairman to repeated, sharp criticism of the FTC's position. By the time the ALJ had finished the remanded hearing and returned it to the Commission for further review, five years later, a number of FTC officials who had been present in the hearing room had themselves become FTC Commissioners. A court of appeals concluded that the hectoring they had witnessed required these Commissioners to have disqualified themselves from this further proceeding. (The Chairman who testified had submitted

---

5. See notes 43, p. 145, and 139, p. 173.
6. Compare pp. 143-49 with pp. 159-74.
7. See the text at note 43, p. 145.
8. United States Lines, Inc. v. Federal Maritime Commission, 584 F.2d 519 (D.C. Cir. 1978). While the court's reasoning depended on the heavily criticized decision in Home Box Office v. FCC, discussed at pp. 169-71, the fact that this proceeding involved adjudication, with individual interests at stake and the idea of the record more sharply defined, gives it continuing influence. Compare the discussion of Sierra Club v. Costle, pp. 172-74.

his resignation to the President at about the time of the Senate hearing, and so was no longer sitting.) "To subject an administrator to a searching examination as to how and why he reached his decision in a case still pending before him, and to criticize him for reaching the 'wrong' decision . . . sacrifices the appearance of impartiality—the sine qua non of American judicial justice."[9]

How is such a result to be reconciled with recognition that judges "have no constituency," and that the political branches that do have constituencies may appropriately bring their influence to bear on those policy matters legislation has left open for agency decision? But for the connection to pending adjudication, there could hardly have been objection to the committee's interest in how the FTC interpreted its governing statute. If agencies can choose to make policy either by rulemaking or adjudication,[10] does their choice of adjudication insulate them from political oversight even as to the general policy content of their decisions, as distinct from the precise outcome of particular cases? Unlike judges, agency heads *do* appear regularly before Congress, and these appearances might be very restrained indeed if responsible agency officials could not be questioned on any general matter that happened to be involved in litigation then pending before their agencies. The working response to this dilemma—ordinarily acceptable to agency and committee alike— is to engage freely in discussion of policy, but to leave out of the conversation any mention of particular proceedings in which the policy issues under discussion may arise. Agency counsel and committee staff may even work together to assure that this occurs. There is "no constitutional violation in a Congressional attempt to influence the regulatory interpretation of statutes," while fairness *is* implicated in an effort to force the outcome of a particular adjudication on individual grounds.[11]

Extraneous factors

The second characterization that may lead judges to disapprove political interventions is that they have introduced extraneous factors into decision, factors that cannot lawfully play a part in the conclusion to be reached. Thus, when convinced that a congressman had used his political control over the appropriations process to coerce the Secretary of Transportation into approving a challenged road project (the congressman threatened to block funds for other work unless the project was author-

9. Pillsbury Co. v. FTC, 354 F.2d 952 (5th Cir. 1966).
10. See pp. 178-82.
11. See U.S. ex rel Parco v. Morris, 426 F. Supp. 976 (E.D. Pa. 1977).

ized), a court reversed the approval and insisted the Secretary reconsider the matter without regard to this inappropriate factor.[12] Of course, one must learn that such political controls have been used, and that the inappropriate factor has played a role in the decision. The reluctance of the courts to inquire "behind the scenes" of the decisional process absent strong indications of impropriety[13] makes this an unlikely outcome. An example arose when a newspaper reported that, during a briefing on rulemaking of importance to his constituency, an important Senator had made remarks "strongly hinting" that he might not support other measures of importance to the administration unless the rulemaking outcome included some recognition of his constituents' interests (as it then did); the court did not find this single account of "strong hint[s]" to be "substantial evidence of extraneous pressure significant enough to warrant a finding of unlawful congressional interference."[14]

"Open government" regulations

Earlier pages have already discussed the impacts on rulemaking of the Freedom of Information Act and the less widely applicable Government in the Sunshine Act.[15] The openness these acts require reflects what is perhaps a peculiarly American political idea, that publicity can serve as an effective constraint on government action—that "sunlight is the best disinfectant." Thus, it seems appropriate here to give a general overview of these acts, and briefly to mention two other statutes with similar legislative motivation, the Privacy Act and the Federal Advisory Committee Act. As has generally been done in this essay, only the federal statutes will be described. But the reader should be aware that open government statutes had their genesis in state law, and that even more forceful legislation of this character is to be found at the state level.

Freedom of Information Act

The Freedom of Information Act was first adopted in 1967 as an amendment to Section 552 of the APA, which previously had been con-

---

12. D.C. Federation of Civic Associations v. Volpe, 459 F.2d 1231 (D.C. Cir. 1971), cert. denied, 405 U.S. 1030 (1972). See note 139, p. 173.
13. See pp. 265-66.
14. Sierra Club v. Costle, discussed at pp. 172-74.
15. See pp. 163-64.

cerned chiefly with publication of materials about agency structure, procedures and policy;[16] FOIA was vastly strengthened in 1974 and has been subject to minor revisions in the years following.[17] The statute requires every federal agency to make "promptly available to any person" any of its records the requester "reasonably describes" in accordance with its published procedural rules, subject to only limited statutory exceptions. The agency may charge a fee for the service, but that fee is a limited one: if the records are sought for commercial use, it may include reasonable costs for search, duplication and review; but if sought by the newsmedia or an educational or noncommercial scientific institution, it may charge no more than standard costs for duplication.[18] The obligation to provide the records is backed by severely limited time for agency response and review,[19] unusually stringent provisions for judicial review,[20] and the assessment of litigation costs including attorney fees and even possible civil service penalties when records are wrongfully withheld.[21]

This is an openness requirement of remarkable breadth. Enacted for its expected contributions to journalistic, scholarly, and political understanding of government, it has also transformed the rulemaking process and benefits all for whom the information available might have economic value; a cottage industry has grown up in Washington to exploit this

---

16. See pp. 137-38 and 157-58.

17. The major treatise on FOIA, looseleaf in two volumes, is O'Reilly, Federal Information Disclosure. An annual developments note has appeared since 1973 in a spring number of the Duke Law Journal.

18. The Anti-Drug Abuse Act of 1986, P.L. 99-570, which amended FOIA in a number of minor respects, changed the Act's fee structure to differentiate between commercial and other requesters; even the higher fees asked of the former are unlikely to approximate the government's actual costs in complying with FOIA. 5 U.S.C. § 552(a)(4)(A).

19. Agencies are given ten working days (subject to a single extension of the same length for described cause) to make their initial response to a request; twenty working days to review an initial denial of materials if agency review is sought. 5 U.S.C. § 552(a)(6). In practice, some agencies have been overwhelmed by requests and not provided the resources to respond to them. Responding to the dilemma created by this situation, courts have permitted delays consistent with reasonable diligence. See Open America v. Watergate Special Prosecution Force, 547 F.2d 605 (D.C. Cir. 1976).

20. Judicial review is to occur "de novo"—that is, without any necessary regard to the application of agency expertise to the decision—and the judge may herself examine the contents of the documents being withheld to determine whether they are within the disclosure requirements of the act. The agency is required to follow an expedited schedule in answering complaints seeking review, and the judge is encouraged (although no longer required) to give the matter priority on her calendar. 5 U.S.C. § 552(a)(4)(B,C).

21. 5 U.S.C. § 552(a)(4)(E,F).

potential. Putting the exemptions aside for a moment, *every* agency record is subject to the Act.

While what constitutes an "agency record" is not statutorily defined, subsequent litigation gives this phrase a broad reach. Four factors have been identified: whether materials were generated within the agency, the presence of materials in an agency's files, the exercise of agency control over materials, and agency use of materials for agency purposes.[22] If materials have been obtained by an agency for its use, and so are in its files, they will be regarded as "agency records" even though not generated by the agency itself. Only if materials are not in official possession or can somehow be characterized as personal to a particular officer rather than relating to the organization are they likely to be found not to be "records."[23]

This leaves, as the only possible basis for maintaining the confidentiality of "agency records," nine exemptions stated in Section 552(b) of the Act. Five of these nine can be described, generally, as embracing differing forms of governmental privilege; the remainder protect private individuals or corporations from the harm that might be caused by publication of information about them or of information that they have supplied. The governmental privileges include (roughly in diminishing order of strength) information properly classified for defense or diplomatic reasons; material specifically privileged by statute; law enforcement information whose disclosure threatens harm to public or private interests; internal, pre-decisional governmental discussions of policy choice; and materials bearing on personnel rules and practices. The remaining exemptions reach "trade secrets and commercial or financial information obtained from a person and privileged or confidential"; personal files, such as personnel or medical files, "the disclosure of which would con-

---

22. Kissinger v. Reporters Committee for Freedom of the Press, 445 U.S. 136 (1980); see also Forsham v. Harris, 445 U.S. 169 (1980). These cases denied "record" status, respectively, to a Secretary of State's handwritten notes of his telephone conversations, consistently treated by him as personal documents and not shared with departmental personnel; and to the raw data a private researcher had amassed under a government contract but had not given into the government's possession (although under the contract the government could ask for it).

23. Thus, in Bureau of National Affairs v. United States Department of Justice, 742 F.2d 1484 (D.C. Cir. 1984), reporters sought the appointment records of the head of the Department's Antitrust division—doubtless seeking evidence of improper contacts. Daily calendars generated by his secretary for distribution to his subalterns, to inform them of his availability, were "agency records"; the appointment calendars she kept for his personal convenience and did not distribute were; not "agency records," even though she might occasionally have let staff glance at them.

stitute a clearly unwarranted invasion of personal privacy"; and two more specific—perhaps special interest—provisions: information generated in regulating or supervising specific financial institutions, such as banks; and geological and geophysical data about wells.

Note that the application of an exemption to an "agency record" does not end inquiry. FOIA also requires that "any reasonably segregable portion of a record shall be provided to [the requester] after deletion of the portions which are exempt." For some of the exemptions this is not an important qualification; judges are not disposed to order line-by-line reclassification of generally sensitive national security documents, and tend to accept that even apparently harmless snippets from investigative files can convey damaging information. For the less forceful forms of privilege, however, it has major impact. As noted in the preceding discussion of rulemaking,[24] the government can withhold pre-decisional discussions of policy, but ordinarily must disclose the factual materials on which those discussions are based;[25] personal files may no longer threaten the invasion of privacy if all identifying characteristics can be stripped from them before their release.[26] Determination of these issues, as of the application of the exemptions themselves, is made uncomfortable by the fact that counsel for the requester cannot be shown the withheld information, since to show it would moot the case. An elaborate practice of government affidavits has grown up, supplemented by occasional judicial inspection of the documents in camera. The government is encouraged to be as forthcoming as possible in its affidavits by the knowledge that it bears the burden of sustaining the withholding of the documents.[27]

Foreign governments and enterprises are doubtless particularly sensitive about the administration of those exemptions bearing immediately on their own interests. Material about an accident at a nuclear generating

---

24. See pp. 163-64.

25. See generally NLRB v. Sears, Roebuck & Co., 421 U.S. 132 (1975). Occasionally, but not invariably, the government has been able to convince a court that revealing the agency's belief about the facts—the sorting and characterizing its staff may have done—will itself reveal the "predecisional process" and so is exempt.

26. Department of the Air Force v. Rose, 425 U.S. 352 (1976); and see Arieff v. U.S. Department of the Navy, 712 F.2d 1462 (D.C. Cir. 1983), where the court felt required to use ex parte affidavits to decide whether embarrassing information could be inferred even from "scrubbed" lists of the prescription drugs that had been supplied by a Navy pharmaceutical office to congressmen, Supreme Court Justices, and others.

27. Vaughn v. Rosen, 484 U.S. 820 (D.C. Cir. 1973), cert. denied, 415 U.S. 977 (1974) is the widely followed source of this procedure; it has been more recently described in Arthur Andersen & Co. v. Internal Revenue Service, 679 F.2d 254 (D.C. Cir. 1982).

station, for example, is not easily classified as either national security data or "trade secrets and commercial or financial information obtained from a person and privileged or confidential." Another nation whose domestic policies would not ordinarily lead it to make such information public—at least not immediately—may be surprised to find it in the American press, and discouraged from subsequent sharing of this important data with American regulators. Foreign corporations are unlikely to share sensitive commercial data that they fear will find its way into a competitor's hands. Much of the most interesting FOIA litigation and legislative consideration today concerns both the reach of the "trade secrets" exemption and the availability of procedures by which the supplier of information may be able to participate in any governmental decision whether to release it.

The reach of the "trade secrets" exemption is in fact a good deal less broad than might be imagined. That a corporation supplying data regards it as sensitive or confidential is not enough. Research plans supplied by a not-for-profit organization, however confidential, were not "commercial or financial information";[28] "trade secrets" may be limited to information about the productive process.[29] And to sustain an agency's invocation of the exemption, a court may have to be convinced not only that the information in question is commercial or financial and of a kind that would not ordinarily be made available to the public, but also that its "disclosure will harm legitimate private or governmental interests in secrecy."[30]

An agency decision to release information that its supplier believes to be within this exemption could be characterized in at least two ways. The agency may be wrong in a judgment that the exemption does not apply. Alternatively, it may agree that it *could* withhold the information by invoking the exemption, but believe as a matter of discretion that it would be preferable to release it. It is important to start by recognizing that neither of these judgments presents a question under FOIA as such. That statute merely creates rights in the requester. If an agency by error or as an act of discretion chooses to reveal more than it has to, FOIA itself provides no relief to the supplier of the information.[31]

The information supplier is not, however, completely without remedy. Other statutes may create legal obligations to maintain information in

---

28. Washington Research Project, Inc. v. Department of Health, Education and Welfare, 504 F.2d 238 (D.C. Cir. 1974), cert. denied, 421 U.S. 963 (1975).

29. Public Citizen Health Research Group v. FDA, 704 F.2d 1280 (D.C. Cir. 1983).

30. National Parks and Conservation Assn v. Morton, 498 F.2d 765 (D.C. Cir. 1974).

31. The leading decision on this matter is Chrysler Corp. v. Brown, 441 U.S. 281 (1979).

confidence, that would be violated by an erroneous judgment or would stand in the way of an assertion on the agency's part that it had discretion to release. As a means of encouraging those subject to their regulation to supply needed information more freely, many agencies have adopted regulations assuring suppliers of both notice when information they have supplied is requested and an opportunity to participate in any consideration of its release. And the courts have developed a "reverse FOIA action," permitting review in accordance with ordinary APA standards of review.[32] While not so generous as the de novo review provided by FOIA itself, the reverse FOIA action provides a possibility of control over agency behavior that has been useful to suppliers and that—to date— has obviated any need for legislative specification. As a practical matter, scholarly studies have revealed little leakage of proprietary information from the government under FOIA.[33] The litigated cases often arise from public interest groups' efforts to secure data on which to base demands for regulation rather than competitive prying.[34]

Government in the Sunshine Act

In 1976, following the perceived success of FOIA in making governmental processes more accessible, Congress enacted the Government in the Sunshine Act.[35] The Act was passed at the height of the movement to enhanced public participation in agency proceedings,[36] and in response also to perceptions that regulated industry groups often had access to agency deliberations the public generally did not share.[37] This Act applied

---

32. See the Chrysler case, cited in the preceding note. On the ordinary APA standards of review, see pp. 239-69. National Organization for Women, Washington D.C. Chapter v. Social Security Administration, 736 F.2d 727 (D.C. Cir. 1984), well states the arguments for and against de novo review on reverse FOIA actions, with the latter prevailing.

33. See an analysis undertaken for the Administrative Conference of the United States, R. Stevenson, Protecting Business Secrets Under the Freedom of Information Act: Managing Exemption 4, 34 Ad. L. Rev. 207 (1982).

34. The Chrysler Corp. and NOW cases, notes 31 and 32, above, both concern efforts to secure data about employment practices for potential use in anti-discrimination actions. While the same data might be used by a competitor to improve its own record in hiring blacks or women at its competitor's expense, there is no indication this has ever occurred.

35. The leading commentary on the act and its history is R. Berg & S. Klitzman, An Interpretive Guide to the Government in the Sunshine Act (1978).

36. See pp. 149-54.

37. The decision in Home Box Office, Inc. v. FCC, described in the text following note 125, p. 169, was made just a year after the Act took effect; the many private meetings described in that opinion were occurring, then, as the legislation took shape.

a regime already common in the states to all the multi-member federal agencies—by and large, the independent regulatory commissions. Under it, commission "meetings" are generally required to be held in public, on advance notice published in the Federal Register; closings are subject both to judicial supervision and to a requirement of transcription that permits after-the-fact revelation should the agency's judgment prove to have been erroneous, or should the reason for closure pass.[38]

Ten exemptions to the open meetings requirement are provided, roughly corresponding to the FOIA exceptions. The one notable exception to this pattern is that no provision is made for closing pre-decisional discussions of general policy issues, as in rulemaking. Despite the implications of publicity both for staff candor and for the effectiveness of the agency's subsequent negotiations with OMB and congressional committees about its needs, even meetings for the development of agency budget proposals have been found subject to the openness requirements.[39]

A more likely basis for a determination that the Act does not apply may lie in the definition of a "meeting." While the courts of appeal had seemed disposed to give that term an embracive meaning, reaching all "meetings at which agency interests are pursued," the Supreme Court recently adopted a narrower view.[40] A committee of the FCC had traveled to Europe to share ideas with European and Canadian counterparts about the enlargement of overseas telecommunications services. The companies already serving the American market sought to compel these meetings to be held openly. The meetings could easily be characterized as deliberative, and bore on agency business. Yet they could not have resulted in the taking of "agency action" within the meaning of the APA. The Court thus concluded they were at best preliminary actions, outside the

---

38. It also permits members of Congress to demand the transcriptions in the course of oversight, and then make whatever use of them they choose. See San Luis Obispo Mothers for Peace v. NRC, 751 F.2d 1287 (D.C. Cir. 1984), vacated in part 760 F.2d 1320 (1985), affirmed 789 F.2d 26 (en banc 1986), where this technique fueled a concerted (and ultimately unsuccessful) effort to go behind the announced reasoning on the Nuclear Regulatory Commission in licensing a power plant, to show what the "real"—and assertedly improper—reasons for that action had been. Perhaps aware of the chilling impact if their own deliberations were transcribed, the majority refused to consider the transcripts in themselves to be sufficient evidence of the "bad faith" that is necessary for a court to go behind an agency's announced reasons for judgment and examine its deliberative processes. See pp. 265-66.

39. Common Cause v. Nuclear Regulatory Commission, 674 F.2d 921 (D.C. Cir. 1982).

40. FCC v. ITT World Communications, 466 U.S. 463 (1984), reversing 699 F.2d 1219 (D.C. Cir. 1983).

notice and openness requirements. The Supreme Court's opinion warned of an "impair[ment of] normal agency operations without achieving significant public benefit" if the Act were applied to preliminary discussions or to "informal conversations of the type Congress understood to be necessary for the effective conduct of agency business." This reasoning was arguably inaccurate as a reading of the legislative history; like that of FOIA, the history stresses the benefits anticipated from openness and the need to curb agency resistance to it. The opinion tracks recent scholarly findings, however, about the Act's impact in fact. An empirical survey undertaken for the Administrative Conference of the United States found

> reasons to believe that there has been a shift in patterns of decision-making behavior . . . away from collegial processes toward segmented, individualized processes in which . . . members are isolated from one another. One reason is a decline in the importance of meetings as decisional vehicles. . . . Another reason for suggesting diminished collegiality is an indication of a sense that collegial bodies are impaired in the performance of the agency leadership responsibilities placed in them by statute . . . [because] speculative exploration of sensitive matters at an early stage . . . is difficult to do in public. . . . [41]

Whether the Court's opinion, roughly contemporaneous with the study, will allow the collegial leadership of the commissions to reassert authority over their staffs will be interesting to watch.

Federal Privacy Act

The Federal Privacy Act[42] was enacted in 1974 to meet growing concerns about the accuracy and availability of governmental files containing information about individuals. Largely, but not exclusively, it was a response to the emergence of the computer data bank, by which it was feared government could vastly magnify the detail and intrusiveness of its knowledge of private lives. Only individuals, not corporations, are protected by the Act. For individuals—especially for federal employees concerned about the contents of their personnel files—the Act provides controls of substantial importance.

The Act in general reflects five principles of "fair information practice" identified by an influential Report of the Secretary of Health, Education

---

41. D. Welborn, W. Lyon & L. Thomas, Implementation and Effects of the Federal Government in the Sunshine Act (1984).
42. 5 U.S.C. § 552(a).

and Welfare's Advisory Committee on Automated Personnel Data Systems:[43]

(1) There must be no personal data recordkeeping systems whose very existence is secret.

(2) There must be a way for an individual to find out what information about him is in a record and how it is used.

(3) There must be a way for an individual to prevent information about him that was obtained for one purpose from being used or made available for other purposes without his consent.

(4) There must be a way for an individual to correct or amend a record of identifiable information about him.

(5) Any organization creating, maintaining, using, or disseminating records of identifiable personal data must assure the reliability of the data for their intended use and must take reasonable precaution to prevent misuse of the data.

As these principles suggest, the Act is more concerned with regularity of information uses than with restrictions on use. Accordingly, information seekers are encouraged to obtain it from the subject of the inquiry or with her knowledge. They must provide notice, actual or formal, of the reasons for which information is being sought, the authority on which it is being sought, and any consequences of failure to respond. Only "relevant" information is to be sought or retained in government files. An individual is entitled to access to identifiable records concerning her, with exceptions reminiscent of the first, third and seventh exemptions of the FOIA (those having to do with restricted access materials and investigations). Procedures are set out by which she may seek to have information she regards as inaccurate corrected. The Act's limitations on acquisition and use of information, while responsive to privacy needs in the computer era,

explicitly recognize the legitimate needs of government departments to acquire, rely on and disseminate relevant personal information. ... A fair reading of [the Act's provisions intended to enhance information quality] reveals that high standards of information quality are by no means inevitable.

... In contrast to the FOIA, the right of access afforded by the Privacy Act is not designed to free up public entry to the full range of government files. Rather, access under the Privacy Act is merely a necessary adjunct to the broader objective of assuring information

---

43. Records, Computers, and the Rights of Citizens 41 (1973).

quality by obtaining the views of persons with the interest and ability to contribute to the accuracy of agency records.[44]

Federal Advisory Committee Act

We have several times encountered the perception common in the late 1960's and 1970's that government agencies operating under traditional procedures had been captured by the very interests they had been intended to control, and that steps were necessary to assure greater visibility and broader public participation in the regulatory process.[45] The Federal Advisory Committee Act of 1972,[46] a precursor of the Government in the Sunshine Act, was one of the early legislative responses to this problem. Advisory committees are boards of experts or community members brought together by an agency to advise on policy issues or serve as a sounding board. They may be local citizens brought together to advise Bureau of Land Management officials about the important uses of federal lands in the area,[47] nationally respected scientists asked to advise the Nuclear Regulatory Commission about technological issues arising in nuclear power reactor regulation, or businessmen and others asked to advise the Department of Commerce on its policy developments. The perception was that these boards did not represent balanced cross-sections of the relevant communities—that they were being used to work out in private discussions regulatory solutions that ought to have been the product of public procedures. Corrective measures imposed by the Act include requirements of balanced membership, open meetings on advance notice, and periodic agency clearance of any advisory committee with the OMB[48] for compliance with the Act.[49]

---

44. Smiertka v. United States Dept. of Treasury, 447 F. Supp. 221, 226-227 (D.D.C. 1978), remanded for consideration of possible mootness, 604 F.2d 698 (D.C. Cir. 1979). See also A. Alder & M. Halperin, Litigation Under the Federal FOIA and Privacy Acts (9th ed. 1984); Report of the Privacy Protection Study Commission, Personal Privacy in an Information Society (1977); Project, Government Information and the Rights of Citizens, 73 Mich. L. Rev. 1323 (1975); J. Hanus and H. Relyea, A Policy Assessment of the Privacy Act of 1974, 25 Amer. U.L. Rev. 555 (1976).

45. See, e.g., p. 153.

46. P.L. 92-463, 5 U.S.C. App. I.

47. See the text at note 36, p. 120.

48. See pp. 76-77.

49. Individual consultations, or one-time reference to a group as distinct from creation of a body for continuing consultations, are excluded from the Act. See R. Wegman, The Utilization and Management of Federal Advisory Committees (1983).

Ombudsmen and watchdog agencies

Ombudsmen form a common and apparently effective non-judicial control over administrative action in parliamentary systems. My colleague Walter Gellhorn's studies of Ombudsmen and their functioning[50] were once thought to be precursors of the emergence of similar institutions in the United States. Perhaps because looking after constituents' problems in dealing with the bureaucracy has become so important a part of the life of members of Congress,[51] a function they would not readily relinquish, the institution has not gained a significant foothold at the federal level. Occasional states and state and local agencies do employ persons so designated, although their actual functions may vary considerably.

Institutional watchdog agencies can be identified, although none intended to be prompted into action by citizen inquiry or for the possible benefit of individuals rather than the public as a whole. Two such agencies that have already been identified are OMB[52] and GAO[53], attached to the President and the Congress, respectively. In 1978, legislation created independent Inspectors General in each of the executive departments to serve as guardians against waste and abuse,[54] and other legislation sought to prevent reprisals against federal employees who brought misconduct or shoddy practice to light.[55] At the state and local levels the audit function is commonly placed in a separately elected official, an Auditor or Comptroller, specifically responsible for assuring the efficiency and honesty of government. And in at least one state, a central agency is responsible for oversight of all agency rulemaking, to assure its proper justification and clear expression.[56]

Procedural oversight: the Administrative Conference of the United States

The Administrative Conference of the United States, whose recommendations have already been encountered in these pages,[57] began op-

---

50. W. Gellhorn, When Americans Complain (Harvard 1966); Ombudsmen and Others: Citizens Protectors in Nine Countries (Harvard 1966).
51. See p. 52.
52. See pp. 76-77.
53. See pp. 58-59.
54. P.L. 95-452, 5 U.S.C. App.
55. Civil Service Reform Act of 1978, P.L. 95-454 § 3.
56. See note 199, p. 189.
57. See, for example, notes 131, p. 171, and 145, p. 175.

erating in 1968 as a body responsible for continuing analysis and development of federal administrative procedure. The Conference is headed by a small permanent staff of government employees, an Administrator appointed by the President, and a council of twelve appointed from public and private life. Its principal work, however, is done by its assembly. This is a deliberative body of about 100 drawn from both government agencies and the worlds of academia and private practice. Twice each year the assembly meets to debate and adopt recommendations for the improvement of administrative procedures. These recommendations will have been drafted on the basis of studies performed under contract by academicians and (occasionally) individual attorneys. While Congress has been less respectful of the results of this (ordinarily successful) consensual process than one might imagine it should be,[58] the recommendations have often produced significant change at the administrative level. As important, the forum has permitted professional views on such matters as hybrid rulemaking[59] and presidential oversight of agency policymaking[60] to coalesce in a fashion that seems then to have informed and influenced subsequent judicial pronouncements.

Similar influences arise from informal sources, notably the American Bar Association[61] and its Administrative Law Section, a group of public and private members of the Association who practice administrative law. This group regularly generates recommendations for legislation and internal changes in administration, and publishes the quarterly Administrative Law Review, a useful source of continuing analysis of practical administrative law issues.

Informal policy oversight: the general and trade press

In many Washington agencies, functionaries scan the national press for stories bearing on the agency and its responsibilities and reproduce

---

58. The United States does not have, at the federal level, any tradition of routine legislative adoption of draft legislation, however carefully or consensually prepared.

59. See notes 131, p. 171, and 145, p. 175.

60. See pp. 70-76 and 171-74; P. Verkuil, Jawboning Administrative Agencies: Ex Parte Contacts by the White House, 80 Colum. L. Rev. 943 (1980) is the ACUS report on the matter.

61. An analysis undertaken by a special commission of the ABA, Commission on Law and the Economy, Federal Regulation: Roads to Reform (1979), was particularly influential in shaping the deregulatory measures of the years following its release.

them for circulation to the agency leadership. One more often learns in this way of failures than of successes, of negative public attitudes, of emerging scandals that may result in legislative oversight hearings unless (or even if) resolutely dealt with, or of tough regulatory problems requiring resolution. The national press generally does not cover agency business on a continuing basis. Emergencies and scandals draw the public's attention more sharply than jobs routinely well done. But the influence of a story or television interview on an agency's agenda can often be substantial.[62]

Where the regulatory stakes warrant it, specialist publications emerge whose undertaking is to provide interested private communities with detailed information about a particular agency's functioning and directions—often at rather high annual cost.[63] These publications, too, are carefully read within the agency; their reporters sometimes learn before agency heads do of developments or problems in the lower reaches of the bureaucracy with which the leadership will have to deal. The leadership uses them, as well, to give regulated industries information about future policy directions that may help guide their course, or bring opposition or contrary views out into the open.

To similar ends, agency heads find it valuable to spend time cultivating relationships with the regulated community—appearing at its conventions, speaking at its lunches. The raised eyebrow can produce desired behavior at a minimal expenditure of agency resources. This intimacy can have its corrupting impact, however, if it begins to appear instead to be the knowing wink of an agency "captured" by those it is supposed to regulate,[64] particularly when the regulator begins to see those with whom he is thus associating as the source of his future career. This problem, described in the literature as the problem of "the revolving door," is one that has been hard to deal with, given the choice to have

---

62. In the writer's personal experience, the Nuclear Regulatory Commission's attention was commanded for the better part of a month by the consequences of the staged televised resignation of one of its engineers, who asserted that his safety judgments were being ignored and then took employment with a prominent group generally opposed to the construction of nuclear power plants. The resignation was, of course, a legitimate story; and preparation for the ensuing congressional hearings caused some self-examination that may have been helpful from a regulatory perspective. It also, however, forced the agency's priorities, requiring personnel to be released from other work to reassess analyses that, in the end, were not significantly changed. See also R. Stewart, The Discontents of Legalism: Interest Group Relations in Administrative Regulation, 1985 Wisc. L. Rev. 655 (1985).

63. Thus, Broadcast Magazine serves those with interests in the FCC's work; Nucleonics Week, those who need to follow the NRC.

64. See pp. 149-54.

political rather than civil service leadership of its regulatory bodies.[65] Nonetheless, informal sources of knowledge about the concerns of both regulator and regulated are essential to the functioning of the enterprise. If the relationship between them is not fully adversary, that is in good part because Congress has not chosen, and would not choose, such a relationship.[66] The regular interactions that some see as lying at the root of the agency "capture" problem are also the lubricant that, by permitting anticipation, reduces the friction of the regulatory process.

"Public interest" model, and actors

The final source of non-judicial controls or influences warranting mention are the groups very largely responsible for the emergence of the public interest model of administrative action in recent years, associations undertaking to represent the interests of those on whose behalf regulation is ostensibly to occur. That "the public" does not often appear separately in administrative proceedings is not due simply to the proposition that the agency is, in some sense, directed to represent their interests; the agency is also to take some account of the interests of the regulated, who do appear. Nonappearance of the public also reflects the economic truth of the matter, that any one individual's interest in effective regulation is both small and highly diffuse. Ordinarily, individuals are not easily organized nor made willing to pay for such representation unless through government itself. The successes the civil rights and civil liberties movements enjoyed in achieving change through litigation in the middle part of the current century, however, encouraged the formation of groups for other purposes, either general[67] or targeted on some specific project or dispute.[68] The footnotes to the preceding sentence call attention to groups responsible for influential environmental cases already encountered in these pages; the examples could be multiplied in other fields.[69]

---

65. See P. Strauss, Disqualification of Decisional Officials in Rulemaking, 80 Colum. L. Rev. 990 (1980) for a general discussion.

66. See L. Jaffe, The Illusion of the Ideal Administration, 86 Harv. L. Rev. 1183 (1973).

67. The Sierra Club, note 135, p. 172; the Natural Resources Defense Council, Inc., notes 72, p. 154, and 140, p. 174.

68. Citizens to Preserve Overton Park, note 112, p. 165; San Luis Obispo Mothers for Peace, note 38, above.

69. E.g., Office of Communication of the United Church of Christ, note 69, p. 153; National Welfare Rights Organization, note 73, below; National Association of Radiation Survivors, note 113, p. 47.

These groups are voluntary associations, supported by membership donations and, occasionally, gifts from wealthy individuals or private foundations wishing to encourage their activities.[70] To some extent, they are supported as well by factors that tend to reduce their costs. Their staff members are willing to work for salaries considerably below those received by equally skilled counterparts representing industry, because of the non-monetary rewards they receive from such representation.[71] The rule on litigation costs ordinarily protects them from having to bear any significant costs other than their own, even if they lose the litigation. And, occasionally, statutes provide for public subvention of their expenses (including attorneys' fees) should they prevail.

The presence of these groups, actual or potential, as participants in the administrative process changes the character of that process. It is not simply that, as former Chief Justice Burger remarked in a passage earlier quoted,[72] they provide an expression of views the agencies themselves perhaps cannot be relied upon fully to represent. Over time, many have become experts in the matters to be decided by the agencies before which they regularly appear, with significant resources for evaluating scientific or economic controversy as well as law. Their principals become known to and, if they are serious and well informed, respected by the agency officials with whom they deal. Moreover, the informal processes of administration, negotiation and adjustment are rendered far more complex when multiple interests must be accommodated.[73] In preparing for

---

70. The Ford Foundation's financial support during the early 1970's, for example, was a major impetus to the formation of many of the "public interest" litigators, especially in the health, safety and environmental fields.

71. The beginning salary for a new lawyer at large Wall Street law firms is now in excess of $70,000 per annum; for a lawyer at the Natural Resources Defense Council, who ordinarily must have professional experience to be considered for a position, less than half of that.

72. See p. 153.

73. Consider, for example, National Welfare Rights Organization v. Finch, 429 F.2d 725 (D.C. Cir. 1970). National welfare legislation is administered by the states, under federal supervision. When a state appears to be departing from applicable federal standards, that was ordinarily a matter for adjustment between federal and state officials. Federal officials could threaten to cut off a state's funds if, after a hearing, they could prove the state out of compliance. For understandable reasons, this extreme remedy was rarely invoked.

When, on one such occasion, federal officials did initiate such a hearing, representatives of welfare recipients (the National Welfare Rights Organization) insisted on being accorded party status in the hearing. The court agreed with this claim. "Without participation," it reasoned, "issues which [NWRO] might wish to raise about the character of the state's plan may have been foreclosed as a topic for review." Recognizing, however, the complications their participation

hearings or explaining rulemaking outcomes, agency staff must look in both directions—whether it can be taken to task for laxness as well as strictness, for failures of action as well as over-aggressiveness.

The groups' participation is not inevitably beneficial to one's largest sense of the public interest. As these groups often do not have economic stakes, as such, in the outcome (and in any event would have difficulty taking instructions from their membership respecting appropriate compromise), they may be prepared to insist on small points that an economic actor would readily compromise. Moreover, no certainty can be had that *all* imaginable public interests in a given proceeding's outcome will be represented when some are; persons interested in scenic beauty or the preservation of a commercial fishery may appear to oppose a new power facility, but not those who would benefit from reduced rates or assured supply.[74] Appreciation of these and like points, it has already been suggested,[75] appears to be contributing to a certain judicial recession from the public interest representation idea. But it is impossible to imagine that any withdrawal will reach the point of abandonment. As a participant in the regulatory process with substantial knowledge, high incentive, and the capacity to inflict large costs upon the agency and other participants in any proceeding, the public interest litigator can exercise major influence—whether or not litigation ensues.

might bring to settlement negotiations, the court added:
> We do not hold that this intervenor status creates in appellants a right to participate in any way in the Secretary's informal effort . . . to bring a state into conformity, nor do we limit his right to terminate a hearing, once called or begun, upon a determination by him that it is no longer necessary because he believes that conformity has been achieved.

74. Scenic Hudson Preservation Conference v. FPC, 354 F.2d 608 (2d Cir. 1965), cert. denied, 384 U.S. 941 (1966).

75. See p. 154; see also R. Stewart, note 62, above.

$\equiv 7$
THE JUDICIAL SYSTEM

A general introduction to the judicial system of the United States is given at another point in this essay.[1] That description makes evident that, like the United Kingdom, the United States (with minor exceptions) lacks a system of specialized courts dedicated specifically to the review of administrative action. Direct review of federal administrative action— that is, a judicial proceeding seeking to enforce an agency action, to deny it legal effect, to require it, or to preclude it—ordinarily occurs, instead, in the national courts of general jurisdiction. One can see in this choice evidence of the American theory of separation of powers,[2] which stresses the importance both of checking among the three branches of government and of avoiding, not competition between the branches, but the possible hegemony of any one. To have an administrative court within the executive would be to invest too much power in the executive—to leave it unchecked.

The present chapter explores the possibilities and some of the mechanics of obtaining judicial review. As in previous parts of this essay, only the federal law is directly discussed; review at the state level generally proceeds on analogous principles, although in some states the traditional common law writs have greater play and in others some of the preliminary issues of obtaining federal review, such as standing, are not much developed. The chapter following this one examines issues respecting the scope of judicial review, once obtained. The final chapter considers issues associated with the indirect review of government action that occurs when monetary damages are sought from the government or one of its officials to redress harm brought about by an asserted illegality.

---

1. See pp. 78-86.
2. Dealt with on pp. 12-18.

Obtaining judicial review

Statutory and non-statutory review of administrative action

The appellate jurisdiction of the federal courts is wholly statutory. From that perspective the title of this section of the essay is paradoxical. Nonetheless, the contrast between "statutory" and "non-statutory" review is used to distinguish between the precisely defined jurisdiction a limited-purpose statute may create over a particular agency's actions, and the extensive jurisdiction created by statutes conferring judicial jurisdiction generally. "Statutory review" occurs pursuant to a statute designating a particular court or courts to exercise review authority over described decisions of a particular agency. "Non-statutory review" is available whenever the party seeking review can frame a complaint that meets the general requirements for invoking the jurisdiction of the courts.

One begins any effort to secure review of an administrative action by searching for "statutory review" provisions in this sense. The APA is specific that *if* statutory review is provided for, it is the preferred form of proceeding.[3] The statute providing for review itself will govern the court, venue, timing and form for review. Such provisions are commonest respecting the outcomes of formal proceedings, those decided on the basis of an identified record. Often, although not invariably, initial jurisdiction over federal statutory review proceedings will be placed in the courts of appeal.[4] When a formal record and elaborate findings result from the administrative process, trial is not required, and permitting several levels of judicial review could be wasteful.[5]

The APA does not itself confer review jurisdiction of the more general character, but strongly endorses the view that non-statutory review jurisdiction should be found. "[I]n the absence or inadequacy" of statutory review provisions, it states, the form of proceeding for judicial review is "any applicable form of legal action, including actions for declaratory judgments or writs of prohibitory or mandatory injunction or habeas corpus, in a court of competent jurisdiction."[6] All "[a]gency action made

---

3. 5 U.S.C. § 703.
4. See pp. 83-85.
5. Partial canvassing of the federal statutes, and an effort at theoretical exegesis, can be found in H. Friendly, Federal Jurisdiction: A General View (1973) and D. Currie & F. Goodman, Judicial Review of Federal Administrative Action: The Quest for the Optimum Forum, 75 Colum. L. Rev. 1 (1975).
6. 5 U.S.C. § 703.

reviewable by statute *and final agency action for which there is no other adequate remedy in a court* are subject to judicial review."[7] What persons are entitled to seek review is dealt with in more detail below,[8] but it suffices to say here that the statute has been read to embrace essentially all those likely to be particularly affected, in fact, by the regulatory action they may wish to challenge. Except for suits for money damages, dealt with in the final chapter below, the statute gives unqualified consent for the United States to be named as a defendant, together with the agency and any responsible officials (in their official capacity).[9] And review is also available to defendants in civil or criminal proceedings brought by the agency or the government for enforcement, unless a statute provides adequately for review at an earlier stage and precludes such consideration on enforcement.[10]

Jurisdiction is in fact readily obtained in the United States district courts. Under the most commonly invoked general provision of the Judicial Code, the district courts have jurisdiction over all controversies raising a "federal question" and not otherwise assigned; that is, they enjoy jurisdiction over all questions that necessarily require the resolution of an issue or issues of federal law.[11] Since the claim that an agency action reviewable under the APA was unlawful necessarily raises such an issue, the establishment of jurisdiction is a trivial matter.[12] A suit may be brought in any district court having venue—generally, where the agency has offices, or the regulatory event in question occurred, or where the plaintiff is located—without regard to the amount in controversy. The only possible hurdle lies in the possibility that the court will find the matter unsuited to judicial resolution—a judgment extremely rare in practice although the subject of much puzzlement for lawyers, scholars and students; these issues, also, are taken up within.[13]

---

7. 5 U.S.C. § 704.

8. See pp. 225-28.

9. 5 U.S.C. § 702.

10. 5 U.S.C. § 703. The effect of provisions limiting review at the enforcement state is ordinarily only to narrow the issues that can be considered then. Thus, the question whether an EPA rule was adequately supported by the materials of the rulemaking, or adopted following proper procedures, may be raised only in a proceeding to challenge the rule, filed within 60 days of the rule's adoption; but the constitutionality of the rule or the appropriateness of its application to a particular defendant is not an issue that must be raised at that time.

11. 28 U.S.C. § 1331.

12. Other general statutes, somewhat more limited in their reach and hardly necessary to invoke given the ease with which 28 U.S.C. § 1331 can be used, include 28 U.S.C. § 1337 ("regulating commerce") and 28 U.S.C. § 1339 (postal matters).

13. See pp. 229-34.

Before the APA had been interpreted in this manner, defining an acceptable cause of action for review required an artificial form of analysis that may be useful to state, since it is still occasionally encountered and used. Under this "legal rights" analysis, one is to analogize the behavior of the government agency or official being complained of to that of a private individual. If a common law action could be brought against a private individual in the circumstances—say, for defamation in the case of an offense to personal reputation, or for trespass in the case of an intrusion on private property—then the official could be sued and made to defend on the ground of the lawfulness or privileged character of her actions.[14] Except for cases in which monetary damages are actually being sought from government officials for allegedly unlawful conduct,[15] this analysis need rarely be pursued today. The APA adequately frames the necessary cause of action.

Jurisdiction may also be claimed on the basis of a number of statutes providing for special remedies, such as suits against the federal government for monetary relief,[16] or against state or local officials for civil rights violations.[17] An often-used remedy permits a district court to "declare the rights and other legal relations of any interested party . . . whether or not further relief is or could be sought," in any "case of actual controversy[18] within its jurisdiction, except with respect to Federal taxes."[19] Another provision of importance for administrative lawyers empowers the district courts to issue the writ of mandamus, one of the writs developed in the English common law, to federal officials.[20] The particular office of a writ of mandamus is to command the person to whom it is addressed to fulfill some duty owed to the plaintiff, a duty which has been violated. This statute, then, confers on the district courts plenary jurisdiction to issue an order directing "an officer or employee of the

---

14. The classic explanation of this theory appears in Associated Industries of New York State v. Ickes, 134 F.2d 694 (2d Cir. 1943).

15. See pp. 276-81.

16. See pp. 274-76.

17. See pp. 276-81.

18. See note 94, p. 78, and pp. 223-24, below.

19. This is the Declaratory Judgment Act, 28 U.S.C. §§ 2201-2. Although not itself a grant of jurisdiction, the Act supplies a cause of action that easily meshes with jurisdictional provisions such as 28 U.S.C. § 1331, the source of general "federal question" jurisdiction.

20. 28 U.S.C. § 1361. The other common law writs—certiorari, prohibition, quo warranto and habeas corpus—are little used in administrative law practice, although the last (a challenge to the legality of personal detention) finds use in immigration proceedings. As to it, see P. Bator, P. Mishkin, D. Shapiro and H. Wechsler, The Federal Courts and the Federal System, ch. 10 (2d ed. 1973).

United States or any agency thereof to perform a duty owed to the plaintiff."

This is one of the remedies already provided for, in effect, in the Administrative Procedure Act, so that one might wonder why a litigant would ever bother using this special provision. It was much more important in an earlier day, when "federal question" jurisdiction could be invoked only on a showing that at least $10,000 was in controversy. Any residual importance (which is disputed) would lie in the absence of any necessity to relate the review being sought to the APA and its standards respecting proper parties, timing, scope of review, etc. To bring a cause of action under the "federal question" statute ordinarily requires invoking APA review; the cause of action under the mandamus statute is, simply, for the writ.

Can this difference create an occasional advantage for the plaintiff? That question is hard to answer without having an understanding of the scope of review under the APA, developed in the chapter following, as well as the further materials of this chapter. Two considerations would argue against there being any substantial advantage: First, one can imagine few reasons why courts charged with operating under both statutes would encourage differentiation between the statutes. That neither was sought by Congress nor is supported by obvious public policy advantages. Thus, the tendency of the courts ought to be (as it largely appears to have been) to merge the two heads of jurisdiction, to make them indistinct. Second, historically the mandamus remedy has been unavailable to review the exercise of governmental discretion; the existence of "discretion" was taken to defeat the argument that there existed any "duty" that could be judicially enforced. This factor has grown less important as courts have accepted that there can be a duty to exercise discretion, to do so considering only appropriate factors, etc.—all of which can be understood as duties owed to particular plaintiffs and enforceable by them.[21] Even so, it lurks as a potential obstacle, one that the courts have less incentive to remove now that APA review is generally available under the "federal question" jurisdiction.[22] Nonetheless, possible differences in the threshold showings necessary to invoke judicial review—for example, the APA's requirement that there have been "final agency action"[23] as a condition for obtaining APA review—raise some chance that the mandamus action would prove useful.[24]

---

21. See, e.g., Work v. Rives, 267 U.S. 175 (1925).
22. Cervase v. Office of the Federal Register, 580 F.2d 1166 (3rd Cir. 1978).
23. See pp. 229-32.
24. Thus, a statutory preclusion of review associated with Medicare legislation

The presumption of reviewability

As a general matter, American law presumes that any administrative action that has reached the point of finality[25] within executive government is susceptible to judicial examination. The APA says as much in two ways: first, by stating that "except to the extent that prior, adequate, and exclusive opportunity for judicial review is provided by law, agency action is subject to judicial review in civil or criminal proceedings for judicial enforcement";[26] second, by stating that "final agency action for which there is no other adequate remedy in a court [is] subject to judicial review."[27] Nonetheless, it was not until 1967 that the Supreme Court decided the case regarded as most clearly endorsing that presumption—and that over vigorous dissent. As prior discussion has already hinted,[28] very recent developments suggest some possibility that, in the special area of executive discretion to set enforcement priorities, the opposite presumption is in course of development.

The 1967 case, *Abbott Laboratories v. Gardner*,[29] involved a challenge to a rule that had been adopted by the Food and Drug Administration, requiring prescription drug manufacturers to include information on their labels that would help consumers identify equivalent (and perhaps cheaper) drugs made by others. The government insisted that review was not available until enforcement proceedings were brought. That stage would never be reached if the manufacturers simply complied and changed their labels as commanded, rather than face the severe costs and penalties that could result from successful enforcement proceedings. For one concerned both with parsimony of government effort and encouraging voluntary compliance with (generally valid) administrative action, the government position is an attractive one. Permitting review of the rule risks delaying its successful implementation for however long the review process takes. It significantly lowers the cost of unsuccessfully seeking review, from suffering a successful enforcement action to the net cost (or gain) of litigating expenses minus any benefits obtained from delay. It thus invites the strategic use of review to postpone the effec-

---

foreclosed APA review, see pp. 219-20, below, but another court concluded that it left open the possibility of mandamus relief. Ellis v. Blum, 643 F.2d 68 (2d Cir. 1981). See, generally, C. Byse & J. Fiocca, Section 1361 of the Mandamus and Venue Act of 1962 and "Nonstatutory" Judicial Review of Federal Administrative Action, 81 Harv. L. Rev. 308 (1967); Note, 1973 Duke L.J. 207.

25. Finality is discussed on pp. 229-32.
26. 5 U.S.C. § 703.
27. 5 U.S.C. § 704.
28. See pp. 151-52.
29. 387 U.S. 136 (1967).

tiveness of requirements that those seeking review might privately concede to be lawful. Nonetheless, the rule, once adopted, constitutes a final "agency action" under the APA,[30] and a bare majority of the Court relied strongly on the presumption that such actions are reviewable in rejecting the government's argument. "[T]he APA's 'generous review provision' must be given a 'hospitable' interpretation . . . [and] only upon a showing of 'clear and convincing evidence' of a contrary legislative intent should the courts restrict access to judicial review."

As this quotation may suggest, the government's argument in *Abbott Laboratories* had relied, in part, on a contention that the particular statute under which the FDA adopted its rule contemplated that judicial review would not occur prior to the rule's enforcement.[31] This contention sought to invoke a threshold provision of the APA's judicial review provisions, that they apply

except to the extent that—
    (1) statutes preclude judicial review or
    (2) agency action is committed to agency discretion by law.[32]

This language states the principal exceptions to the presumption of reviewability, which will be taken up in turn in the following paragraphs. At the outset, note two features of the provision: First, it qualifies or modifies everything that follows. Those provisions that permit review (the main focus of this chapter and the chapter following) apply only where this preclusion language does not. Second, it is open to applications that preclude judicial review only in part. That is, "to the extent that" suggests the possibility of a statute that precludes some but not all review, or commits some but not all decision to agency discretion.

Statutory preclusion of review

Explicit preclusion. Occasional statutes will state, in terms, that some or all decisions taken under them are not subject to review; or severely constrain review in one way or another. One way of illustrating the strength of the presumption of reviewability is to remark that the courts do not easily assume that this has been done; a provision that an administrator's judgment is to be "final" or "final and conclusive," for example, has been taken not to preclude review altogether, but to restrict

---

30. " 'Agency action' includes the whole or a part of an agency rule. . . . " 5 U.S.C § 551(13).

31. Its other principal contention, that the dispute was not "ripe" for judicial resolution, is treated below, at pp. 233-34.

32. 5 U.S.C. § 701(a).

the scope of review given.[33] Thus, these courts have given less than ordinary attention to the question whether sufficient factual support existed for the administrator's judgment; but they still have considered issues of statutory authority and necessary procedure.

Even explicit formulations have been resisted to a degree. Thus, the claims of military veterans for benefits are decided by an agency, the Veterans' Administration, whose decisions "on any question of law or fact under any law" it administers are made final and conclusive. "[N]o . . . court of the United States," the statute adds, "shall have power or jurisdiction to review any such decision." But whether either the classifications Congress has created or the procedures it has chosen for distributing benefits meet *constitutional* standards, the Supreme Court concluded, is not a question that arises "under" such a law, and so these questions remain available for judicial review.[34]

It would be a mistake to ascribe this resistance simply to judicial imperialism. Separation of powers theory[35] cannot admit that Congress has the power effectively to deny the courts their constitutional standing and role. Control of some forms of legislative and executive action seems a necessary element of the courts' position. To be sure, Article III of the Constitution states that the Supreme Court's appellate jurisdiction over (inter alia) "cases . . . arising under this Constitution, the Laws of the United States, and Treaties . . . " is conferred subject to "such exceptions, and under such regulations as the Congress shall make"; this language seems to place Congress in full control. Yet what is an "exception" in the constitutional sense is a question for judicial as well as congressional interpretation, and the phrase can be taken to presuppose a remaining body of authority that permits the judiciary to fulfill its role as one of the three branches of government.

Thus one finds a murky body of caselaw, certainly inappropriate to explore here,[36] that on some occasions appears unquestioningly to accept

33. These cases often, but not invariably, involve issues (such as deportation, or military status) with important personal consequences. See Shaughnessy v. Pedreiro, 349 U.S. 48 (1955) (deportation); Harmon v. Brucker, 355 U.S. 579 (1958)(military discharge); cf. Gonzalez v. Freeman, 334 F.2d 570 (D.C. Cir. 1964)(agricultural credit).

34. Johnson v. Robison, 415 U.S. 361 (1974)(classification); Walters v. National Association of Radiation Survivors, 105 S. Ct. 3180 (1985)(procedures); Traynor v. Turnage, 108 S. Ct. 1372 (1988)(hearing of another statute). The ensuing debate in the courts of appeals, looking toward expanded review, is captured in the majority and dissenting opinions in Gott v. Walters, 756 F.2d 902 (D.C. Cir. 1985), an action subsequently dismissed on joint motion of the parties, 791 F.2d 172 (1985).

35. See pp. 12-18.

36. A well-regarded academic treatment of this confusing topic appears in P.

congressional judgments precluding judicial participation,[37] on others to insist that only judges may find certain types of facts, or conduct certain types of proceeding.[38] Perhaps the most important point for our purposes—not clearly stated in the cases, but in the judgment of the writer nascent there—is that some provision for judicial review may be the quid pro quo that persuades the courts to tolerate a grant of discretion elsewhere in government, that they would otherwise find inconsistent with continued assurance that the government would act pursuant to the rule of law.[39] Absent some possibility of an effective judicial check on its legality, that is, Congress' delegation to the President (or, more broadly, to the government) of some forms of authority might be regarded as suspect.[40] While the courts have tended not to be confrontational about this, the concern animates their approach to such issues as review-exclusion and even gives rise (as it did in the first of the Veterans' Administration cases) to remarks about a "serious constitutional question."[41]

Bator, P. Mishkin, D. Shapiro & H. Wechsler, The Federal Courts and the Federal System 313-75 (2d ed. 1973); see also G. Gunther, Congressional Power to Curtail Federal Court Jurisdiction, 36 Stan. L. Rev. 201 (1984), and pp. 241-43.

37. Marbury v. Madison, 5 U.S. (1 Cranch) 137 (1803), Ex Parte McCardle, 7 Wall 506 (U.S. S. Ct. 1869).

38. See pp. 242-43.

39. Yakus v. United States, 321 U.S. 414 (1944), sustaining the World War II price control legislation against a delegation argument, see pp. 20-23, may come closest. Special limitations on the time and manner for securing judicial review of price orders were part of the scheme, and were upheld. These limitations did admit of the possibility of review, however. The Court's general conclusion was that the delegation was sustainable so long as it permitted *courts* to ascertain— that is, to review—whether the administrator had "kept within [his authority] in compliance with the legislative will." Reliance on Yakus was later questioned by one Supreme Court Justice, on the grounds that its review constraints were sustainable *only* in light of the severe emergency posed by the war. Adamo Wrecking Co. v. United States, 434 U.S. 275 (1978) (Powell, J., concurring), discussed at note 44, below.

40. Thus, the cases on the problem of delegation of legislative power are consistently dealt with by the courts as problems of judicial review: when the courts are able to assert (however loosely) that they are in a position to assess the legality of challenged governmental conduct, no delegation problem arises. See pp. 21-23. The case has not arisen in which judicial *authority* to review such a matter had been directly denied by the legislature. The contentions have uniformly been that vagueness of statutory language rather than statutory preclusion disabled the courts from exercising their role. Yet there is no reason to think the outcome would be different. Faced with a governmental function that could be valid only if exercised in accordance with law, and unavoidably denied the chance to assure that it was being so exercised, a court could only find it invalid.

41. See Weinberger v. Salfi, 422 U.S.749, 762 (1975); Bowen v. Michigan Academy of Family Physicians, 106 S. Ct. 2133 (1986); cf. Thomas v. Union Carbide Agricultural Products Co., 105 S. Ct. 3325 (1985).

Less serious issues are presented when the issue concerns the shaping of review rather than total preclusion—as by referring matters to a designated court, or indicating that review of some rulemaking issues must be sought immediately following the rulemaking and may not be raised defensively in an enforcement action. Thus, one court of appeals was able to avoid the difficult questions it thought posed by the statutes governing national medical insurance, which appeared to deny review jurisdiction even over constitutional claims, when it concluded that the same issues could be raised in an action for monetary damages brought in the Claims Court.[42] "Only the relief granted would be different [from the equitable and declaratory relief plaintiffs sought], and Congress has power over the relief granted suitors against the United States and its officers."[43] Similarly, the Supreme Court upheld the Clean Air Act's provision that an EPA "emission standard" could only be reviewed only in the D.C. Circuit, and then only if review was sought by a petition filed within 30 days of the standard's promulgation. It first noted, however, that issues about the proper application of the standard *would* be appropriate to review at the enforcement stage. Even this caveat failed to satisfy one Justice, who questioned the fairness of so limiting the arguments available to "small contractors scattered across the country," persons he thought unlikely to learn of the rule's adoption quickly enough to seek review at the designated time.[44]

Implicit preclusion. One of the arguments rejected in the *Abbott Laboratories* case briefly discussed above[45] was that the explicit provision for review at the enforcement stage implied a congressional wish to preclude review at the rulemaking stage. Such implied preclusion arguments have not often been availing, as the general emphasis on a presumption of reviewability would suggest. When they have succeeded, it has generally been in the presence of special circumstances. In one case, for

---

42. The Claims Court is a court of specialized jurisdiction hearing monetary claims (principally contractual actions) against the United States. See pp. 85-86.

43. American Ass'n of Councils of Medical Staffs of Private Hospitals, Inc. v. Califano, 575 F.2d 1367 (5th Cir. 1978), cert. denied, 439 U.S. 1114 (1979); to similar effect, see United States v. Fausto, 108 S. Ct. 668 (1988).

44. Adamo Wrecking Co. v. United States, 434 U.S. 275 (1978). In choosing the D.C. Circuit Congress was doubtless choosing an expert and perhaps favorable forum. It was also choosing a forum to which trade associations and other institutional litigators centered on Washington, D.C. (if not potentially affected individual businessmen) would have little difficulty gaining access. On the striking difference between the reception of EPA rulemakings in the D.C. Circuit and the reception of its enforcement proceedings in district courts scattered around the country, see R.S. Melnick, Regulation and the Courts: The Case of the Clean Air Act (1983).

45. See pp. 216-17, above.

example, a "complex" statute specifically authorized the producers and handlers of milk products to seek review after they had exhausted detailed procedures; but review had been sought by milk consumers, before those procedures had taken place. Although ordinarily one would expect the consumers to be recognized as possessing "standing"[46] to challenge the administrative action, the Supreme Court directed that the action be dismissed. It based its decision that the consumers could not seek review upon preclusion of review that it implied from Congress' careful specification of administrative procedures that might otherwise be circumnavigated.[47] In another, much earlier case, the Court inferred the inappropriateness of review from Congress' choice of the informal and unstructured techniques of mediation rather than litigation as the technique for dealing with particular labor problems.[48] A more recent statement, however, forcefully reaffirmed "the strong presumption that Congress intends judicial review of administrative action."[49]

Matters committed to agency discretion by law

The second significant exception to APA review concerns those cases in which the court is convinced that the decision in question has been "committed to agency discretion by law." While this might be viewed as just another way of saying that judicial review has been precluded, the formula suggests a different focus of inquiry—one that stresses the characteristics of agency function and the impact of judicial review upon them, rather than the intended judicial role. Here the constitutional inhibition just discussed[50] becomes especially prominent. To conclude that a matter has been "committed to agency discretion by law" does not imply that such a commitment is itself lawful—that is, constitutional—under a scheme of government that ordinarily insists upon the maintenance of shared controls over governmental actions. One finds, correspondingly,

---

46. See pp. 225-28.

47. Block v. Community Nutrition Institute, 467 U.S. 340 (1984). That the Court described its reasoning in terms of "preclusion" rather than "standing," might seem to be, simply, an error of characterization on the Court's part. However, a later decision, supporting rather than denying reviewability in the context of a "standing" argument, insisted that the preclusion label was the apt one. Clark v. Securities Industry Association, 107 S. Ct. 750 (1987). In any event, the reasoning process chosen demonstrates a willingness to see the presumption of reviewability overcome on the basis merely of implication from such matters as the complexity of a legislative scheme.

48. Switchmen's Union v. National Mediation Board, 320 U.S. 297 (1943); cf. Leedom v. Kyne, 358 U.S. 184 (1958).

49. Bowen v. Michigan Academy of Family Physicians, 106 S. Ct. 2133 (1986).

50. See pp. 218-19, above.

that the courts are most likely to find such commitments in cases concerning executive conduct for which judicial review appears to have the least to contribute to governmental legality and stability: decisions raising issues of defense and foreign relations policy,[51] of government management of contracts,[52] or of allocation of prosecutorial effort.[53] In its most recent and extended discussion of the matter, earlier described at some length,[54] the Supreme Court described decisions not to prosecute or enforce as "generally committed to an agency's absolute discretion," entitled to a rebuttable presumption of *un*reviewability.

It is important to note how even this strong statement was qualified. The presumption can be overcome by a showing of judicially manageable standards for review—in the Court's phrase, of "law to apply." The situations in which the presumption applies generally do not involve a complaint that the government has wrongly used its coercive power against a citizen. The complaint, rather, is that the government, by declining to act, has failed to do enough for public protection. And the Court reserves in a footnote the possibility—insisted upon in separate opinions in the case, and well established in the lower courts—that review *would* be available if the issue were not an agency's incremental decision how to expend its resources, but an apparently mistaken belief about its authority under governing law or a conscious policy of refusal to enforce the law in question.[55] However difficult the two motives may be to distinguish in fact, executive abnegation of law would present different issues than the executive's day-to-day working judgments how most effectively to deploy the limited resources Congress has placed at its command. Here, the "to the extent that" qualification of the statutory language quoted at the head of this section acquires special significance. It suggests outcomes in which some aspects of agency action are found to have been "committed to agency discretion by law," while others remain within reach of APA review.

---

51. E.g., Curran v. Laird, 420 F.2d 122 (D.C. Cir. 1969).

52. E.g., Langevin v. Chenango Court, Inc., 447 F.2d 296 (2d Cir. 1971), which found the Federal Housing Administration's approval of a federally subsidized landlord's request for a rent increase to be within the exception. Note, however, that the finding was made on a petition of *tenants* for review; if the landlord had sought review of a denial of its proposed increase one can easily imagine a different result. Thus the analysis, like the implied preclusion analysis discussed at note 47, above, could also be framed in terms of "standing."

53. See Heckler v. Chaney, 105 S. Ct. 1649 (1985), discussed at pp. 151-52; NLRB v. United Food and Commercial Worker's Union, 108 S. Ct. 413 (1987).

54. Heckler v. Chaney, note 53, above.

55. See Adams v. Richardson, 480 F.2d 1159 (D.C. Cir. en banc, 1973); see also note 154, p. 178.

Even when one has identified some aspect of a matter as involving agency "discretion," it does not follow that judicial review is, to that extent, precluded. The APA contains two references to discretion, the one we have been considering and a later provision specifically authorizing review for "abuse of discretion."[56] The resulting linguistic puzzle is generally solved by the courts in favor of review. "Committed to agency discretion by law" is taken to be a "narrow" exception applicable only where the court finds judicial review unmanageable—whether because there is "no law to apply" or for other important reasons of state.[57] The reason for this result is the quasi-constitutional limit already suggested. The assertion that there is "no law to apply" can raise such serious questions about the legality of the underlying delegation of authority, that government attorneys are as unlikely to make the argument as courts are to reach that finding.[58] Thus, the bulk of matters that might be described as in some sense "committed to agency discretion by law" are nonetheless subject to a fairly rigorous review for abuse of that discretion.

Preliminary issues on judicial review

The subject matters of the following section concern preliminary issues on judicial review, that may work either to deny, to postpone, or sharply to limit the review provided. They are as arcane and complex as any in the American lexicon. Although they loom large as intellectual puzzles, however, and so consume inordinate amounts of time for law students and scholars, they can and will be dealt with briefly here. The questions they ask can be stated clearly. And, most importantly, for the great bulk of cases the answers also are not problematic; the difficulties arise only at the margins, when attorneys seek to push for additional review.

In general, these issues arise out of the judiciary's concern for its own proper function. In a legal system that sharply distinguishes legislative, executive and judicial branches, what are the characteristics of a "judicial"

---

56. 5 U.S.C. § 706(2)(A); the scope of review under this provision is discussed on pp. 261-69.

57. The formula and the narrowness of the exception were stated in the Overton Park case already discussed on pp. 165-67, and returned to on pp. 261-67.

58. The types of action for which the finding is most commonly made, the exercise of prosecutorial discretion for example, can be understood as the constitutionally central functions of the executive.

act? Article III of the Constitution provides some structure for this inquiry by repeatedly describing judicial business as involving either a "case" or a "controversy."[59] This has been taken by the courts to involve a number of interrelated elements:

- There must be a genuine, not a contrived, dispute, arising out of an injury-in-fact alleged to have been suffered or palpably threatened;
- The dispute must be between distinct parties, each of which has a definite stake in its outcome;
- Courts must be capable of resolving the dispute, including the provision of effective relief for the alleged injury;
- The judicial outcome must not be subject to revision by non-judicial authority.

The stated rationale for these conditions, believable as a general matter if not for every case in which they are said to have been met, is that they contribute to achieving the conditions needed for informed judicial judgment: adversary parties, with real stakes, who will be driven by their interest in the outcome to present the court with the fullest possible evidence and argument. If the need to resolve a controversy, rather than the wish to generate doctrine, is the legitimate basis for judicial action, these conditions tend to assure that that need is present.[60]

In addition to these constitutional issues—this is where the waters grow especially murky—the courts have developed a series of supplementary "prudential" ideas for denying, limiting, or postponing review thought to be inopportune. For example, a court may conclude that although review seems formally proper at the moment, it should be postponed because further development of the facts through additional administrative processing would "ripen" the matter, aiding judicial consideration, without imposing untoward costs on the parties. If one of these prudential standards is met, then the court may decline to exercise or may limit its review jurisdiction even though there is no constitutional

---

59. The "case or controversy" problem is generally pursued in our legal literature in the context of constitutional rather than administrative law, and even more in treatments of federal court jurisdiction. Useful sources include A. Bickel, The Least Dangerous Branch (1962); G. Gunther, Cases and Materials on Constitutional Law (11th ed. 1985); L. Tribe, American Constitutional Law (1978); P. Bator, P. Mishkin, D. Shapiro and H. Wechsler, Hart and Wechsler's The Federal Courts and the Federal System (Foundation Press; 2d ed. 1973 and Supp. 1981).

60. Relatively little thought has been given, to date, about the impact of the Supreme Court's discretionary review function on this vision of the judicial process. See pp. 81-82; P. Strauss, One Hundred Fifty Cases Per Year: Some Implications of the Supreme Court's Limited Resources for Judicial Review of Agency Action, 87 Colum. L. Rev. 1093 (1987).

barrier to its undertaking that review. Adherence to these prudential standards has been variable, giving rise to occasional suspicions that they are simply manipulated in the service of attaining, or avoiding, review on essentially political grounds. In part for this reason, the legitimacy of these prudential bases for avoiding review is disputed by some. In any event, they are not often significant in ordinary administrative matters. The distinction between constitutional requirements for review and these prudential considerations should be kept clearly in mind.

Standing[61]

The basic question addressed by the issue of standing is, *who* is entitled to seek review of governmental action. There is an elaborate, turgid and badly conflicted body of constitutional law on this question, which at the moment appears to have settled on three constitutionally based elements: the person seeking to challenge government action must have suffered an "injury in fact"; that injury must have been caused by the government action of which she complains; and a judicial decision must be capable of remedying the injury. An additional "prudential" element has been stated, and adhered to with varying enthusiasm and fidelity: the federal law the complainant invokes in support of her lawsuit must be seen to have, as one of its arguable purposes, the protection or regulation of the interest whose injury she is seeking to redress. This prudential element is illustrated by a government decision to increase the zinc content of the penny under a statute passed to relieve a situation caused by hoarding of all-copper coins. The decision injured copper fabricators in fact, by depriving them of a market that tended to keep copper prices up. Their injury was caused by the decision, and a finding that the agency had acted unlawfully would have remedied the injury. Nonetheless, protecting the economic interests of copper fabricators was not even arguably among the factors to be taken account of in the administrative scheme. Thus, the fabricators were unable to establish the prudential element of standing.[62]

This is, however, an unusual outcome. In general, the requirements of standing have been interpreted in recent years so as not to pose a significant obstacle to—indeed to encourage and enlarge the availability

---

61. In general, see K. Scott, Standing in the Supreme Court—A Functional Analysis, 86 Harv. L. Rev. 645 (1973); G. Nichol, Rethinking Standing, 72 Cal. L. Rev. 68 (1984); Administrative Law: Cases and Comments 1036-81; R. Pierce, S. Shapiro & P. Verkuil, Administrative Law and Process 141-63.

62. Copper & Brass Fabricators Council, Inc. v. Department of the Treasury, 679 F.2d 951 (D.C. Cir. 1982).

of—*conventional* administrative review. The litigant who has been a party to an administrative action, or is its direct object, and complains of some illegality in the agency's judgment which she wishes corrected, generally meets all of the requirements. What is an "injury in fact" can be established by statute, and since 1970 the courts have considered general language of the APA, quoted in the margin,[63] to establish that such a person has been so injured.[64] Thus, in its most recent statement, the Supreme Court explained that the "zone of interests" test is strongly associated with Section 702 of the APA. The Court described what that test asks in a manner broadly supportive of "standing" findings. "Not meant to be especially demanding," it inquires only whether "the interest respondent asserts has a plausible relationship to the policies underlying" the statutes it seeks to invoke.[65] In the context of an (arguably) illegal administrative action to be corrected under the APA's provisions for review, causality and remediability also present no obstacles—the injury is caused by the illegality, which can be remedied by an order directing the agency to redress its error.

The developments of the 1960's and 1970's, encouraging broader public participation in administrative processes, were perhaps nowhere so evident as in the willingness of courts to find that the requirements of standing to secure review of federal administrative action had been met. The cases in which significant disputes over standing remain likely today arise outside the APA, when persons or associations not directly implicated in administrative action seek its correction. Even here, obtaining standing is usually a matter of careful pleading. The Court has been

---

63. "A person suffering legal wrong because of agency action, or adversely affected or aggrieved by agency action within the meaning of a relevant statute, is entitled to judicial review thereof." 5 U.S.C. § 702. While "legal wrong" suggests a traditional approach, that the complainant must be able to show that the government's action would be a tort if undertaken by a private person, see note 14, above, "adversely affected or aggrieved" is understood as requiring simply an injury in fact that is arguably related to what the statute in question was intended to deal with.

64. The leading cases are Association of Data Processing Service Organizations v. Camp, 397 U.S 150 (1970) and Barlow v. Collins, 397 U.S. 159 (1970), and, most recently, Clarke v. Securities Industry Association, 107 S. Ct. 750 (1987). Note, in relation to the copper fabricators' case discussed in the preceding paragraph, that if that case had arisen from an administrative proceeding to which they were parties, their consequent interest in having a lawful outcome to the administrative proceeding would clearly have established standing to raise such questions as procedural regularity, the existence of requisite factual support for the decision, etc. Since, however, the Secretary had reached his judgment informally—in the absence of statutorily required procedures, see pp. 141-43—their economic interest was the only basis of their complaint.

65. Clarke v. Securities Industry Association, 107 S. Ct. 750 (1987).

willing to accept aesthetic as well as economic injury as "injury in fact"; attenuated as well as direct causality.

Thus, when a federal agency decision permitted railroads to increase their rates for shipping recyclable materials, some Washington, D.C. students asserted that this would impair their enjoyment of area parks by encouraging both the depletion of natural resources and increased litter in the parks. Although required to prove their assertions, the students were held to have stated grounds that, if proved, would provide them with standing.[66] The injuries to their sensibilities in using the park, while not economic, were "a specific and perceptible harm that distinguished them from citizens who had not used the natural resources that were claimed to be affected." The attenuated chain of causality was not disqualifying, but a matter for proof.

To be distinguished was a case in which an environmental association had omitted any claim either that its members used the parklands whose proposed future as a ski resort it sought to block, or that they would be harmed in that use.[67] To have found that the association had standing merely because, as it argued, it was an established organization dedicated to environmental protection would have permitted simple interest in a problem to suffice, and the Constitution insists upon "a direct stake . . . even though small." One might even have believed that the omission was deliberately made, in the hope of establishing the proposition that the association could sue over environmental injury occurring anywhere in the United States. Although American cases, like the British, speak of review in cases such as these as being brought by "private attorneys general,"[68] federal law stops short in theory at permitting any interested citizen to sue. One with nothing more at stake than the citizen's general interest in seeing the law upheld has no "controversy" with the government. But so little is required to establish the "personal stake" that passes constitutional muster—surely much less than would lead even the extraordinary citizen to pursue a matter as far as the Supreme Court merely to vindicate that stake—that in practice matters are the same.

With the waning, already suggested,[69] of the public interest representation movement, some elements of conservatism over standing are appearing. While a number of examples could be given,[70] perhaps the

---

66. United States v. Students Challenging Regulatory Agency Procedures (SCRAP), 412 U.S. 669 (1973).

67. Sierra Club v. Morton, 405 U.S. 727 (1972).

68. The classic American statement appears in Associated Industries of New York State, Inc. v. Ickes, 134 F.2d 694 (1943).

69. See p. 154.

70. United States v. Richardson, 418 U.S. 166 (1974); Warth v. Seldin, 422 U.S. 490 (1975). Political lines are clearly drawn in the lengthy opinions filed in two

most striking are two cases seeking APA review of rulings by the Internal Revenue Service (the administrators of tax collection), which the plaintiffs asserted were inconsistent with the Internal Revenue Code. In one, some poor persons sought to challenge the legality of a revenue ruling respecting the conditions necessary for a hospital to retain tax-exempt status. They asserted that it had resulted in their being denied needed medical care they would previously have received as charity.[71] In the other, the parents of black children attending public schools challenged rulings that they asserted unlawfully granted tax benefits to private schools practicing racial discrimination, thus supporting racial segregation and making it less likely their children would receive a fully integrated education.[72] Even such brief statements should make clear that these are marginal cases. Plaintiffs' basic complaint is about the objectionable conduct of other individuals which, they assert, has been promoted by tax treatment unlawfully favorable to those others. Perhaps it is not surprising that the Court resisted permitting outsiders, even appealing ones, to intrude into tax issues involving others. The reasoning in both cases stressed the absence of clear lines of causation, or of certainty that judicial relief, even if granted, would redress the injury complained of. Yet one's sense, animated by the vigorous dissents filed in both opinions, is that a few years earlier the Court would, without much difficulty, have found standing to be present.

It seems important to reiterate, in conclusion, that the standing issue speaks to the qualification of the individual plaintiff seeking review, and not to the reviewability of the decision, as such. The decisions on tax matters briefly discussed in the preceding paragraph, for example, would have been fully open to review, to the extent they affected the interests of the taxpayers themselves. If one looks at the transaction arguably subject to review in terms of the universe of litigants that might possibly be permitted to seek that review, one sees with clarity the relationship between expanded standing and the public participation movement.[73] Expanded standing enlarges the class of potential litigants, requiring the agency to anticipate having to defend the legality of its decisions from more perspectives than that simply of the regulated party. It is in this sense, as suggested earlier,[74] that some of the cases on implied preclusion of review, those implying a preclusion just for the particular parties before the court, sound standing themes.

recent decisions of the D.C. Circuit en banc, dividing 5-5 over standing questions. Hotel & Restaurant Employees Union v. Smith, 846 F.2d 1499 (1988); Center for Auto Safety v. Thomas, 847 F.2d 843 (1988).

71. Simon v. Eastern Kentucky Welfare Rights Organization, 426 U.S. 26 (1976).

72. Allen v. Wright, 468 U.S. 737 (1984).

73. See pp. 149-54.

74. See pp. 220-21.

Finality, exhaustion, ripeness

The requirement for exhaustion of administrative remedies prior to seeking review, the requirement that administrative actions be "ripe" for review, and the requirement that only "final" agency actions are reviewable all pertain to the *timing* rather than the fact of review. All share a concern for proper allocation of effort as between agency and court. In particular, they seek to avoid the disruptive and potentially adventitious interruptions to agency processes that would be caused by premature or repeated judicial proceedings. The administration of each is complicated by the realization that in some cases or for some issues, however, the postponement of review can occasion significant injustice. Consequently, these often emerge as doctrines requiring postponement only of some of the issues presented for review. Even in asserting that full judicial review must await the exhaustion of administrative procedures, further ripening, or a final agency judgment, that is, courts often reach limited but helpful judgments about the course of the proceedings already in train. At the margins, too, these doctrines are frequently indistinct, merging into one another—and also into the problems of preclusion and standing, already discussed.

Finality

The basic idea of "finality" is simple enough, and is given explicit statement in the APA. Only agency judgments that are "final agency action" are eligible for review. One easily understands the basis for this rule. As in a civil trial, one awaits the conclusion of proceedings rather than initiate a stream of appeals as potential errors occur. Many may wash out in the ultimate result, or be corrected by the tribunal itself. The considerable disruption of repeated appeals is itself an evil to be avoided.

Yet a limited class of interlocutory appeals are provided for in civil judicial proceedings. Such appeals may be taken from judicial orders that finally dispose of the interests of one participant, although not the entire proceeding. Interlocutory appeals may also be taken from judicial orders that dispose of issues collateral to the main proceeding, too important to be denied review and too independent of the main proceeding to be required to wait.[75] And review may be sought on permission of the trial court concerning issues of such evident importance and controversiality that the costs of proceeding in error appear to be greater than the dis-

---

75. Cohen v. Beneficial Loan Corp., 337 U.S. 541 (1949).

ruption caused by an appeal to determine whether an error has in fact been committed.[76]

Efforts to secure similar review in administrative proceedings will occasionally succeed,[77] although there is no statutory provision for interlocutory review similar to that applicable to civil trials. At this writing, however, the courts seem defensively aware of the delays and disruption threatened by even permitting such claims to be made; success is rare.[78]

The larger question in the administrative context may be what *completed* acts, "agency action," will be regarded as having sufficiently formality to be designated "final agency action." In the *Abbott Laboratories* case previously discussed,[79] the Supreme Court easily concluded that a legislative rule was "final agency action." How should courts treat the less formal interpretive rules,[80] which are not legally binding on agency or private parties but nonetheless may significantly shape both conduct and judicial outcomes? How shall they treat an agency's formal decision to issue a complaint initiating administrative proceedings, which have yet to run their course? Or an agency's failure to act in a timely manner, in response to a petition or a statutory mandate?

The staff of the Wage and Hour Division of the Department of Labor annually issue 750,000 letters of advice about the application of federal fair labor standards. Of these, 10,000 are designated as having been signed by the Administrator of the Division, and result from processes in which outside presentations are welcomed. Although the smaller group (having had more careful consideration) are more likely to be followed by the agency and respected by the courts, all 750,000 letters could be characterized as agency action. Making them reviewable could discourage the agency from issuing them at all. The D.C. Circuit found only the smaller group to be "final agency actions" subject to judicial review. It reached even this conclusion in a manner careful to preserve agency

---

76. 28 U.S.C. § 1292(b). No corresponding statutory provision exists for interlocutory review of administrative proceedings.

77. Gulf Oil Corp. v. United States Department of Energy, 663 F.2d 296 (D.C. Cir. 1981).

78. Pepsico, Inc. v. Federal Trade Commission, 472 F.2d 179 (2d Cir. 1972), cert. denied, 414 U.S. 876 (1973) is the exceptional case. The court indicated, in dictum, a willingness to consider interlocutory appeals from agency errors so obvious and gross that the proceeding in question "must prove to be a nullity." Other courts faced with precisely the same merits question as elicited the discussion in Pepsico declined to offer any such formula of hope. Coca-Cola Co. v. Federal Trade Commission, 475 F.2d 299 (5th Cir.), cert. denied, 414 U.S. 877 (1973); Seven-Up Co. v. Federal Trade Commission, 478 F.2d 755 (8th Cir.), cert. denied, 414 U.S. 1013 (1973).

79. See p. 216, above.

80. See pp. 157-58.

control over that outcome: it said that it would not regard as "final" an opinion not signed by the Administrator, or explicitly labeled as tentative or subject to reconsideration. It would reach this conclusion even though, for the moment, nothing was left to do. Finality, in effect, was the price the Administrator was required to pay to purchase the added weight and formality of an opinion he had signed without reservation.[81]

The issuance of a complaint to initiate administrative proceedings can be a formal agency act, and one with severe consequences for its subject. It must undergo the considerable expense of defense, and face the indirect costs to reputation of having been so charged. Once a hearing has resulted in findings for or against the defendant, any question whether issuance of the complaint was justified seems likely to have disappeared. But permitting review of the existence of proper cause for the issuance of a complaint would allow any defendant to force the delay of any hearing. Courts find their way past this puzzle with the observation that "the expense and annoyance of litigation is part of the social burden of living under government." The complaint, having no *direct* impact beyond the imposition of those costs, is not a "final agency action."[82] One can understand this as a general judgment about the relative balance of claim between agency and accused; in general, it might be concluded, the accused is more likely to abuse the initiative that would come from having the review question decided in its favor. When concrete evidence of corruption in agency behavior can be supplied, then, one might expect this judgment to come under significant pressure.[83]

Agency "failure to act" is explicitly defined as "agency action,"[84] but on the surface significant problems can arise in deciding when such a failure is "final." Other language of the APA provides that a court may "compel agency action *unlawfully* withheld or *unreasonably* delayed,"[85] and this establishes at least a framework for argument. In early years of the public participation movement, this language provided a major impetus for what might be described as agenda-setting litigation. A would-be public interest representative would petition an agency to undertake what it regarded as necessary action; then, after an interval, it would sue to compel action on its request.[86] While the mechanism remains available

---

81. National Automatic Laundry and Cleaning Council v. Shultz, 443 F.2d 689 (1971); see also Kixmiller v. SEC, 492 F.2d 641 (D.C. Cir. 1974).

82. Federal Trade Commission v. Standard Oil Company of California, 449 U.S. 232 (1980).

83. Gulf Oil Corp. v. United States Department of Energy, 663 F.2d 296 (D.C. Cir. 1981).

84. 5 U.S.C. § 551(13).

85. 5 U.S.C. § 706(1).

86. Environmental Defense Fund v. Hardin, 428 F.2d 1093, 1097 (D.C. Cir. 1970); Environmental Defense Fund v. Ruckelshaus, 439 F.2d 584 (D.C. Cir. 1971).

where statutes establish a duty to act, the recently established general presumption that agency decisions on enforcement matters are not reviewable[87] seems likely to have diminished considerably the utility of the approach.

Exhaustion

In its most common appearance, the requirement for exhaustion of administrative remedies can be seen as a restatement of the finality principle: this matter is not yet ready for review, because there remain administrative procedures that might resolve it, or further develop the facts for judgment. The question commonly arises collaterally. Plaintiffs are not seeking review of an agency action, as such, but to enjoin the further pursuit of agency proceedings that, they contend, can only result in a nullity and thus will inflict on them costs from which they are entitled to be protected.

In the classic case, the Bethlehem Shipbuilding Corporation sought to enjoin National Labor Relations Board hearings that Bethlehem asserted were beyond its jurisdiction. Acknowledging that the Board's jurisdiction was a proper issue, the Court held that it must first be decided by the Board and so declined to consider the question itself.[88] Important to note, however, is that the Court *did* consider and decide a number of preliminary legal questions: whether the Labor Relations Act, on its face, was constitutional and authorized a proceeding of the kind to which Bethlehem had been called; whether the procedures before the Board, to which Bethlehem was required to submit, were on their face sufficient to permit a fair outcome; and whether judicial review following the Board's judgment had been adequately provided for. Had these preliminary questions been decided favorably to the plaintiff, that would have led to the relief demanded in the complaint. In other words, Bethlehem did get a rather full review of the general legality of its being required to submit to this administrative scheme. This was a matter as to which neither agency judgment nor further factual development would be useful, and as to which its costs in having to go through a proceeding would be unusually high. The availability of this partial, early review is a common, although not always noted, feature of the exhaustion cases.[89]

87. See pp. 151-52.
88. Myers v. Bethlehem Shipbuilding Corp., 303 U.S. 41 (1938).
89. Touche Ross & Co. v. Securities and Exchange Commission, 609 F.2d 570 (2d Cir. 1979); Leedom v. Kyne, 358 U.S. 184 (1958); Allen v. Grand Central Aircraft Co., 347 U.S. 535 (1954). The presence of a constitutional challenge to agency jurisdiction does not always defeat exhaustion arguments; if the claim is marginal, or may be mooted or illuminated by the agency proceeding, and if being required

Occasionally, exhaustion requirements assume the guise of a penalty, not merely a principle for ordering judicial and agency effort. This happens when a statute in effect precludes judicial decision of any matter that has not been ventilated before the appropriate agency. Thus, in two criminal prosecutions for draft resistance, the government asserted that the defendants could not claim in defense that they were statutorily entitled to be excused from the draft, when they had not fully pursued these matters before the responsible administrative authorities. In one of the cases, the Court thought only statutory construction was required, and held that the defense should have been entertained in light of the "harsh" consequences of now requiring the defendant to have exhausted his administrative remedies.[90] Decision in the other case "depended upon the application of expertise by administrative bodies," and the defendant, having failed to exhaust that remedy, was not entitled to make his defense.[91]

Ripeness

The idea of partial review is particularly prominent in relation to the question of ripeness, which permits postponing (some aspects) of the review of agency action that is concededly final, when the advantages of requiring further development of the controversy are seen to outweigh the imposition on the parties of that postponement. The authoritative statement occurred in the *Abbott Laboratories* litigation already discussed.[92] After evoking the presumption of reviewability and determining that the FDA's legislative rule constituted "final agency action," the Court addressed the government's argument that review would nonetheless be premature. The government asserted that review would not "ripen" until an enforcement action was brought (if ever), whose particular facts would illumine what was otherwise an abstract challenge to undeveloped language. The "basic rationale" of ripeness doctrine, the Court agreed, "is to prevent the courts, through avoidance of premature adjudication, from entangling themselves in abstract disagreements over policies, and also to protect the agencies from judicial interference until an administrative decision has been formalized and its effects felt in a concrete way by the challenging parties." This rationale suggested a two-part inquiry: whether

to submit to the agency proceeding is not, in itself, an evident constitutional harm, exhaustion will nonetheless be required. Rosenthal & Co. v. Bagley, 581 F.2d 1258 (7th Cir. 1978).
90. McKart v. United States, 395 U.S. 185 (1969).
91. McGee v. United States, 402 U.S. 479 (1971).
92. See pp. 216-17.

the issues were "fit" for judicial decision, and what would be the "hardship to the parties" of withholding consideration.

In the case before it, the Court found both legs of the inquiry to suggest review. If review were denied, the parties would likely be forced by practical considerations to make large investments to comply with the rule, rather than face the drastic consequences of non-compliance. And the Court was able to characterize the legal issue presented as one simply of statutory interpretation, which did not require significant factual development to be decided. The last is the decisive point. It answers the concerns expressed in a vigorous dissent written by a Justice who had had considerable experience in private practice with the behavior and motivations of clients such as Abbott Laboratories. If companies were able to attack rules in the abstract, the dissent argued, they would conjure up outlandish facts and interpretations that could distort the judicial sense of the real application of the rule.

This last point is central to understanding the partial review that ripeness considerations entail. The majority's response to the dissenting arguments was, in effect, to limit the review provided at the pre-enforcement stage to what can be decided *on the face* of the rule. The question of facial validity is whether any state of facts is imaginable to which the rule could validly be applied. That question is ripe, but questions of particular application are not. While this response tends to avoid the problem of distorted perspective, it does (as the dissent also noted) somewhat lower the costs of seeking review. The party seeking review now faces only its litigating costs, possibly offset by gains from non-compliance in the interim, rather than the substantial costs that could result from successful enforcement against it. In a nation that had elected to foster declaratory judgment arguments generally, the majority argued, this effect was unobjectionable.

In a companion case, the Court concluded it could not properly appraise the challenge made to a different rule in the absence of specific factual development; the practical impact of being required to await review in that case was also less. Review was found not ripe, and submission to enforcement proceedings was required.[93] Here, too, the Court had gone far enough to assure itself that the requirement of postponed review was a fair one. Other ripeness cases, while often confusing in tone and reasoning, can generally be understood along these lines.[94]

---

93. Toilet Goods Association v. Gardner, 387 U.S. 158 (1967).

94. See, e.g., National Automatic Laundry & Cleaning Council v. Shultz, discussed at p. 230, above; Better Government Association v. Department of State, 780 F.2d 86 (D.C. Cir. 1986); Eagle-Picher Industries v. United States Environmental Protection Agency, 759 F.2d 905 (D.C. Cir. 1985).

Primary jurisdiction

It can occasionally happen that in ordinary civil litigation, that would not be characterized as administrative review as such, a court is presented with a dispute or issue it recognizes as falling comfortably within some agency's jurisdiction. It may be asked, for example, to assess the reasonableness of a railroad's rate,[95] or to decide which of two rates stated in a railroad's tariff structure properly applies to particular goods.[96] Both these questions are within the ordinary ken of the Interstate Commerce Commission. If one conceives the usual assignment of such issues to the agency as in a sense jurisdictional, the situation may be analogized to that arising when a federal court is faced with the need to decide complex issues of state law, likely to be far better understood within the state judicial system primarily responsible for them. In both situations, American jurisprudence embodies judge-made doctrines of reference, that require the parties to seek answers from the other system, either in lieu of the federal action or as a condition to further consideration of it.

The doctrine of "primary jurisdiction," which had its largest application in the now-fading domain of economic regulation, addresses the court's proper course in the administrative context.[97] Is it to dismiss an action because it could be, and more properly should be, initiated before the expert agency? Postpone decision while a particular issue better suited to agency determination is referred to the agency? Or simply plow ahead on its own? There is no fixed formula for resolving these issues,[98] which can be regarded as a means for policing (and preventing parties from wreaking havoc upon) the very complex jurisdictional allocations of federal law. Three factors have been identified as suggesting invocation of the doctrine: the existence of specialized agency expertise; a need for uniform national resolution of the issue; and any prospect that judicial decision of the matter would adversely affect the agency's ability to perform its functions.[99]

---

95. Texas & Pacific R. Co. v. Abilene Cotton Oil Co., 204 U.S. 426 (1907).

96. United States v. Western Pacific Railroad Co., 352 U.S. 59 (1956).

97. The analog in federal-state relations is the doctrine of abstention. See Shapiro, Abstention and Primary Jurisdiction: Two Chips Off the Same Block?—A Comparative Analysis, 60 Cornell L. Rev. 75 (1974).

98. See the Western Pacific decision, note 96, above, for a general discussion.

99. R. Pierce, S. Shapiro and P. Verkuil, Administrative Law and Process at 206; the classic scholarly treatment (as for so many of these issues) is in L. Jaffe, Judicial Control of Administrative Action, Chapter 4 (1965). As primary jurisdiction doctrine has seen relatively little development since publication of Jaffe's work, it is more timely on that subject than might ordinarily appear.

Preliminary relief

A different kind of question concerning the timing of judicial involvement arises when a party seeks to maintain the status quo, or obtain other auxiliary judicial assistance, during the pendency of administrative action or while it is awaiting review. Two decisions of the D.C. Circuit warrant mention in this regard. The first in point of time, widely regarded as authoritative, identifies four factors to govern issuance or denial of a stay of effectiveness of an agency order (say, granting an immediately effective license to operate a nuclear power station) pending judicial review: probable success on the merits; irreparable injury if a stay is not granted; whether the issuance of a stay would significantly harm others; and what may be suggested by public interest considerations.[100] The second decision, quite recent, concerns the court in which such relief is to be sought. Among a number of statutes (including the APA) that authorize judicial granting of interim relief, the All Writs Act[101] is prominent. That Act authorizes federal courts to "issue all writs necessary or appropriate in aid of their respective jurisdictions. . . . " The import of this provision, the D.C. Circuit reasoned, is that where statutory review[102] is provided, only the court given exclusive review jurisdiction is in a position to "aid" that jurisdiction by providing preliminary relief; no other court, in its view, has jurisdiction to intervene.[103]

Available judicial remedies

With the exception of a brief discussion of mandamus,[104] we have thus far been generally assuming that review is occurring under the Administrative Procedure Act. That Act provides a unified and usually fully adequate structure both to review "final agency action" and to preserve, in the interim, the conditions necessary for effective ultimate judicial relief.[105] In connection with APA review, the court may issue any but monetary relief: orders of enforcement, declaratory judgments, compulsory orders directing the agency or its officials either to act[106] or to refrain

100. Virginia Petroleum Jobbers Ass'n v. FPC, 259 F.2d 921 (D.C. Cir. 1958).
101. 28 U.S.C. § 1651.
102. See p. 212.
103. Telecommunications Research and Action Center v. FCC, 750 F.2d 70 (D.C. Cir. 1984).
104. See pp. 214-15, above.
105. 5 U.S.C § 705 is the APA analog of the All Writs Act, note 101, above.
106. See p. 231.

from acting, or—most commonly—judgments upholding or setting aside, in whole or in part, the results of agency action. To the extent agency action is found legally deficient, the court will take one of two courses. If the flaw is one that cannot be corrected, it will simply be found unlawful and set aside. If administrative reconsideration could yield a valid result, however, the proceedings are remanded to the agency for fresh or supplementary attention. In this respect, the matter resembles appellate review of a lower court's decision more than a lawsuit between private parties. The "record" transmitted by the agency in support of its action is simply returned to it for further attention, as it would be to the lower court.

As the last few paragraphs have suggested, however, one may sue an agency in federal court independent of the APA—so long as another cause of action can be defined. The Bethlehem Shipbuilding Corporation[107] and others who seek to avoid having to exhaust judicial remedies urge as their cause of action that illegal agency action is inflicting otherwise irreparable harm, and seek the ordinary judicial remedy in such circumstances, an injunction against its continuance. Jurisdiction is established if the asserted illegality presents a "federal question," arises under statutes "regulating commerce," or otherwise meets the constraints of the Judicial Code.[108] Questions of preclusion, standing, and timing would still arise. That the action is brought outside the APA framework may produce somewhat more conservative responses on these issues, on the ground that *that* framework is the one Congress has chosen for review.[109] As no record is before the court in these cases, as such, the remedies available are limited accordingly: a mandatory or declaratory order may be obtained, but a remand is not to be anticipated.

Similarly, review issues may arise defensively, when an agency seeks enforcement of an order or rule. Here, subject to the preclusion possibilities already discussed,[110] the APA is explicit that its review provisions attach. The remedies available in this context may include a remand as well as simple loss of the proceeding (or enforcement) for the government. Finally, monetary damages may be available in actions not brought under the APA. Those actions are discussed in the final chapter of this essay.

---

107. Note 88, above.

108. See the text at notes 14-15, above.

109. Thus, for example, the recent decision in Community Nutrition Institute v. Block, note 47, above, where the fact that the would-be plaintiffs were not involved in the complex administrative procedure set up in the governing statute seemed to be an important element in the conclusion that review at their behest was precluded.

110. See pp. 217-23 and 232-33; 5 U.S.C. § 703.

$\equiv 8$

SCOPE OF JUDICIAL REVIEW

"The availability of judicial review is the necessary condition, psychologically if not logically, for a system of administrative power which purports to be legitimate, or legally valid."[1] So observed the author of a complex study that, two decades later, remains the best general account of judicial control of administrative action in American law.[2] The preceding pages ought to have demonstrated that such review is broadly available. Conveying in a few pages how that review is exercised is not a simple matter. The nature of the problem is easily enough stated: permitting the court to control the lawfulness of agency action without allowing it to displace agency responsibility. But the difficulty of producing trustworthy verbal formulae that will accomplish that end, adjusted to the variety of settings in which the task arises, ought not be underestimated. "[T]he rules governing judicial review," other scholars despairingly wrote, "have no more substance at the core than a seedless grape."[3] As if to illustrate the point, the principal treatise-writer in the field presented as his "adequate summary," "more reliable than the many complexities and refinements that are constantly repeated in judicial opinions," the following:

> Courts usually substitute judgment on the kinds of questions of law that are within their special competence, but on other questions they limit themselves to deciding reasonableness; they do not clarify the meaning of reasonableness but retain full discretion in each case to stretch it in either direction.[4]

---

1. L. Jaffe, Judicial Control of Administrative Action 320 (1965).

2. Id. For a contemporary restatement of the technical law, characterized by considerable sophistication, see R. Levin, Scope of Review Doctrine Restated: An Administrative Law Section Report, 38 Ad. L. Rev. 239 (1986). R.S. Melnick, Regulation and the Courts: The Case of the Clean Air Act (Brookings 1983) provides a close and interesting analysis of the impact of judicial review on the functioning of one agency, the EPA.

3. E. Gellhorn and G. Robinson, Perspectives in Administrative Law, 75 Colum. L. Rev., 771, 780-81 (1975).

4. K.C. Davis, 5 Administrative Law Treatise 332 (2d ed. 1984).

That is, this formula suggests, courts intervene or not essentially as the circumstances move them, and not in accordance with any set of fixed and objective principles.

The writer's view is a more pragmatic, perhaps less despairing one, that detects certain regularities in judicial practice, informed by statute and prior judicial statement, and enforced to a degree by the Supreme Court.[5] Historically, the development of judicial review can be seen as a progression from plenary judicial involvement in a limited range of cases and issues, to broad but restrained involvement, as allocations between agency and court have acquired clearer definition. Initially, that is, the courts intervened only if the person seeking review could demonstrate a rather stark illegality in the behavior of some government agent. Such illegality warranted treating the official as if he were a private citizen *and* granting the complaining party one of the standard judicial remedies— an injunction, or an award of damages for tort. While such remedies remain available, the predominant mode of judicial review today assumes the official character of the act, and asks a more discriminating series of questions. These questions assume a sort of partnership or distribution of authority between agency and court, in which each actor has a unique and protected role.

Whenever the scope of review is at issue, the first step is to say precisely what error the complaining party claims the agency committed. Next is the inquiry about the "partnership agreement": so far as the relevant statute indicates, just what is the extent of the power delegated to the agency for the function under review? Much turns on precisely what agency function is under review: Is it adjudication or rulemaking— and in either case, is it on a formal record or not? If rulemaking, was it pursuant to an express grant of power, or was it pursuant to a general grant of power to "make rules to carry out the purposes of this Act"? Was the agency finding a fact? making a prediction? exercising discretion? applying the statute to the situation? construing aspects of the statute not affected by the particular situation? or deciding its procedure for performing such functions?

The brief discussion early in this essay of the developing understanding of executive "discretion,"[6] and the consequent broadening of the mandamus remedy,[7] form one prominent example of the historical development of review. Mandamus (or its equivalent) is far more widely available today than it was in Chief Justice Marshall's time. This is so substantially because we now feel confident that judges can exercise

5. See Administrative Law: Cases and Comments 348-544.
6. See pp. 61-63.
7. See pp. 214-15.

review functions that check but do not supplant the authority of others—
that an order to exercise discretion, or to exercise it under some particular
constraint, does not entail directing the agency what decision it must
reach. Of course judges may fail from time to time. Occasionally they do
issue orders that in effect supplant the authority of agencies. Yet, one
may believe that this reflects human failings these understandings generally succeed in keeping in check, rather than the self-conscious and
cynical manipulation of an empty formula.

Constitutional issues

At the outset one meets again the question whether, and if so to what
extent, the Constitution affirmatively requires that judicial review be available. That is, is there a constitutional minimum amount of review that
must be provided, and if so how could it be described? The question can
appear in at least three guises. First, whether judicial decision of some
matters is required by formal separation of powers considerations—that
is, because the matter is inherently "judicial" in character, and so *must*
be assigned to the judicial branch. Second, more broadly, whether legislative provision for judicial review is a condition necessary to the validity
of the delegation of authority to an administrative agency. Third, whether
review in some form over a decision depriving a person of "life, liberty
or property" is a necessary element of due process of law.

The first[8] and second[9] of these questions have already been the subject
of some discussion in the preceding pages. As has already been suggested,[10] the tendency of the Supreme Court has been to avoid giving
direct answers to these questions. In substantial part, this avoidance
reflects the potential embarrassment arising out of the Constitution's
explicit provision of congressional authority to shape the Court's appellate jurisdiction. The absence of clear doctrine on these issues also reflects
the infrequency with which they arise. The strong presumption of reviewability, together with Congress' general practice of making administrative action reviewable, permit their easy avoidance.

Current indications are that a Due Process Clause entitlement to judicial review is more sharply limited than might seem to be implied by
the usual lists of "due process" factors,[11] or by the reasoning of *Goldberg*
v. *Kelly*.[12] References to findings and on-the-record proceedings, and *Gold-*

---

8. See pp. 78-86.
9. See pp. 221-23.
10. See pp. 218-19.
11. See pp. 47-48.
12. Discussed at pp. 38-40.

berg's dicta make it appear that a proceeding governed by due process considerations must be subject to judicial review of some character reaching all normal issues that may arise from it—issues of application as well as problems arising on the face of the governing statutes. Yet the Supreme Court carefully avoided endorsing the *Goldberg* expectation on one recent occasion when it might have done so,[13] and seems unconsciously to have contradicted it on another. The potential issue in the first case concerned the review of mandatory arbitration proceedings, which could be thought to give it a special character, and the Court stated that the parties had raised no due process issues as such; the review provisions it found to satisfy the other concerns that had been raised, however, were extremely limited—essentially independent of the merits as such.

The second case involved proceedings to terminate a veteran's continuing receipt of statutory benefits, an entitlement the Court understandably found to warrant application of the Due Process Clause.[14] As we have seen,[15] review of Veterans' Administration judgments about veterans' benefits is generally precluded by statute. Because the particular question the Court had to decide was whether an aspect of the statute shaping procedures before the agency was consistent with the requirements of due process, the Court was able to avoid this preclusion by applying the rationale we previously noted. For present purposes, however, the noteworthy point is that use of this special reasoning implicitly accepts that review of the merits of that decision was not available. Although the point seems not to have been directly faced in the Supreme Court,[16] what appears is that the Due Process Clause does not invariably prevent Congress from establishing administrative procedures to which the clause applies, but under which judicial review of the administrator's decisions as such is precluded. Facial review of the constitutionality of the scheme—the sort that can be obtained without need to exhaust administrative remedies[17]—is insisted upon;[18] but review of issues of application is not.

Finally, brief mention should be made of the courts' occasional insistence that, as a constitutional matter, certain facts must be found by the courts—even, by the Supreme Court itself. "Regarding certain largely

13. Thomas v. Union Carbide Agricultural Products Co., 105 S. Ct. 3325 (1985); see pp. 79-80.

14. Walters v. National Association of Radiation Survivors, 105 S. Ct. 3180 (1985), discussed at p. 47.

15. See pp. 217-18.

16. Gott v. Walters, 756 F.2d 902 (D.C. Cir. 1985).

17. See pp. 232-33.

18. This step is necessary to avoid the "positivist trap" briefly discussed at pp. 41-42.

factual questions in some areas of the law," the Supreme Court recently remarked in reviewing ordinary civil litigation raising free speech issues, "the stakes—in terms of impact on future cases and future conduct—are too great to entrust them finally to the judgment of the trier of fact."[19] Obviously, the Court is not referring to the concrete, historical, primary facts of the underlying situation. These sensitive "largely factual questions" concern the proper characterization to be placed on primary facts under the applicable legal regime. Although the task is ordinarily one for the trier of facts, at times it assumes a significance requiring that it be freshly done, not merely reviewed, by the appellate tribunal.

During the first third of this century, a series of enigmatic Supreme Court decisions made similar pronouncements concerning issues of arguable constitutional significance arising in administrative hearings: whether a rate was confiscatory;[20] whether persons involved in deportation proceedings were citizens;[21] or whether an injury for which workmen's compensation was sought had occurred, as was jurisdictionally necessary, upon "navigable waters."[22] Later developments made clear that only the characterization, not the raw fact-finding, need be freshly appraised in court.[23] In ordinary administrative contexts the idea is now regarded as moribund.[24] Still, the recency of the quoted language suggests that, in the context of individual rights matters, it retains significant force.

The APA framework

Section 706 of the Administrative Procedure Act sets the general framework for review of administrative proceedings at the federal level. It warrants quotation in full:

§ 706. Scope of review

To the extent necessary to decision and when presented, the reviewing court shall decide all relevant questions of law, interpret constitutional and statutory provisions, and determine the meaning

---

19. Bose Corp. v. Consumers Union of U.S., Inc., 466 U.S. 485 (1984); similar reasoning appears to underlie Court practice respecting various criminal procedure issues, for example whether a confession was coerced.
20. Ohio Valley Water Company v. Ben Avon Borough, 253 U.S. 287 (1920).
21. Ng Fung Ho v. White, 259 U.S. 276 (1922).
22. Crowell v. Benson, 285 U.S. 22 (1932).
23. St. Joseph Stock Yards Co. v. United States, 298 U.S. 38 (1936).
24. See Administrative Law: Cases and Comments, 530-38; the issues are generally treated in H. Monaghan, Constitutional Fact Review, 85 Colum. L. Rev. 229 (1985).

or applicability of the terms of an agency action. The reviewing court shall—

(1) compel agency action unlawfully withheld or unreasonably delayed; and

(2) hold unlawful and set aside agency action, findings, and conclusions found to be—

(A) arbitrary, capricious, an abuse of discretion, or otherwise not in accordance with law;

(B) contrary to constitutional right, power, privilege, or immunity;

(C) in excess of statutory jurisdiction, authority, or limitations, or short of statutory right;

(D) without observance of procedure required by law;

(E) unsupported by substantial evidence in a case subject to sections 556 and 557 of this title or otherwise reviewed on the record of an agency hearing provided by statute; or

(F) unwarranted by the facts to the extent that the facts are subject to trial de novo by the reviewing court.

In making the foregoing determinations, the court shall review the whole record or those parts of it cited by a party, and due account shall be taken of the rule of prejudicial error.

If one looks particularly at the sub-paragraphs of Section 706(2), one can see that the provision addresses three separable areas of concern. Sub-paragraphs (E), (F) and, in part, (A) suggest three different standards for review of agency conclusions of fact. Sub-paragraphs (B), (C) and (D), as well as the introductory sentence to Section 706, address review of agency conclusions of law. Sub-paragraph (A) speaks to review of an agency's judgment, its exercise of the discretion conferred on it by law in a particular state of facts. These matters are dealt with, in turn, in the following pages.

Questions of fact

In writing about judicial review of agency determinations of fact, it is important to distinguish at the outset between those concrete historical or scientific assertions that can be made without any necessary reference to the legal order, and those characterizations or conclusions about the significance of historical or scientific fact, that almost inevitably take on its coloration. "Mrs. Jones was driving at 45 miles per hour on an ice-covered road" and "ingestion of 1 part per million diacetyphamine for two months produced a 20% increase in stomach cancers among a population of 1000 white mice" are the first sort of assertion. "In the circumstances, Mrs. Jones was being negligent" and "a concentration of 1 part per million diacetyphamine in foodstuffs intended for human consumption imposes a significant risk of causing human cancer" are the second.

It would be easier if judges (and others) described only the first kind of assertion as involving a "question of fact" and consistently saw the second for what it is, the exercise of judgment. But there remains some tendency to ascribe to both assertions the quality of "fact," and this somewhat confuses the law on review of questions of fact. Judicial review of both agency fact-finding and agency judgment (taken up below) is considerably more permissive than judicial review of legal questions. Early practice tended to conflate the two. It recognized the distinction, if at all, as a contrast between "basic" and "ultimate" fact, and stated only two standards for review: review of questions of fact, and review of questions of law. One of the contributions of the Supreme Court's decision in *Citizens to Preserve Overton Park, Inc.* v. *Volpe*, earlier discussed in another context,[25] was to elucidate the standards for reviewing the exercise of judgment or discretion in ways that sharply distinguished them from the standards for reviewing conclusions about strictly factual issues. The opinion thus firmly established "review of judgment and the exercise of discretion" as a third field for inquiry.

Indeed, the *Overton Park* opinion appears to have been taken by the Court as an opportunity to make a catholic statement about review, one that quite exceeded any necessities of the case. As part of that statement, the Court called attention to the way in which paragraphs (E), (F), and (A) of Section 706 establish three different statutory standards for review of "questions of fact": de novo review, or retrial by the court; substantial evidence review; and review to determine whether the agency's action was "arbitrary" or "capricious" in light of the information it possessed.

De novo review really is not review at all. It requires the court's independent determination of the matter at issue, on the basis of a record made in court (although it may incorporate the agency's record). As the Court remarked, the statute makes it available only in very limited circumstances.[26] It does not warrant further examination here.

---

25. See pp. 165-67; the case is also discussed at pp. 261-66, below.
26. The rare judicial determinations of "constitutional" or "jurisdictional" fact, pp. 242-43, above, can be regarded as a form of partial de novo review.

Substantial evidence

As the statutory formula of Section 706(2)(E) suggests, the "substantial evidence" test characterizes judicial review of fact-finding in on-the-record agency proceedings. Both its aspiration and its application in that context are well understood. An appeals court would be warranted in reversing a trial court's determination of some factual issue only if persuaded there had been a "clear error." In this way the appeals court's time is saved for matters of greater general interest than simple redeterminations (on a cold record) of what particularly concerns the parties. The "substantial evidence" test incorporates a similar, somewhat more permissive, approach to the fact-finding of an agency. As long as the court can determine that, viewing the record as a whole, there is evidence on the basis of which a reasonable person might have reached the agency's conclusions, it must accept those conclusions.[27]

The meaning of the "record as a whole" qualification can be illustrated by considering from the perspective of judicial review the importance of the administrative law judge's initial opinion in an on-the-record administrative adjudication. Recall that when an agency decides a matter that has already been before one of its ALJs, the agency is regarded as having reached *its* decision de novo. Unlike the court that will review the agency's factual judgments, the agency is under no obligation to respect the ALJ's factual judgments.[28] Yet the ALJ, of course, will be the only hearer to have observed live witnesses. Moreover, her limited responsibilities and freedom from political oversight in the agency give a substantial assurance of objectivity in judgment; the agency members, in contrast, have many tasks, and policy-oriented tasks; they are deeply enmeshed in political considerations and exercises from day to day.[29] The reviewing court recaptures the ALJ's contributions by regarding her initial decision as a part of the record. If an agency's ALJ had reached a conclusion opposite to her agency on some factual matter, that fact—together with whatever the record might offer in the way of support for her conclusion—would detract from whatever else in the record may support the agency's factual conclusions. In that way, it would make it less likely that "substantial

---

27. Universal Camera Corp. v. National Labor Relations Board, 340 U.S. 474 (1951). The test has been analogized to the standard for appellate review of jury determinations of fact, which is more permissive than the "clear error" test applied to judicial fact-finding.

28. See pp. 146-47.

29. And see note 51, p. 147; while staff assistance for ALJs is provided on occasion, the literature provides no basis for believing ALJ opinions are not their own.

evidence" support for the agency's conclusions could be found on the record as a whole.

In well-established understandings how this test is applied, one also finds reflected the distinction already drawn, between fact and judgment. The ALJ's judgment will carry a good deal of weight in the former category. She is in position to hear witnesses, has fewer distractions, less incentive to cut corners for the sake of achieving policy ends, and so on. But what judgments are to be drawn from scientific or historical facts, questions of inference or ultimate fact as they are sometimes called, is a matter inescapably tied up with the policy for which the agency, not the ALJ, is responsible. In a proceeding concerning unfair labor practices, for example, the first kind of issue might be whether a management or a union witness is to be believed in testifying about what words were uttered at a given meeting. The second kind of issue is presented if one needs to decide what inferences are to be drawn about management's state of mind in uttering the words, or the impact on persons present of hearing them. The National Labor Relations Board's sense of what the carrying out of national labor policy requires, and its general experience with labor-management relations, will shape the way in which these questions are answered. Here, an ALJ's inference ought not play a significant role in a court's assessment of the agency's differing judgment; the court should ask only whether the agency's judgments of this character were irrational or insufficiently grounded.

Legislative provision for use of a "substantial evidence" test also has been understood, from the outset, to serve a signaling function. It indicates Congress' wish for somewhat more intensive review of the agency's work than might otherwise be expected. When first adopted in 1946, it came against the backdrop of a supposed judicial practice of sustaining agency findings so long as the record contained *any* materials that might support them, without regard to the "record as a whole." More recently, Congress has occasionally used the formula in describing judicial review of particularly important informal rulemakings, for example those under the Occupational Safety and Health Act.

The use of a "substantial evidence" test for informal rulemaking initially produced a good deal of intellectual consternation. How could one properly review for support by substantial evidence on the record as a whole, a proceeding that was not required to be decided "on the record"? With the developing sense of what constitutes the record in rulemaking[30] and of what constitutes judicial review of fact-finding under the "arbitrary, capricious" standard, next to be discussed, the question has re-

---

30. See pp. 159-74.

ceded in importance.[31] As with the initial development of the test, Congress' choice of words is taken to express a mood, an expectation of relative intensity, rather than a precise test to be applied. This expectation is substantially responsible for the development of the "hard look" idea explored below.[32] In the rulemaking context, particularly, the distinction between fact and judgment has had major importance. The most significant issues before the rulemaking agency invariably involve projection or judgment. While the courts have wanted to assure themselves that this is accomplished in an open and thoughtful manner (again, the "hard look" idea), they have easily perceived that these are not factual judgments in the ordinary sense.

"Arbitrary, capricious"

When a decision is not required to be taken on the record, and the "substantial evidence" test is not specially and misleadingly invoked by statute, the formula of Section 706(2)(A) is the only one that applies. The "arbitrary, capricious" element of that formula is taken, inter alia, to express the standard the reviewing court should apply in judging the agency's treatment of the facts. Here, too, one has the problem of what constitutes the "whole record" against which the agency's conclusions are to be assessed. The nature and resolution of that problem in the context of informal rulemaking is addressed at some length earlier in this paper.[33] Here it may be enough to say that for informal adjudications, at least outside the context of the Due Process Clause, the demands on agencies for involving the public in creation of a record are less significant. Review is to occur on the basis of whatever record the agency presents.[34]

Assuming the record somehow identified, one might imagine "arbitrary, capricious" to state a considerably less demanding test than "substantial evidence." At times courts have behaved as if an agency finding was not "arbitrary" or "capricious" so long as the agency had any factual basis at all for its position, without regard to what might oppose it. Yet this view is confounded by the explicitly applicable "whole record" qualification of Section 706's concluding sentence. The D.C. Circuit recently

---

31. The initial, and still important, decision is Industrial Union Department, AFL-CIO v. Hodgson, 499 F.2d 467 (D.C. Cir. 1974).
32. See pp. 267-69.
33. See pp. 159-74.
34. Camp v. Pitts, 411 U.S. 138 (1973). The Freedom of Information Act, pp. 195-200, and any statutory provisions for public participation will permit external identification of the "record" to some degree.

made the following observation on the subject, an observation it aptly described as "the emerging consensus":

> When the arbitrary or capricious standard is performing [the] function of assuring factual support, there is no *substantive* difference between what it requires and what would be required by the substantial evidence test, since it is impossible to conceive of a "nonarbitrary" factual judgment supported only by evidence that is not substantial in the APA sense. . . . The distinctive function of paragraph (E)—what it achieves that paragraph (A) does not—is to require substantial evidence to be found *within the record of closed-record proceedings* to which it exclusively applies. The importance of that requirement should not be underestimated. . . . [The administrative record in an informal proceeding] might well include crucial material that was neither shown to nor known by the private parties in the proceeding. . . . [35]

Arguably this simplifies matters excessively. Yet any differences are subtle matters of intensity in assessing an aspect of judicial review that all would concede is not expected to be an especially rigorous one. The understanding that review will *not* be rigorous, particularly in contrast to judicial review of legal judgments, is the central proposition.

Questions of law

The American practice of statutory interpretation

A discussion for readers not familiar with our judicial practice concerning "questions of law" had best start with a sketch of our approaches to statutory interpretation. While "questions of law" in general include common law (or judge-made law) as well as statutory issues, in the administrative context questions of law almost invariably raise issues of statutory meaning. Statutory interpretation in federal courts is highly attentive to the history of a law's development within the Congress, and over time this in turn has generated a good deal of respect for administrators' views about issues of statutory meaning. The complexity of many regulatory schemes, daily managed by the agencies but only rarely encountered by the courts, contributes to this sense of dealing with the

---

35. Association of Data Processing Service Organizations, Inc. v. Board of Governors of the Federal Reserve System, 745 F.2d 677 (1984).

experts. Federal courts frequently give presumptive validity to an administrative agency's construction of the statutes that are particularly within the agency's charge, both in consequence of what courts find in the legislative histories and because of the agency's experience.

The process of federal legislation briefly described in chapter 3 produces a variety of public documents of greater or lesser availability:

- The enacted law, printed both in an annual volume of statutes at large and (ordinarily, for those of importance to administrative agencies) in the United States Code;

- Transcripts of any debates and votes on the bill and proposed amendments to it in the House of Representatives and

- Senate;[36] Reports generated by the responsible legislative committees of the House and Senate, explaining the bill's provisions and important choices that may have been made in committee to help their colleagues prepare for the House and Senate debates;[37]

- If the House and Senate produced differing bills, requiring a conference committee, a conference committee report explaining the choices were made;

- Committee prints of the bills as they took shape at varying stages; and

- Occasionally, printed transcripts of Senate or House committee hearings.

- If the president vetoes legislation, his veto message is also a public document, appearing both in the Congressional Record and in the weekly compilation of presidential documents.

Congressional debates are printed in the daily Congressional Record, a widely circulated official gazette to be found in most libraries. The committee and conference reports are fairly widely available in large municipal and university libraries located throughout the country and often

---

36. Readers from parliamentary democracies should remember that party discipline is highly variable in American practice; a Senator or Representative is free to vote his conscience on every vote and ordinarily will do so. While he will vote with party more often than not, amendments to proposed legislation are generally expected. Most successful legislation *begins* as a draft supplied by the executive administration, but it is the rare such draft that is not extensively amended before final enactment.

37. Studies of the legislative process indicate that these reports are, in fact, the principal source of information about pending legislative matters for congressmen who are not members of the responsible committees. See M. Malkin, Unelected Representation (1979).

also (for important legislation) in commercial publications.[38] The availability of hearings and of committee prints of bills is much more haphazard, generally being limited to large "depositary" libraries to which all congressional documents are sent. The practices about to be described are of much lesser significance respecting state legislation, for which comparable historical materials are rarely if ever available.

For an agency whose daily work will be controlled by particular legislation, as may easily be imagined, recordkeeping about legislation of interest begins at an early stage and reaches more broadly. If the agency is already in existence during initial drafting stages within the administration, its officials will be deeply involved in those processes, and will generate institutional memories about them. When the draft reaches Congress, the agency will be careful to maintain its own records of all the documents already mentioned, and perhaps others—transcripts or notes of unprinted hearings, detailed records of all agency testimony on legislative matters, etc. Often enough, bills must be submitted to a number of sessions of Congress before any one is enacted. The agency will possess a rather detailed sense of this history and of the political changes and compromises, explicit and unspoken, that ultimately produced success. It has, as well, a continuing relationship with the responsible congressional committees and their staff. This relationship continues after the bill becomes law and is likely to be influenced, for good or for ill, by the committee's reaction to the manner in which the new legislation is implemented. The agency must be prepared at every step to defend its choices, politically as well as in court, in terms of its statutory authority. This generates a continuing attention to issues of statutory meaning *in the context of legislative history* that, outside government, can be difficult to appreciate.[39]

Faced with the problem of interpreting a congressional statute, a court will of course first consider its direct language. This will include sophisticated reference to context, structure, and all the usual tools of understanding written language. Occasionally, judges will assert that they are adopting the "plain meaning" of statutory language. This formula sug-

---

38. The most important such source is the U.S. Code, Congressional and Administrative News published by the West Publishing Company, which makes available all congressional legislation within a few weeks of its enactment, together with excerpts from the more important committee reports.

39. I tell my classes that the real impact of the "delegation" doctrine, discussed on pp. 18-23, is experienced in the daily work of thousands of government lawyers striving to show that proposed agency conduct lies within statutory authority. That work—as likely to be exposed to congressional committees or the GAO, pp. 58-59, as the courts—can invest a commissioner's testimony in hearings with the seriousness of a treaty.

gests that the judge finds only one reading of language to be sensible, whatever the parties may think. But in a matter parties have thought important enough to argue about in litigation, the language alone often will not put an end to the controversy. It will be susceptible of two or more readings from which a choice must be made. Indeed, persuading the judge that an ambiguity exists in a statute is the threshold that must first be crossed in any interpretive setting. But once that threshold is crossed, no formal rules of construction must be used to determine which is the preferable reading. Rather, the judge is to choose that meaning that most closely fits the purpose of the legislature.[40]

In doing so, she is encouraged to refer to the publicly available materials of legislative history. To the extent this is done to acquire a sense of the problems with which the legislators expected their work to deal—the "mischief" to which the statute responded—it seems unlikely to appear controversial to the readers of this essay. Preliminary studies, committee reports and debates can all set a context for understanding the troubles that called forth particular language, and in that way contribute to its construction. But the judge also will be looking for indications of what the legislature considered—"intended," in some formulations—the language chosen would accomplish. Here, practice may be somewhat surprising. Speakers in committee hearings, writers of committee reports, and participants in congressional debates may each state, with greater or lesser clarity, what they expect particular language to mean, and the judge is to take some account of these expressions. The footnotes give hints about how that is done,[41] and about the justifications for[42] and the difficulties of[43] the practice, but this is hardly the place to go into detail.[44]

---

40. "Purpose of the legislature" is a loose phrase that conceals a great deal of imprecision. How long is historical purpose to govern contemporary (and arguably unforeseen) developments? How much realism is appropriate in assessing about the detail with which problems were considered and acted upon? Is it rational to ascribe "purpose" (beyond language officially adopted) to an act adopted on the votes of 535 politicians, who are informed and motivated in sharply varying degrees and who lack the opportunity to persuade and be persuaded by more than a fraction of their total number? etc.

41. In general, greater formality is attached to the documents with the greatest exposure and significance in the legislative process. Conference reports have the highest regard in this respect, as they are the basis for votes in both houses on matters already shaped by extensive debate. Most give next rank to committee reports, the written and universally available products of the most intensive view given the draft legislation. Next come floor debates, which embody high seriousness (votes) but may at any given moment be poorly attended; also, the transcripts of debates are subject to extensive editing by the speaker. Among the debates, statements by those most responsible for the legislation—for example, a committee chairman—will be given the most attention. The least attention is

Administrative readings of statutes are also among the considerations that the judge is to take into account. They bear in at least four differing ways, discussed in the paragraphs immediately following. Note that the first three of these arguments for considering administrative readings preserve the judge's ultimate responsibility for determining the meaning of the statute as a question of law. The fourth, however, seems to place important elements of that responsibility in the agency.

First, testimony at congressional hearings by agency officials who will be responsible for implementing the legislation being considered is often thought more useful than other hearing testimony in understanding legislative purpose. This is perhaps the most readily understood of the ways in which administrative readings are to be taken into account. These

---

paid to what transpired at hearings, which is both preliminary and, typically, far less readily accessible.

42. The chief justifications are that the material is available, that its use serves as a partial check on judicial subjectivity in interpretation, and that it serves also as a reminder of legislative supremacy. Judicial insistence on using only linguistic techniques of interpretation is associated with attitudes such as that statutes must be narrowly construed to avoid interference with the judicially created and managed common law. Johnson v. So. Pac. RR, 117 F. 462 (8th Cir. 1902), reversed 196 U.S. 1 (1904) is a notorious example.

In the regulatory context, where principal responsibility for a statute's administration lies with an agency rather than the courts, legislative materials give a set of common external points of reference to both agency and court. It could be thought that this has a tendency to control the subjectivities of both. For the agency, it recognizes the legitimacy of the indicia of meaning that politics would in any event require it to consult; that is, Congress will require agencies to pay attention to these materials through oversight, *whether or not the courts will do so*. For the courts, use of these materials is a reminder of the agency's responsibility. For the system of government as a whole, it avoids competition between overseers of the administrative process as to the proper standards of meaning to be applied.

43. Legislatures vote on statutory language, not reports and certainly not on hearings. As it has become known that reports, debates and hearings are used to decide issues of meaning, participants in the legislative process who might not be able to win a direct vote have used these devices to convey purposes and intents that are, at the least, controversial as implications from statutory language as such. As congressional staff has grown in size, reports have become less a repository of legislators' thinking, and more an expression of the legislative bureaucracy, whose contents are often influenced by private lobbyists. The printed reports of congressional debates carry no indication how widely they were heard, and in any event are subject to such extensive editing and enlargement after the fact as to be unreliable evidence of what was heard. Committee hearings are often attended by only one or two legislators, or even just staff.

44. Highly regarded sources on statutory interpretation include H. Hart and A. Sacks, The Legal Process: Basic Problems in the Making and Application of Law (Tent. ed. 1958); F. Frankfurter, Some Reflections on the Reading of Statutes, 47 Colum. L. Rev. 527 (1947); J. Kernochan, Statutory Interpretation: An Outline of Method, 3 Dalhousie L.J. 333 (1976).

officials are often the drafters, and in any event their continuing relationships with the responsible committees and the importance of the outcome to their own functions give their understandings particular credibility.[45]

Second, and relatedly, decisions an agency makes in its immediate implementation of new authority are regarded as probative indicators of meaning. Once again, the reasoning is that agency officials will likely have been involved in drafting and the hearing process; they will have had a deep interest in following the legislative debates. And just as this important and intensive exposure to the legislative process makes apt understanding probable, their continuing relationships with the responsible committees make it unlikely that they would depart sharply from congressional understanding.[46]

The third area of judicial attention to administrative readings is concerned with long-term statutory administration rather than formation. The interpretations an agency makes even in later years are frequently said to be entitled to significant deference. This is in recognition that statutes must be kept dynamic instruments, capable of response to changing social circumstances without need for explicit legislative revision. Their wording often permits such adaptation. As the years pass, an agency with continuing responsibility for administration of a statutory scheme (particularly a complex one) is often in a better position than a court to maintain the scheme's integrity as new circumstances arise requiring attention. One could expand on this observation about comparative advantage by noting two additional considerations. First, the agency has greater incentive and capacity to understand the particular scheme as a whole. Second, the agency's continuing legislative relationships could be understood to suggest that Congress' failure to revise the statute is (at least in part) the product of satisfaction with the agency's continuing stewardship. These factors are, of course, highly variable. Many other explanations—inattention, controversiality—can be given for congressional failures to act, and the risk may appear substantial that an agency's course of interpretation will be self-interested.

One might expect, then, that judicial attention to this third factor would be highly variable, and it is. It may be helpful to look particularly at the situation of the taxing authorities, whose interpretations tend in fact to be highly respected by the courts. Understanding the reasons for this can assist the analyst in locating other administrators on the continuum of agency and court responsibility.

---

45. Securities and Exchange Commission v. Collier, 76 F.2d 939 (2d Cir. 1935) provides a useful example of this approach.

46. Norwegian Nitrogen Prod. Co. v. United States, 288 U.S. 294 (1933) is the decision customarily cited for this proposition.

The relationships between the taxing agencies and the Congress are unusually close, with small changes constantly occurring in the tax laws as problems come to light, and unusually detailed committee oversight of tax administration generally. The Internal Revenue Service has long had a reputation for rigorously professional administration. It publishes its interpretations in unusual detail, and engages in vigorous professional discussion of them, in addition to its oversight relations with Congress. The tax laws are an unusually complex and interdependent body of technical statutes, an intricate web which a judge who visits only occasionally could not confidently traverse without risk of causing unintended consequences and disruptions. Finally, recognizing IRS authority tends to promote rational uniformity in tax administration, as against a court system that, beneath the Supreme Court, is geographically organized. National uniformity is particularly needed in tax administration; differing results in San Francisco and New York regarding a citizen's obligation to pay the costs of government would create enormous discontent. And so judges generally respect interpretations of the tax codes that can be made to appear reasonable to them.[47] Absent some or all of these factors, a different result might be expected.

Finally, the fourth respect in which courts may pay special heed to administrative readings differs from the three just described, in that it recognizes in the agency a primary role. The court may conclude that the law places in the agency, to some extent, the responsibility to say what the statute means. In its own way, of course, this conclusion also requires a court's independent judgment on an issue of law. It is the court, not the agency, that decides when and subject to what constraints such authority has been conferred. Nonetheless, it should be apparent that any such conclusion crosses a significant threshold. In each of the prior examples, the court has been responsible for deciding the meaning of the statutory language in question, taking such guidance as administrative conduct may offer. The question of meaning is then fixed by the judicial reading, unless later reexamined by another court or the legislature. Under this fourth approach, the question of statutory interpretation is, to a certain extent, given to the agency. The judicial control is only to determine whether the choice it has made is a "reasonable" one. Other "reasonable" meanings might be attached by the agency at another time (if suitably justified), and those are equally entitled to be upheld.

As the Supreme Court recently explained this fourth approach in one of the most strongly stated of these cases:

> When a court reviews an agency's construction of the statute which it administers, it is confronted with two questions. First,

---

47. See, e.g., Cammarano v. United States, 358 U.S. 498 (1959).

always, is the question whether Congress has directly spoken to the precise question at issue. If the intent of Congress is clear, that is the end of the matter; for the court, as well as the agency, must give effect to the unambiguously expressed intent of Congress. If, however, the court determines Congress has not directly addressed the precise question at issue, the court does not simply impose its own construction on the statute, as would be necessary in the absence of an administrative interpretation. Rather, if the statute is silent or ambiguous with respect to the specific issue, the question for the court is whether the agency's answer is based on a permissible construction of the statute.

. . .

In this case, the Administrator's interpretation represents a reasonable accommodation of manifestly competing interests and is entitled to deference: the regulatory scheme is technical and complex, the agency considered the matter in a detailed and reasoned fashion, and the decision involves reconciling conflicting policies. Congress intended to accommodate both interests, but did not do so itself on the level of specificity presented by this case. Perhaps that body consciously desired the Administrator to strike the balance at this level, thinking that those with great expertise and charged with responsibility for administering the provision would be in a better position to do so; perhaps it simply did not consider the question at this level; and perhaps Congress was unable to forge a coalition on either side of the question, and those on each side decided to take their chances with the scheme devised by the agency. For judicial purposes, it matters not which of these things occurred.

. . .

When a challenge to an agency construction of a statutory provision, fairly conceptualized, really centers on the wisdom of the agency's policy, rather than whether it is a reasonable choice within a gap left open by Congress, the challenge must fail. In such a case, federal judges—who have no constituency—have a duty to respect legitimate policy choices made by those who do. The responsibilities for assessing the wisdom of such policy choices and resolving the struggle between competing views of the public interest are not judicial ones: "Our Constitution vests such responsibilities in the political branches." TVA v. Hill, 437 U.S. 153, 195 (1978).[48]

---

48. Chevron, U.S.A., Inc. v. Natural Resources Defense Council, Inc., 467 U.S. 837 (1984). For recent elaboration on this language, which has proved controversial, see NLRB v. United Food and Commercial Workers Union, 108 S. Ct. 413 (1987); INS v. Cardoza-Foneca, 107 S. Ct. 1207 (1987).

Agency or court?

The language just quoted may seem the more surprising when compared with the language of Section 706, and also with a line the Supreme Court often quotes from its early, and foundational, decision about judicial review, *Marbury* v. *Madison*.[49] Both the preamble to Section 706 and its paragraphs (B), (C) and (D) appear to stress the primacy and independence of judicial judgment. They reflect in this way the *Marbury* assertion, "it is emphatically the province and duty of the judicial department to say what the law is." That courts have plenary authority to determine legal questions is the orthodox view and is a proposition suggested from time to time even as a matter of constitutional necessity.[50] The following paragraphs are intended to illustrate the lines along which this paradox is likely to be resolved.

An independent judicial role will invariably appear when the question to be decided is larger than the agency's responsibility. Thus, if the question concerns the constitutionality of a statute or of its application, one would expect that to be decided strictly by the courts; this is reflected in the special judicial practice respecting "constitutional facts" mentioned briefly above.[51] Similarly, if the question is one of ascribing meaning to a statute of general application, not one specially within a particular agency's charge, the judiciary will naturally enough decide the matter on its own, without any particular guidance from the judgment of an agency that may have had occasion to confront it. Thus, the Federal Trade Commission, whose responsibilities include conducting formal administrative hearings implementing laws protective of competition, might well have to decide questions about the meaning of a provision of the APA, or of the Sherman Anti-Trust Act. Yet there is no reason to think a court would be much persuaded by the FTC's judgment about the meaning of such statutes, which could easily have arisen before another agency or in a judicial trial.

Where the agency has not been delegated (or has not used) formal authority to bind others in its implementation of a statute, even one uniquely within its own responsibility, any question of interpreting the statute that reaches the courts will, of necessity, have to be resolved by the courts. Often, however, the court will resolve the matter on a basis according substantial deference to the views the agency may have developed. Thus, the work of the Wage and Hour Division of the Department of Labor in implementing fair labor standards legislation, discussed

---

49. 1 Cranch 137 (1803).
50. E.g., Crowell v. Benson, 285 U.S. 22 (1932); pp. 218-20; and pp. 241-43.
51. See pp. 242-43.

briefly above,[52] is almost exclusively interpretive. Advice is given through letters of greater or lesser formality and through the issuance of interpretive rules or bulletins. None of this is binding, but the courts have experienced no difficulty in describing the Administrator's judgments as appropriately influential; his

> rulings, interpretations and opinions . . . , while not controlling upon the courts by reason of their authority, do constitute a body of experience and informed judgment to which courts and litigants may properly resort for guidance. The weight of such a judgment in a particular case will depend upon the thoroughness evident in its consideration, the validity of its reasoning, its consistency with earlier and later pronouncements, and all those factors which give it power to persuade, if lacking power to control.[53]

One way of rationalizing this practice is to recall that although federal agencies are organized nationally and the law they apply is national in scope, the first two levels of the federal judiciary are geographically limited. Moreover, the Supreme Court's capacity to enforce uniformity upon the lower federal courts is severely restricted by the small size of its docket.[54] The tendency produced by having courts in Maine, Florida and California each believe it should respect the Administrator's judgment about statutory meaning in reaching its own conclusions is to enhance the probability of uniform national administration of the laws.

The language just quoted, which frequently appears in judicial opinions, conveys a sense of its own limits. At the outset, the Administrator in taking a position must be able to convince the court that his is a possible or sensible position in light of the statutory language. Thus, the same statute authorized the Administrator to define an "area of production" for agricultural products as an element of exemption from reputation. The Administrator read this language as permitting distinctions between large and small enterprises performing the same work in the same locality. In context, however, the Supreme Court believed that "area" necessarily referred geographical and/or work-related factors, and so it easily rejected

---

52. See p. 230.

53. Skidmore v. Swift & Co., 323 U.S. 134 (1944); for a similar contemporary case, see Ford Motor Credit Co. v. Milhollin, 444 U.S. 555 (1980).

54. See pp. 81-82; P. Strauss, One Hundred Fifty Cases Per Year: Some Implications of the Supreme Court's Limited Resources for Judicial Review of Agency Action, 87 Colum. L. Rev. 1093 (1987). If the Supreme Court hears only 160 full arguments yearly, questions arising under the fair labor standards legislation can hardly come before it more than once each few years; recall, however, that the Administrator issues about 10,000 opinions annually that have the dignity warranting judicial review. (The actual incidence of judicial review, of course, is very much lower than that.)

the Administrator's reading.[55] The courts, that is, retain independent judgment on the question *what possibilities of meaning* statutory language opens up. Only when it comes to choosing among the possibilities that language offers, must attention be paid to administrative constructions.

This same distinction is readily seen in cases in which agencies do exercise statutory authority to bind others by their interpretations, and the question is whether (or under what circumstances) courts must also accept those interpretations. This can be seen in a pair of roughly contemporary formal NLRB adjudications of the 1940's; and more recently in two rulemaking proceedings, the *Chevron* case quoted above[56] and another involving the Federal Reserve Board.[57] In each of these pairings, one case appears to state a principle of judicial obligation to respect the agency's interpretation; the other seems oblivious to the fact that the agency has interpreted the statute at all. One may offer as an explanation for both pairs that *all* of these cases started with examination of the question what possibilities of meaning the statutory language in question opened up. In only two of the cases, one in each pair, was the Court required to reach the question who was to choose, and how, among the possibilities thus revealed.

In *NLRB v. Hearst Publications, Inc.*[58] the question was whether certain men who sold Hearst's newspapers on the streets of Los Angeles were "employees" within the meaning of the National Labor Relations Act. In *Packard Motor Car Co. v. NLRB*,[59] the question was whether foremen in Packard's plants—that is, workers responsible to some extent for supervision of other workers—could be regarded as employees. In both cases the Court sustained a finding by the Board that the workers *were* employees. In *Hearst*, it did so because the "task [of determining who is an employee] has been assigned primarily to the agency . . . Congress entrusted to it primarily the decision whether the evidence establishes the material facts. Hence in reviewing the Board's ultimate conclusions, it is not the Court's function to substitute its own inferences of fact for the Board's, when the latter have support in the record. . . . Where the question is one of specific application of a broad statutory term in a proceeding in which the agency administering the statute must determine it initially, the reviewing court's function is limited." In *Packard*, however, the question whether the foremen could be regarded as "employees" was de-

---

55. Addison v. Holly Hill Fruit Products, Inc., 322 U.S. 607 (1944).
56. See p. 256.
57. Board of Governors, Federal Reserve System v. Dimension Financial Corp., 106 S. Ct. 681 (1986).
58. 322 U.S. 111 (1944).
59. 330 U.S. 485 (1947).

scribed by the Court as "a naked question of law," and the agency's view was essentially ignored.

If one looks more deeply, however, the suggested pattern emerges. In *Hearst* the question for the Court was choosing among three possible systems for investing meaning in "employee." First, because the question who is an "employee" commonly arose in state law, it might be decided on that basis, from state to state. Second, because being an "employee" was important to a variety of federal statutes, each with a different aim, the Court might have chosen to give the term a uniform and judicially administered national interpretation. Finally "employee" could be regarded as a term that would take its color from the particular policies of the National Labor Relations Act, the responsibility for which was placed primarily in the Board. The Court independently and sensibly concluded that the last was the proper choice. That choice having been made, it followed that the Board should be primarily responsible for investing meaning in the term. In *Packard*, however, the question was not what system Congress had chosen to give general meaning to the statutory term "employee." It was whether workers with management responsibilities were, or were not, specifically excluded from the possibility of falling within it. The very hypothesis of the question is that Congress did not commit judgment about it to the NLRB. Having answered that question, the Court had no occasion to consult the Board's judgment. Even though it is for the Board to choose among possible meanings, in other words, it is for the courts to say what meanings are possible.

Similarly, in *Chevron*, the initial judgment reached independently by the Court is that Congress' delegation of rulemaking authority to the EPA left open the possibility that it would, by rule, permit the approach to pollution control challenged in that litigation. The court independently decided, first, that the approach was neither compelled nor foreclosed by the legislation, but remained a possibility under its terms. Having reached this conclusion, its obligation to accept the agency's choice then follows.[60] The Federal Reserve Board, on the other hand, attempted to use rulemaking to give the term "bank" a meaning the Court believed Congress had specifically excluded.[61] Having reached that conclusion, the

---

60. If there is a surprising element to the *Chevron* formulation, it may be that the Court states the interpretive proposition so broadly: *whenever* legislation is found to permit a choice among given constructions, agencies with power formally to bind citizens by legislative rules or other measures are to be regarded as having the power "reasonably" to make that choice. *Hearst* is the product specifically of a reading of the National Labor Relations Act; the *Chevron* statement states a more general proposition about how Congress expects issues to be decided that it has not resolved, and that are committed in the first instance to powerful administrators.

61. Note 57, above.

Court had no reason to talk about what the Board's authority would have been if the meaning the Board wished to adopt were one among several permissible options. The reader will understand from this analysis that the characterization of the questions presented to the court on review is of the utmost importance.

Judgment and the exercise of discretion

Doubtless the most challenging aspect of judicial review, that aspect courts worry about most openly in their opinions, concerns the judicial function in reviewing agency judgment and exercise of discretion. Agency findings of this character are more involved with the legal system (and have more implications for society as a whole) than the most basic of facts about a particular situation. Yet they fall in the particular area of responsibility assigned to the agency, and do not implicate those general questions about the legal order that are inescapably the courts'. On the one hand, court action must respect the statutory assignment of responsibility. The agency, not the court, has been directed to make judgments about whether a given road should be built, reactor licensed or environmental protection rule adopted. Assuring that respect is not a simple task, since judges commonly share the passions of their community on such matters. On other hand, the agencies' responsibility is intended to be constrained by procedures, by substantive law, by expectations of rationality and openness. Assuring the success of those constraints *is* a judicial task. The APA's formula for this judicial role is that of Section 706(2)(A), quoted above.[62] The Supreme Court's most elaborate discussion of its meaning and application, already discussed at some length in another context,[63] was its decision in *Citizens to Preserve Overton Park, Inc. v. Volpe*.[64]

Citizens to Preserve Overton Park v. *Volpe*

The elements of review

As has already been mentioned, the Supreme Court used the occasion of its opinion in *Overton Park* to write a kind of Baedeker of judicial review.

---

62. The text is quoted on pp. 243-44.
63. See pp. 165-67.
64. 401 U.S. 402 (1971).

Recall that the issue in that case was whether the Secretary had properly authorized federal funds to be provided the state of Tennessee to assist it in building a road that was going to traverse an important municipal park, in the face of a recent federal statute whose purpose was to discourage the use of parklands for such purposes. The Court's tour of judicial review principles began with what was perhaps an unconscious re-creation of the tension animating the task generally:

> Certainly the Secretary's decision is entitled to a presumption of regularity. [The Court here cited a case[65] that would be taken by most American lawyers to state an extremely permissive approach to judicial review of the rationality of agency rulemaking, equating it with review of the rationality of statutes.][66] But that presumption is not to shield his action from a thorough, probing, in-depth review.

It then elaborated a series of tasks.

"The court is first required to decide whether the Secretary acted within the scope of his authority." This, the Court explained, requires a reviewing court to delineate that authority and to determine whether, on the facts, the Secretary's judgment can reasonably be said to fall within it. Even if the judgment is thus a possible one, the court must inquire to some degree whether it has been correctly reached: Did the Secretary correctly understand his authority? Could he reasonably have believed that the statutory conditions necessary to permit the proposed use of this parkland had been met? Thus, the "scope of authority" question is more complex than asking, simply, whether the decision the Secretary made is a kind of action he is authorized to take. In the simple sense, it is easy to say that this was a decision about supporting state road-building, that involved making judgments between the use of parkland for the road and other possible routings. But the court is also to learn how the Secretary understood the statute; and if he did so correctly, whether the facts before him "reasonably" could support the conclusion he reached.

A second inquiry the Court required exposes the Secretary's reasoning process in another sense:

> Section 706(2)(A) requires a finding that the actual choice made was not "arbitrary, capricious, an abuse of discretion, or otherwise not in accordance with law." To make this finding the court must consider whether the decision was based on a consideration of the relevant factors and whether there has been a clear error of judgment. . . . Although this inquiry into the facts is to be searching and

---

65. Pacific States Box & Basket Co. v. White, 296 U.S. 176 (1935).
66. See, as to the constitutional overtones arising on review of the constitutionality of *statutes*, pp. 24-25.

careful, the ultimate standard of review is a narrow one. The court is not empowered to substitute its judgment for that of the agency.

While the distinction between this inquiry and the second aspect of the inquiry described in the preceding paragraph may strike the reader as somewhat ephemeral, its focus is less on the objective circumstances under which judgment was reached, and more on the actual process of judgment. "Consideration of the relevant factors" invites attention, not only to whether the Secretary asked all the right questions, but also to whether he asked any wrong ones. Did, for example, political "blackmail" play a role?[67] Does the reasoning process represented to the reviewing court reveal gaps in thought or other irrationality?

A prominent recent example of this form of review can be found in litigation challenging a decision by President Reagan's Secretary of Transportation to rescind a rule that would have required automobile manufacturers to install "passive restraints" in all passenger cars.[68] Passive restraints are devices, like air bags or pre-attached seat belts, that protect a car's driver and passengers against accidents without their having to take any action to engage them. The rule had been adopted during the previous administration after lengthy and harrowing rulemaking proceedings. In rescinding it, the new Secretary of Transportation relied on studies indicating that many drivers would disable the pre-attached belts. She expressed doubt whether the safety benefits from a requirement that could so easily be defeated would exceed the costs of installing the belts in all cars. Clearly, this is the kind of decision the Secretary is authorized to make, and it would be hard to say in the abstract that the underlying facts compelled a decision one way or the other.

Reversing, the Supreme Court expressed some doubts whether the studies the Secretary relied upon supported her judgment. More important, the Court relied on two failures of reasoning. First, the Secretary had failed to consider whether, if seat belts could be so easily defeated, the better alternative would not be to require air bags or other less easily defeated devices. Second, she had not considered the effect of driver inertia on the use rate even of the pre-attached belts. Even though they could be disabled, that is, those belts would remain in place until someone took the trouble to disable them. If ever reattached—say, for a longer trip—they would remain in use until, again, someone affirmatively undid them. The result did not deny that the Secretary might on a proper showing be able to rescind the rule. Rather, the Court found that she

---

67. See pp. 193-95.
68. Motor Vehicle Manufacturers Association of the United States, Inc. v. State Farm Mutual Automobile Insurance Company, 463 U.S. 29 (1983).

had failed adequately to justify her decision to do so, and must reconsider the matter.

The reader may think (as a concurrence charged, and as could not be proven wrong) that as to the second of these matters the Court *did* substitute its judgment for the Secretary's. Yet the form of judgment, inviting reconsideration, denies that. One's general experience is that such reassessments as were invited here are, when made, accepted by the courts.

The problems of record, findings, and reasons

As we earlier discussed,[69] the *Overton Park* opinion voiced (and generated) expectations about the administrative record, agency fact-finding, and agency reasoning that would be hard to justify on the face of the APA or in light of prior practice. The process that it describes seems to demand a fairly complete record, and full agency explanations both of facts found and of reasons for judgment. Yet in other settings the Supreme Court has insisted that reviewing courts must accept the record more-or-less as provided by the agency.[70] It has yet to confront the difficulties introduced by institutional styles of decision. The administrative record in an informal proceeding, as the D.C. Circuit remarked,[71] "might well include crucial material that was neither shown to nor known by the private parties in the proceeding." As important, it will often be interlaced with projections and judgments based on nothing more tangible than the agency's expert "feel."

As for the issue of explanation, the Court conceded in *Overton Park* itself that findings were not legally required (although the failure to make them had a consequence shortly to be explored). Two years later, the Court decided a case in which the Comptroller of Currency's decision to deny an applicant permission to open a new bank had been explained in one paragraph of an informal letter.[72] The Court remarked:

---

69. See pp. 164-69.

70. Camp v. Pitts, 411 U.S. 138 (1973); Vermont Yankee Nuclear Power Corp. v. Natural Resources Defense Council, Inc., 435 U.S. 519 (1978).

71. See the text at note 35, above.

72. Camp v. Pitts, 411 U.S. 138 (1973). The letter read in part:
On each application we endeavor to develop the need and convenience factors in conjunction with all other banking factors and in this case we were unable to reach a favorable conclusion as to the need factor. The record reflects that this market area is now served by the Peoples Bank with deposits of $7.2MM, The Bank of Hartsville with deposits of $12.8MM, The First Federal Savings and Loan Association with deposits of $5.4MM, The Mutual Savings and Loan Association with deposits of $8.2MM and the Sonoco Employees Credit Union with deposits of $6.5MM. The aforementioned are as of December 31, 1968.

Unlike Overton Park, in the present case there was contemporaneous explanation of the agency decision. The explanation may have been curt, but it surely indicated the determinative reason for the final action taken: the finding that the new bank was an uneconomic venture in light of the banking needs and the banking services already available in the surrounding community. The validity of the Comptroller's action must, therefore, stand or fall on the propriety of that finding, judged, of course, by the appropriate standard of review.

The manner in which these problems have been dealt with, and the manner in which requirements respecting record, findings and reasons have been considerably elaborated, have already been explored in the context of rulemaking.[73] Occasional tendencies in the same direction can be noted for informal adjudication,[74] even though a statutory peg, like that provided for rulemaking by APA Section 553, is harder to find. Whatever the formal justifications for these tendencies, the very fact of having to distinguish judicial oversight from the substitution of judicial judgment supplies an important practical incentive. Agency heads can see as easily as a court can, that the *Overton Park* standards will work to keep the court in its place, but only if the agencies provide the kind of data about their decisionmaking that will permit the court to conduct the analyses described. Having to restrict review to the reasons the Comptroller gives not only leads to demands for additional data about agency processes and tends to prevent courts from substituting judgment; it also encourages the Comptroller to give reasons. It is not unusual for a court to remand a matter to an agency for further explanation, asserting that the explanations given are insufficient to permit it to follow, and thus review, the agency's reasoning process.[75]

Inquiry into mental processes

A more pointed incentive for the Comptroller to state his findings and reasons at the time he decides is that the parties may be able to force a judicial trial about them if he does not. Review must *always* occur on the basis of the agency's findings and reasons. If those are not given at the

---

73. See pp. 164-69.

74. Independent U.S. Tanker Owners Committee v. Lewis, 690 F.2d 908 (D.C. Cir. 1982).

75. It is well to recall that this effect is not without its costs for administrative process. The experience of having to generate relatively elaborate explanations for each rule is said to be a significant disincentive to use rulemaking generally. See J. Mashaw and D. Harfst, Regulation and Legal Culture: The Case of Motor Vehicle Safety, 4 Yale J. Reg. 257 (1987).

moment of decision, they can be supplied afterwards only by a process of reconstruction. In *Overton Park* the Secretary sought to accomplish this by submitting sworn statements—affidavits. The Supreme Court thought this improper, because it generated too large a risk that the reasons would simply be generated by lawyers after the fact, rather than reflect the Secretary's actual bases for judgment when he acted. Just as courts are not to substitute their judgment for the agency's, they must also be alert that agency lawyers do not substitute *their* judgments or reasons for the agency's during the review process.[76] Thus, in *Overton Park*, the Court called for an active judicial inquiry into the Secretary's reasoning. This inquiry that could (and in the event did) transform itself into a lengthy and rather exacting trial.

In the ordinary case, administrative officials are protected against any such examination of their "real reasons" for acting. This is, at root, the meaning of the "presumption of regularity" recited by the Court in the quotation from *Overton Park* given above. "[W]here there are administrative findings that were made at the same time as the decision," the Court remarked in *Overton Park*, "there must be a strong showing of bad faith or improper behavior before such inquiry may be made.[77] But here there are no such formal findings and it may be that the only way there can be effective judicial review is by examining the decisionmakers themselves." It can easily be imagined that a busy federal official would happily take "unnecessary" formal steps such as making findings, if doing so would eliminate the risk of being forced to submit to a judicial trial of his actual reasoning process. Prior discussion has already suggested that "strong" showings of bad faith or improper motivation are not easily made.[78]

Consistency

One common demand on the agency reasoning process warranting special mention here is that the agency explain its decision in light of other actions taken in like circumstances. One wants to be careful in stating this. While the ordinary controls exist against abusive relitigation in matters involving the same party,[79] the courts repeatedly affirm that agencies may change the policies they apply from time to time as political

---

76. SEC v. Chenery Corp., 318 U.S. 80 (1943); see p. 147.

77. The statement was based on a series of decisions involving agricultural regulation from the 1930's, that culminated in United States v. Morgan, 313 U.S. 409 (1941). An excellent treatment appears in D. Gifford, The Morgan Cases: A Retrospective View, 30 Ad. L. Rev. 237 (1978).

78. See pp. 171-74 and 191-95.

79. Administrative Law: Cases and Comments 517 ff.

or other circumstances change, so long as they do not exceed the scope of discretion accorded them. In making such changes, however, agencies must be able to articulate reasons for doing so. They must adhere to what might be described as a requirement of momentary consistency—undertaking to treat all matters of the character now before them as they are treating this one, until they have found some reason to change their view. (At that time, the new view will have to be consistently applied.) What would be "arbitrary" would be to apply two inconsistent rules at the same time, having no acceptable reason for choosing one or the other in any particular instance. From this derives what sometimes appears to be a special obligation of explanation: "[w]hatever the ground for [a] departure from prior norms, . . . it must be clearly set forth so that the reviewing court may understand the basis of the agency's action and so may judge the consistency of that action with the agency's mandate."[80] A concrete showing of apparent and unexplained inconsistency of treatment provides challengers with one of the strongest bases for interesting a court in judicial review. One must also expect, however, that the courts will be realistic about the capacity of agencies having to decide high volumes of cases to achieve perfect consistency of application; reasonable effort to attain it will suffice.[81]

Hard look review

The problem of consistency is not the agencies' alone. The reader will already have remarked to himself that the variety of inquiries described leaves a good deal of room for a court to pursue review aggressively or permissively, as the particular circumstances before the court or the court's political inclinations may suggest. Some empirical studies appear to have demonstrated such effects,[82] which may appear to give point to earlier quoted remarks about seedless grapes.[83] One can find in the cases, however, indications of structure concerning the issue of intensity. Agency decisions smacking of priority-setting, or that have relatively little impact on individuals, or that are unusually dependent on judgments of a political character, all warrant a permissive judicial approach. Decisions setting standards carrying important consequences for the private realm, heavily reliant on judgments about physical fact, or responding to a spe-

---

80. Atchison, Topeka & Santa Fe Ry. Co. v. Wichita Bd. of Trade, 412 U.S. 800 (1973).

81. Davis v. Commissioner, 69 T.C. 716 (1978).

82. One recent, excellent study of this character is R.S. Melnick, Regulation and the Courts: The Case of the Clean Air Act (Brookings 1983).

83. See note 3, above.

cific statutory command, by contrast, call for a more aggressive judicial stance.[84] In the context, particularly, of judicial review of agency rule-making to regulate health, safety and environmental concerns, the aggressive mode of judicial review has acquired a name, "hard look" review. In origin the idea thus expressed was that the court's sole obligation was to be sure the *agency* had taken a hard look at the problems before it. In popular usage and probably reality today, the idea is understood to be that in such cases the *courts*, too, ought to take a hard look.

The earlier discussion of the "paper hearing"[85] has substantially outlined the development of this idea, employed by the Supreme Court itself in the air bag/seat belt case described toward the beginning of this section.[86] Both its extent and its problems may be suggested by the 125-page opinion of the D.C. Circuit reviewing EPA regulations governing the use of coal by electric generating stations. One aspect of that opinion, already discussed,[87] concerned a procedural question, the participation of the President and an influential senator in the decision process; the resolution of that issue well illustrates the point just made about judicial reluctance to inquire into the actual agency motivation for a decision that appears to be well explained. The bulk of the massive opinion, however, addressed issues concerning the substantive outcome of the rulemaking: whether the agency properly understood its authority; whether computer models on which the agency was relying had been adequately justified; whether the studies and other factual material in the vast record of the rulemaking supported its outcome; whether the proper factors (and only the proper factors) had been considered; and so forth. As the size of its opinion makes apparent, the court examined these issues with care and in substantial detail—yet always from an outsider's perspective: Was the agency being reasonable? Had it adequately explained its thinking? Where uncertain (because it had to make projections from necessarily incomplete data), had it acknowledged its uncertainty and indicated how and why it was being resolved?

This aggressive policing of the reported thought process ended in enforcement, defeating any thought that it might have been the product simply of a disposition to upset the result. "In this case," the court concluded, "we have taken a long while to come to a short conclusion: the rule is reasonable." The process was not without costs—in time, in effort, and in risks of misunderstanding. The rulemaking had been begun

---

84. See, for a helpful recent canvas of the problem, C. Koch, Judicial Review of Administrative Discretion, 54 Geo. Wash. L. Rev. 469 (1986).

85. See pp. 159-74.

86. See pp. 263-64, above.

87. Sierra Club v. Costle, 657 F.2d 298 (D.C. Cir. 1981); see pp. 172-74.

in 1973; the rule came into effect only in 1979; review proceedings were not finished until 1981. Its results were subjected to vigorous intellectual as well as political criticism.[88] Whether judges who are not engineers, computer modelers, economists or statisticians can vouch for the intellectual integrity of a reasoning process that requires those attainments and more is, to say the least, open to grave doubt.[89] The warrant for such a high degree of engagement is found, in part, in arguable propositions about the favorable impact on *agency* decision processes of having to expect such intense review.[90] It is found, as well, in a view well stated by the scholar whose remarks also opened this chapter: "[T]here is in our society a profound, tradition-taught reliance on the courts as the ultimate guardian and assurance of the limits set upon executive power by the constitutions and legislatures."[91]

---

88. B. Ackerman and W. Hassler, Clean Coal/Dirty Air (Yale 1981).

89. M. Shapiro, Administrative Discretion: The Next Stage, 92 Yale L.J. 1487, 1507 (1983): "Courts cannot take a hard look at materials they cannot understand nor be partners to technocrats in a realm in which only technocrats speak the language." Cf. B. Ackerman, Reconstructing American Law 67-68 (Harvard 1984).

90. An unusually thoughtful bureaucrat wrote, "The effect of such judicial opinions within the agency reaches beyond those who were concerned with the specific regulations reviewed. They . . . give those who care about well-documented and well-reasoned decisionmaking a lever to move those who do not." W. Pedersen, Formal Records and Informal Rulemaking, 85 Yale L. J. 38, 60 (1975). Less favorable views appear in B. Ackerman and W. Hassler, note 88, above, R.S. Melnick, note 82, above, and J. Mashaw and D. Harfst, note 75, above.

91. L. Jaffe, Judicial Control of Administrative Action 321 (1965).

═9
LIABILITY OF PUBLIC AUTHORITIES AND THEIR AGENTS

The subject matters of this chapter, the civil (monetary) liability of government and government agencies for wrongful acts and contractual default, are distinctly subsidiary elements in administrative law, as that subject is conventionally understood. If they appear in law school curricula at all, they are as likely to be treated as specialities of the law of torts (civil wrongs), the law of contracts, or even constitutional law (civil rights actions) as they are to be thought matters of "administrative law." The treatment here will be correspondingly sketchy and brief.

The reader should be aware at the outset that these subjects suffer not only from their somewhat haphazard historical development, but also from the influences of federalism.[1] When dealing with the subject of relief involving the sovereign, one should not be surprised to find issues of sovereignty close at hand. Thus, the Eleventh Amendment to the federal Constitution, ratified in 1798 (the very first adopted after the Bill of Rights), prohibits the federal courts from entertaining actions brought by citizens of one state (or foreigners) against a state other than their own;[2] the result is to preclude federal actions for monetary damages to be paid by a state or its agencies.[3] This stricture may be avoided, however, if the suit is brought against a state officer individually—even for acts committed in his official capacity. Such remedies have long been available. In recent years, interpretation of the Civil Rights Act,[4] a statute passed in the wake of the Civil War, has led to a tremendous growth in lawsuits against state and municipal officials seeking the payment of monetary damages for acts alleged to have violated federal constitutional or statutory norms. The success of these actions, in turn, created pressure for

---

1. See pp. 7-8.
2. U.S.Const. Amendment XI. As written, the Eleventh Amendment appears to prevent only diversity actions, p. 78, and not actions a citizen of the same state might bring, relying on "federal question" jurisdiction. It has been interpreted, however, to forbid *all* federal actions that, if successful, will require a judicial order to the state to pay money damages. Hans v. Louisiana, 134 U.S. 1 (1890).
3. Quern v. Jordan, 440 U.S. 332 (1979).
4. 42 U.S.C. § 1983; the Act is discussed below at pp. 277-78.

the recognition of similar remedies against federal officers, whose behavior was not directly regulated by the Civil Rights Act. For the federal courts to be enforcing against state officials a remedy they did not provide against federal officials was transparently problematic.

Relief against the sovereign

Historically, American courts have declined to entertain law suits that sought to require the expenditure of public money or to compel the transfer of public property.[5] The idea on which they relied, perhaps surprising for a republic born of revolution against monarchy, was sovereign immunity. This is the proposition that the polity cannot be brought into its own courts and there be compelled to answer for its wrongs. This idea won universal acceptance at both state and federal level; indeed, the speedy adoption of the Eleventh Amendment[6] resulted from the federal courts' failure to recognize that principle in dealing with a state.[7] While in formal terms a state would not be the "sovereign" entitled to immunity in federal courts, in political reality the states insisted on the same immunity there as they enjoyed in their own courts.

The years following have seen a steady, but not always rational, recession from this idea.[8] Suits might be brought against individual officers acting beyond their legal authority, as if they were private citizens; their success depended on whether such behavior by a private citizen would have been an actionable wrong. Statutory provisions were made for special courts to hear such suits for monetary relief as the legislature might authorize. Individual statutes authorized judicial review of the decisions of particular agencies, or of defined types of governmental action more

---

5. An exception was recognized for the remedy of mandamus, in the very narrow circumstances in which that was first thought available. See pp. 61-63. If payment of a certain sum was a ministerial duty of a governmental official, respecting which he enjoyed no discretion whatever, mandamus was available to compel the payment even though it would come from the public treasury. Kendall v. United States, 37 U.S. (12 Pet.) 524 (1838).

6. See note 2, above.

7. Chisholm v. Georgia, 2 Dall. 419 (1793).

8. It is not meant to suggest that the doctrine is itself in all respects irrational. Public resources are limited. Giving tort claimants priority in obtaining public resources, in a way that cannot be mediated by politics, may deprive other members of the polity whose need is equal but who lack a conventional legal claim. Cf. National Board of YMCA v. United States, 395 U.S. 85 (1970). Moreover, judicial refusal to order delivery of government property may serve to protect the public generally against the effects of official mismanagement of public resources.

generally. As liability insurance became more readily available, judges in the states frequently overturned the sovereign immunity defense to tort actions. The insurance meant the defense was no longer justified by the rationale of protecting the public treasury.[9]

At the federal level, these results have largely been rationalized since 1976, when amendments to APA Section 702 waived the defense of sovereign immunity, absent special circumstances, for any "action in a court of the United States seeking relief other than money damages and stating a claim that an agency or [its] officer or employee . . . acted or failed to act in an official capacity or under color of legal authority." Thus, sovereign immunity, as such, is no longer a defense for non-monetary actions brought against the United States in federal district court. Actions for monetary damages are controlled by other statutes, such as the Federal Tort Claims Act (civil wrongs)[10] and the Tucker Act (breach of contract and other non-tortious legal wrongs).[11]

The specific provisions for monetary relief may be taken, in some cases, to create what is in effect an implied preclusion[12] of suits for other-than-monetary relief in the district courts, despite the 1976 legislation. We saw earlier that congressional shaping of available relief is thought to avoid the constitutional problems that might be presented by total denial of review.[13] A prominent example of such an implication may be found in the Tucker Act's authorization of breach of contract actions. The availability of money damages in such an action carries the implication—readily supported in public policy terms[14]—that *no* remedy for specific performance is authorized. Thus, an action seeking specific performance from a district court, even though it is for relief "other than money damages," will be dismissed as not having been consented to.[15]

---

9. A recent overview of the development of state practice on sovereign immunity may be found in W. Prosser and P. Keeton, Prosser and Keeton on the Law of Torts 1044-45 (1984).

10. The Act is discussed below at pp. 274-76.

11. 28 U.S.C. §§ 1346, 1491.

12. See pp. 220-21.

13. See pp. 219-20.

14. See note 8, above.

15. Senate Committee on the Judiciary, Judicial Review of Agency Action, Sen. Rep. No. 94-996 on S. 800, 94th Cong., 2d Sess. 11-12 (1976); Spectrum Leasing Corp. v. United States, 764 F.2d 891 (D.C. Cir. 1985).

Tort actions as a form of review[16]

Against governmental units

The Federal Tort Claims Act[17] permits citizens to sue the federal government directly for a wide variety of intentional or negligent behaviors by civil servants, particularly those to which the ordinary citizen is most likely to be exposed—automobile accidents with postal vehicles, lawless police behavior, carelessly maintained beacons, etc. The general test for this liability is whether "the United States, if a private person, would be liable to the claimant in accordance with the law of the place where the act or omission occurred."[18] Note that, remarkably for a federal system, this formula ties liability to state tort law, which varies from state to state, rather than to a uniform national standard; the variations, however, are not major. The liability is also limited in two important procedural respects: the jury trial a plaintiff could expect in suing a private citizen is unavailable; and punitive damages, generally available under tort law in the case of particularly egregious behavior, are also precluded.

Yet the Act's coverage is at best haphazard, and consequently the subject of frequent criticism. It makes no provision for governmental liability in the absence of fault, a form of liability now common (as for dangerous activities) under state tort law. It also explicitly excludes liability for some intentional torts, such as misrepresentation, deceit, defamation, and interference with contract rights. To recover from the government itself, persons suffering these harms must rely on the willingness of federal administrators to settle their claims nonetheless (for example, to avoid public appearances of injustice that might shame an administration

---

16. An excellent modern literature exists on the tort action as a form of review, including an analysis that, thanks to the efforts of my colleague George Bermann, offers a comparative perspective well informed about the treatment of the subject in European legal systems. E.g., G. Bermann, La Responsabilité Civile des Fonctionnaires au Niveau Fédéral aux États-Unis: Vers la Solution d'une Crise, 1983 Revue Internationale de Droit Comparé No. 2, p. 319 (1983). See also Shuck, Suing Government (Yale 1983); R. Cass, Damage Suits Against Public Officers, 129 U. Pa. L. Rev. 1110 (1981); G. Bermann, Integrating Governmental and Officer Tort Liability, 77 Colum. L. Rev. 1175 (1977); Symposium, Civil Liability of Government Officials, 42 Law & Contemp. Prob. 1 (1978).

17. The FTCA first appeared in 60 Stat. 842 (1946). Then it was reenacted without substantive changes in the revision of the Judicial Code, 62 Stat. 869 (1948). Now its provisions are scattered widely in the Code—28 U.S.C. §§ 1346, 1402, 1504, 2110, 2401, 2402, 2411, 2412, and 2671-80. Most of the substantive provisions appear in §§ 2671-80.

18. 28 U.S.C. § 1346(b).

or provoke unwanted legislative action)[19] or on the willingness of Congress to adopt a private law for their relief. Both outcomes occur with some frequency.

The most important exception to the Torts Claims Act, from a theoretical perspective at least, preserves the government's immunity from suits relating to its agents' discretionary acts. The exemption has two aspects. The less controversial denies liability for an employee's act or omission in executing a statute or regulation "whether or not such statute or regulation be valid," so long as the employee was otherwise acting with due care. This bars litigants from using tort suits as a vehicle for challenging the bare legality of a law or regulation, and has produced little debate; the standard techniques of judicial review remain fully available.[20] More problematic is the provision that government liability cannot be based upon the performance of (or failure to perform) "a discretionary function or duty . . . whether or not the discretion involved be abused."[21] This has been taken to excuse the government from direct fiscal responsibility from the consequences of official judgments, even when they have the most catastrophic outcomes. In effect, this limits liability to damage occasioned by carelessness in routine operations.

Thus, governmental liability has been found when a maritime accident resulted from carelessness in maintaining a specific navigational aid and when carelessness in attempting to control a forest fire led to significant destruction of private property.[22] But a judgment that France's immediate and pressing need for fertilizer in the years following World War II warranted taking certain risks in packaging and shipping that fertilizer produced no liability when a terrible explosion resulted, killing hundreds and wounding thousands.[23] And policy judgments by the Federal Aviation Administration about how intensively to inspect aircraft design and manufacture prior to certification of airplanes as safe for commercial use—a certification known to be widely relied upon outside as well as inside the United States—could not result in liability for airplane accidents a more thorough review would have prevented. "Judicial intervention in such decisionmaking through private tort suits would require the courts to

---

19. A detailed report of federal practice can be found in G. Bermann, Federal Tort Claims at the Agency Level: The FTCA Administrative Process, 35 Case West. Res. L. Rev. 509 (1985). Of course, the agency must have authority to pay the claim, either because its liability under the FTCA is colorable, or because (as many agencies do) it enjoys additional claims or benefits payment authority.

20. G. Bermann, La Responsabilité, note 16, above.

21. 28 U.S.C. § 2680(a).

22. Indian Towing Co. v. United States, 350 U.S. 61 (1955); Rayonier, Inc. v. United States, 352 U.S. 315 (1957).

23. Dalehite v. United States, 346 U.S. 15 (1953).

'second-guess' the political, social, and economic judgments of an agency exercising its regulatory function. . . . In administering the 'spot-check' program, . . . FAA engineers and inspectors necessarily took certain calculated risks, but those risks were encountered for the advancement of a governmental purpose and pursuant to the specific grant of authority in the regulations and operating manuals."[24]

One may see the "discretionary function" exemption, in part, as the obverse of the implication previously noted, that the availability of monetary relief sometimes connotes the unavailability of other forms of relief.[25] Conversely, it could be suggested, the exemption reflects that some matters are better suited to consideration under the ordinary forms of judicial review than to actions seeking to establish monetary liability. These tend to be settings in which the "if a private person" condition of FTCA liability would, in any event, be problematic. In part, too, it can be suggested that the exemption serves to protect from "tort action" review judgments that also are excluded from review, or at least difficult to test, under the ordinary APA provisions for judicial review. Who would have standing to challenge an FAA judgment how intensely to inspect commercial aircraft before certification,[26] and whether that judgment should be found one "committed to agency discretion by law,"[27] are themselves knotty questions. One can understand that if standing rules and the belief that agency action is indeed "committed to agency discretion" are to have meaning and validity, then one cannot allow them to be circumvented through tort actions. One sees here a recognition that for some governmental actions, so much the product of budgetary considerations, controls must be left wholly in the realm of politics—even when, as in war, the outcome of official judgments may be, for some, the most dreadful of consequences.

Against government officials

Theories of liability

If one cannot always sue the government to redress harm occasioned by official (mis)conduct, it may be possible to sue a particular government official for tort damages he has caused. That remedy, which at the federal level at least is not a statutory one, has two different sources. The first

---

24. United States v. S.A. Empresa De Viacao Aerea Rio Grandense (Varig Airlines), et al., 467 U.S. 797 (1984).
25. See p. 273.
26. See pp. 225-28.
27. See pp. 221-23.

source is the ordinary common law of torts. It has long compensated for the "sovereign immunity" of government itself by treating the government officer as authorized only to act lawfully. To the extent he acts beyond his lawful authority, he exposes himself to liability as if he were a private citizen. Thus, an official meat inspector authorized summarily to seize and destroy tainted chickens being held in a cold storage warehouse for later sale exercised that authority at the risk of having to show, in defense of a later tort action for the destruction of property, that the chickens were in fact unwholesome.[28]

The second source, already briefly noted,[29] lies in implication from constitutional or statutory provisions. Since the American Civil War, state and local officials have been subject to potential tort (as well as criminal) liability for actions under color of state law that deprive any "person . . . of any rights, privileges or immunities secured by the Constitution and laws."[30] Such Section 1983 actions, as they are called after the provision of the federal code containing this language, have exploded in recent years; they represent the substantial part of some 30,000 civil rights actions pending in district courts in 1986 (the most recent year for which figures are available),[31] largely as a by-product of the civil rights movement. While most commonly used to seek monetary damages from the violation of civil liberties guaranteed by the federal Bill of Rights,[32] Section 1983 permits remedies as well for violations of statutory rights, and forward-looking equitable relief along with retrospective damage awards.[33] Ten years after the explosion in Section 1983 actions began, the Supreme Court implied a similar principle of tort liability to control the actions of

---

28. North American Cold Storage Co. v. Chicago, 211 U.S. 306 (1908). This potential for tort relief answered any objection that the seizure could occur without a prior hearing. See pp. 44-48. Later state cases have recognized a qualified privilege for such official judgments. Gildea v. Ellershaw, 363 Mass. 800, 298 N.E. 2d 847 (1973).

29. See the text at note 4, above.

30. 42 U.S.C. § 1983.

31. Annual Report, Administrative Office of the U.S. Courts, 115 (1986) shows 11,929 private civil rights actions not classified under particular substantive civil rights statutes, and 19,502 prisoner petitions classified as "civil rights" claims.

32. E.g., Monroe v. Pape, 365 U.S. 167 (1961)(unlawful search and seizure); Pembaur v. Cincinnati, 106 S. Ct. 1292 (1986)(unlawful arrest); Hudson v. Palmer, 468 U.S. 517 (1984)(deprivation of prisoner's rights).

33. See Edelman v. Jordan, 415 U.S. 651 (1974); Maine v. Thiboutot, 448 U.S. 1 (1980). There is a certain potential here for using § 1983 to control or review state administrative actions for compliance with federal standards. See Wright v. City of Roanoke Redevelopment and Housing Authority, 107 S. Ct. 766 (1987); Middlesex County Sewerage Authority v. National Sea Clammers Association, 453 U.S. 1 (1981); C. Sunstein, Section 1983 and the Private Enforcement of Federal Law, 49 U. Chi. L. Rev. 394 (1982).

federal officials, in a case arising out of a violent, destructive, and apparently lawless search of a private home during early morning hours. In the absence of any legislative provision to the contrary or of any "special factors counselling hesitation 'that implication was compelled.' 'The very essence of civil liberty certainly consists in the right of every individual to claim the protection of the laws, whenever he receives an injury.' "[34]

Defenses to liability

The two different bases on which one might be able to establish officer liability must be kept in mind when considering the question, to what extent an official thus made subject to the possibility of tort liability may claim a privilege or immunity based on his official status. Development of the law on that subject has not been smooth under either heading. More confusing is that, at the moment, it appears to differ as between the two.

Judicial recognition of common law tort liability has carried with it three possible outcomes on the issue of immunity: that the officer is protected from civil liability only for those acts that are in fact lawful; that he has a "qualified privilege" for acts reasonably believed to be lawful exercises of the authority conferred on his; and that he has an absolute immunity for all acts done under color of office. The qualified privilege has both objective (could the act reasonably be thought a lawful exercise of authority?) and subjective (did the officer believe he was acting lawfully?) elements, the latter of which, at least, would often require a trial to resolve. Choice among these three possible outcomes, as well as precise definition of the character of the "qualified privilege," has rested on a readily grasped tension between desirable policies. On the one hand, the citizen should be protected from official lawlessness, especially from abuse of office. On the other, the conduct of public business often requires fearless action by public servants, who should be neither dissuaded nor distracted from their work by the risks and interruptions of lawsuits, and whose general probity can be controlled in other ways.

Although initially some civil servants were required to demonstrate the actual lawfulness of their decisions,[35] it is now generally recognized that at least a qualified privilege is appropriate. If the civil servant reasonably could, and did, believe himself to be acting lawfully, that will suffice to defeat a tort action. Whether out of particular familiarity with its own functions or a more self-serving motive, the Supreme Court early

---

34. Bivens v. Six Unknown Named Agents of the Federal Bureau of Narcotics, 403 U.S. 388 (1971), quoting Marbury v. Madison, 1 Cranch 137, 163 (1803).
35. See note 28, above.

awarded judges (and by extension prosecutors and others acting within the judicial system)[36] an absolute immunity from civil liability. In part, this judgment relied upon the usual availability of alternative remedies, such as judicial review, of the merits of the action complained of to correct the asserted wrong. In part, it relied upon the judge's need to be "free to act upon his own convictions, without apprehensions of personal consequences to himself."[37]

Similar reasoning underlay a federal trend in ordinary tort actions toward recognition of an absolute privilege for matters requiring the exercise of official discretion. In 1959, this development found fruition in a case in which a middle-level bureaucrat was alleged to have defamed two of his subordinates in a press release issued in response to congressional oversight. The Court found that he was absolutely immune from suit, reasoning that freedom from the fear of being sued and the distractions of having to defend were necessary to promote "fearless, vigorous and effective administration of policies of government."[38] In effect, the Court had extended the "discretionary function" exemption from the Federal Tort Claims Act[39] from government itself to executive officials.

Developments under Section 1983, as distinct from common law tort suits, pointed toward only a qualified privilege for executive officials. In the states, executive officials generally were accorded only a qualified privilege. When the Supreme Court came to consider the issue of privilege under Section 1983, it held that state officials, even a governor, were entitled to no more than a qualified privilege under that statute. That privilege might vary with "the scope of discretion and responsibilities of the office" but nonetheless could be defeated by a showing of bad faith, or that there did not exist reasonable grounds for belief in the legality of the action taken.[40] Plainly enough, this is a compromise position. It hopes to provide sufficient protection for the honest official while defeating the

---

36. See Gregoire v. Biddle, 177 F.2d 579 (2d Cir. 1949).

37. Bradley v. Fisher, 13 Wall. 335 (1871); Stump v. Sparkman, 435 U.S. 349 (1978), is an ugly and dramatic confirmation of the force of the principle. The case found to be immune a judge who had authorized a daughter's sterilization on her mother's petition—without notice, hearing, representation for the child, or explicit statutory authorization. Arguable jurisdiction was present, and that was enough. Forrester v. White, 108 S. Ct. 538 (1988), accorded only qualified immunity to a judge's administrative actions concerning a court employee.

38. Barr v. Mateo, 360 U.S. 564. The quoted language was subscribed by only four of the Court's nine Justices; another was particularly moved by the fact that the alleged tort involved public criticism of the way civil servants had performed their function; a sixth indicated agreement in principle; the remaining three would have found a qualified privilege only.

39. See pp. 274-76.

40. Scheuer v. Rhodes, 416 U.S. 232 (1974).

manipulations of the unscrupulous. The necessity for such a position may have seemed particularly compelling given the adamant resistance to the civil rights movement by officials in some parts of the country.

When, in 1978, the Secretary of Agriculture and other lower level federal officials were sued for alleged constitutional torts, the Court found that most of them, also, could claim only a qualified privilege. "Surely, *federal* officials should enjoy no greater zone of protection when they violate *federal* constitutional rules than do *state* officers."[41] Administrative adjudicators and prosecutors, however, were found still to enjoy an absolute immunity, both on account of their special needs for protection from "harassment or intimidation" and because of the tendency of the hearing process to provide its own checks against abuse.

As of this writing, these two lines of development have not been reconciled. Absolute immunity appears to be available in common-law based actions; only qualified immunity, in those that arise from so-called "constitutional torts."[42] A possible line of accommodation is suggested, however, by a 1982 decision involving alleged "constitutional torts" by White House officials. In its 1978 opinion, the Court had admonished the lower courts to see that insubstantial claims should not proceed to trial. It now admitted that the subjective, good faith element of the qualified privilege it had defined stood in the way of this outcome. Malicious intention was easy for a plaintiff to claim, and it is in the nature of the discretionary actions likely to be the subjects of such litigation that the defendant's judgments "almost invariably are influenced by [her] experiences, values, and emotions." To avoid the resulting, and highly disruptive, inquiries, the Court redefined the "qualified privilege" to encompass the objective element only. The privilege would attach unless a government official performing a discretionary function had acted in a manner violative of "clearly established statutory or constitutional rights of which a reasonable person would have known."[43] The validity of such a claim of privilege, it thought, could usually be determined without the need for civil discovery, and consequently would avoid most of the feared disruptions. If this projection is born out by experience, it seems reasonable to believe that the common-law privilege will be adjusted to the same point.

---

41. Butz v. Economou, 438 U.S. 478 (1978) (emphasis in original).

42. Only however, if a "discretionary function" was involved. Westfall v. Erwin, 108 S. Ct. 580 (1988). For a strong critique, giving a convincing account of the difficulties of distinguishing "constitutional" from ordinary torts, see G. Bermann, La Responsabilité . . . , note 16, above.

43. Harlow v. Fitzgerald, 457 U.S. 800 (1982); Mitchell v. Forsyth, 472 U.S. 511 (1985); Anderson v. Creighton, 107 S. Ct. 3034 (1988).

Integration with tort action against government

While this discussion should suffice to suggest certain, but inexact, parallels between the Federal Tort Claims Act and the tort liability of individual federal officials, it has not yet mentioned what is perhaps the more remarkable point—that the availability of a remedy against government itself does not generally exclude a suit against the individual officer.[44] The point was made in an action brought by the mother of a former federal prisoner against prison officials; she asserted her son had been killed by their intentional cruelty. In an action arising out of the alleged constitutional tort of inflicting "cruel and unusual punishment," the Supreme Court specifically found that the existence of an FTCA remedy for intentional torts committed by federal law enforcement officials did not preclude the judicially implied remedy. It found no purpose in the statute to preclude a judicial remedy, and thought that the constitutional tort remedy had signal advantages over the FTCA: greater deterrence; the availability of punitive damages and a jury trial; and the application of uniform national, rather than state, law.[45] This failure of coordination, indeed of protection of individual officers from disabling personal liability, has been widely seen as a matter requiring reform, in the direction of expanded governmental and reduced individual liability.[46]

The implied cause of action

Judicial implication of a tort remedy in relationship to administrative action is also possible in private tort actions brought by one citizen against another, where the tort action seeks to enforce a rule of conduct that could also be the subject of administrative enforcement. The appropriateness of such implied private rights of actions is well established where the rule of conduct in question is enforced by criminal law. Thus, the owner of a farm whose livestock was poisoned by improperly manufactured feed was able to sue his supplier, on the ground that the supplier had violated a criminal provision intended to prevent just such consequences. Until recently, the courts appeared to be generally willing to imply similar remedies based on the rights or interests protected by

---

44. A statutory provision that actions for motor vehicle accidents *are* to be brought exclusively under the FTCA, 28 U.S.C. § 2679(d) can be taken to imply the opposite for other torts.

45. Carlson v. Green, 446 U.S. 14 (1980).

46. See the works cited in note 16, above; also, Federal Officials' Liability for Constitutional Violations, Recommendation 82-6 of the Administrative Conference of the United States, 1 C.F.R. § 305.82-6.

administrative regimes. If a citizen violated an administrative norm, he could be held liable in a suit by another citizen, just as if he had violated a criminal law norm. In the past few years, however, one has noted a distinct reluctance to draw such implications, in a variety of contexts. The possibility of explaining this reluctance in general terms suggestive of the changing nature of relationship between agency and court warrants a few words on the subject here.

We can start with a case that marks a contrast to the FTCA case discussed at the very end of the next preceding section. While the Supreme Court did not think that the Tort Claims Act precluded application of its implied constitutional tort remedy for "cruel and unusual punishment," it concluded that another federal employee's constitutional tort remedy for having been demoted in retaliation for his public criticism of his agency *was* precluded by the federal civil service statutes.[47] The civil service statutes offered more limited relief for the harm of retaliatory discipline he asserted. The Court assumed that the agency's actions violated the plaintiff's rights of free speech, and so comprised a constitutional tort. Here, as in the FTCA case, there was no reason to think Congress had reached any specific judgment whether a tort remedy should or should not be provided. It had, however, provided an "elaborate, comprehensive scheme" for the resolution of civil service disputes. Even though the remedies available under this scheme were in many respects inferior to the constitutional tort remedy, the Court concluded that implying a tort remedy would raise too many risks of disrupting the balance Congress had struck.

One can see in a similar light a case refusing to recognize a Section 1983 claim that would have created a judicial remedy in competition with the elaborate enforcement provisions of the Federal Water Pollution Control Act and the Marine Protection, Research and Sanctuaries Act. Again, one had no reason to think Congress had faced the question whether a judicial remedy should be implied under Section 1983 when state officials violated the statute, threatening to damage the interests of private citizens. But Congress had provided in such detail for the administrative scheme, that judicial improvisation of additional remedies seemed likely to disrupt it.[48] In a more recent case, all indications were that Congress and the agency expected and even welcomed private enforcement.[49]

In yet another series of cases, the Court has addressed the problem of implying private remedies from federal regulatory statutes in the same

---

47. Bush v. Lucas, 462 U.S. 367 (1983).

48. Middlesex County Sewerage Authority v. National Sea Clammers Association, 453 U.S. 1 (1981); see also C. Sunstein, Section 1983 and the Private Enforcement of Federal Law, 49 U. Chi. L. Rev. 394 (1982).

49. Wright v. City of Roanoke Redevelopment and Housing Authority, 107 S. Ct. 766 (1987).

terms. Where it thought Congress had anticipated or accepted implication of a private remedy supplementary to that provided by statute, the implication was made. Thus, for example, a private remedy for violations of Securities and Exchange Commission regulations, long recognized in the lower courts, was sustained.[50] But, as a general matter, the Court cautioned that courts ought not to imply such remedies in the face of complex and detailed administrative schemes, whose operation might be disrupted by the intrusion of a supplemental judicial remedy.[51]

The common element should be apparent, and may be found in other contexts as well.[52] It is the appearance of complexity and integration in an administrative scheme, that judicial implication of a separate remedy may disrupt. One may see here more than arguably appropriate judicial modesty. One difference between judicial and administrative relief is that the latter is more likely to be administered with national uniformity. It is in the nature of the geographically dispersed federal system, and the Supreme Court's extremely limited resources for supervision of the lower courts, that a judicially administered remedy is likely to show some geographic variation. This need not be objectionable, of course. Recall that the FTCA explicitly accepts such variation; that helps understand why the FTCA is not taken to exclude an implied remedy. In other settings, however, the prospect would be a disturbing one. The Court may be moved, too, by the possibility that courts, which encounter detailed statutory schemes only occasionally, might well be less accurate in their reading, less full in their comprehension, than an agency with daily responsibility for the matter. One can find here, then, as in the Court's decision in the *Chevron* case, both a rather striking recognition of the limitations of the judicial remedy, and acceptance of the administrative endeavor that, in the American context, is rather new.[53]

Liability in contract

This essay is not the place for a discussion of public contract law, a body of law that is specialized, subject to detailed control by statute and

---

50. Blue Chip Stamps v. Manor Drug Stores, 421 U.S. 723 (1975).

51. Merrill, Lynch, Pierce, Fenner & Smith v. Curran, 456 U.S. 353 (1982); for a general discussion, see M. Field, Sources of Law: The Scope of Federal Common Law, 99 Harv. L. Rev. 881, 930 ff. (1986).

52. E.g., Block v. Community Nutrition Institute, briefly discussed at pp. 150-52 and 220-21.

53. See P. Strauss, One Hundred Fifty Cases Per Year: Some Implications of the Supreme Court's Limited Resources for Judicial Review of Agency Action., 87 Colum. L. Rev. 1093 (1987).

regulation, and subject also to the pervasive oversight of the GAO and the OMB.[54] (For all that control, especially of defense procurement—or perhaps even because of the costs it engenders—America seems not to have been able to avoid the $600 hammer or toilet seat.) It may be possible, however, to suggest some of the ways in which that law may vary from the ordinary law of contract administered in the state courts.

The subject here is procurement, as in the government's purchase of military equipment, rather than the individual's contractual relations with government. In the latter setting, it is often the citizen who contracts with government for delivery of services to him, and the legal regimes are not unusually complex. One need not file elaborate forms to obtain express mail service for a valuable package, or federal insurance for one's crops. There is simply the hazard that, because one has purchased the service from government, the possibilities of recovery when something goes wrong are less than they would otherwise be. Ideas of apparent authority and estoppel, commonplace in the private law of contracts, are more problematic in litigation against the government.[55]

Procurement and subsequent contract administration is generally performed by specialized federal decisionmakers, who apply a distinctly federal law. As in military supply contracts, the relationships in question are frequently enduring ones, for which reaching mutually acceptable modifications can be as important as redressing past harms. From the public's perspective, these relationships create hazards of waste and self-dealing that must be controlled for, as well as benefits. In any event, they are planned relationships, permitting (and from the government's perspective requiring) constant oversight and a national body of law rather than, as in the Tort Claims Act, sporadic litigation to enforce obligations that may vary from state to state to reflect the differing expectations of citizens in each place about the conduct the law regards as injurious.

Government contracts are reached, and initially administered, through specialized contracting officers within the responsible agencies. As may be imagined, these contracts are not freely negotiated in all respects for each transaction. Procurement procedures are subject to

---

54. A general introduction for lawyers, W. Keyes, Government Contracts (West 1979) was published before the Federal Courts Improvement Act of 1982, P.L. 97-164, 96 Stat. 25 and the Competition in Contracting Act of 1984, P.L. 98-369, altered administrative and judicial assignments. More detailed information can be found in the Commerce Clearing House Government Contracts Reporter; in J. McBride and I. Wachtel, Government Contracts (Matthew Bender); in Judge Advocate General's School, Procurement Law; and in J. Whelan, Federal Government Contracts—Cases and Materials (1985).

55. Portmann v. United States, 674 F.2d 1155 (7th Cir. 1982); Federal Crop Insurance Corp. v. Merrill, 332 U.S. 380 (1947).

elaborate regulation. In addition to standardized forms of the usual sort, a variety of provisions are often required to be included in completed contracts as a means of promoting an assortment of affirmative policies: for example, protecting the confidentiality of sensitive information, combatting discrimination, maintaining decent wages, providing employment for the handicapped, or favoring small or minority-owned businesses. Each of these policies may have its own agency, or office within the contracting agency, responsible for its enforcement. The actions of these bodies often provide grist for the ordinary mills of administrative law.

Disputes involving the contract proper (including requests for modification during performance) will ordinarily be determined, within the agency, by a special contracting officer. His determination can be appealed either to a board of contract appeals within the agency or, in a suit for monetary damages, to the Claims Court (formerly the United States Court of Claims), which sits in Washington, D.C. The result of either proceeding may be appealed to the Court of Appeals for the Federal Circuit.[56] Recall that the remedy given, usually limited to monetary relief, excludes the possibility of suit for specific performance or other equitable forms of relief in the federal district courts, under the APA.[57]

The public character of the contracts is reflected not only in their specialized (and frequently regulatory) terms, but also in the possibility of legislative oversight and of litigation initiated by outsiders to the contracts, challenging the terms of their formation. Such contracts are frequently let under a bidding process intended to be administered in accordance with stated standards. As would not often be the case after formation of a private contract, disappointed bidders may be able to sue to avoid a choice wrongfully made,[58] although the standard of review articulated in such actions is highly deferential.[59] More practically, perhaps, they can invoke the oversight of the General Accounting Office, the congressional agency that in this as in other respects oversees governmental contracting.[60] While the Comptroller General cannot avoid a contract as such, his view respecting the legality of an agency's commitment to spend its appropriated funds in a particular way is highly influential; and Congress has provided special remedies for staying the effectiveness of proposed, but disputed, contract awards to await his review. These remedies were recently upheld in a persuasive

---

56. See p. 86.
57. See p. 273.
58. Scanwell Laboratories, Inc. v. Shaffer, 424 F.2d 859 (D.C. Cir. 1970).
59. Gull Airborne Instruments, Inc. v. Weinberger, 694 F.2d 838 (D.C. Cir. 1982), noting in particular that bidders who can connect their failure to win a government contract to illegal agency action may be able to recover their bid preparation costs by suing in the Claims Court.
60. See p. 59.

opinion by the United States Court of Appeals for the Third Circuit, despite separation-of-powers arguments prompted by the Supreme Court's recent decisions.[61]

The public character of the contracting process is equally reflected at what might be considered the other end of the contracting process, when the issue is the potential disqualification of a private party from some or all future governmental contracting. Again, in private law one cannot easily imagine as the occasion for legal complaint that a company (however large) had decided and instructed its agents never again to contract with a given bidder. In public contracting, the issue of debarment—used as a sanction for improper conduct—raises important issues of due process.[62] The result has been to encourage both more formal agency procedures and much closer judicial supervision for such issues than for issues arising out of the ordinary course of contracting.[63]

---

61. Ameron, Inc. v. U.S. Army Corps of Engineers, 809 F.2d 979 (3d Cir. 1986); see pp. 17-18.

62. See pp. 32-48.

63. Gonzales v. Freeman, 334 F.2d 570 (D.C. Cir. 1964); Transco Security, Inc. v. Freeman, 639 F.2d 318 (6th Cir.), cert. denied, 454 U.S. 820 (1981).

INDEX